PENGUIN BOOKS

AMPHIBIOUS THING

Lucy Moore was born in 1970 and educated in Britain and the United States before reading history at Edinburgh University. She is the editor of *Con Men and Cutpurses: Scenes from the Hogarthian Underworld*, and the author of the critically acclaimed *The Thieves' Opera: The Remarkable Lives and Deaths of Jonathan Wild, Thief-Taker, and Jack Sheppard, House-Breaker.* Lucy Moore lives in Gloucestershire.

Amphibious Thing

The Adventures of a Georgian Rake

LUCY MOORE

PENGUIN BOOKS

PENGUIN BOOKS

Published by the Penguin Group
Penguin Books Ltd, 80 Strand, London WC2R ORL, England
Penguin Putnam Inc., 375 Hudson Street, New York, New York 10014, USA
Penguin Books Australia Ltd, Ringwood, Victoria, Australia
Penguin Books Canada Ltd, 10 Alcorn Avenue, Toronto, Ontario, Canada M4V 3B2
Penguin Books India (P) Ltd, 11 Community Centre, Panchsheel Park,
New Delhi – 110 017, India
Penguin Books (NZ) Ltd, Cnr Rosedale and Airborne Roads,
Albany, Auckland, New Zealand
Penguin Books (South Africa) (Pty) Ltd, 5 Watkins Street, Denver Ext 4,
Johannesburg 2094, South Africa

Penguin Books Ltd, Registered Offices: 80 Strand, London WC2R ORL, England

First published by Viking 2000
Published in Penguin Books 2001
1

Set in Monotype Bembo
Printed in England by Clays Ltd, St Ives plc

The quotation from Winston S. Churchill on p.vii
is reprinted by kind permission of Curtis Brown
Group Ltd. Copyright Winston S. Churchill

Contents

We are all worms – but I do believe that I am a glow-worm

Winston S. Churchill

Introduction

Satire or Sense, alas! can Sporus feel?
Who breaks a Butterfly upon a Wheel?

In 1734, Alexander Pope published the vicious poem 'Epistle to Dr Arbuthnot'. His venom, while it splattered many, soaked one man: thirty-eight-year-old John, Lord Hervey, heir to the earldom of Bristol, Vice-Chamberlain to the second Hanoverian monarch, George II, favourite of his buxom wife, Queen Caroline, loyal supporter of Great Britain's first Prime Minister, Sir Robert Walpole, and model for Sporus, Pope's most enduring satiric creation.

As well as being a skilled speaker in Parliament and perhaps the best political pamphleteer of his generation, Lord Hervey was a noted amateur classical scholar and connoisseur of art. He counted as friends some of the most brilliant men and women of his age: Lady Mary Wortley Montagu, Voltaire, Lord Chesterfield, William Hogarth, Henry Fox. His *bons mots* were reported in the letters of people he hardly knew; his good looks earned him the nickname 'Hervey the Handsome'. For a few heady years in the 1730s his closeness to Walpole and the Queen made him one of the four or five most influential people in the country.

But it was not Lord Hervey's worldly success that had turned Alexander Pope against him. Although Hervey was a Whig, and Pope a Catholic, and therefore a Tory, their rift ran deeper than mere politics. What Pope despised about Hervey (and, arguably, also envied in him) was his bisexuality, an open secret among the five hundred or so people who made up aristocratic society in early eighteenth-century England. Amphibious thing, Pope called him, implying that his sexual duality – 'Now trips a Lady, and now struts a Lord' – masked a more sinister threat:

A Cherub's Face, a Reptile all the rest.
Beauty that shocks you, Parts that none will trust,
Wit that can creep, and Pride that licks the Dust.

Pope transposed Hervey's courtliness into obsequiousness and his effeminacy into evil, all the while creating a contrasting image of himself, as poet and narrator, as a man of honour and virtue.

In some ways, Pope's malevolent portrait of Lord Hervey is an accurate one. Hervey could be vain, selfish, cruel. His treatment of his wife is just one example. Throughout their life together he ignored and belittled her, consistently rejecting the devotion she showed him, mocking her attempts to please him, betraying her with other lovers. Even as he lay dying, he could not bring himself to soften towards her. He did not leave her a penny. He bequeathed his money to her children 'born in wedlock', which was not a common legal term, mysteriously implying that she had borne children out of wedlock. He tried (unsuccessfully) to prohibit his wife from bringing up their youngest daughter, entrusting her to the care of another woman, the mother-in-law of the love of Hervey's life.

A different contemporary image of Lord Hervey is William Hogarth's 1738 group painting with Hervey at its centre (*Lord Hervey and his Friends* plate. 1). Hogarth shows Hervey gazing out at the onlooker with an expression of amused detachment on his pale china-doll face. He stands at a three-quarter angle, his legs slightly apart, one hand resting on the back of a chair, the other gesturing gracefully away. His urbane elegance – Hogarth painted him wearing a violet velvet coat – was commended even by his enemies. It is not difficult, looking at this picture, to imagine Hervey's characteristic mincing gait, or the wit and scepticism which pervade his writing.

But Hogarth's portrait of Hervey, while fond, still does not contradict the negative image propagated by his detractors. Hervey was well aware that his brittle charm did not appeal to everyone. He joked that his coat of arms should be, 'a cat scratchant, with this motto: "For my friends where they itch, for my enemies where they are sore."' Even in Hogarth's painting, which he commissioned,

Hervey chose to show himself surrounded not by a loving family (he would not have been the first bad husband and father to try to atone for his sins by portraying himself as a family man) but by his most intimate male friends, including the man who almost certainly – and, scandalously for the time, almost openly – was his lover.

'It is no great matter what posterity thinks or says of one,' Hervey wrote in his *Memoirs*, 'but if it were I would pay less deference to truth and more to my own reputation in the characters I give of people.' Only one scrap of poetry in his hand survives which shows that he was stung by his enemies' barbs, despite his efforts to appear untouched and untouchable:

> Few Men he lik'd, and fewer still believ'd,
> Fewest of all he trust'd, none deceiv'd;
> But as from Temper, Principle or Pride,
> To gain whom he dislik'd he never tried.
> And this the Pride of Others disapprov'd,
> So lik'd by many, few by he was lov'd.

Lord Hervey refused to be cowed by his detractors and refused to answer them. He was too proud to show his wounds or modify his behaviour. And so we remember him today as his rivals (Pope was not the only one) portrayed him over two and a half centuries ago. But Hogarth's enigmatic group portrait survives, and great sheaves of private letters, as well as two volumes of memoirs of his years at court: these are Hervey's posthumous defence, his ambiguous justification. They reveal a man more complex than the caricatures drawn by his enemies, which are circumscribed by their topicality as well as their spite. This is the man who has drawn me in over the past years, keeping me fascinated even though I still cannot decide whether or not I like him.

As my choice of title suggests, what stands out about Lord Hervey for me is his ambiguity. He juggled his private and public personas, presenting one face to the world, another to his wife, and still others to his lovers and friends. He hid behind a web of artifice and deception, of affectation and wit, never letting anyone get close enough to see his inmost self.

Another angle for us, reading so long after his death, is the question of what Hervey – whose extensive, deliberately preserved correspondence and memoirs serve almost as an autobiography – hoped to show of himself to future generations. Sometimes one gets the sense he cared not a jot for posterity's reckoning; at other times, he seems almost painfully conscious of his legacy.

Ultimately, we can empathize with Hervey, because the façades he erected around himself served only to cut him off from the people he cared about; but he was not always a sympathetic character because his self-absorption interfered with the veneer of detachment behind which he tried to hide. He is compelling, though, because he was never neutral, never passive. He felt everything deeply. His skin was thin. Hervey progressed from bright young thing to has-been, from ambition to disillusion, from being loved and beloved to dying alone; and all the way along, his writings reveal the contradictions of the inner man.

Lady Mary Wortley Montagu, who knew Hervey better than anyone, famously remarked, 'This world consists of men, women and Herveys.' She was probably referring to Hervey's sexuality – about which he confided in her – but she was right in more ways than one. Her friend was not only an unusual but an exceptional man who lived beyond the parameters of his age. Although he chose to be portrayed by Hogarth as the consummate eighteenth-century gentleman, and conversely was depicted by his enemies as a freak of nature or a bitchy opportunist, the picture of Hervey that emerges from his life and letters is that of a quintessentially modern man: curious, contemplative and independent; troubled by internal conflicts between his public hopes and private desires; and ultimately all too aware of his own human inadequacies and imperfectibility.

Lucy Moore
January 2000

PART ONE

When I consider life, 'tis all a cheat,
Yet fooled by hope, men favour the deceit;
Trust on, and think, tomorrow will repay;
Tomorrow's falser than the former day;
Lies more; and whilst it says we shall be blest
With some new joy, cuts off what we possessed;
Strange cozenage! none would live past years again,
Yet all hope pleasure in what yet remain,
And from the dregs of life think to receive
What the first sprightly running could not give.
I'm tired with waiting for this chymic gold,
Which fools us young, and beggars us when old.

John Dryden

1. Childhood

In 1695, John Hervey (the father of our Hervey) took as his second wife the overbearing heiress Elizabeth Felton. Hervey's beloved first wife, Isabella Carr, had died in childbirth two years previously, leaving behind a daughter and one surviving son, his heir, named Carr for his mother. But Hervey, although he mourned Isabella's loss, was a practical man who believed that man's natural state was the married one, and he lost no time in finding a new bride. Within a year, on 15 October 1696, Elizabeth Hervey's first child, named John for his father, was born. To distinguish between the two, John and Elizabeth called their baby Jack.

When young Jack was four, John Hervey inherited from his own father the family estate of Ickworth, near Bury St Edmunds in Suffolk. These lands became the lifelong passion of their new owner, who after moving to Ickworth left it as seldom as possible, preferring his simple rural life there to the fast pace of London society that his wife adored. His diary entries refer variously to sweet, peaceful, innocent Ickworth, his beloved 'centre of rest'. Although the house was 'a tenant's old house in the park, so very bad a habitation that I am astonished how so large a family have made so long a shift in it', according to one visitor, Ickworth's park was beautiful: 'much the finest park I ever saw' with its gentle hills and ancient trees.

In the year following his family's move to Ickworth, John Hervey was created Baron Hervey, largely thanks to the patronage of the irascible Sarah, Duchess of Marlborough. He was rewarded again for his loyalty to the Hanoverian dynasty in 1714 with the Earldom of Bristol when King George I came to the throne. 'I have a double interest in the security and prosperity of the royal family,' he declared with his customary loyalty to the Whig cause, 'both as a subject and an original stickler for settling the succession in their

House, where I would have it remain in full fame and true glory till time shall be no more.'

After this second elevation, the new Earl considered building a grand seat that would reflect his new status. Sir John Vanbrugh, who designed Blenheim Palace for Bristol's friend and patron the Duke of Marlborough, was consulted about Ickworth in 1703 and again in 1718; but Bristol, possibly because of his wife's fondness for high play at cards, decided it would be too expensive a procedure and resigned himself to the humble existing lodge.*

This cannot have pleased the upwardly mobile Lady Bristol. For the first years of their marriage she and the Earl wrote passionately to one another of their love – she concluded one letter, 'Oh! 'tis in vain to struggle with desires [as] strong as my love to thee; for every moment I'm from thy sight ye heart within my bosom moans like a tender infant in its cradle whose nurse had left it; come & with the songs of gentle love persuade it to its peace' – but by the 1710s her protestations of devotion rang increasingly hollow as she immersed herself in life at court. Lady Bristol snatched moments between engagements to write to her husband describing long nights of gambling and dancing, including accounts of her admirers; detailing her ailments (which often sound more like hangovers than serious illnesses); and always concluding with extravagant declarations of love.

---

* It was not until the 1790s that the fourth Earl of Bristol began work (completed by his son, the first Marquis of Bristol) on what is now Ickworth House. The first Earl was succeeded by Lord Hervey's eldest son, his grandson George, who was unmarried and died childless. On George's death his brother, Augustus. became Earl; but his purported son by his bigamous wife, Elizabeth Chudleigh, had died in infancy. Frederick, Hervey's third son, and Bishop of Derry, succeeded Augustus as fourth Earl of Bristol. Horace Walpole called him 'that mitred Proteus'; Emma Hamilton, Nelson's lover and the wife of the Earl-Bishop's best friend, Sir William Hamilton, said he treated 'even the immortality of the soul as an article of doubt and indifference'. Frederick's daughter was Lady Elizabeth Foster, who lived for many years in a *ménage à trois* with the Duke of Devonshire and his wife Lady Georgiana Spencer. Bess, as she was known, was said to combine in her person 'all the wit, all the subtlety, all *les agréments*, and all the wickedness of the Herveys'. See also Brian Fothergill's *The Mitred Earl* and Amanda Foreman's *Georgiana Duchess of Devonshire*.

Miserable as I am in body and mind, to whom should I complain but to the dear kind partner of all my happiness and distress, which indeed at this time is very great, for I am hardly able to stand or go, for we did not come home from Epsom till six o'clock this morning, but I must say, to make amends for the fatigue, I never saw people in so good humour as the Prince & Princess [the future George II and Caroline], and consequently all the rest of the company; but I am so much out of order that my company [friends] that dined with me today have made me lie down till this minute that I got up to make my complaint where I know I shall be pitied [i.e., by her husband]; and now I think I am easier [feeling better], but that will not be lasting, for the coaches are come to go to Kensington [Palace], so that I must bid my dear dear life, Adieu.

In 1723, Lady Mary Wortley Montagu observed Lady Bristol's indiscretions with a critical eye:

The Countess [of Bristol] is come out a new creature; she has left off the dull occupations of hazard and basset [games; one card, one dice] and is grown young, blooming, coquette and gallant; and to show she is full sensible of the errors of her past life, and resolved to make up for time mis-spent, she has two lovers at a time, and is equally wickedly talked of for the gentle Colonel Cotton and the superfine Mr Braddocks.

The one person whom Lady Bristol seemed to care for more than herself was her eldest son, on whom she doted. Her letters to her husband typically send her blessing to all their children (eleven in total), 'and something particular to Jack'. He had all the confidence of an adored child and loved using his skills of mimicry and word-play to attract the attention of his parents and siblings.

Jack's upbringing was typical of a boy of his age and class. He attended Westminster School in London, where he was well tutored in the classics by Dr Freind, and then Clare Hall, Cambridge, from 1713 to 1715. Holidays were spent between Ickworth and nearby Newmarket, where his father, who loved racing, had a second house. Jack was a fearless jockey, whose exploits made Bristol glow with pride but gave his overprotective mother sleepless nights. When she forbad him from racing, Bristol, who hoped Jack's intellectual proclivities would be counteracted by sport, protested vigorously. If you cosset him, he wrote to her, 'your . . . weakness . . . tends to nothing but effeminacy . . . you must determine to be content to see him live a shrimp or risk something to enable him to commence [to become] a man'. But Bristol's prophetic argument availed nothing.

Despite his bravery at Newmarket, Jack was a frail child. His mother's Felton blood was the source of the delicacy of health that plagued subsequent generations of Herveys. Lady Bristol called it her 'hysteric disorder', and treated herself with large doses of rhubarb and laudanum (opium dissolved in alcohol). Jack's ailments – rheumy eyes, headaches, fevers, colic and, at his worst, fits and delirium – were probably a mild form of epilepsy, compounded by general physical weakness. He was highly strung, plagued by his nerves. But for most of his life, as long as he took vigilant care of himself, Hervey was able to lead a relatively normal life.*

---

* He did have to follow a stringent regime, though. In 1732, Hervey wrote an angry letter to his doctor refuting charges that he was not an obedient patient.

If you were as just to *my* practice as I am to *your* doctrine, it would be impossible for you, whilst I always acknowledge and revere you as the great Aesculapius of this age and country, to speak of me as an apostate, a heretic or even a schismatic in your medicinal religion. In order therefore to set you right, and let you know who is one of your most pious votaries, I write this letter to tell you the method I am in. In the first place, I never taste wine or malt-drink or any liquid but water and milk-tea. In the next, I eat no meat but the whitest, youngest and tenderest; nine times in ten, nothing but chicken; and never more than the quantity of a small one at a meal. I seldom eat any supper; but, if any, absolutely nothing but bread and water. Two days in the week I eat no flesh. My breakfast is dry biscuit not sweet, and green tea. I have left off butter as bilious. I eat no salt, nor any sauce but bread-sauce. I take a Scotch pill once or twice a week, and thirty grains of Indian root, when my stomach is loaded, my head giddy and my appetite gone. I have been ill lately; but it was by an accident, and such a one as would have made a coach-horse sick. I bled, vomited, purged and sweated by my own prescription, and by these means in four days got rid of a sore throat, cough and fever, that would have stuck by a true beef and pork-eater as many months. After this account of myself, I expect you should compare me no more to *Mahomet's Tomb*, because I think my rigid perseverance in this faith entitles me, in the Heaven of Health, to the place immediately next to the Angel Gabriel (Ickworth, 9.12.32, to Dr Cheyne).

In 1716, after coming down from Cambridge, Jack was sent to Europe 'in order to his further travels', his father reported, 'wherein I beseech God almighty to protect and perfect him ye man I wish to see him [become]'. A letter written to Jack, aged twenty, in France, demonstrates Bristol's blinkered devotion to his son. Since the French had been so kind to Jack, he said, he could think almost as well of them as they do of themselves. Arrogance, that typically Gallic failing, was one Bristol was sure Jack lacked entirely, 'notwithstanding you possess as many tempting endowments to betray you into that vice as most young men'. This modesty was one of the beauties of his son's nature, he concluded, 'whenever a general survey is taken of you by ye pleased imagination of your most affectionate father'.

While Jack was away, his parents argued about whether or not he should be allowed to travel on to Italy, as he desired. Predictably, Bristol was forced to prohibit it at his wife's request: 'I find your Mama's tears and fears are both so very predominant whenever Italy is but mentioned, that rather than put myself into ye uneasy situation of standing answerable for all accidents that may happen in such an expedition, I am forced not only to sacrifice my own judgement but your improvement to her foolish fondness.'

The Grand Tour was a rite of initiation, not only in classical art and learning, but in sex as well; and Italy – as Defoe said, 'where blood ferments in rapes and sodomy' – was where many a young English nobleman developed a taste for sexual deviance. There, homosexuality was viewed with tolerance and experimentation considered natural. Alexander Pope described the young Aeneas's travels in Europe,

> Where, eased of Fleets, the Adriatic main
> Wafts the smooth Eunuch and enamour'd Swain.
> Led by my hand, he saunter'd Europe round,
> And gather'd ev'ry Vice on Christian ground.

It may be that Lady Bristol was aware of Italy's reputation and feared for the corruption of Jack's innocence; more likely, though, her motivation was venal rather than moral. Instead of going to the

land of culture and sin, Jack was sent to Hanover to lay 'ye foundation in Prince Frederick's [the son of George, Prince of Wales]
favour'. His parents knew that Jack would have a head start at court
when George came to Britain if he had already become friends
with the royal family. As a younger son, Jack could not rely on an
inheritance for his living. For a young man of his rank, there was
no better opportunity to make his own fortune than at court; and
with his parents' contacts and wealth he was well placed to make a
success of a career as a courtier. Sure enough, when the future
George II arrived in England in January 1717, the twenty-one-year-
old Jack Hervey was in his train. Lady Bristol, no less ambitious for
herself than for her son, used her connections to wangle a position
as Lady of the Bedchamber to George's wife, Caroline of Ansbach.

2. Jeunesse Dorée

Jack Hervey's intelligence and astonishing – if effete – good looks soon made him a favourite in the glamorous, tight-knit circle of young courtiers which included the witty Lord Chesterfield, the poets Alexander Pope and John Gay, and Carr, Lord Hervey, Jack's dazzling but dissolute half-brother and their father's heir. These bright young men, bored by the staid Germanic court of George I and frustrated there in their desires for office and honours, welcomed the arrival of his small, blustering son George, Prince of Wales, who professed to love the English and clearly revelled in his courtiers' attentions to him. Jack – now known as John – Hervey, famed for his charm and wit, became one of the brightest stars in this firmament, attracting the admiration not just of women but also of men as eminent as Voltaire, who spent his years of exile from France between 1726 and 1728 in England, and formed a friendship with Hervey that was to last the rest of Hervey's life.

The courtiers of the Prince and Princess of Wales formed a glittering, intimidating, debauched group. Their parents – if they were anything like Lord Bristol – must have deplored their morals and mores. In 1722, one observer was shocked at the girlishness of courtiers' attire: 'I believe the gentlemen will wear petticoats very soon for many of their coats were like our mantuas [dresses]. Lord Essex has a silver tissue coat, and pink colour lutestring [a glossy silk] waistcoat, and several had pink colour and pale blue paduasoy [another type of silk] coats, which looks prodigiously effeminate.' The age of the Macaronis, the height of eighteenth-century dandyism, had not yet dawned, but fops already strolled London's streets, red heels click-clacking, clouds of scented powder from their wigs issuing out behind them as they minced along waving scraps of lace masquerading as handkerchiefs. Englishmen were usually very simply dressed, in frock-coats without facings or pleats, unfussy wigs and plain hats; when people saw a well-dressed man, said the Swiss tourist Cesar de

Saussure (who had clearly been subject to this kind of attention), in 'a braided coat, a plume in his hat, or his hair tied in a bow', they would shout 'French Dog' at him. At court, though, extreme fashions were the norm. Hervey, called 'Hervey the Handsome', and always noted for his sartorial splendour, blossomed in this hothouse atmosphere. He was admired for the elegance of his slight figure and graceful hands, and his expressive, mobile face. For some months when he was twenty-three, he made a flamboyant feature of an eye-patch he was forced to wear by his weak, stinging eyes.

Princess Caroline's Maids of Honour were no less famous for their beauty and style than George's attendants:* there was Mary Bellenden, described by her contemporaries as 'the most perfect creature they ever knew' and by Hervey as being 'made up of every ingredient likely to engage or attract' a man; the flighty Sophia Howe, who ran away to London amateurishly disguised as a boy to be with her lover, announced her identity and desire to be with him to a large and interested mob which followed her to his house

---

* The royal chaplain, Bishop Burnet, complained to Princess Caroline that her pretty young Maids were causing distractions during his sermons in the Chapel Royal at St James's Palace. Caroline tried to discipline the girls, but to no avail. High panelling had to be erected around their pew to prevent them making eyes at the gentlemen of the court. Lord Peterborough, a great admirer of the Maids, wrote this poem about the incident:

> Bishop Burnet perceived that the beautiful dames
> Who flocked to the chapel of hilly St James'
> On their lovers alone did their kind looks bestow;
> And smiled not on him while he bellowed below;
> To the Princess he went, with pious intent,
> This dangerous ill to the church to prevent.
> 'Oh Madam,' he said, 'our religion is lost,
> If the ladies thus ogle the knights of the toast.
> These practices, Madam, my preaches disgrace:
> Shall laymen enjoy the first rights of my place?
> Then all may lament may condition so hard,
> Who thrash in the pulpit without a reward.
> Then pray condescend such disorders to end,
> And to the ripe vineyard the labourers send
> To build up the seats that the beauties may see
> The face of no brawling pretender but *me*.

and witnessed his undignified – and dishonourable – escape out of the back door; and the sweet, pretty Molly Lepell.

Days at court were filled with walking, riding and hunting in the royal parks, while the evening's entertainments were dancing and gambling. Wit was valued as highly as charm or beauty among these bright young things, and much time was spent in composing verses on love or topical gossip. Hervey's first published work was an allegorical verse entitled 'Monimia to Philocles' about the tragic early death of his friend Sophia Howe in 1726. When John Gay wrote a poem to commemorate his friend Alexander Pope's triumphant completion of his translation of the *Iliad* in 1720, he included Hervey among the celebrated figures at court:

> Now Hervey, fair of Face, I mark full well,
> With thee, Youth's youngest Daughter, sweet Lepell!

Hervey's companion, 'Sweet Lepell', was if not the most beautiful then one of the most popular of Princess Caroline's 'Virgin Band'. Mary, or Molly, Lepell was the daughter of a Danish courtier, Nicholas Lepell, who had come to England in Queen Anne's entourage, and then married an Englishwoman with lands in Suffolk. Molly was a slight girl with grey eyes and soft brown hair; her nickname among the other Maids of Honour was Schatz, meaning 'treasure' in German. She was celebrated in verse by Gay, Alexander Pope and Voltaire, and eulogized by Lord Chesterfield as the ideal eighteenth-century female:

She has been bred all her life at courts, of which she has acquired all the easy good breeding and politeness without the frivolousness. She has all the reading that a woman should have, and more than any woman need have: for she understands Latin perfectly well, though she wisely conceals it. No woman ever had more than she has *le ton de la parfaitement bonne compagnie, les manières engageantes et le je ne sais quoi qui plaît.**

* The style of the perfect companion, the engaging manner and the certain something that pleases.

But Chesterfield's description is ambivalent, although he did not intend it to be so: politely living all one's life at court pretending to be less well educated than one is smacks of the insincerity of which she was later accused.

In October 1720, when Gay described them together, Hervey and Molly Lepell had been secretly married for nearly six months. The first record of their acquaintance comes in a letter from Lady Bristol to her husband a year earlier. She and Jack, she reported, had dined at Lady Grizel Baillie's with Lady Grizel's daughter Griselda Murray, Molly's best friend and a former Maid of Honour, and Molly herself. Then the party had gone to the theatre. Lady Bristol made no comment on Miss Lepell, or on 'Jacky's' (as she still referred to her son) friendship with her. It would be unlikely if this was their first meeting, since by 1719 both had been at court several years; and the few surviving references to their friendship (in April 1720 Hervey was said to be terribly worried about Molly, who was ill) suggest it was well established by this time.

In May 1720, Lord Bristol wrote to welcome his pretty daughter-in-law to the family, 'with safety to ye secret'. J. W. Croker, the nineteenth-century compiler of Hervey's memoirs, speculates reasonably that their wedding was kept secret at first so that Molly could continue to receive her salary as Maid of Honour. Hervey, his father's second son, had no money of his own; perhaps at first they could not afford to give up Molly's court income.

Their marriage was a union of beauty and wit, but not fortune, and this, combined with the mystery which initially surrounded the match, suggests that the couple married for love. Bristol, writing to Molly in October 1720, spoke of knowing his son 'loves you so much above himself that he will even value my affection [for Molly] ye more for its being so much better disposed of [than on him]'. If fecundity is also an indication of conjugal happiness, then they were well satisfied with each other; their first child, tactically named George, was born in August 1721, and three more quickly followed.

Alexander Pope had been one of Molly Lepell's most ardent admirers before she married, but a letter he wrote to her in 1722 showed that he was beginning to see in her an affectation – which perhaps he attributed to her husband – that he regretted:

Now let me tell you I don't like your style; 'tis very pretty, therefore I don't like it . . . Methinks I have lost the Mrs L[epell; unmarried women were commonly addressed as 'Mrs'] I formerly knew, who writ and talked like other people (and sometimes better) . . . As I am too seriously yours and his [Hervey's] to put turns upon you instead of good wishes, so in return I should have nothing but honest plain how d'ye's and pray remember me's; which not being fit to be shown to anybody for wit, may be a proof we correspond only for ourselves, in mere friendliness.

Pope praised Molly's intelligence, but he was always quick to take umbrage. The new pretentions he complained of, Molly's airs and graces, drove a wedge between them; and his friendship with Hervey, still in evidence in this letter to Molly, deteriorated over the subsequent years from resentment to bitter jealousy.

Pope's feeling of being condescended to by the Herveys may have been exacerbated soon afterwards by their change of fortunes. In November 1723 Carr, Lord Hervey, the heir to the earldom of Bristol, died unmarried;* and his twenty-seven-year-old brother assumed the courtesy title of Lord Hervey and became heir to the Ickworth estates. From being the prospect-less younger son, John Hervey became, in his own words, 'a lazy titled heir to an estate'. But his marriage to a society beauty without a dowry now took on a new significance. Bristol had for some years before Carr's death been urging him to marry well to prevent 'ye crisis of our family's fate'. Hervey's failure to marry an heiress when the burden of his family's hopes was on Carr may not have mattered; it did matter when he would one day inherit the Bristol title and lands.

Bristol, rather than give way to misery on his bereavement, instead focused all his expectations on to his second son. God had taken Carr away from him, he told Hervey years later, so that Hervey could replace him in his heart. Bristol admitted his errant eldest son's debauched lifestyle had brought him more misery than his love for Carr had ever made him happy. Hervey's lifelong

---

* But not childless, according to contemporary gossip: it was rumoured he was the real father of Horace Walpole, born in 1717. This would help explain why Horace Walpole, who was devoted to his father Sir Robert but was remarkably unlike him, so detested Hervey.

endeavour to replace Carr's memory in their father's heart had succeeded, Bristol told him, by his achievements 'towards the credit and interests of our whole family'.

In the first years of their marriage Molly and Hervey seem to have lived together happily enough. According to Horace Walpole, Voltaire wrote an epigram (no longer extant) on seeing Hervey and his wife in bed together, 'in which he speaks of the beauty of both'. Lady Mary Wortley Montagu mentioned to her sister, the Countess of Mar, the 'ardent affection that Mrs Hervey and her dear spouse took to me' soon after their wedding (before Carr's death in 1723 when Mrs Hervey became Lady Hervey). They visited Lady Mary two or three times a day, and were 'perpetually cooing' in her rooms. Grown 'at last so weary of those birds of paradise', she was forced to flee to her riverside villa in Twickenham.

By as early as 1725 Lady Mary, one of Hervey's dearest friends, had become equivocal in her admiration of Lady Hervey. 'Lady Hervey is more delightful than ever, and such a politician, that if people were blind to merit, she would govern the nation,' she wrote to her sister. The next year she reported that '*Lady Hervey* makes the top figure in town, and is so good as *to show* twice a-week at the Drawing-room [the bi-weekly royal assemblies], and twice more at the opera, for the entertainment of the public'. The Duchess of Marlborough concurred with Lady Mary's judgement; she thought Molly Hervey, 'my Lord Fanny's wife', as she referred to her, 'extremely forward and pert'.

Lady Bristol did not like her new daughter-in-law either. While Bristol wrote with typical warmth and effusion to welcome Molly into the family, one suspects his request that 'since then yee have made yourselves so completely happy in each other, I hope and earnestly desire that yee would think of making my wife and me so too by living with us' would not have gone down well with Lady Bristol. She could not bear to be replaced in her favourite son's affections by another woman. Just months after Hervey and Molly's wedding, she ended a letter written to her husband, 'Jack is just arrived [at her apartments], so everybody is happy but poor me; I know ye time when I should have been so too at ye sight of him;

But now nor that nor nothing else can please;
Those were enjoyments for a mind at ease.'

Lady Bristol's animosity was not one-sided: Molly felt equally strongly about her mother-in-law, as she wrote to her best friend, Griselda Murray, describing her as 'hard as flint', and 'the oddest, and I fear the worst woman that ever lived'. In 1725, reported Lady Mary, Lady Bristol and her new daughter-in-law were almost at each other's throats, quarrelling publicly 'in such a manner that they have given one another all the titles so liberally bestowed amongst the ladies at Billingsgate [fish market]'.

By the mid-1720s Hervey, too, was increasingly disenchanted with the vain, pretty wife whom he had married a few years earlier in such romantic secrecy and haste. It is hard to tell as none of their correspondence survives, but it seems likely that as Molly's mannered charm began to grate on Hervey, he began to seek distraction in the endless round of entertainments available in London to a handsome young man of fortune and rank. Often leaving Molly with her in-laws at Ickworth, Hervey preferred to remain in town. He attended the theatre and the opera, masquerades and parties on the Thames. Blithely ignoring his physical delicacy, he would stay up until dawn several nights a week, talking, drinking and playing cards for high stakes. In Florence in 1740, the young Horace Walpole said his days consisted of slipping 'out of my domino into bed, and out of bed into my domino' and Hervey's life, like that described by Walpole, had become little more than an endless round of parties and routs. And this existence could begin to wear.

3. Stephen Fox

By the mid-1720s his dissipated lifestyle was taking its toll on Hervey's health, as well as depressing his spirits. As his marriage lost its allure, stimulated by late nights and overindulgence, and living in an emotional and intellectual void, Hervey became ill again. In November 1726, he went to Bath to consult the celebrated Dr Cheyne about his assorted ailments.

Hervey had been frustrated for years by the inefficaciousness of his doctors, many of whom were little more than quacks.

They all jog on in one beaten track; a vomit to clear your stomach, a glister to give you a stool, laudanum to quiet the pain, and then a purge to cleanse your bowels, and what they call 'carry it off'. This was their method in every attack; and, during the intervals, if bitters to restore my appetite, spa-water to raise my spirits, and ass's milk with powder of crab's eyes and oyster-shells to sweeten my blood, would not prevent the returns of my distemper, they none of them knew what else to try,

he wrote in 1731 as part of a treatise on his health intended 'merely for the benefit of my own family' that they might learn about the infirmities which he was convinced were hereditary.

Dr Cheyne found in Hervey a willing convert to his methods. Unusually for the period, Cheyne believed that most medicines were 'palliatives, but not remedies' and advised his patients to change their diet instead of depending on being blooded or given purgatives to relieve their ailments. He recommended eating as little meat as possible and avoiding alcohol: singular advice in an age when men were hardly considered men if they did not eat the greater part of a cow washed down with several bottles of claret each day.

There at Bath – or 'the Bath' as it was referred to by the aristocratic visitors who congregated there to bathe in and drink its mineral waters while enjoying the social life for which the town was also famous – Hervey met the twenty-one-year-old Henry Fox. The two quickly became firm friends, as Hervey's first letter to him, written on 23 November just after Fox left the spa-town, revealed.

I have an unbounded curiosity with regards to those I love; but your reservedness, I fear, will make it live upon as slender a diet as a patient of Dr Cheyne's . . . I think with pleasure on everything you have ever said to me, but never find so much satisfaction in reflecting on our short past acquaintance, as when I think of it an earnest [pledge] of a long future friendship.

Henry Fox's detachment, one of the patterns of the long friendship so accurately predicted by Hervey, was evident even during the first weeks after they met.

The following week Hervey was back in London, writing again to Fox at Redlynch, his elder brother Stephen's house in Somerset, in a vain attempt to lure his new friend up to the fleshpots of the capital. 'What amusements you find now in the country I cannot conceive. I take the season to be rather too cold for the diversion of swimming. I'm sure 'tis too wet for any other without doors. The floods must have confined you to your Ark; and if your brother still shoots, it must be out of his window.' Henry, unmoved, remained at Redlynch several weeks, and Hervey, by this time a little petulant, was forced to write again: 'I hate your brother [Stephen] without knowing him, (which is perhaps the only way one can hate him) for postponing another week the pleasure I have waited for so long, and expected with so much impatience.'

Henry and Stephen Fox were the only sons of Sir Stephen Fox, who had made an immense fortune (from nothing) as Paymaster General to Charles II.★ In 1703, as an elderly widower, he married the companion of one of his daughters from his first marriage, Miss Christian Hopes. Three of their four children survived to

★ He was in the same department as Samuel Pepys.

adulthood: Stephen, born in 1704, Henry, in 1706, and Charlotte, the youngest. Sir Stephen died in 1713, followed three years later by his wife. At the age of twelve young Ste (as he was called at home) became the head of the family, responsible for his orphaned siblings. The children, drawn together by their shared loss, became, and remained, intensely close.

Ste and Henry were sent to Eton, and then Christ Church, Oxford. In 1723, Ste came down from Oxford and went to Europe with his tutor, Dr Wigan, while Henry stayed behind at Oxford to finish his studies. Dr Wigan wrote to Henry from Brussels that Ste was passing 'his time here to his satisfaction; but he is, as I am afraid you are, very lazy in lying abed, and makes me lie as long as himself for fear of disturbing him. But then I must needs say he is very sober and virtuous, which I hope rather than believe you are.' Charlotte Fox wrote to her brother Henry while he was in London at this time, teasing him about being a 'good-for-nothing toad' who spent all his nights at the Cocoa Tree coffee-house gambling and drinking. These early assessments of the two brothers' natures are accurate: Stephen was modest, moderate, self-sufficient; Henry was more flamboyant, more obviously brilliant, and wild.

Bored by his wife, pestered by his parents, exhausted by London, Hervey was searching for an attachment that would satisfy him as his marriage and his social life no longer did. He needed something to devote himself to, and the Fox brothers became his new passion. Over the following few months, when Henry Fox finally came to London, bringing Ste with him, Hervey threw himself at his new friends. Together they attended grand assemblies and royal levees, gambled in smoky chocolate-houses, and gossiped at political dinner parties. They walked through the streets of London's West End, past the imposing mansion being built by the Earl of Burlington on Piccadilly (now the Royal Academy), down to Westminster and through the ranks of tawdry streetwalkers towards the Houses of Parliament where both Ste and Hervey sat as MPs. They rode in the afternoons through Hyde Park, shopped for heavily embroidered silks in Jermyn Street (where Hervey's father had his London house), and watched the rival Italian prima donnas, Cuzzoni and Faustina, sing in theatres so opulent that it was not uncommon for wicker cages full of songbirds to be opened on the stage so the birds could take flight above the singers' heads.

Gradually it became clear to Hervey that although he liked Henry, and enjoyed the challenging political and intellectual discussions in which they engaged, it was the gentle Ste to whom he was emotionally drawn. Slight (like Hervey), country-loving and charming, Ste was calmer than his brother Henry, the kind of man about whom a harsh word is never spoken, yet who avoids being thought boring. Hervey found his fondness for Ste so well confirmed by others, he told him that 'everybody's good opinion of you is proportioned to the degree in which they are acquainted with you'. According to Hervey, Ste combined in his person all the qualities of the ideal eighteenth-century man: 'parts', which meant intelligence, honour and virtue; warmth of affection; the ability to sympathize; a sense of humour; and 'good breeding', or tact and moderation. 'I dote on the negligence of your style,' Hervey told Ste in 1729, two years after they met, 'it has a double merit when one wishes so heartily to have the things you say natural.' The traits that stand out most clearly from Hervey's letters to him,* over two and a half centuries later, are Ste's unaffected ease of manner and his self-containedness. Ste filled his days at Redlynch as agreeably, said Hervey (slightly surprised), as he himself did in London.

Ste tolerated London, but only felt truly himself in the country. He was absorbed, when Hervey met him, in improving Redlynch (which had been built by his father), erecting new buildings and a park wall, and redesigning the park, adding woods and a lake. Redlynch was a comfortable, plainly built stone house situated halfway up a hill, well aspected and surrounded by trees; higher up the hill was a little chapel set in a grove. Inside, when Horace Walpole visited Redlynch in later years, were portraits of the three

---

* Only two of Ste's letters to Hervey survive, in the Holland House Papers in the British Library. Both men's letters were written on thick, cream paper, often edged with gold, in black ink which has faded with age. Many still retain particles of glitter from the sand used to blot the ink. They were folded up and sealed with red wax; Hervey used his family crest (three clubs diagonally across a shield) as his seal, Ste a Fox.

Fox children, Ste, Henry and Charlotte; Sir Robert Walpole; and Lady Hervey, dressed in white, accompanied by a dog. In the hall was a bust of Hervey made by Bouchardon in Rome in 1729, its classical pose echoing the bas relief of the huntress Diana over the fireplace, copied from another copy of the antique original at Sir Robert Walpole's Norfolk house, Houghton.

As Molly Hervey wrote to Henry Fox, Ste 'is such a country gentleman that unless one could be metamorphosed into a bird or hare he will have nothing to say to one'. He was a brilliant shot: the game book from Maddington, his hunting-box on Salisbury Plain, records him on one day bagging twenty-two partridges, one pheasant and a wild duck – without missing a single shot. One entry in 1739 reads, 'Memorandum: Mr H. Fox a great boaster of his shooting. S. Fox made such a shot today that H. Fox could not, nor ever will.' This boyish, wholesome way of life was a far cry from the drawing rooms, gambling and politicking that Hervey loved. But, jaded and ill when he met Ste, Hervey found his lack of sophistication a relief, his naturalness a tonic. And he was impressed by Ste's sense of self: despite his youth, Ste seemed unmoved by others' opinions of him; Hervey, who craved attention, must have found this quality not only refreshing but intriguing.

By the end of May 1727 Stephen had returned to Redlynch from London, and Hervey's letters followed him there with a mixture of sadness at his leaving and a sense of wonder at the intensity of their friendship. 'I have thought of you and wished for you a thousand times since you went,' he marvelled. What Ste had said to him as they bid each other goodbye had allowed Hervey to hope, for the first time, that Ste might return his affections with something of his own passion. 'I begin to doubt whether you have not a heart susceptible of some impressions, and if great perseverance and a faithful attachment might not in length of time eat into that adamantine outside which I once thought impenetrable.' If this miracle should take place, Hervey continued, he was encouraged to think that just as impressions were more difficult to make on hard surfaces, so too are they more difficult to erase, and 'possession will be sure, in the same way that acquisition was difficult'. Love, then, rather than mere friendship, was what Hervey undisguisedly hoped for from Ste.

4. Sir Robert Walpole

Despite his apparently single-minded pursuit of Ste Fox in the early summer of 1727, Hervey was distracted at the same time by unfolding political events. This dichotomy between private and public interests – and Hervey's ability to become consumed by one at the expense of the other, at the same time as trying to retain his hold over both – was to become a pattern for him. On 15 June, Hervey wrote to inform Henry Fox of George I's death, adding that the new Parliament this necessitated would mean that, as MP for Shaftesbury, Stephen would have to come up to London, and 'I shall be an early gainer of one pleasure at least by the new reign'.

The King had had a stroke in his coach near Osnabrück, in Hanover, and died soon afterwards. On hearing the news, George I's first minister, Sir Robert Walpole, rushed from dinner at his house in Chelsea to Richmond to inform George II of his father's death. He was rumoured to have ridden two horses to their deaths on the way, in his haste to reach the new monarch before anyone else. In a farcical scene, Walpole knelt to pay homage to his new master as the dapper George was buttoning up his breeches before dinner. Walpole asked the King whom he would like to have draw up the declaration to the Privy Council; George, who had loathed his father, and by extension was determined to loathe his chief servant Walpole, curtly replied, 'Sir Spencer Compton.' So Sir Robert galloped back to London and informed Spencer Compton, the Speaker of the House of Commons, of George's choice. 'My time has been, yours is beginning,' he said to Compton; but soon after, Walpole warned his political ally, Sir William Yonge, not to give up hope of remaining in power. 'I shall certainly go out; but let me recommend you not to go into violent opposition, as we must soon come in again.'

Sir Spencer Compton was a dull, complaisant man whose ambitions far exceeded the attributes he needed to achieve them;

he was known more for his propensity to burst into tears in moments of stress than for his political nous. Hervey described him at this time as 'dazzled with the lustre of so bright a prospect' being held before him. He was so politically ignorant that, unsure of the correct form of the declaration he had been asked to draw up, he enlisted his rival Walpole's aid. Walpole gladly drafted the paper and gave it to Compton, who took it to read to the new King. When he reached a point he did not understand he was forced to call out to Walpole, standing nearby, to explain it to him. It was clear, even to a man as predisposed as George was to dislike Walpole, who was the superior politician.

But it was finances, rather than political acumen, that clinched it for Walpole in the end. He was able to guarantee George a civil list of over £900,000 per annum, £40,000 more than Compton offered, and a rise of over £200,000 a year from George I's list. Sir Robert had risen to prominence during the South Sea Crisis in the autumn of 1720 (a mess from which Hervey emerged one of the few winners; he was said to have made £20,000, presumably by selling his shares early). George I had consulted Walpole on how best to deal with the bursting Bubble, and Walpole, responding with calm, confident leadership, had restored public credit. In the following year he was rewarded with two offices: Chancellor of the Exchequer and First Lord of the Treasury. He was now, *de facto*, the first Prime Minister, even though the position did not yet exist by that name. From 1721 Walpole consolidated his grasp of power not by moving into the Upper House but by dominating the House of Commons and working tirelessly to retain the King's favour. These tactics were the basis for his domination of British politics that was to last over twenty years.

Queen Caroline, who recognized Walpole's talents – and appreciated that Walpole paid his court to her rather than to Mrs Howard, her husband's mistress – was instrumental in convincing her husband to retain him as first minister; indeed, she let Walpole know that Compton had managed to scrape together only £60,000 for her jointure, enabling him to outbid his rival. 'New leeches would not be less hungry,' she told her husband. In the first official Drawing-room she held as Queen, Caroline looked around her

and saw Lady Walpole lost in the vast crowd. 'There I am sure I
see a friend,' she said, making her way over to her. The Queen's
attentions distinguished Lady Walpole with the badge of royal
favour. As she said to her son, Horace, years later, when she arrived
that day no one had bothered to speak to the wife of the former
first minister, 'in returning I might have walked on their heads so
eager were they to pay their court to me'. So Walpole retained his
place at the Treasury, and Spencer Compton was kicked upstairs
to the House of Lords to sugar-coat his political failure. But, said
Hervey, Compton was so pathetic he 'did not seem to feel the
ridicule or the contemptibleness' in his promotion; he failed to
notice the dishonour of 'a title which was the mark of his disgrace'.

Early eighteenth-century politics were highly personal. The
character of the King's mistress, for instance, might sway affairs;
and Queen Caroline wielded power because of the personal control
she maintained over her husband, George II. One of the best
examples of the subjective nature of politics at this time is the
importance that was attached to opera. Both George II and his
estranged son, Frederick, adored opera, and they attended the
London theatres regularly. The stars of these performances inspired
passionate support in their fans. In 1727 the rivalry between two
Italian prima donnas, Cuzzoni and Faustina, was so intense that it
was said 'no Cuzzonist will go to a tavern with a Faustinian'.
Senesino, a male contralto, was so jealous of the attention paid to
his female counterparts that he took 'it for a mark of contempt
that he was not distinguished with a cat-call'. In 1734, the most
celebrated contralto of the moment was Carestini, whom Hervey
patronized, and who had made Hervey's friend Thomas Winnington, 'who has been all his life an atheist to the power of music,
a bigot to it'. But on the arrival of the castrato Farinelli in London,
Carestini's ascendancy was over. Prince Frederick patronized Farinelli, and his impresario Porpora; his father remained loyal to
Carestini and Handel, his composer. 'An anti-Handelist,' said Hervey, 'was looked upon as an anti-courtier.' The Princess Royal told
Hervey she expected soon to see half the House of Lords in their
robes and coronets playing in the orchestra to demonstrate their
support for Handel – and, thus, for the King.

Lord Bristol lost no time in paying his respects to the new monarch on behalf of his beloved son. Less than a week after George I's death, Bristol was somewhat inappropriately congratulating his successor on the 'happy occasion' that had brought him to the throne, and urging him to make use not of his own services – though Bristol assured George of the 'zeal and steady adherence I have always had and shall ever have for your Majesty and your royal family' – but of Hervey's. His son's establishment 'in your Majesty's favour is ye thing in this world I have most at heart', he explained, begging George to 'promise some way or other to provide for him; his affection and fidelity I will stand bound for; his abilities I hope will answer for themselves'.

Despite his father's hopes, Hervey's interest in the jostlings that attended George II's accession was keen but, as yet, impersonal. Although he supported Walpole in the House of Commons – and prided himself on having refused to pay court to Spencer Compton when he looked certain to replace Sir Robert as Prime Minister – Hervey's role was still that of observer of events rather than parti-cipator in them. He was disappointed at first not to receive a place in Walpole's initial batch of appointments, but he let Walpole know he was interested in becoming more involved in government, and awaited the moment when affairs should have settled down enough for the reinstated Prime Minister to make changes to his administration.

The choice of Walpole as political mentor was an unusual one for a man like Hervey of such delicate sensibilities. Walpole, twenty years Hervey's senior, was a vast, hearty figure whose coarseness belied his penetrating insight, administrative genius and skills of persuasion. Even Queen Caroline, who relied utterly upon his political perspicacity, was repulsed by his person, '*avec ce gros corps, ces jambes enflées, et ce vilain ventre*';* she and the King referred to their chief minister as '*le gros homme*'.† For all his vulgarity, Sir Robert possessed enormous charm to which even his political adversaries were not immune: Alexander Pope, describing Walpole

---

* With its fat body, its swollen legs and its vile belly.
† The fat man.

'unencumbered with the venal tribe', saw him 'smile without art, and win without a bribe'.

His opponents objected to the cavalier attitude with which Walpole controlled and dispensed patronage. His followers – later known as 'Walpole's Whelps' – were criticized for sacrificing their honour to serve an opportunistic minister whose policies were despoiling England and denegrating her king. Just as the arch-criminal Jonathan Wild lured boys into a life of crime with promises of rewards and favour, so too Walpole was thought to have set out to pervert the morals of the men, like Hervey, who served him. In the words of the nineteenth-century editor of Hervey's *Memoirs of the Court of King George II*, Sir Robert 'made a point of debauching the political morals of his boys, preaching a rationalized scoundrel-ism, systematically deriding political decencies, and using his pres-tige and influence, with considerable success, to lower the tone of public life'. The most explicit contemporary illustration of public perceptions of Walpole's corruption is John Gay's *The Beggar's Opera*, which compares Walpole to both Peachum, the greedy thief-taker, and Lockit, the corrupt gaoler. Even Whig loyalists like Lord Bristol distrusted Walpole's opportunism and feared for the security of the constitutional changes they had helped establish. But despite all the controversy he engendered, the King and Queen soon came to depend entirely on Sir Robert.

The streets around Westminster Abbey were packed by 4 a.m. on the autumn day the new monarchs were crowned. Cesar de Saussure left his lodgings early to watch the proceedings. The peers and their wives processed past in long crimson kirtles lined in white satin and edged with flame-cut green silk, over which they wore heavy green cloaks edged in ermine and fastened with thick silver tassels. 'When the Duchesses were in front of our seats, the pro-cession was for a time brought to a stop,' Saussure wrote. 'The Dowager Duchess of Marlborough took a drum from a drummer and seated herself on it.' The crowd, he continued, went wild at the incongruous sight of the aged wife of their national hero plonking herself down for a rest in the middle of this most solemn event.

Lady Mary Wortley Montagu, writing to Hervey in Bath, was

less flattering in her descriptions of the peeresses attending the event.

The business of every walker there was to conceal vanity and gain admiration. For these purposes some languished and others strutted; but a visible satisfaction was diffused over every countenance, as soon as the coronet was clapped on the head. She that drew the greatest number of eyes was indisputably Lady Orkney [William III's *maîtresse en titre* after Mary died]. She exposed behind, a mixture of fat and wrinkles; and before, a very considerable protuberance which preceded her. Add to this, the inimitable roll of her eyes, and her grey hairs, which by good fortune stood directly upright, and 'tis impossible to imagine a more delightful spectacle. She had embellished all this with considerable magnificence, which made her look as big again as usual.

But everyone had made as much effort as Lady Orkney. Another visitor, Mrs Delany, who like Saussure had set out at the crack of dawn to secure a good vantage point – and survived the crowds which at one point threatened to squash her 'flat as a pancake' – thought it a little conceited of the exquisite Duchess of Queensberry to scorn ornamentation. She depended so much upon her native beauty that she despised all adornments, and 'had not one jewel, riband, or puff to set her off, but everybody thought she did *not* appear to advantage'.

George and Caroline were, of course, highly embellished. The Queen's dress was made of gold and silver tissue, brocaded with large bunches of different coloured flowers, its skirt thickly embroidered with jewels. George's cap, as Saussure called it, was made of crimson velvet, with a gold circlet and a border of ermine which did not stop it falling over his face into his eyes. Apparently he did not mind this, as Hervey in his *Memoirs* commented that George adored 'all the pageantry and splendour and badges and trappings of royalty'; but he must have presented an amusing spectacle, a small man, dwarfed by his crown and rich clothes. Caroline's jewels, the splendour of which so impressed Saussure, were, added Hervey, many of them borrowed to create this effect. This 'mixture of magnificence and meanness [was] not unlike the *éclat* of royalty in many other particulars when it comes to be nicely examined and its sources traced to what money hires or flattery lends', he concluded.

5. Remembrances

Throughout these months of political activity, Hervey continued to write to assure Ste of the profundity of his feelings for him. 'Though I have lived ever since I saw you in a constant hurry and a perpetual succession of different company, I don't find any change can produce so great a one in me, as to make me less regret the loss of you,' he lamented on 3 July 1727, going on to thank Ste for his last letter and the warmth of his assurances of friendship. Hervey would not tell Ste how much he cared about him, in case it seemed mere *politesse*, but to him the written word was as sacred as an oath. He would think worse, he said, of a man who lied in a court of justice than one who lied in a letter to a friend. 'I insist therefore on your never doubting what I convey to you that way; that you take it all for gospel, and never send me anything apocryphal in return.' By emphasizing his sincerity, and challenging Stephen to return it, Hervey was implicitly raising the stakes. He wanted to force Ste into declaring that he cared as much about their relationship as Hervey did.

Although eighteenth-century letter-writing convention decreed that extravagant protestations of love were common, whether the relationship was familial, platonic or sexual, Hervey's letters to Stephen Fox were unusual in the strength of passion they conveyed. The principal characteristic of eighteenth-century letters was their 'sentimentalism', the eagerness to communicate mutual affection, and the belief that to do so was the expression of man's innate benevolence. 'What charming advantages, what high delights,' wrote Samuel Richardson in 1747, 'flow from the familiar correspondences of friendly and undesigning hearts.' It was quite common for friends to talk of living together in intimacy, and it did not mean that the pair were lovers; vows of love and devotion abound in letters from men to men and women to women, and do not necessarily indicate a sexual relationship. But Hervey's letters to

Stephen are utterly different in style from those he wrote to friends such as Lady Mary Wortley Montagu and Henry Fox, or to his parents – all of which are marked by love and fondness, but lack the intensity which permeates every word he wrote to Ste.

The early eigheenth century was called the Augustan Age as a self-conscious reference to the glorious Roman age of the Emperor Augustus, in which the arts flourished in an atmosphere of enlightenment and political stability. This was the era of Addison and Steele's *Spectator*, of Hogarth's painting, of the poetry of Pope and the satirical genius of Swift; all of these, in their differing ways, intended to illuminate the era for posterity – to make, in the words of the poet Horace (one of the brightest lights of the Roman Augustan Age), their 'monument more lasting than bronze'. English Augustans believed that they lived in a second golden age, and they sought to emulate the civilization of the ancients. In their turn, they strove to record their age for the generations that would succeed them. The art that epitomizes this era is that of letter-writing.

The ideal letter was thought to be one which combined both literary form and conversational spontaneity: an artful artlessness. 'The beauty of writing,' believed Mrs Delany, 'consists in telling our sentiments in an easy natural way.' Letters should read like Pope's 'talking upon paper,' yet had also to have enough stylistic merit to render them worthy of the attention of future generations. In the 1710s the diarist Dudley Ryder praised John Locke's writing style for the qualities admired by his own generation: 'it seems to have come from him without any study or choice of words, but to have writ his thoughts down as they presented themselves to him at different levels, much such language as a man that is full of a subject and had a command of words would use in conversation'. This effect, however, was easier to discuss than to achieve. Alexander Pope – notorious for the dullness of his conversation – prided himself on the simple intimacy of his letters, yet he was criticized by his first biographer Samuel Johnson for writing letters 'always with his reputation in his head'.

The refreshing thing about Hervey's letters to Stephen Fox is that though he recognized their literary value (many of them survive as transcripts written in a secretary's hand), they were written with the eyes of only one person in mind. Usually letters, such as Lady Mary Wortley Montagu's describing the coronation, were treated like newspapers, written to be passed around and discussed. But unlike Chesterfield's letters of advice to his heir, or Pope's to his friends and enemies, the only reader Hervey cared about influencing or impressing was Ste. His passionate outpourings reveal a man unaffected by the opinion of others and marked by a profound sense of scepticism for everything but the object of his affections. Hervey's detachment, which in the letters is tempered – almost concealed – by his love for Fox, is the predominant tone in all his other writings, especially the *Memoirs*. This is the voice by which Hervey became known in his own generation; and its contrived coolness must partly explain the ambivalence with which Hervey has been regarded since his death.

During a period in which the highest accolade that could be bestowed upon a man was a comparison with Atticus or Seneca, the classical ideals of reason and moderation were extolled above all others. In Alexander Pope's words, a man must be, 'though learned, well-bred', his primary care to put others at their ease. La Rochefoucauld's paradigm of the *honnête homme* was embraced by his eighteenth-century readers. Like the classical concept of *virtu*, this model of behaviour encouraged men to be educated, amusing, honourable and always in control. As Lord Chesterfield reminded his son, 'The Graces! The Graces! Remember the Graces!' The perfect eighteenth-century gentleman was good at everything, and excessive in nothing. In Jonathan Swift's words, he would be,

> Blest with each talent, and with each art to please
> And born to write, converse, and live with ease.

This standard is ever-present in Hervey's correspondence, apparent both in the way he judged others and in the way he tried to behave himself.

Like the sixteenth-century French essayist, Michel de Mon-

taigne, whom he greatly admired, Hervey strove to control his
passionate nature. Montaigne, whose outpouring of grief at the
death of his lover reveals him as a man of intense emotion, wrote
in his essay 'On Sadness' (apparently more in an effort to convince
himself), 'I am little subject to these violent passions (love, or
grief, &c. that can produce numbness or fire). My susceptibility is
naturally tough; and I harden and thicken it every day by force of
reason.' As he matured, Hervey tried to deal with life's blows with
Montaignian philosophical indifference; but the detached ideal he
strove towards always eluded him.

At the end of August 1727, when his sister Betty Mansel, 'whom
I loved better than all the rest of our nursery put together', finally
died after a long illness, Hervey was unable to stop himself surren-
dering to inconsolable grief. His father wrote to urge him to seek
solace in 'submission to ye will of God' especially since, as he added,
'you ought to adore rather than accuse his providence for bereaving
you only of a second-rate treasure, where his goodness hath yet
spared your wife and all your hopeful children'. This was what he
was doing, wrote Bristol, to console himself: 'though I have borne
a most sensible share in our common loss, yet I can never make
myself so completely wretched as to think ye chief ornament of my
family gone, as long as God vouchsafes to spare your more valuable
life'.

Fears about his own ill-health (aggravated by Betty's death) and
disappointment at not being offered a position in Walpole's newly
formed government brought Hervey back to his sick-bed in the
autumn of 1727. He admitted that his physical symptoms were caused
as much by his nerves as by any specific disease, and had resorted to
laudanum in order to calm them: he was far from well. His relationship with Ste was established enough after six months of intimacy
that Fox, rather than Molly, took over the responsibility of nursing
Hervey back to health. Ste, he reported in his treatise, 'who loved
me too well not to take a part in anything that made me uneasy and
do all in his power to alleviate the weight of it', took Hervey first to
Redlynch in early October and then on to Bath for two months.

Hervey ordered his wife to stay at Ickworth while he was in
Bath, explaining that the added expense would be too much for

him and that he did not think her presence would help him feel better. Molly Hervey was miserable without her husband – "tis impossible for anyone to be more destitute of spirits than I am' – telling her friend, Griselda Murray, that the only pleasure she found at this time was in writing to and hearing from him; but she never questioned Hervey's decision to remain apart, or that she live with the mother-in-law who made no secret of her loathing for Molly.

And so, abandoned in Suffolk by her husband, Molly had little outlet for her feelings but the letters she incessantly penned. But she never blamed Hervey for her isolation. Indeed, her trust in him was so absolute that she wrote, again to Griselda, that she was afraid her friends and family were conspiring against her, pretending that Hervey was not seriously ill so that she would not worry. It was hard not to be with him, she continued sadly, but she knew it was out of consideration for her that he had asked her to stay at Ickworth; though she could not refrain from adding, 'yet I think I should in his case rather have desired, than forbid, one I loved to be with me'. Even if Hervey was no longer in love with Molly, she remained so besotted with him that she readily justified his neglect to herself.

Ste and Hervey spent their time in Bath drinking the waters, playing quadrille and attending the assemblies. Hervey amused himself by writing witty letters to Lady Mary Wortley Montagu. 'I will not make the common excuse for a dull letter, of writing from a dull place,' he began one letter. If a letter fails to be entertaining, it is not because the writer lacks material, but that the writer lacks 'genius'. But, Hervey continued with stunning understatement, he was not passing his time disagreeably despite Bath's monotony, for his temper was one which allowed him to be happy whomever he happened to be with, whatever he happened to be doing.

What came after this passage is cryptic, at best, and was written to follow on from a conversation the two had had at an earlier time; but it seems to be a veiled defence of homosexual love, capped with a perfunctorily conventional compliment to his reader.

As to your manner of living at Twickenham, I entirely disapprove [of] it. Nature never designed you to perform the offices of a groom and a nursery-maid; if you would be sincere, you must own, *riding* is inverting her [Nature's] dictates in your search of pleasure [Lady Mary had a reputation for lasciviousness], or you must confess yourself an example of the maxim which I laid down, and you controverted so warmly two nights before I left London. I have met with several accumulated proofs since I saw you [since Hervey had been with Ste], that confirm me more and more in that faith; and begin to think it impossible I should change my religion, unless you will be so good to take my conversion into your own hands.

The only letter Hervey wrote to Fox that actually mentions a physical relationship was written soon after they met, in June 1727. Hervey chided Ste for not coming to London – 'you will not find it quite so easy to make me believe you, when you say you wish you were in town again. If your wishes were very strong (since your horses are so very sound), what hinders your gratification of them?' – and went on to complain that he couldn't write intelligibly about how much he missed Ste; and even if he could, Ste would not understand him. 'I might as well talk to a blind man of colours, an atheist of devotion, or an eunuch of f—' [sic].
He continued,

You have left some such remembrances behind you that I assure you (if 'tis any satisfaction to you to know it) you are not in the least danger of being forgotten; the favours [bruises] I received at your honour's *hands* are of such a nature that though the impression might wear out of my mind, yet they are written in such lasting characters upon every limb, that 'tis impossible for me to look on a leg or an arm, without having my memory refreshed: I have some thoughts of exposing the marks of your *polissonnerie* [naughtiness] to move compassion, as the beggars that have been slaves at Jerusalem do the burnt crucifix upon their arms; they have remained so long I begin to think they are equally indelible.

Considering how frequently letters were opened and read at this time, either by greedy servants hoping to bribe their indiscreet employers, or curious politicians, this was probably as direct as one could be about sex. Hervey's letters are littered with references to other readers.* He never signed his letters to Ste, relying on his correspondent to recognize his writing, and this practice was also endorsed by Lady Hervey, writing to the tutor of her sons in 1743: 'Do not, for the future, use the formality of signing your letters: you may possibly have the occasion to write such news as may be better unsigned.' 'There is a great deal of news in town,' she told Griselda Murray in 1729, 'but as I know I'm writing to the Post-masters as well as to my dear Grisy I shan't impart it to them, though I would to you.' Lord Chesterfield was even more direct and blasé in his approach to the problem, concluding a letter to George II's mistress Mrs Howard (later Lady Suffolk) with, 'I make my compliments likewise to those who will open and peruse this letter before you do.'

Despite the frequency with which letters, especially those to and from people involved in politics, were opened, they were still the only form of long-distance communication and often a more reliable source of news than newspapers. When Ste was at Redlynch, or Henry Fox was abroad, Hervey's letters brought them the news from London sometimes as often as twice a week. Hervey chaffed them about their 'quidnunc lechery' but loved being so depended upon, filling his letters with hints about things that were occurring in their absence, but that he could not commit fully to paper. It is a mark of his insecurity that he felt he had to make the Foxes believe that he was the repository of news they could not hear elsewhere, as if in order to guarantee their friendship for himself.

* One interesting point is that Hervey saved copies of his letters to Ste at Ickworth. After his death, both his wife and father, who survived him, might have read them. Did Hervey care? And further, the first twenty-seven pages of the letter-book containing his letters to Ste have since been cut out. By whom? When? And what scandal did they contain that was considered worse than Hervey's letters to Fox? They may have been destroyed by the first Marquis of Bristol, who removed the years 1730–32 from Hervey's handwritten *Memoirs*; or by Hervey himself. Hervey's first modern biographer, Robert Halsband, speculates that they may have been letters to another lover, with whom Hervey corresponded more openly about sex than he later did with Ste. What happened to Ste's letters to Hervey is another point of interest: the most likely explanation is that Hervey's son returned them to Fox after Hervey's death, as he did Lady Mary Wortley Montagu's letters to her, and that Ste then destroyed them.

If Hervey restrained from any further mention of sex, however oblique, in his other letters to Ste, he never felt the need to do so with regard to declarations of love and analyses of Ste's temperament and his affection for Hervey. Writing to Ste at Redlynch after his own return to London in December 1727, Hervey spoke of the sacrifice he had made in not insisting that Fox stay in town with him. 'You once told me, you never were so convinced 'twas impossible for you to be happy or even easy when you were from that [which] you had resolved for the future, never to be out of long sight whenever it was avoidable.' He had this promise in Ste's own writing, Hervey reminded Ste, even though it was written at such a time – in the heat of passion, perhaps – that would make it as wrong for Hervey to insist upon holding Ste to his word as if he had sworn it while he was drunk.

Hervey went on to develop a rhetorical argument that he was to use frequently over the subsequent years of their relationship, describing Ste's make-up as one that did not allow him to feel things as deeply as Hervey did, and placing himself in the role of supplicant as well as mentor. 'After all I have said,' he concluded,

do not imagine me so injust as to impute your journey [back to Redlynch] entirely to a cooler way of thinking towards me; neither would I have you flatter yourself that 'tis solely *l'ennui de Londres* that made you undertake it; there is more owing to the inquietitude *de votre tempérament* than you would be willing to find out, or to allow if you did . . . Adieu. [Dr] Amyand has put a fresh caustic to my cheek but the pain I am most sensible under is from the caustic your absence has put to my heart.

The last letter that survives from 1727 was dated two days later, 30 December. Hervey reported that he and Henry Fox had looked at a house in Grosvenor Square which might do for Stephen; in planning to rent a house in London Ste was clearly hoping to spend more time with Hervey, as he had promised him he would.

I have told you all that made my writing seem necessary; yet I feel as unsatisfied with what I have said and as unwilling to conclude, as if I grudged every word that related to anything but the state of my heart, or as if the thought of my writing forever could make you acquainted with it. It is charitable in me to believe you do not guess at it for if you did, what must I think of your being able to leave me!

Hervey's letters to Fox were beginning to express not simply the initial attraction that had marked his early letters, but a new intensity in their relationship. Hervey's correspondence with Ste and Lady Mary indicates that he and Fox had become lovers soon after they met, but Hervey's first letter to Ste in 1728 reflects his desire for a deeper, more lasting attachment: this was more than a passing fancy. Written on 2 January from London to Redlynch, Hervey at first refused to reproach Ste for disappointing his hopes of a letter by the post of the day before. He did not want Ste to write to him just because Hervey had asked him to; as soon as Ste ceased to want to be with him Hervey would cease to desire his presence. 'I would no more stay in a heart, than I would in a house, if I wanted those supports; 'tis neither an easy, a safe, a comfortable or a creditable dwelling; and I should take it much kinder of my landlord . . . to give me warning and bid me to decamp.'

Fox, whom Hervey liked to portray as the more hesitant (or fickle, depending on his mood) partner in the relationship, responded, to judge from Hervey's reply, both offensively and defensively. 'As to your reproaching me with the love of London, I am very ready to plead guilty to that charge; but you know it was not that which hindered me accompanying you to Redlynch,' he asserted, and then went on to describe his recent activities as proof of his devotion. 'Perhaps you expect an account of the transactions at court last night; there was dice, dancing, crowding, sweating and stinking in abundance as usual; but I had the prudence . . . to absent myself, and . . . I went to supper, with a little coterie which only you could have improved.' It would be natural for Ste to think that the part of the evening Hervey most enjoyed was that which resembled the time he spent in the country with Ste, he said, just as it was natural for Hervey 'to think every place agreeable in proportion to the resemblance it bears to that which you inhabit'.

Although Hervey loved London life – his description of Henry Fox and Thomas Winnington doing 'nothing but *politiquer* from morning to night; I hear of nothing but petitions, journals, treaties, alliances &c. whenever I see them' might just as easily describe some of his own letters to Henry – he could also see the attractions of the countryside, particularly if they involved Ste. Hervey may never have fully understood this aspect of Ste's life, but he did make an effort to fit in at Redlynch. 'Pray make my compliments to Miss [Hervey's nickname for Charlotte Fox, Stephen and Henry's sister], I envy you both,' Hervey wrote to Ste. 'The serenity, the uninterrupted, unalloyed full satisfaction that two people have in a country life is to be equalled or rivalled by no other.'

Despite Ste's ministrations the previous autumn, Hervey's health was increasingly bad in the spring of 1728; a letter from Mrs Delany to her sister in April reported him to be 'past recovery'. Ste rushed to London when he heard how ill Hervey was. Worried about the effects of the amount of opium Hervey was taking, Fox extracted a promise from him never to take laudanum again except by prescription; but the short-term effect of this ban only made Hervey worse. As soon as he was well enough to be moved, Ste took him to Redlynch where they stayed two months, but Hervey continued unwell despite the fresh Somerset air. 'Mr Fox never left me but to eat and sleep, and not always for that,' Hervey remembered gratefully; Ste's faithful nursing meant much more to him than the combined efforts of Doctors Arbuthnot and Cheyne.

When, in mid-June, they were separated for the first time in five months, Hervey wrote to Ste almost every other day, his wistful words about Redlynch betraying how much he missed being there and how far his relationship with Ste had developed during the months they had spent so closely together. 'Walk often through the Hervey-grove,' he instructed Fox on 18 June, 'and now and then visit the ash by the *pas-glissant*; I want no memorandums,' he continued in a conceit that shows both the depth of his love for Ste and the delicacy of his writing style,

even your picture is useless in that character; my imagination is so much a better painter than Link [a contemporary portraitist] that I find you're drawn there not only more like than by his hand, but also in colours fixed by so much a better fire, that 'tis impossible they should ever fade till everything on which they are so lovingly laid is itself destroyed; nor is that all, for this painter not only describes your figure but your voice, 'tis an echo to your words as well as a mirror to your form, and so extraordinary a performer in each capacity, that I hear you in deadest silences and see you in deepest darkness.

Despite his fondness for Redlynch and its inhabitants – 'I beg my compliments to Miss; make her curl her nose, repeat my name, and say, well I do love him Ste, though he does carry you away' – Hervey was delighted to be back in London in June, telling Ste that he was 'grown a great rake; I sup and sit up, and in a little time I believe you will hear of my getting drunk, breaking windows, beating the watch [parish-watchman], being knocked down by a constable, and lying all night in the Roundhouse [a London prison]'. But he had decided that the only remedy for his continuing weakness was a warmer climate, and so had determined to travel to Europe leaving England on 10 July, as he wrote to inform Ste at the end of June. He hoped, he concluded, that Ste 'would find it necessary to be in town longer than you thought before I go'.

Three days later he wrote to Ste again, in response to a letter of Fox's in which he seems to have chastized Hervey about something – probably for sitting up too late at dinner parties and jeopardizing his health – and gone on to apologize for what he saw as his lack of wit, compared to Hervey's sparkling missives. How could Ste be so naive as to think Hervey valued his letters for their intellectual content, when what he loved about him – and flattered himself he was alone in possessing – was Ste's devotion, Hervey demanded in reply.

I prefer the pleasure of a thing I engross [Ste's love] to one I enjoy in common with the rest of the world [Ste's understanding]. When you talk of talents for writing letters I should rather have thought you were beginning a critique on Voltaire and Bentivoglio, than alluding to any [letters] that had passed between us; what talents are requisite to make these agreeable but affection and sincerity?

Ste, worried by Hervey's new-found independence and obvious enjoyment of London's pleasures, had allowed his insecurities to show, and Hervey immediately wrote back to reassure him of his fidelity.

He was, he said, getting nothing done in London, since he divided his time between being distracted by other people from thinking of Ste, and being distracted from seeing other people by his thoughts of Ste. 'They have no good of me, nor I of myself; I am absent from them without being present to you,' Hervey wrote a few days later, seeking to show Ste how much he missed and needed him. Hervey's assurances convinced Ste of his devotion, because when he came up to London as planned he allowed Hervey to persuade him to go with him to Europe. 'With an affection and friendship I am as incapable of forgetting, as any nature but his is incapable of feeling, [Mr Fox] offered to go with me to any part of the world, and for as long as I pleased,' Hervey recalled years later.

Ste's decision to accompany Hervey to Europe reveals that, over a year after they had first met, he had become as attached to Hervey as Hervey was to him. This was no one-sided affair. Although Hervey had pursued Ste, Ste had responded to his pursuit. Despite the independence that Hervey loved in him, Ste needed Hervey. Orphaned at twelve, he must have felt a new security within the affection that Hervey showed him; eight years younger than Hervey, he must have been impressed by Hervey's worldly sophistication and intellectual interests; and then, Hervey was intensely attractive, to both men and women, as well as persuasive. It would have been hard for Ste to resist him.

6. Eros and Agape

Travelling with their friends the Duke and Duchess of Richmond, Hervey and Fox set off across the Channel towards Ostend on 12 July, and from thence to Spa in what is now Belgium. Life at Spa was simple and revolved around the health-giving properties of the celebrated waters:

We rise at five in the morning, drink the waters three miles from the village, and starve with the cold; reading and writing is prohibited (so that what I am doing is absolutely against directions). One must not sleep [during the day], though the effects of the waters are such as make it hardly possible to avoid it; if one does sleep, it is a chance if one ever wakes. At dinner, we are to eat nothing but roast meat, as dry as a stick; at supper, a little weak broth, with bread pretty thick; go to bed at nine; dine at twelve, sup at seven. Thus us poor mortals breathe for living it is not.

For three weeks, this regime benefited Hervey, but then the weather turned cold and he and Ste escaped to Paris. Writing in the frivolous, gossipy tone he assumed in letters to his mother, Hervey described the latest French styles – always more extreme than those adopted in England. 'Fashions are come to such extravagance that unless they wear their petticoats over their heads as often in public as they do in private I can't comprehend what they can invent next to make people stare.'

In Paris, homosexuality, like fashion, was regarded with more tolerance and amusement than in England. Madame de Maintenon, Louis XIV's pious mistress, had a well-known lesbian affair with Henriette d'Angleterre. Louis's brother, the Duc d'Orléans – fondly known as Monsieur – quite openly had a male lover, Philippe, Chevalier de Lorraine, in addition to two wives and several mistresses. Like a transvestite Marie Antoinette, Monsieur adored dressing up as a highly rouged and bejewelled shepherdess; his antics were recorded with interest (but not shock) by Madame de Sévigné in her famous letters, and the King himself seemed to have found the affair little more than a diverting foible of his charming but eccentric brother. Although sodomy was illegal, and punishable by death if proven (as in England),* aristocratic dabbling in homosexuality was largely tolerated in France. In 1722, Mathieu Marais recorded with disapproval but not outrage watching the young Duc de Bouffiers try to sodomize the apparently willing Marquis de Rambure. Bouffiers could not manage it, so his brother-in-law, the Marquis d'Alincourt, took over and finished the job for him. Rambure had made 'no attempt to defend himself'.

The English attitude towards homosexuality – 'this foreign vice' – was more ambivalent. The historical legacies of Piers de Gaveston and Edward II, of Richard II (although probably not homosexual he was thought to devote too much patronage to his effeminate acolytes), of James I and his favourites Somerset and Buckingham, had created an explicit association between homosexuality, degeneracy, and political sophistry and corruption. The effete, sycophantic courtier was, by the eighteenth century, a familiar stereotype, a stock character of Restoration comedy. When Pope wrote about fops in 1716 it was clear to what type of man he was referring, the use of the word 'worm' only underlining his point:

> The fops are painted butterflies,
>> That flutter for a day;
> First from a worm they take their rise,
>> And in a worm decay:

To the majority of the English population, though, homosexuality was a sin against God and nature, something to be viewed with disgust. Henri Misson, a French observer of English customs, wrote on buggery, 'the English say, both the word and the thing came to them from Italy, and are strangers to England. Indeed they love the fair sex too well to fall into such an abomination'. However,

---

* Although in both countries incontrovertible 'proof' was hard to come by.

there is little evidence of the English especially loving the fair sex. 'Englishmen do not spoil their women by flattery and attentions, generally preferring drinking and gambling to female company,' reported Cesar de Saussure. In fact, there were two groups in early eighteenth-century England who accepted homosexuality: a new urban subculture, predominantly lower and middle class; and the intellectual élite.

At this time, a homosexual society was beginning to emerge in London. Homosexual men of the middle rank solicited in certain recognized areas: Moorfields, known as 'Sodomite's Walk'; the latrines of Lincoln's Inn; and Birdcage Walk, in St James's Park, which the Earl of Rochester fifty years earlier called 'this all-sin-sheltering grove'. It was quite common at dusk to stumble across a couple having sex in a remote corner of the park; and the pair might just as easily be two men as a man and a woman. A gentleman sticking his thumbs in the armpits of his waistcoat and drumming his fingers upon his chest was signalling his availability for a quick encounter, as was one wearing a white handkerchief tucked into the skirt of his coat. Mother Clap's, in Holborn, was the most famous homosexual brothel, where Mollies (as homosexual men were known) dressed up as women, curtsied, sang and danced for one another before retiring to upstairs rooms to get 'married'. Mother Clap was arrested and tried for keeping a 'sodomitical house' in 1726; she died from the injuries sustained in the stocks as part of her punishment. But places like this were risky for men of aristocratic background: they were too vulnerable to blackmail to start with, and for a fastidious man like Hervey, who insisted on bathing once a day, one suspects it would have been a bit rough (although that may well have been one of its attractions). This is not to say that these two groups never overlapped, simply that there were two distinct groups.

The second type of homosexual man belonged to the educated, aristocratic élite. In the licentious tradition of Lord Rochester, these men saw themselves as above society's conventions. They held that sexual freedom was not for the lower classes, who might allow themselves to get carried away; but they believed they could control their own dabblings in homosexuality or sado-masochism.

In the eighteenth century, these libertines included the necrophile George Selwyn; Charles Johnstone, the author of the pornographic novel *Chrysal*; the MP John Wilkes; and the founder of the Medmenham Monks, Sir Francis Dashwood. Many of the brightest men of Hervey's generation – from Richard Steele and Joseph Addison to Voltaire, Jonathan Swift and Alexander Pope – were rumoured to have homosexual proclivities.

Their heightened sense of masculine identity was encouraged by the all-male environment in which they lived. Eighteenth-century gentlemen like Hervey could have as little contact with women as they chose; and they did not often choose to have much, for women were seen as men's inferiors. From Juvenal's *Sixth Satire*, a tirade against the vices of women, to Pope's 'Epistle to a Lady', which details women's faults from affection to sentimentality, cunning to whimsy, and wit to stupidity, the masculine literary culture which dominated eighteenth-century thought allowed for no native feminine virtues. Even Lady Mary Wortley Montagu, one of the few classically educated women of her generation, tacitly accepted her age's misogyny almost as a mark of her own superiority. 'I am never pleased to think I am not a man but when I think I can never be married to a woman.'

The rise of the gentleman's club was one manifestation of this all-male Augustan self-consciousness: the gathering together of like-minded men, discussing their relationships to the world and to each other. In this era were founded the scientific Royal Society, the convivial Beefsteak, and the political Kit-Kat Club, as well as Sir Francis Dashwood's Society of Dilettanti, of which Hervey was a member, and which toasted 'Grecian taste and Roman spirit', and Dashwood's irreverent, debauched Medmenham Monks who met at a ruined abbey in Berkshire. Parliament was just one more of these masculine institutions. In March 1739, a troupe of ladies led by the Duchess of Queensberry pushed their way into the gallery of the House of Commons to watch a debate, which was supposed, related Lady Mary Wortley Montagu, to be 'the true reason why poor Lord Hervey spoke miserably'.

For young men of the English upper classes, the emphasis on a classical education as essential to the making of a gentleman often steered them towards an intellectual justification for their homo-sexuality. As Voltaire observed in his *Letters on England*, 'the govern-ments of Greece and Rome are the subject of every conversation, so that every man is under a necessity of perusing such authors as treat of them, how disagreeable soever it may be to him; and this study leads naturally to that of polite literature' – which led naturally to a tolerant attitude towards homosexuality.

Plato argued in the *Phaedrus* that soldiers fight better if their comrade-in-arms is also their lover. Plato's Pausanius (who, like Aristotle, believed women were incapable of virtue) extolled homosexual love as the means to a deeper spiritual union than was possible between a man and a woman. Aristophanes, working on the principle that each soul is searching for its other half, decreed that a male–male union was stronger than a male–female union, which would be weakened by the inherent inferiority of the woman. Socrates believed an older man might educate his younger lover in the ideals of honour, beauty and truth. This was the classic Greek pederastic relationship: an older, active lover, the *erastes*, playing tutor to a younger, passive beloved, the *eromenos*, who was not expected to return the adoration lavished upon him. It was thought to be the highest ideal of virility for the older man and an essential rite of passage for the younger. The love between Achilles and Patroclus did not demean their masculinity, but enhanced it.

As in the Chinese concept of yin and yang, in Ancient Greece men were thought to be hot and dry, proactive and creative, while women were cold, moist and soft. A man's strength could only be diluted by combining with a woman, whereas sex between two men – rubbing and fondling one another – stimulated their masculine energy. The physical relationship between men in classical times varied. In the pederastic model the younger man took the passive role, because it was considered emasculating and therefore demeaning for an adult male.* In a relationship of equals, they

* However, I imagine that this rather Victorian theory would not have influenced Hervey: he seems to me unconventional enough – and madly in love enough – not to care whether he played a passive or active sexual role. For a new analysis of whether or not the Greeks perceived the passive role to be demeaning, see James Davidson's *Courtesans and Fishcakes*.

either had intercrural sex – where the two men faced each other, naked, and derived pleasure from friction rather than penetration – or not at all, in the true platonic spirit. Physical love was thought to be the lowest aspect of homosexual love which, in its highest form, was made up of 'mutual devotion, reciprocal sacrifice, emulation, and the awakening of sensibility, imagination and intellect'.

Philosophy's approval – even advocacy – of homosexuality was reflected in literature up to (and beyond) the eighteenth century. Sodomy was known as the 'philosophical sin'. Michel de Montaigne wrote his essay 'On Friendship' as a paean to his dead lover, Etienne de la Boétie. Although he allowed that 'licentious Greek love is justly abhorred by our morality', he believed that ultimately morality must be defined by the individual: 'I do not make it my business to tell the world what it should do – enough others do that – but what I do in it.'

Hervey, like Montaigne and many of his contemporaries, was an accomplished amateur classical scholar; his correspondence with Dr Middleton on the Roman Senate was collected and published in 1735. Hervey's classical studies, combined with his innate sense of intellectual superiority, can only have justified and reinforced his love for Ste. He considered himself above other men, and thought of his love for Ste as being separate from earthly, degraded lusts. To use Montaigne again to express Hervey's thoughts, there was no rhyme nor reason to their attachment to one another: it simply existed, an inevitable entity that consumed them both. 'If I were pressed to say why I loved him, I feel that my only reply could be: "Because it was him, because it was me."' But the philosophical context in which Hervey placed his love for Ste did justify the physical aspect of their relationship too.

The only other personal letters in the eighteenth century which approach Hervey's in their expressions of homoerotic love are those from the poet Thomas Gray. He was a close friend of Horace Walpole, and travelled through Europe with him after the two left Eton; when they argued, Gray returned to England broken-hearted. His letters to Walpole reflect the classicism and sense of the sublime which characterize Hervey's to Ste, quoting the Roman poet Horace to Horace Walpole: 'While I was dear to thee and no more favoured youth flung his arms around thy dazzling neck, I lived in greater bliss than Persia's king.' Later in life, he met the Swiss Charles Victor de Bonstetten, who revived in him the feelings Walpole had originally inspired and to whom he wrote, longingly, 'My life is now but a perpetual conversation with your shadow.'

Gray and Montaigne, like the classical authors, wrote about the cerebral ideal of friendship between equals, rather than about physical lust. Hervey too was aware of this philosophical tradition, writing to Ste at the end of 1727 that he consented to Fox's leaving him 'to show you how disinterestedly I love you'. This is a reference to Plutarch's essay, 'How to Distinguish a Flatterer from a Friend', in which the true friend places his friend's interests above his own. A poem written for Ste by Hervey while they were in Italy celebrated the foundation of their love:

> Thou dearest Youth, who taught me first to know
> What Pleasures from real Friendship flow;
> Where neither Interest nor Deceit have part,
> But all the Warmth is Nature of the Heart.

When Hervey and Fox left Paris for Italy in October 1728, they were heading towards the country which, in its preservation of classical art and culture, was a celebration of the philosophical ideals they held dear. Less than thirty years later, the great classical scholar Johann Winckelmann proclaimed from Cardinal Albani's villa in Rome, of which he was librarian, that 'There is only one way for the moderns to become great and perhaps unequalled: by imitating the ancients.' Winckelmann's own interest in Greek homosexuality* – a flourishing cult of Antinous was revived at the Villa Albani during his tenure – fostered a new aesthetic: lovers of classical art were assumed to have, by association, homosexual tendencies, however deeply buried they might lie. By using Italy as a sanctuary, Hervey and Ste unwittingly formed part of an eighteenth-century trend.

* Winckelmann's sordid death belied the classical spirit in which he had lived: he was stabbed, aged fifty, by a young male prostitute in a cheap hotel in Trieste.

But for them it was more than that. Travelling together was a chance for Fox and Hervey to enjoy their relationship in an unpressured atmosphere far from the censure of disapproving – or jealous – family and friends.

7. In Sickness and in Health

Hervey and Ste arrived in Rome in December 1728, having crossed the Alps at the end of October and headed south via Turin and Florence. Disappointingly, the first stages of their journey were marred by the ill-health of both men, and by the severity of the winter they were experiencing. Molly Hervey wrote anxiously from Ickworth to Stephen to inquire about her husband's health, adding in a postscript, 'I beg my Lord mayn't know about this letter.' 'I'm afraid you'll think me very troublesome,' she began, 'and indeed I think myself so, but the concern I have been in ever since I had my Lord's last letter, has got the better of every other consideration, and has determined me to beg you'll give me an account of what I fear his good-nature has softened to me.' She urged him to use all his influence with Hervey to persuade him to take a mercurial medicine recommended by a doctor in England which he had not had the patience to persist with before.

Molly was willing to play the devoted, submissive wife, too afraid of upsetting her husband to write to him directly. There is no sign of her resenting Hervey's dependence on his lover rather than on her to bring him back to health. But she did not mention Ste at all in the letters she wrote to others while Hervey was away; she was, she said, turning her 'thoughts as much as possible from the disagreeable to the pleasing parts of my Lord's absence, and figur[ing] him in my imagination recovering his health very fast and returning home without any complaints, with much spirit, and some fat'. Even if she suspected Ste of being a rival for Hervey's love, she was determined to conquer her fears for her husband's sake. 'How does he sleep?' she demanded in another letter to Fox. 'Does he ever sweat o'nights? Pray let me know how his looks and spirits are. I beg, Sir, you'll excuse my being so troublesome, if you can conceive the anxiety I am in, and the continual fear and uneasiness I suffer on his account, I am sure you will forgive it.'

Ever since Hervey's departure Molly had been closeted at Ick-worth, fending off verbal attacks and competition for her children from her jealous mother-in-law and nursing Hervey's invalid sister Nann. In October 1729, exhausted, Molly told a friend that her spirits were so low that she doubted that even a return to their youthful days as Maids of Honour could restore them, 'or revive the *Schatz* [her old court nickname], who is extinguished in a fatigued nurse, a grieved sister, and a melancholy wife'. But she could not resist asking her correspondent to address her letters to her in mysterious handwriting to provoke the curiosity of the nosy Countess.

Hervey, ever his ambitious mother's son, wrote to order his wife to go up to London late in 1728 to greet Prince Frederick when he arrived in England for the first time. People who depend on royal favour for their fortunes must not stay away from court long enough to be forgotten, he told her, because those in power forget so quickly. Molly wrote disconsolately to her friend Griselda Murray, worried that her spirits were so low that she would not sparkle sufficiently at court. 'I know laudanum can at any time lend me a stock [of good spirits] for present use, but that will run me greatly in arrear, and considerably lessen my principal, which is already too much impaired to bear a further diminution'.

Going to court did not improve Molly's mood. Early the follow-ing year, the beautiful Duchess of Queensberry (who, two years earlier, had appeared unadorned at the Coronation to Mrs Delany's disapprobation) was banished from court for her attempts to sell subscriptions to John Gay's new play, *Polly*, the sequel to his successful satirical musical *The Beggar's Opera*. The Duchess had been banished from court once before, when she wore an apron to one of the royal assemblies, despite the fact that they were pro-hibited, and, when stopped by a Lord-in-Waiting, tore off the offending item and threw it in his face before stalking out. This time, she said she was glad of an opportunity to show her contempt for the 'German Court'; the letter she wrote in reply to George's order that she stay away was deliberately insulting. She hoped, she said, 'that by such an unprecedented order as this is, the King will see as few as he wishes at his court, particularly such as dare to think

or speak truth'. Mrs Delany reported that the Duchess was 'still the
talk of the town' two weeks later.

> She is going to Scotland: she has great reason to resent her usage, but she
> was provoking first, and her answer though it shows spirit was not worded
> as her friends could have wished; good manners ought to be observed to
> our equals, and our superiors certainly have a right to them. My Lady
> Hervey told her the other day, that '[since] she was banished, the court
> had lost its chief ornament.' The Duchess replied, 'I am entirely of your
> mind.' It is thought my Lady Hervey spoke to her with a sneer, if so her
> Grace's answer was a very good one.

While his wife faced London society, Hervey was languishing in
Rome, unable to travel further south to Naples because the roads
had been rendered impassable by the weather, alternately bewailing
his own ailments and nursing Stephen through his. Their friend
Thomas Winnington's letters to Henry Fox, in between jokes
about Ste having to put on his own breeches because his valet had
died, report Hervey 'tolerably well' at this time. During their stay
in Rome Hervey visited the famous Dr Stosch, who diagnosed his
illness as hypochondria; needless to say, Hervey did not record this
judgement in the treatise he later wrote on his health.

Ste, on the other hand, was gravely ill. Hervey said he had been
out of his room only once since they arrived in Rome, and he was
nursing his friend back to strength. For the first time he was able to
repay Ste for all the care and attention Ste had lavished on him in
the eighteen months since they'd met. By the end of January,
Winnington had received a letter saying that Ste was 'out of all
danger and in a fair way of being perfectly well'. The pair left Rome
for Naples as soon as Ste was strong enough, to take advantage of the
warmer weather in the south. But while Ste convalesced Hervey, in
his turn, grew steadily weaker once again.

Hervey's condition improved as summer approached. Lord
Bristol wrote to his son to express his joy at the news of his
new-found good health, and to warn him not to persist in drinking
'that poisonous plant, tea' which he believed had destroyed Hervey's constitution. Of his ordeal, Hervey remembered, 'I looked

so dreadfully that he [Fox] has sometimes come to my bedside and doubted if I was living or dead . . . Mr Fox never left me night or day; I saw nobody but him and servants; he went out with me whenever I was able to go out, read to me at home when I had not spirits to talk, and constantly lay in my room.'

This last suggests that only in extenuating circumstances did the two men share a room; but then again, Hervey's account was part of a treatise written on his health for the benefit of his children. It is unlikely in this context that he would have admitted sharing a room except under the necessity of illness or the constraints of travel. It was quite usual for men or women to share a bed with a friend or stranger of the same sex in a crowded inn. This may mean that Hervey and Ste did not have sex when they were forced to share a bed or a room; or, that they benefited from this custom to sleep together all the time they were abroad.

The two men travelled slowly up through Italy from Naples, stopping in Rome in April for Ste to have his portrait painted by Antonio David and Hervey to sit for a marble bust by the French sculptor Bouchardon.* His grave, classical pose reveals both Hervey's reverence for antiquity and his political ambitions. Hervey, who had a passion for antiquities, was busy searching out 'very fine things' to bring home; he expanded his collection of classical seals (which are still at Ickworth) and broadened his knowledge of art. Roman, and some Greek, seals, medals, friezes and statues could be had for a song in Italy and were, like the fine private collections of art throughout Europe, one of the major attractions of the Grand Tour for cultured Englishmen.

Hervey and Fox must have seen the Medici statue of Antinous which Lady Mary Wortley Montagu described when she visited Florence in 1739.

I was stopped short at viewing the Antinous, which they have placed near that of [the Emperor] Hadrian, to revive the remembrance of their preposterous loves, which I suppose the Florentines rather look upon as

---

* He must have given the bust to Ste at some point (or maybe Ste had it done in order to keep it) for it is at Melbury rather than Ickworth, although the terracotta model and another marble copy are still there.

an object of envy, than of horror and disgust . . . When I saw the Venus I was wrapped in wonder – and I could not help casting a thought back on Antinous. They ought to be placed together. They are worthy of each other. If marble could see and feel, the separation might be prudent.

Though Lady Mary may have felt 'horror and disgust' at the thought of the relationship between Hadrian and Antinous, her comments implicitly recognize a tradition of homoeroticism in classical art, a tradition of glorifying the male body that had been revived by Renaissance and Baroque artists such as Donatello, Michelangelo and Caravaggio. Youths were portrayed, such as Rubens's *Ganymede* (from whose Greek name the word 'catamite' derives), as objects of male lust. Artists drew on classical and Christian iconography to justify their subject matter, often using sexual imagery to depict religious ecstasy, as in Mantegna's *Saint Sebastian*.

For Hervey and Ste, the art surrounding them in Italy would have served as some compensation for the various illnesses that had plagued them both at the start of their trip. By the early summer of 1729, though, they had grown well enough to enjoy their time together. Hervey and Ste must have looked back on these months as the halcyon days of their relationship: the first (and only) long period of time they spent alone together, freer in Italy than they could ever hope to be in England, soaking up the rich atmosphere of a Tuscan summer and the beauties of Italian culture. For once, there was nothing to distract them from their love for one another.

Like travellers in any age, they were also amused by the national eccentricities they observed. In Florence they were surprised to experience a series of earthquakes. Nobody, wrote Ste to Henry in early July, knew whose sin was to blame for this unexpected incidence of divine anger. 'The clergy say they have happened because there is not that respect paid to the Church as formerly. The laity say they have been occasioned by the extraordinary wickedness of the clergy.' 'Within an hour after that [shock] of yesterday morning all the squares and streets were full of people confessing themselves in their shirts and smocks,' Ste wrote when the first tremor happened. 'The motion was so disagreeable that it made everybody sick; and I believe the dogs, for they howled in a most terrible manner.' He added that he was

better every day, my spirits revive, and my *embonpoint* returns. We don't talk of leaving this place till the end of August; but if you will have my private opinion on that head, it is that we shall be very near England by that time, for *la maladie des Suisses* [homesickness was thought to be a Swiss national characteristic], and *la maladie* of a fine English gentleman (*c'est a dire ennui*) [that is to say boredom], are so prevalent at present that I am apt to think we shall ne'er hold it till then in Florence.

Despite his love for antiquity, as Ste predicted, by July, Hervey had had enough of travelling. He wrote to Lady Mary of his boredom. Italians were so proud that it was difficult to make friends; social rituals made their acquaintance a burden; and ignorance made them unworthy of cultivation. 'If you had not been in Italy 'twould be impossible for you to imagine how little satisfaction a sociable animal can receive amongst these people,' he complained. Painting, sculpture, music and architecture were well and good in their way but meant nothing without the stimulation of conversation and interesting people. The fact that he was robust enough to be *ennuyé* shows how much better he was; Ste thought him at this time 'as well as I ever knew him'. It was, perhaps, an unhappy indication for the future of their relationship that Hervey was so easily bored by being away from London, even in the company of his lover.

A week later Hervey was writing in similar vein to his mother, his frustration at his health as well as the seclusion in which he and Fox had been living apparent.

Bad health, or bad objects, I don't know which, or perhaps both, have quite cured me of flirting; 'tis so long since I have seen a toilet [dressing-room], that I have hardly the idea of one; and if I venture ever again to accost a fine lady, I believe it will be blushing, stuttering, twisting my thumbs . . . and in much greater confusion to ask her the last favour, than any woman in France or Italy I believe ever felt in granting it. Your Ladyship perhaps won't credit this change, and I wish I did not feel it, but I am absolutely an old fellow . . . I begin to tell stories of what I was;

pretend to despise pleasures I am past taking; rail at wine because I can't drink; [and] condemn gaming because I have no money to play.

The tone of this letter is that of assumed bravado and gaiety, despite its melancholic message, as opposed to the sincerity and intelligence that marked his letter on the same subject to Lady Mary.

In spite of their restlessness, Hervey and Fox stayed in Florence until the end of August, while Hervey had a cyst removed from his throat (the doctor used caustic powder to eat it away) and the wound healed. They travelled up the leg of Italy, being bitten by ever more persistent fleas from Pisa to Lerici to Genoa, where they were welcomed by the British consul. He took them sightseeing by day and fed them ortolans by night. Their journey up to the Alps was chronicled by Hervey in a long, amusing poem written for Molly, describing the musty beds and bugs and unshuttered windows of the inns they stayed in along the way, and their torturous crossing at Mount Cenis in sedan chairs. The poem concluded in a manner that cannot have pleased her,

> But sick or well, where'er I move,
> In every Hardship that I prove,
> *Fidus* Achates still is near,
> And makes my Welfare all his Care.

They stopped in Paris for a few days on their way home, there dining with Cardinal Fleury, and were taken to Versailles to meet the Dauphin. They also renewed their friendship with Voltaire, recently returned from exile in London. On reading the poem Hervey had written to Molly, Voltaire praised its 'delicacy and politeness', saying it reminded him of the work of the Earl of Rochester; he included it, translated by him into French, in his *Lettres Philosophiques* as an example of the work of a cultured English *milord*.

Hervey's gratitude to Ste for accompanying him through Europe was boundless, and he credited Ste as much as the warm weather for his recovery. 'His good sense made his company a constant amusement and his care never a trouble. His spirits enlivened and comforted but never oppressed me. He showed an incessant reasonable and tender concern for me, without all the fiddle-faddle impertinence of officious attention, which is often affectation, always teasing, and never useful.' What a refreshing contrast, one senses, to the way he was treated when he was ill at Ickworth: the overweening fussing of his wife and mother; their sniping at one another, and at him; and the weight of his father's hopes for him always on his mind.

Hervey was so much better for his trip that in Paris people he had met there eighteen months earlier were astonished at the change in his appearance, strength and spirits; and his friends in England were even more surprised. Even though in the eighteenth century there was no cure for Hervey's epilepsy, his other (probably nervous) ailments had been much relieved by the long spell abroad and the pleasure he took in being with Ste. Mrs Delany, who saw Hervey at a party in London soon after he got back in November, thought he was 'quite recovered and looks better than ever I saw him'. Aged thirty-four, secure in his relationship with Ste, eagerly anticipating his return to public life, Hervey was entering the prime of his life.

PART TWO

8. Allegiance

On his return to London Hervey flung himself into social and political life with an enthusiasm unprecedented in his younger days. He wrote to Lady Mary Wortley Montagu begging her to come and visit him in London and share his excitement at being back.

I don't send you this to reproach you for not answering my letter from France, or taking no notice of the hundred and fifty times I have been and sent to your house in Covent Garden since I came to England; I know enough of court doctrine to be sensible how necessary it is to overlook ill-usage whenever one solicits better, and only write to know when you will be visible in town, or if the sacred recess of Twickenham is ever accessible to the unhallowed feet of a Londoner. If your passion for follies and absurdities continues I can't conceive what you mean by keeping Lent in the country and living in abstinence when the market is so well-stocked in this good city.

Hervey was indulging his own passion for absurdities to the full, he told Ste; but it did not fill the void created by Fox's unaccustomed absence.

I am already quite an English fine gentleman. I do a hundred different things of a day and like none of them; yawn in the faces of the women I talk to; eat and drink with men I have no friendship for, play despising the court and live in the Drawing-room [royal assembly], rail at quidnuncs [gossip] and go hawking about for news, throw the faults of my constitution upon the climate, flatter awkwardly, railly worse, and in short make none of my actions conducive to the pleasure or profit either of myself or anybody else. You are in part responsible for this; if I regretted less what I have lost, I should be less indifferent to what I possess . . . As things now stand, I look upon you as my dwelling and feel the inconveniences of these other animals as I did those of Italian inns, hate all their filth, and would no more make friends of the one than I would my home of the other.

The talk of the town in the winter of 1729 was of the young Lady Abergavenny, one of Prince Frederick's first conquests on his arrival in London the previous year. She had married one Lord Abergavenny, who died soon after their wedding, and before they had a child; thereupon she married his cousin and heir, and became Lady Abergavenny a second time. 'It seems her little, pretty, silly Ladyship has been catched in bed with an unlicensed bed-fellow (one Mr Lydal) under her husband's roof,' Hervey wrote to Ste.

Her lover lived in the house with them, was my good Lord's Pylades, or rather his Paris; for whilst the good Menelaus was sunk under the charms of sleep and wine, he was diverting himself with those of his Helen, who with more love than discretion stole from the bed of her insensible Lord, and sought that of her undoer (as some tell the story) at five a clock in the morning.

Her steward and butler came upon the pair, so Hervey related, '*en flagrant delit*'; apparently they had been directed by the suspicious Abergavenny to do so. Lady Abergavenny was sent up to London 'as fast as a coach and six horses could carry her', and her servants given orders that if her father would not take her in, to set her down in the streets. But, Hervey added, 'money she has none, not a guinea, and *pour comble de malheur* [the worst of it] is within a fortnight of lying-in. So that her dear, little, amorous ladyship must be as fresh and brisk (to speak in jockey's style) at the distance post as she was at starting.'

Two weeks later, Lady Abergavenny was brought to bed; her child died immediately, and she followed it after two weeks. Her widower sued for and received £10,000 in damages from Mr Lydal in February 1729. Lydal was forced to flee the country, impoverished, while, so Hervey told Henry Fox, Lord Abergavenny 'sits down contented with the grateful fruits of unfelt infamy'. Hervey said that if he were Abergavenny, he would simply 'have her whipped, and her servants hanged'; to him, their betrayal of their mistress was just as bad as her indiscretion, and Abergavenny's desire for 'vengeance and divorce' worse. What incensed him most about the whole affair was the hypocritical attitude of the society gossips who passed comment on the unhappy situation, railing at her in public but themselves sleeping 'with some necessitous gamester or indebted little Captain of Foot, in private'.

Prudes wonder how she could be such a beast, and coquettes how she could be such a fool; the old practitioners take up on such an example whilst the young ones take warning; and 'tis to be hoped since pacific husbands have so reasonably and judiciously resolved (like old Gomez [Abergavenny]) to demand satisfaction by way of plaintive and defendant in Westminster Hall, rather than by sword and pistol in Hyde Park, that our embroidered, powdered undoers will, for the future, be as industrious to keep their success a secret, as they used to be to publish it.

Adultery was not unusual – or even particularly scandalous – but discovery of it in so public a way was. Because arranged marriages upheld the aristocracy – ensuring penurious peers married heiresses, using money from trade to restore crumbling estates – extra-marital affairs were largely tolerated, if not accepted. Cesar de Saussure observed that if an Englishman has a mistress, his wife is not usually unhappy, but 'will probably console herself with a friend, and thus both husband and wife are happy'. 'The appellation of a rake is as genteel in a woman as a man of quality,' wrote Lady Mary Wortley Montagu. The children of the Countess of Oxford, whose family name was Harley, were known as the 'Harleian miscellany', after her husband's famous collection of books, because all were reported to have different fathers. 'It is the way, and all who understand genteel life think lightly of such matters,' wrote Mrs Thrale's daughter Cecilia of her husband's infidelity. What caused scandal, as in Lady Abergavenny's case, was when one was found out.

As well as playing the social butterfly, Hervey was keen to begin life as a political animal. He had written mistily about his desire to retire to the country while he was away:

O would kind Heaven, these tedious Sufferings past,
Permit me, Ickworth, Rest and Health at last!
In that loved shade, my Youth's delightful Seat,
My early Pleasures and my late Retreat,
Where lavish Nature's favourite Blessings flow,
And all the seasons all their Sweets bestow,
There I might trifle carelessly away
The milder Evening of Life's clouded Day,
From Business and the World's Intrusion free,
With Books, with Love, with Beauty and with Thee!

But Lady Mary, who knew Hervey better than he knew himself, added a mocking 'Continuation' to his sentimental vision of a rural idyll:

So sung the Poet in an humble Strain,
With empty Pockets and a Head in pain,
When the soft Clime inclined the Soul to rest,
And pastoral Images inspired the Breast;
Apollo listened from his heavenly Bower,
And in his health *restored*, expressed his Power.
Returning vigour glowed in every Vein,
And gay Ideas fluttered through the Brain;
Back he returns to breathe his native Air,
And all his late Resolves are ended there.

Hervey turned to politics at this time for the same reason he had become involved with Stephen Fox: to give his life greater meaning. His knowledge of court life, combined with his education and intelligence, allowed Hervey to slip easily into this new role. Chameleon-like, Hervey was able to adapt himself to any situation – an intimate supper in Somerset with Ste, a duchess's masked ball or a fierce debate in the House of Commons – never realizing what was at stake in trying to be so many things to so many people.

Hervey had pledged his allegiance to Sir Robert Walpole before leaving England in 1728, and on his return prepared to make good his promise of service. Within days of arriving in London Hervey wrote to Walpole to restate his old desire to join the government. He was resigning the court pension of £1,000 a year that he had been granted in 1727 or 1728 (there is no record of when the pension was given to him but this period seems most likely), as reassurance that his services were appreciated and would one day be rewarded with a position, because he wanted to support the ministry in Parliament without being seen to be paid to do so.

Hervey's first public foray into politics had been a pamphlet in defence of Sir Robert Walpole, written in response to an article by the Tory Viscount Bolingbroke in February 1727. Hervey had entered Parliament as member for Bury St Edmunds in 1725, and began playing an active Whig role in 1727.* Walpole recognized Hervey's wit and took him under his wing; he needed good writers to defend his ministry because in active opposition were the writers Jonathan Swift, Alexander Pope and John Gay, as well as William Pulteney, one of the best pamphleteers of his generation. Hervey had been disappointed not to receive a post in the new government Walpole formed in 1727, but his loyalty to Walpole remained unshaken and he had moved the Commons address of thanks to George II at the opening of the new Parliament in January 1728.

Political pamphlets, believed Hervey, were at their highest expression of learning, strength of diction and elegance of style at this period. 'It might very properly be called the Augustan age of England for this kind of writing.' They were accessible – the circulation of the Opposition newspaper, the *Craftsman*, sometimes reached 10,000 for an issue – without losing any of their sophistication and erudition: in a debate with the *Craftsman* in 1733, Hervey created an extended metaphor between the English political scene and a game of chess. Horace Walpole, for all his dislike of Hervey, was forced to admit his pamphlets were 'equal to any that ever were written'. Writing in 1743, Molly Hervey agreed; her husband's work, she said, was 'no more to be mistaken or forgot than to be imitated, being indeed inimitable'. But although she admired the wit, art and ingenuity of pamphlets in general, 'yet

* Although MPs did have party affiliations, they were not expected, if they did not want to, to do much more than vote in the House of Commons.

there is something so coarse, so rude, so rough, so ungentlemanly in most of them that I cannot but think they are like porters fighting with cudgels rather than gentlemen with swords'.

Although Hervey saw writing pamphlets as an intellectual, as well as a political, exercise, and admired the art form, he was intolerant of the poor efforts of many of his rivals. Their inferior work brought disgrace to the whole genre.

Every day produces some heavy, unspirited venom of verse or prose in the same style; men and women promiscuously, in their political and moral capacity, in their public and domestic characters, in their own persons and those of their whole family, friends or acquaintance, are one and all brought upon the stage, and forced alternately to represent the vile parts given them by their enemies in every low fare they think fit to publish,

he complained early in 1728, little realizing how large a part these 'venoms of verse or prose' would come to play in his own life.

Hervey had not held an official role before he left England in 1728, but he had enthusiastically developed his rhetorical skills for the government in Parliament. He spoke in reply to the Opposition's calls for the number of the government's Hessian troops to be reduced early in 1728, arguing that the balance of power they supported ensured peace in Europe. He was exhausted the following day, he wrote to Henry Fox – 'I am so stupid, my eyes, ears, thoughts and every sense so clouded that I cannot utter one syllable more' – because the debate had gone on until 11 p.m. The army was one of King George's great passions,* which Walpole knew he had to allow him to retain in magnificence in order to keep his favour. George was known as 'the Little Captain', because of his short stature and obsession with military affairs and history. He had the Guards' regimental records sent to him every week to examine personally, and he used to stay in Caroline's room every morning before going back to his own apartments to dress, until he had

---

* George II was the last British monarch to lead his troops into battle, on the field of Dettingen against the French in 1743.

watched through the blinds the changing of the guards. Despite the unprecedented size of the army (and civil list) Walpole allowed the King, Hervey believed that 'the Crown was never less capable of infringing the liberties of this country than at this time, and that the spirit of liberty was so universally breathed into the breasts of the people, that, if any violent act of power had been attempted, at no era would it have been more difficult to perpetrate any undertaking of that kind'; the Opposition, for its part, claimed 'the King loved nothing but an army, and his Parliament nothing but money'.

Hervey's was 'a long and studied speech', recorded Viscount Percival in his diary after the debate over the Hessian troops, that was impressive because of the way in which he replied to the objections and arguments of the Opposition. Hervey's great skill as a speaker was his ability to think on his feet, although he was often forced to defend himself against critics and political rivals who claimed no one could speak as well as he did extemporaneously.

Hervey also continued writing pamphlets in defence of the government, mainly in answer to the *Craftsman*, a vehicle of Lord Bolingbroke and Hervey's old friend, William Pulteney. Pulteney was a family friend of the Herveys, with whom, as Hervey later recorded, he had lived 'in friendship and intimacy' for many years; he led the Commons' Opposition to Walpole. Hervey's 'Observations on the Writings of the Craftsman' attacked the Opposition as treasonous, claiming

its private views wore the mask of public good; ambition clothed itself in popularity; the spirit of resentment took the title of the spirit of liberty; and the welfare of the nation, and loyalty to the King, were made the plausible pretences for throwing amongst his people the seeds of clamour against his ministers and his measures; for preaching sedition, and endeavouring to infuse discontent into the hearts of all his subjects.

After the civil war and disputes over succession that marked the seventeenth century, George II's unchallenged accession to the throne in 1727 demonstrated the strength of the Hanoverian dynasty and its acceptance by the British nation. The Glorious Revolution of 1688 had created a constitutional monarchy which was, by

Hervey's time, firmly established. Nearly two decades of stable Hanoverian rule had marginalized Jacobite opposition to their regime. The division in politics was now between supporters of Walpole and his opponents. They differed more over individual policies than the nature of the roles of Parliament and the King.

Sir Robert Walpole had based his career on the principle that England would become great through trade, which he tried at all costs to promote and protect. This policy included as a corollary the idea that peace in Europe, if maintained, would help English interests to prosper. Lord Bolingbroke, the highest-ranking peer in opposition (and, in Lady Mary Wortley Montagu's words, 'a glaring proof of how far vanity can blind a man') believed that England's greatness should stem from a vigorous, interventionist foreign policy. Domestically, Bolingbroke thought Walpole's active, modern mercantilism was tarnishing the traditional values of English public life. The mystery of government had been reduced to mere administration; power increasingly derived from money, rather than land or rank; it was a regime run by utilitarianism rather than principle. Walpole answered that these complaints were merely the feeble remonstrations of those excluded from authority and patronage. 'What was there but lamentations on the ruin of England, in the era of its peace and prosperity, from wretches who thought their own want of power as a proof that their country was undone?' asked Horace Walpole, looking back on his father's ministry. 'Sir Robert Walpole and Mr Pulteney are very hot every day about the debts of the nation,' observed Mrs Delany, 'and nobody understands them but themselves.'

Hervey loved Pulteney as a friend, but he agreed with Walpole's politics. On his return from Europe, Hervey realized he would have to choose between the two men because Pulteney and Molly Hervey had hatched a plan to woo him away from Sir Robert. Molly, who hated Walpole – she later accused him of having made advances towards her, which she had rebuffed – had allied herself with Pulteney during Hervey's absence. They persuaded Lord Bristol, who disapproved of what he saw as Walpole's shameless opportunism, to promise to give Hervey an income of £600 a year to compensate him for the court pension he would lose by forsaking his mentor.

When Pulteney approached him with this offer, Hervey, who did not want to refuse outright and anger his friend, avoided the issue by saying that he was sure his father would not really give him the money. Pulteney, encouraged by these words to believe Hervey would accept if the money was forthcoming, redoubled his efforts. He argued that Walpole 'was false, loved nobody, and would never suffer any man that had parts to rise or make any figure under him'; the implication was that Pulteney, when he came to power (aided by Hervey), would grant him high office as a reward for his support. Hervey was 'at last forced to say with an ill grace what he might have said with a good one', that he had given up his court pension in hopes of serving Walpole honourably in government, and would not be distracted from his intended path. Although Pulteney and Hervey remained friends for the time being, their previous intimacy had been destroyed by this misunderstanding and politically they were squared firmly against each other.

Hervey's efforts to obtain a political office did not, at first, reap results. 'I began the day by a *tête-à-tête* with the man [Walpole] to whom I showed you a letter. Caresses, fine words and professions were not spared,' he told Ste, in language usually reserved for seduction rather than politics, 'but you know ministers promise, as Lady Bolingbroke commends, *assez volontiers* [willingly enough]. In short, I was, what perhaps your opinion of my vanities will make you think impossible, mightily flattered and not at all pleased.' For the moment, Walpole was content to keep Hervey waiting. 'My own affairs are at a full stand, as well as every other body's that has any expectations of tenure from the court; no alterations of any kind, they say, will be made there until the end of the session [of Parliament],' Hervey wrote exasperatedly two months later.

It was perhaps because Walpole was considering Hervey for an official role in government that his letters were so keenly censored. Hervey had ten thousand pieces of news for Ste, he said, who was apparently burning with curiosity about Hervey's activities, but could not write them to him because every letter he wrote or received was opened and examined.

I have been very often in the street you mention and have many things on that subject for your private ear; this conveyance [a letter] is become so little so [private], that I have some thoughts of saving the expense of wax for the future, myself the trouble of sealing, and the Post Master that of opening my letters: at least then I may have a chance (if my correspondents do the same) of receiving one untorn if not unread.

Although Hervey was relishing his return to active life, his pleasure in it was tempered by his sadness about being without Ste for the first time in fifteen months, and his concerns for his friend's health. Ste was ill again; but Hervey, instead of rushing to be with his friend as Ste had rushed to his side when Hervey was ill, remained in London, contenting himself with writing to Ste to tell him how worried he was about him.

If these [first] four days [apart] are a specimen of what I am to feel in the many, I fear my ill-fortune if not your choice will force me to pass at a distance from you, [and] I shall pay dear for the pleasure of those few we have lived together. You are grown like my native language to me, I am constrained in any other commerce and speak my thoughts as much by halves when ever they are addressed to anybody else, as I do when I would explain them in anything but English.

By his 'ill-fortune' Hervey meant the political position he hoped soon to occupy; for despite his love for Ste Hervey seemed to have no intention of giving up his worldly ambitions in order to spend more time with him.

9. Perceptions

Ste travelled on to Bath to drink the waters and recuperate while Hervey remained in London. He wrote,

One should never have you, or never be without you, such changes make one's life too unequal, and liable to the same objection that I have to the Italian climate where 'tis always summer or always winter, and where the warmth of the one serves only to make one more sensible of the cold of the other. My mind requires you as constantly as my constitution does the sun.

He wished Ste's constitution enabled him to feel as deeply for Hervey as Hervey did for him, which would ensure that they spent as much time as possible together. But Ste's balanced nature allowed him to enjoy any company. 'Your spirits are no more depressed by a Mr Ward or a Captain Fry than they are by a fog or an easterly wind; which is perhaps the only happiness I grudge you, the only pleasure I would deprive you of and perhaps the only thing I wish altered in you.' This repeated complaint of Hervey's – that Ste barely noticed if Hervey was not with him – was not fair: Hervey was simply trying to convince Ste to come to London by making him feel guilty.

Two days later Hervey wrote again. 'I *must* see you soon, I can't live without you, choice, taste, habit, prejudice, inclination, reason and everything that either does or ought to influence one's thoughts or one's actions makes mine centre in and depend on you.' Hoping so much to see Ste kept the memory of being with him so fresh in Hervey's mind, he wrote, that he felt an impatience to see him again which would be unintelligible to 'those who have not such a companion to regret and to wish for'.

The untutored style of Ste's devoted replies filled Hervey with undisguised joy. 'Your letter of yesterday gave me a pleasure which

I thought the frequency of my own would have prevented me from ever tasting,' he wrote gratefully to Fox on 27 November. 'How could I foresee that it would ever be possible for you to prove that my assiduity to force myself into your remembrance was not necessary to secure me so constant and distinguished a place there?' Ste's naturalness threw the affectation of the people Hervey was seeing in London into sharp relief.

I am just come from court where I saw nothing but blue noses, pale faces, gauze heads and toupees among the younger gentry: and lying smiles, forced compliments, careful bows, and made laughs amongst the elders. People talk of nothing but foreign peace, and think of nothing but domestic war. For my own part, I am quite sick of hearing the same things over and over again from morning till night. Quid-nuncing is more my abhorrence than ever. I despise the actors, hate the piece and dislike the theatre so much, that 'tis making you no great compliment to say I long to get into the easy commerce of such a conversation as yours.

No doubt Hervey meant all this; but it did not prevent him doing all he could to play a bigger part in this glittering, superficial arena.

At the beginning of December Hervey had to give in; he was desperate to see Ste after a month apart. He wrote to Lady Bristol to let her know he was leaving London for Redlynch the following day. The tone he used to express his intentions shows how he tried to mitigate for her the importance of Ste's place in his life. 'A letter I received yesterday from poor Mr Fox (who I find is still complaining) had determined me to go to him tomorrow; his coach is now waiting for me upon the road.' To Lady Mary Wortley Montagu, however, Hervey was more direct. He had always been honest with her about his feelings for Ste, even if she didn't quite understand them:

A *guignon* [bad luck] that attends almost all my wishes and pleasures, prevents my having the honour your Ladyship was so good to allow me of waiting on you tomorrow morning; I have promised Mr Fox a visit in Somersetshire, his coach is at this moment waiting for me on the road, and before your Ladyship receives this note I shall be above twenty miles from London.

So Hervey and Fox were reunited. They spent two months at Redlynch together, living quietly and contentedly in each other's company, as they had abroad. Lady Mary wrote, evidently wondering how they spent their days, and slyly inquiring about rumours she had heard of one of the Fox boys getting engaged. 'As to our manner of living here I can't imagine what you mean by talking of matrimony, holy bands, worldly fetters &c. – there is not a female here but Mr Fox's sister and she you know was executed several months ago [Charlotte Fox had married Edward Digby earlier in 1729],' Hervey replied vehemently. 'If anything else preparatory to that miserable state [marriage] had been going on here, I assure you I should just as soon have taken it into my head to make a party of pleasure in the condemned hold [of a prison] as at Redlynch.' Hervey was explicit in his denunciation of the married state, playing on contemporary slang that used the same words for getting married and being hanged at the gallows. 'I have always professed that if I loved a man never so well, unless I had hopes of rescuing him from the hangman [saving him from marriage], I would never attend him to the scaffold [church or altar].' He could not know how prophetic later events would prove his words to be.

Hervey's surviving letters to Lady Mary imply that she was aware Hervey and Ste were lovers. But she is the only one of his correspondents, apart from Ste, who seems to have known of their affair; or at least, the only one who was let in on the secret. Molly became friends with Ste rather than lose her husband altogether, but she may not have guessed they were lovers; the idea of a homosexual relationship cannot have entered old-fashioned Lord Bristol's ken; bear-like Sir Robert Walpole, who was to become increasingly important to Hervey, treated him with the good-natured roughness he showed everyone close to him. But Hervey must have been aware that as he moved into the public sphere, public perceptions of him would begin to matter.

It was obvious that Hervey and Ste were exceptionally close. The length of time they had spent together abroad was not remarkable –

almost everyone who did the Grand Tour went with a friend or a tutor – but the amount of time Hervey spent at Redlynch, and Ste at Hervey's London house in Great Burlington Street (now Old Burlington Street), was unusual. Hervey had refused an invitation to hunt in Sussex with his friend the Duke of Richmond the previous November, telling Ste, 'I shall *Fox*-hunt only towards the West: 'tis the chase I am most eager after.' They went to the same house parties, staying with Lord Bateman at the end of January 1730, and at other times with the Duke and Duchess of Richmond at Goodwood House in Sussex, and when apart, spoke of one another like lovers. Hervey was aware of how others might perceive their friendship, as he wrote to Ste, but he justified it by describing his love for Ste as originating from a mental attachment rather than a physical one.

I have often thought, if any idle body had curiosity enough to intercept and examine my letters, they would certainly conclude they came from a mistress rather than a friend; but it must be people that were unacquainted with you who made that conclusion. Otherwise, they might know that reason would make one as fond of your society, as passion could make one of any other body's.

It is not clear the extent to which Henry Fox was aware of the depth of Hervey and his brother's friendship. Hervey wrote to Henry several times early in 1730 complaining that he was passing his 'time in a hum-drum way, neither to be envied nor much to be pitied'. The solution, he continued, was to be in love.

But for my sins, that happy privation of one's senses I am cured of, and labour in vain to be reinfected by so charming a disease that I should be glad to keep to my bed of it the rest of my life. You see by what I have said that I am incorrigible, and that neither precept nor example can influence my opinion. There may be some amusement in the pursuit of other points, but there is no pleasure in the possession of anything but that.

Hervey may have been trying to throw a red herring across Henry's path, and assure him obliquely that his relationship with his brother was innocuous, but it is more likely that he simply did not look on his friendship with Ste as something that would preclude his falling in love with a woman. In his view, a woman's inherent inferiority would automatically mean that a mistress, like a wife, could never threaten their relationship, which was on a higher level than that to which any female might hope to aspire.

Despite moaning to Henry Fox about not being in love, Hervey was feeling very well early in 1730, his health apparently still upheld by the beneficial effects of the Italian climate. He told Henry that he had stayed late in Parliament to vote in favour of England's support of Louis XV's demolition of the fortifications at Dunkirk, 'went afterwards abroad to dinner, sat up till six, rose again at ten, walked to Kensington, and was as well the next day (and have continued so ever since) as ever I was in my life. Are not times well mended with me?'

10. The Back Stairs

As Hervey had predicted, the new and changed government appointments were announced in the spring. Robert Walpole had strengthened his position by replacing Lord Townshend with Lord Harrington as Secretary of State. Although Townshend was Walpole's brother-in-law, as well as his neighbour in Norfolk, they had nearly fought a duel the previous year after Sir Robert told Townshend, 'My Lord, there is no man's sincerity which I doubt as much as yours.' Townshend resigned before any more damage was done, and through his wife he and Walpole were able to remain on cordial terms. Years later, Horace Walpole suggested that their quarrel was not to do with them disliking one another, but incited by Queen Caroline, who distrusted Townshend and wanted him out of government. This opinion was shared by Henry Fox's grandson, the third Lord Holland, who said that Walpole never forgave Queen Caroline for this interference in his affairs. Hervey thought that their disagreement was due to the fact that Walpole based his power on the Queen's support, Townshend on the King's. Walpole's customarily concise analysis of the situation was that, 'As long as the firm of the house was Townshend and Walpole, the utmost harmony prevailed; but no sooner it became Walpole and Townshend, than things went wrong.'

Harrington, who replaced Townshend, had been given a barony after the success of his negotiation of the Treaty of Seville in 1729. A cousin of Lord Chesterfield, the new Lord Harrington was a lazy, stubborn man who, so Hervey said, was forgotten as soon as he became Secretary of State. If Caroline's description of his typical day was accurate, he can have had little time to attend to business; she said he needed 'six hours to dress, six more to dine, six more for his mistress, and six more to sleep'. But Hervey owed him his thanks because it was the position Harrington vacated at court that Walpole awarded to the expectant Lord Hervey. He was created

Vice-Chamberlain in April 1730, with a salary of £1,000 a year.

The court to which Lord Hervey was now attached was one of pomp and pageantry, creating an appearance of absolute power which belied the reality behind it. The 'alchemy of ritual' performed by the royal court was essential to transform a man – quite an ordinary man, in George II's case – into a supreme monarch; a royal household of over a thousand officials was required to effect and maintain this illusion. Hervey's role, as one of two Vice-Chamberlains, was to handle the day-to-day organization and upkeep of the royal palaces under the authority of the Chamberlain, the Duke of Grafton, for whom he had also to officiate if Grafton were absent on important court occasions such as St George's Day. His other duties included assigning lodgings to courtiers, arranging the transport and moving the court from palace to palace, and co-ordinating the arrangements for special events at court, or special requests from the King or Queen. Probably his most important (though undefinable) role was as constant companion to the royal family.

While previous rulers received their ministers and courtiers in their private apartments, George I had restricted access to his private rooms, and his son continued this policy, thus emphasizing the separation between the private and public personas of the royal family. Access to the King, except at official times, was guarded by the Gentlemen of the Bedchamber, who guided the monarch's visitors up the back staircase to a closet off his bedroom (which, theoretically, was a public chamber) where he would receive them; this role made courtiers especially vulnerable to jealousy – and bribery. As Vice-Chamberlain, Hervey's strategically placed lodgings at St James's Palace were at the foot of the Queen's back stairs.

The physical layout of George II's palaces reflected this division between public and private roles, best exemplified at Kensington, which was rebuilt by his father. This newly built palace was one of Caroline's favourites, and its rural setting was much admired by contemporaries. 'Nothing is more beautiful than the road from London to Kensington, crossing Hyde Park,' wrote de Saussure. 'It is perfectly straight and so wide that three or four coaches can drive abreast. It is bordered on either side by a wide ditch, and has posts put up at even distances, on the tops of which lanterns are hung and lamps placed in them, which are lighted every evening when the court is at Kensington.'

Rambling St James's Palace was the principal London residence of the royal family. It had been in regular use only since the grand palace at Whitehall was destroyed by fire in 1697; there was not the money to remodel it, as George wished to, in the style of the magnificent European palaces, such as Versailles, which were being built around this time. Cesar de Saussure described St James's as not giving 'the impression from outside of being the residence of a great King'.

The daily routine at court was predictable, changed only by the seasons. 'We jog on here *le vieux train* [in our usual fashion]. A little walking, a little hunting and a little playing, a little flattering, a little railling and a little lying; a little hate, a little friendship, and a little love; a little hope and a little fear, a little joy and a little pain,' as Hervey described it to Ste soon after his arrival in 1730. In the mornings, members of the court walked in the palace grounds, or rode or hunted, except on the days of formal Drawing-room assemblies. Every afternoon – after dinner, between five and seven in the summer, and before dinner, between one and three in the winter – the ladies of the court promenaded through the royal parks, either Hyde Park or St James's; their husbands and suitors accompanied them and they were the subject of much attention from the common people of London who gathered to watch the celebrities of the court gossiping and flirting. The evenings were more intimate, if competitive: the King played backgammon or commerce; the Queen, with the Princess Royal and a lady-in-waiting, played quadrille; and the younger princesses played at lottery with the Duke of Grafton.

'No mill-horse ever went in a more constant track,' wrote Hervey. The court spent the winter at St James's, roughly from the King's Birthday at the end of October until Parliament was dissolved in April. The royal Birthday was the opening event of the London season, and one which everybody with any tie to the court attended in their most extravagant outfits; but, 'one Birthday is so like another . . . excepting the colour of people's clothes', wrote the jaded Hervey in 1732. In the summer months, George tended to return to Hanover, leaving Caroline as regent. She would move between Windsor, Hampton Court and Kensington, taking her courtiers with her from palace to palace.

Winter was the official season, in which every moment the King and Queen were in public was regimented and ceremonial. The royal family dined in state each Sunday, watched by members of the public who had purchased tickets for the honour of gazing on their annointed leader as he ate his chops. Assemblies, known as Drawing-rooms, because they were held in the royal drawing-rooms, were held two or three times a week. The guests, an assortment of peers, gentlemen, and their ladies, entered the palace through a courtyard, and proceeded up a grand staircase to the guard chamber, the first of the state rooms. There they were ushered through to the presence chamber and privy chamber to the drawing-room; beyond the drawing-room were the royal family's private apartments.

These receptions were held in great state, with the King, Queen, Princes and Princesses processing into the drawing-room preceded by six Yeomen of the Guard, carrying halberds over their shoulders; the Master of the Household and the Chamberlain bearing their long white wands of office; a pair of mace-bearing sergeants-at-arms; and finally by a courtier carrying the sword of state. 'This weapon is very long and broad; the scabbard is of crimson velvet, the hilt of massive gold, enriched with some precious stones,' recorded Cesar de Saussure.

Saussure was

surprised at seeing everyone making a profound reverence or bow as the King went by, which he in turn acknowledged by a slight inclination of the head. The English do not consider their King to be so very much above them that they dare not salute him, as in France; they respect him and are faithful to him, and often sincerely attached to him.

Although compared to the French court protocol was relatively relaxed, there were still no chairs at the Drawing-rooms, so that people did not (even inadvertently) sit down in the royal presence. People kissed one another in greeting – often on the lips, in contrast

to the continental style, which was on the cheek: 'let not this mode
of greeting scandalise you,' wrote Saussure, 'it is the custom in this
country, and many ladies would be displeased should you fail to
salute them thus'.

Drawing-rooms were the central, regular court event. No in-
vitations were issued – people simply came as they pleased, when
they wanted to show off, or curry favour – but most of the peerage
(just under two hundred families at this time) attended at least
semi-regularly throughout the season, and would have been well
known to the footmen who ushered them into the receiving rooms.
The eighteenth-century aristocracy was a small, insulated group,
its members bound to one another by ties of marriage and kin
stretching back over generations. Theoretically, though, anyone
who could afford the clothes (and pass muster with the royal guards)
could attend a Drawing-room or a Birthday and meet the King.

At the Queen's Birthday in 1729, Mrs Delany admired Prince
Frederick's spirited dancing and his costume of 'mouse-colour
velvet, turned up with scarlet, and very richly trimmed with silver'
but thought less of the Princess Royal's gown, 'it being only faced
and robed with embroidery'. She herself had dressed 'in all my best
array, borrowed my Lady Sunderland's jewels, and made a tearing
show'. Her clothes for the Birthday, she said, had cost her £17;
they were of French silk, 'the ground dark grass green, brocaded
with a running pattern like lace of white intermixed with festoons
of flowers in faint colours'. To top it all off, she wore pink and
silver ribbons, with a French headdress and a cockade.

For the women of court, dressing could take several hours, and
became a social ritual, a sort of informal salon. Ladies received
visitors *en déshabillé*, wearing uncorseted silk 'night-dresses', as they
had their hair powdered and put up, or placed beauty spots on their
bosoms or cheeks. Formal dress, a corset and wide hoop skirts, was
worn for official occasions, like a royal Drawing-room, or a dinner
party or ball. During the day, when walking in the park or shopping,
ladies wore simple dresses, their petticoats 'only of a size to lift the
dress from clinging', with white aprons and straw hats or lace caps
tied with broad coloured ribbons. In the words of the French-
woman Madame du Boccage, English ladies looked like nymphs

in this guise – far better, she added, than they did in the evening, for the natural English beauty did not suit the elaborate French styles ladies adopted in pursuit of the latest trends. Mrs Delany's letters reveal a passionate interest in fashion typical of her age. Everybody pleased themselves in matters of style, she commented in 1727: 'there is great liberty taken in dress'. This liberty might take unusual form: Hervey described a male friend, recently returned from Paris, wearing a pair of shoe-straps around his ankles which looked like Mercury's wings covered in black shoe-polish.

Court life was expensive, and only those with large incomes – usually derived from royal or political office, as well as revenues from estates – could afford to attend with any regularity. Particularly for the major royal assemblies and balls, such as the King or Queen's Birthdays, astonishing finery was required; on Caroline's Birthday in 1731, an Italian count wore twenty-four large diamonds on his coat instead of buttons.* Suitable clothes (which, of course, could not be worn more than once) for the royal Birthdays alone might cost £200 a year, which was the annual salary of the lowest officials at court. As Hervey said in his *Memoirs*, the 'necessary expenses incurred in dangling after a court' were prohibitive for all but the richest families.

One's importance (often correlative to the magnificence of one's clothes) was sized up and analysed not only by courtiers but by the masses, for whom the inhabitants of the court occupied the status of twentieth-century movie stars. Newspapers reported with interest the comings and goings at court, and of the aristocracy; poems, plays and satires of aristocratic life were published almost weekly. Because of the explicit association of court life with politics – as Walpole himself said, 'Nobody can carry on the King's business if he is not supported at court' – events there often assumed a relevance beyond their real import.

---

* In 1734, Lady Mary Wortley Montagu half-joked to Hervey that she was pleased to be absent from the King's Birthday in order to miss seeing the Queen wearing pink,

> Superior to her waiting nymphs,
> As lobster to attendant shrimps.

But something more than mere clothes or money was necessary to make an *entrée* into society; breeding was also vital for social acceptance. Although the English system was more flexible than its European counterparts, accessible to the ambitious (and loyal) newly rich in a generation or two, blood still mattered. Men such as the poet Alexander Pope, who were valued by their aristocratic friends for their intelligence, were still looked down on for their origins – especially if they seemed to question the legitimacy of the nobility's exclusive right to power. As Lady Mary Wortley Montagu said of Pope and Jonathan Swift, 'It is pleasant to consider that had it not been for the good nature of those very mortals they condemn, these two superior beings were entitled by their birth and hereditary fortune to be only a couple of link-boys [boys who were paid to carry torches to light the way of passers-by through the dark streets of London].' Although Lord Chesterfield urged his son not to 'be proud of your rank or birth, but be as proud as you please of your character', the assumption was that rank and birth did contribute to one's character, and could only be discounted where they were present in the first place.

With its emphasis on appearance rather than substance, court life was notoriously superficial, as the introduction to Pope's *The Rape of the Lock* reflects:

> Hither the Heroes and the Nymphs resort,
> To taste awhile the Pleasures of a court;
> In various talk th'instructive Hours they pas't,
> Who gave the Ball, or paid the Visit last:
> One speaks the glory of the British Queen,
> And one describes an Indian Screen;
> A third interprets Motions, Looks, and Eyes;
> At ev'ry Word a Reputation dies.
> Snuff, or the Fan, supply each pause of Chat,
> With singing, laughing, ogling and all that.

It was a criticism even courtiers levelled at themselves, and had ever done so. The Marquis of Halifax used the phrase, 'mere Drawing-room compliments', to describe the vacuity of the softly spoken words at James II's court. Timeless, too, were the accusations of venality and corruption. Courtiers, Hervey said in his *Memoirs*,

like cautious and skilful sailors, see every cloud as soon as it rises and watch every wind as fast as it changes . . . [and] set their sails in such a manner as should enable them to shift to the gale that was most favourable, and put them in a readiness to pursue the course they were on or tack about, just as the weather should require, and to the point of the compass where sunshine was most likely to appear.

Dependent for their livelihoods on the whims and moods of the King and Queen, courtiers soon learned to be not only responsive but fawning, not just obedient but obsequious. They would swallow anything if it meant they were seen to be in favour, as Swift demonstrated in *Gulliver's Travels*, describing the antics of the ministers at the Lilliputan court who danced on tightropes or crept under and jumped over sticks to gain a ribbon or an office. But 'there is one article in which you must allow a court office to be very unlike matrimony', Hervey wrote to a friend soon after his arrival at court. Though courtiers were often as ill-used as wives, and complained as often of the treatment they were accorded, unlike wives they never wished to be divorced. Indeed, courtiers lived in fear of being sent away from the place where they were forced to 'wipe the shoes that kick 'em, and kiss the hands that cuff 'em'.

The flattery and bribery that were accepted parts of court life were little more than institutionalized corruption: it was the way things worked, everyone knew it, and so everyone could use the system if they cared (or could afford) to. According to Lord Chesterfield, some people were better suited to this system than others:

courts are unquestionably the seats of good breeding; and must necessarily be so; otherwise they would be the seats of violence and desolation. There all the passions are in their highest state of fermentation. All pursue what but few can obtain, and many seek what but one can enjoy. Good breeding alone restrains their excesses. There, if enemies did not embrace, they would stab. There, smiles are often put on, to conceal tears. There, mutual services are professed, while mutual injuries are intended; and there, the guile of the serpent simulates the gentleness of the dove.

For all this, he still advised his son to take up a position at court. 'It is the best school for manners, and whatever ignorant people may think or say of it, no more the seat of vice than a village is; human nature is the same everywhere, the modes only are different.'

Despite Chesterfield's caveat, the court was undeniably a hotbed of intrigue and immorality; no one who hoped to advance could hold himself apart from it. Horace Walpole remembered a story of Lady Sundon, Caroline's Mistress of the Robes and therefore powerfully close to the Queen's ear, visiting the old Duchess of Marlborough wearing a pair of diamond earrings she had received in return for placing Lord Pomfret in the lucrative position of Master of the Horse. As soon as she had gone, the Duchess turned to Lady Mary Wortley Montagu and erupted at Lady Sundon's impudence, 'to come hither with a bribe in her ear'. 'Madam,' replied Lady Mary, 'how should people know where wine is sold, unless a bush is hung out?'

For all the Duchess of Marlborough's indignation (and she was no angel in that respect, having helped secure Lord Bristol's peerage, among many others), Hervey thought Lady Sundon was one of the best of a bad lot. By her conduct, he said, she

reversed the manners and maxims of most courtiers and politicians, as she seemed generally in the obligations she conferred to consider more who wanted her than whom she wanted, a way of thinking very different from that of her master and mistress, who looked upon humankind as so many commodities in a market, which, without favour or affection, they considered only in the degree they were useful, and paid for them in that proportion, Sir Robert Walpole being sworn appraiser to their majesties at all these sales.

In the role of appraiser, Walpole had selected Hervey and placed him at court. He needed an ally close to the King and Queen, who could inform him of their opinions and try to influence them if necessary. Bright, charming Lord Hervey, who had been brought up with the dealings of courts, and had proven his loyalty in Parliament the year before, was the perfect choice.

11. Gilded Cages

Hervey arrived at Windsor in June 1730 to take up his new duties. He wrote to Ste almost immediately to let him know how much he was missing him. 'I cannot help writing to you though I am sure a journal of my actions here can be no great entertainment to you and a diary of my thoughts would be nothing but a recapitulation of a thousand things you have said, and a thousand more that I have told you before a thousand times.' Hervey marvelled that he felt when he was with Ste nothing of the indifference which is the usual response when one spends too much time with another person. 'I begin to believe the whole of what I am either when I am with you, or from you, is a sensation which I only ever knew and you only ever imparted. Nobody's conversation amuses me but yours,' he continued, 'nobody's jokes enliven me but yours, nobody's confidence pleases me but yours; and what is stranger than all the rest, nobody's flattery pleases me but yours, and though you may think my vanity keen enough to feed on any other, I assure you if it does, it is only eating to satisfy its hunger, and not to gratify its taste.'

He had, he said, been thrust straight into his new role, as the Duke of Grafton was to be away on St George's Day and Hervey was to take his place in the proceedings. 'I have already had my lecture of instructions, as to bows, steps, attitudes etc.,' he told Ste. His actual duties were more wearing than mere bowing and scraping, as he wrote to Ste a month later. From seven o'clock until 2 a.m. he had been on his feet, going from a dull reception to a dinner to a dance with only half-an-hour's nap to keep him going. Henry Fox and Charles Hamilton had been at Windsor for the proceedings, but went to London before the ball: Lord Sunderland (later Duke of Marlborough; pictured in *Lord Hervey and His Friends*, see plate 1) was to dine with Hervey that day. 'Why are you not of the party?' Hervey wrote to Stephen. 'What are you doing at

Redlynch? You are as much present in my mind as if I had seen you but this morning; and yet it seems as long as if I had not seen you these seven years.'

Stephen came to Windsor from London several times in June and July to visit his friend, but he never stayed long enough to satisfy Hervey. Ste would hardly have left Windsor before Hervey would be summoned back to his duties, which by their formality and ritual were a constant reminder of the freedom and ease of Ste's much missed company. 'I have you now only by accidents and starts, and instead of having it a miracle to pass an hour from you, 'tis grown the work of contrivance to pass an hour with you.' Hervey's letters railed against their separation, yet he never accepted responsibility for it. He seems to have been unaware of, or blinded to, the fact that it was his own ambition that made it so difficult for them to be together.

Ste felt the lack of Hervey's company as much as his was missed, for Hervey wrote on 21 August to assure him that life at court could not make up for his absence.

What are the royal pleasures you talk of, my dear Ste, which are not given equally to every subject? Do the trappings of royalty make the amusements of the country more agreeable? Are our chaises easier or our boats safer for being gilt? Is the air sweeter for a court, or the walks pleasanter for being bounded with sentinels? What entertainment does Windsor afford that cannot be found at Redlynch?

But ask whether Redlynch contains anything that Windsor lacks, he continued, 'and I should quickly answer – the greatest joy I ever did or can know.' Do not be ungrateful to me, Hervey urged Ste, or unjust to yourself, by imagining that my lack of you does not corrode every other pleasure I might find here without you.

Ste did have a point: if Hervey wanted to be with him as desperately as he claimed to, his accepting a station at court would seem directly to oppose this aim. But just as Ste fulfilled Hervey's emotional needs, his position at court satisfied his intellectual and worldly objectives; he needed both elements to make his life complete. The tragedy unfolding was that each began to preclude his possession of the other.

In 1730, though, Hervey still believed a compromise was possible. He had written to Ste in July to say that if their separation 'sits as uneasily upon you as me, sure it might be better palliated, if not quite cured'; and in August he wrote again to suggest a solution.

I beg you would not encourage yourself in supposing that the walks of life we are thrown into have so few paths of communication, that one of us must go out of his way whenever we meet. Why should we only see one another by visits, but never have a common home? Think, if you please, that it is not easy to contrive it, but take care of concluding it impossible.

He was convinced, Hervey said, that people more often fail to possess what they desire from the weakness of their desire, rather than from the obstacles to it. In other words, if they wanted to be together badly enough, they could make it happen.

What Hervey had in mind was that Ste should have Hervey's house in Great Burlington Street. Then he could be in London without feeling any obligation to anyone, and he and Hervey might see each other as much as they pleased, on their own, mutual, territory. Hervey no longer needed the house – as Vice-Chamberlain he had a permanent suite of apartments in St James's Palace, and he had the use of his father's London house if he wanted it – and giving it to Ste would enable him to be in London close to the court more often. Their shared arrangements would also allow a new level of domesticity to enter their relationship; over the following year, Hervey's letters were littered with references to visiting upholsterers or hiring valets to ready the house for Ste. A year later, when it had been newly redecorated, Hervey told Ste,

It is quite finished, and looks the snuggest, sprucest, cheerfulest thing I ever saw. Nothing can improve it but a piece of moveable goods of my acquaintance, which I expect home with more impatience than I can tell you or that you deserve I should feel since the 10 (January 1732; Hervey was writing three weeks earlier, on 21 December) is the soonest you design to bring it.

In November 1730, Ste paid £4,000 into Molly Hervey's account at Hoare's bank and the deal was done. The reason Molly, rather than Hervey, was paid, is unclear. It is possible that the house had been bought with her money in the first place in October 1725, although Hervey told his mother at the time that he had paid for the house by calling in all his old gambling winnings. It was whispered that Molly had been given £4,000 in 1725 by the Duchess of Kendal, George I's aged mistress, to stop flirting with the King. Most people believed that nothing had happened; Horace Walpole thought that the King had made advances to her, but that she had not yielded. 'Lady Hervey, by aiming too high, has fallen very low,' commented Lady Mary Wortley Montagu at the time, 'and is reduced to trying to persuade folks she has an intrigue, and gets nobody to believe her.' A ballad written in the mid-1720s by two of Molly's admirers, Lord Chesterfield and William Pulteney, attested to George I's admiration of her:

> Or were I the King of Great Britain,
> > To choose a Minister well,
> And support the Throne that I sit on
> > I'd have under me Molly Lepell . . .

> Heaven keep our good King from a Rising,
> > But that Rising who's fitter to quell
> Than some Lady with Beauty surprising,
> > And who should that be but Lepell?

More likely, though, the money was Hervey's way of giving his wife her financial independence, and perhaps an ambiguous means of compensating her for his lack of interest in her.

But Molly and Hervey were not completely estranged even after Ste bought their house. Their fifth child, Frederick Augustus (named for the Prince of Wales), was born exactly nine months after Hervey's return from Europe. Hervey had been with Molly

in London for the delivery, and wrote cynically to tell Griselda
Murray in Scotland that his wife had 'suffered a good deal, but not
more than I think every woman deserves at the hands of a poor
mortal that she throws involuntarily into an existence where it has
so few chances to be happy and so many to be miserable'. During
her pregnancy, Molly had been at court with her husband over the
previous winter, for Bristol wrote to her in October to reproach
her gently for the delicacy of his new grandson. He would admit
that little Frederick was pretty, for he was the image of his mother,
but in all honesty he could not tell her that the baby was 'large,
strong and well-nourished'. Frederick's slightness was, Bristol
claimed, the consequence of Molly's indulging in 'dancing,
morning suppers, sharp wines, china oranges, &c.' while she was
pregnant.

Hervey hardly mentioned Molly (or their children) in his letters,
so that even when she was with him, she seems to have been an
irrelevance in his life. All Hervey's emotional energy was bound
up in Ste. When, in September 1730, two of Ste's letters in a row
were delayed in reaching him, Hervey wrote to Fox in a panic.
'How this happened I know not but I was terribly afraid by the
long interval in our correspondence that you were sick; sometimes
I hoped it was a sign you were on the road, and every night came
home to my lodgings flattering myself it was possible to find you
there.'

Between Ste's longed-for visits, Hervey was kept busy with his
court obligations. He went out hunting with the royal party – but
only as a spectator when it rained, as he told Ste ('we chickens . . .
chose the ignoble safety of a dry coach with glasses drawn up'); he
gossiped and gambled, and went up to London if he was needed
there. On one day, he stopped in at Lady Mary Wortley Montagu's
house in Twickenham, having left Prince Frederick shooting in
Richmond Park. He had hoped to dine with Lady Mary while
Frederick hunted, because he had seen her so little recently. 'I have
been so tied by the leg this summer at Windsor, that I conclude
you have forgot there is such a body in the world [as Hervey], but
whilst I am in it, 'tis impossible I should ever forget you enough
not to think you one of the most agreeable things it contains.'

Hervey's joking reference to being 'tied by the leg' was an allusion to his court duties, playing down his pleasure in the marks of royal favour. He had begun to spend a great deal of time in the company of the callow Prince of Wales. In the beginning of September, he wrote to tell Ste the latest gossip: Frederick's pursuit of Henrietta, the young Duchess of Marlborough. 'They are so taken with one another, that I am sure it will not end in a flirtation,' he predicted. Henrietta had had a long-standing affair with the poet William Congreve, who died in 1729. After his death, she ordered a life-size waxen model made of her lover, which she dressed in his clothes, sat at her table, and talked to as if it were alive.

The ups and downs of life at court took their toll on Hervey, but Ste was his salvation.

I write today merely because it is writing to you, and not for your sake but my own, to try if it is possible for any employment to please me; two or three things happened to vex me as much as anything can do if it does not relate to you (which I own is not a great deal) and I have a mind to try if your influence is strong enough at a hundred miles' distance to disperse those clouds which I know if you were here would vanish in a moment; for I do not only look upon you as the source of all my pleasures, but take you always as an antidote to the poison of all my pains.

The problem with depending on a single thing for his happiness, he concluded, was it had become impossible for him to live without it.

Stephen planned a visit to Hervey at the end of September, and Hervey arranged for their friend Lord Bateman to be at Windsor to keep Ste entertained when Hervey could not be with him. 'Not that I will lend you for a moment of the day or night when I can have you; but in order, if I can so contrive, that the hours you are not with me may not lie as heavy upon your hands, as I always find in those when I cannot be with you.' He added as a postscript, 'If you are not impatient to see me, don't come, but I am sure you are.'

Ste stayed in London with Hervey until the beginning of December. They had already made plans for Hervey to join Ste at

Redlynch for Christmas. He could think of nothing but their meeting, he said after Ste had left, but was anxious that Ste not lose two days' shooting to meet him halfway. 'I long to be with you again, for though some considerations may make it necessary for me to be absent from you sometimes, yet I look upon those hours as lost in point of happiness as much as those in which I sleep.'

Ste was missing Hervey, too; so much that when he arrived back at Redlynch from London he was disappointed to find no letter from Hervey waited there to greet him. But in order for Hervey to have got a letter to him that quickly, he said, he would have had to write it the day Ste left town, 'which I told you the night before you left, I was to pass with the Prince at Kew'. If Frederick needed him, Hervey's tone implied, Ste could not expect to distract him.

Before leaving London, Ste told Hervey that he disliked one of his new friends – probably Anne Vane, a Maid of Honour to Queen Caroline. 'I thought you seemed at dinner by what you said to be sorry I was acquainted with the lady you hate, but can you know me so little as to imagine that it is possible for any acquaintance to lessen the pleasure I have in yours?' Hervey asked Ste. Ste knew the contempt in which Hervey held most of his acquaintances. This 'must secure you the profession of a heart, which, (if you were to abdicate your empire there) yet from its own make and bent could never venture to admit a successor. When it ceases to open itself to you it will be shut forever.' But despite these assurances of loyalty, Hervey's heart had indeed admitted a rival to Ste.

12. Miss Vane

Ste's suspicions were not unfounded, for Hervey was, over the winter of 1730–31, pursuing the Honourable Anne Vane, Maid of Honour to Queen Caroline.* In 1728, Molly Hervey, comparing the present generation of Maids of Honour to books, had described Miss Vane as 'a folio-collection of all the court ballads, and all jokes and witticisms of the fashionable world, this book is very diverting, and may easily be read by those of the meanest, as well as by those of the best understanding being writ in the vulgar tongue'. By 1730, rumours about Miss Vane's chastity, or lack thereof, had been circulating at court. In October, she had written to Mrs Howard, the King's mistress, from Bath, denying that she was with child. 'I confess the knowledge of this piece of malice has done infinite mischief with regard to my health, but none, I hope, to my reputation, because thousands daily see the contrary; for this story, however groundless soever, has forced me frequently into public.' Horace Walpole later described Anne Vane as 'a Maid of Honour who was willing to cease to be so at the first opportunity'; Lord Percival thought she had nothing to recommend her, 'neither sense nor wit'.

Life at court was a notoriously corrupting influence on young girls; unmarried women were involved in scandals almost as often as married ones like the unfortunate Lady Abergavenny. 'No one is shocked to hear when Miss So-and-So, Maid of Honour, has got nicely over her confinement,' wrote Lady Mary Wortley Montagu. Mary Bellenden agreed with her, writing to Mrs Howard after her marriage in 1724 for court gossip: 'And pray tell . . . if our maids are like to lose what they are weary of [their virginity].' It may have been the young and ambitious Anne Vane, newly arrived at court, to whom she was referring.

---

* I cannot find a reliable birth-date for Miss Vane; one source says 1705, another 1710.

The romance between Hervey and Anne Vane had started late in 1730, and Ste, as his barbed comments to Hervey in December showed, was clearly jealous. But Hervey did nothing to assuage his fears. Even in Hervey's long protestation of love for Ste, written during a drunken evening in court soon after his return from Redlynch in January 1731, he had taunted his lover with the veiled suggestion of a rival at court:

I shall always find far inferior pleasures to amuse me in those less grateful hours when you are absent; . . . [there are] people that have enough sense for me to laugh with them, and with such ingredients one may make up a little *ragout* that though it is not just one's favourite dish will prevent one either dying of hunger or choosing to fast.

Hervey, it seems, was as vulnerable as any naive Maid of Honour to the blandishments available at court.

None of Miss Vane's letters or responses to Hervey from this period or later survive, so the motivation behind her involvement with him must remain unclear. Satirical pamphlets written after the affair was over describe her as being overwhelmingly in love with Hervey. She started when his name was mentioned, and took care to place herself in his path whenever she could. Besides his influence at court and importance as Walpole's ally, Hervey was devastatingly attractive: handsome, elegant, witty and learned. Perhaps Miss Vane, whose name was already sullied by rumour at least – as her letter of 1730 to Mrs Howard shows – had determined to follow her heart, and damn the consequences to her reputation. But gossip at this time also linked her to Lord Harrington, a Secretary of State; she may just have been generous with her favours.

There is no extant evidence that Hervey ever directly alluded to the affair in his correspondence with Ste, though one tantalizing, partially destroyed note, dated by a later archivist 4 April 1731, ends, 'I was engaged tonight at ten a clock to *you know who*' just above the tear. But, realistically, Hervey could have meant any number of people. Very few letters from Hervey to Ste survive from early 1731 because they were still spending as much time as possible together; and perhaps also because the other events they would have recorded – such as Hervey's duel (see below) – necessitated their being destroyed as well. It is this period, the period of Hervey's intimacy with Prince Frederick as well as his affair with Miss Vane, that was torn out of the handwritten manuscript of Hervey's *Memoirs* by his grandson, over fifty years after Hervey's death. It is unclear whose reputation the first Marquess of Bristol was trying to protect by this act of censorship: his ancestor's, or that of his monarch's family.*

Despite Hervey's new interest, Molly was still forced to write to Ste (not Miss Vane) in order to keep tabs on her husband, just as she had done while they were abroad. She directed her letters to 'Mr Stephen Fox at his house in Burlington Street, London' – where Hervey, in all likelihood, was also staying, and where she and Hervey had once lived together. From one letter, written from Ickworth on 14 June, it sounds as if Ste had been passing on Hervey's political gossip to Lady Hervey: 'I have kept your secret so well that I deserve to be trusted next time your little newsmonger tells you any more which to be sure he'll soon do, for if I guess right (and I am vain enough to think I do) the little man [Hervey was physically slight] can't keep his tongue in his mouth.'

Her interest in politics, one of her husband's obsessions, reveals a touching desire to be included in a group that scorned to notice her despite her intelligence and grasp on public affairs. Stephen was more approachable than her husband, which is perhaps why she wrote to him rather than to Hervey; although even to him she professed to feel herself at an intellectual loss. 'One must have more wit, or vanity, than I have, to be, or think oneself, capable of answering your last letter,' she wrote on 3 July. 'I write therefore to acknowledge, not to answer, it; and to endeavour to pique your generosity into continuing a correspondence I can't make it your interest to keep up.' Ste took care to be kind to Molly, sending

---

* Hervey apparently began the *Memoirs* in 1733, first going back over the events from 1727 until 1733, then writing from day to day, describing events 'just as they occur and while they are fresh in my memory'. He seems to have given sections to his friends to read, telling Henry Fox on 3 October 1734, 'It is impossible for me to speak by letter my sentiments on the present state of affairs, but I write every day *for* you though not *to* you.'

her the odd brace of pheasant or some other little delicacy from
Redlynch or Maddington; she responded via her husband. 'As to
the cheeses Lady Hervey says better late than never and better few
than none,' Hervey told Ste just after their return from Italy, his
literal reporting making Molly sound not sweet (as no doubt she
had intended) but tart.

Molly had been hoping that Hervey and Fox would come down
to Ickworth, she told Ste, but had just heard their plans had changed.
''Tis impossible to tell you how much I was disappointed last night
to hear from my Lord that the Norfolk journey is put off. I never
thought any letter from him could be so disagreeable to me. 'Tis
too much in one week, to see what one does not like [Lady Bristol],
and to hear one shan't see what one does.' How was Hervey, she
demanded, did he look well, and were his spirits high? Living
together had not improved relations between Hervey's wife and
mother. Molly told Ste to tempt him to bring Hervey to Ickworth
that the park was at its peak of beauty, but added, 'There's something in the house extremely disagreeable.'

Molly's wishes were fulfilled a few days later – only for a short
time, but long enough for her to conceive her fourth son, William,
born in May 1732. Hervey and Ste arrived at Houghton, Sir Robert
Walpole's lavish new house in Norfolk, on 12 July after a brief stop
at Ickworth en route. Within two hours of dismounting from his
horse Hervey was writing to Prince Frederick, to whom he was
becoming increasingly close as he spent more time at court.

Houghton, Hervey told Frederick, was a classically inspired
house that combined Palladian beauty with modern luxuries.

The base, or rustic storey, is what is chiefly inhabited at the Congress.
There is a room for breakfast, another for supper, another for dinner,
another for afternooning, and the great arcade with four chimneys for
walking and quid-nuncing. The rest of the floor is merely for use, by
which your Royal Highness must perceive that the whole is dedicated to
fox-hunters, hospitality, noise, dirt and business.

Walpole's home and its contents celebrated all that he stood for
politically and personally. Sir Robert was also known as 'Sir Blue

String' because of the efforts he had made to have the blue ribbon, star and medal of the Order of the Garter painted on to his existing portraits after he received the honour in 1726; similarly his house was thought by many to display 'very great expense without either judgement or taste'. No cost had been spared to make Houghton perfect during the seven years it had taken to build. Even the local village was uprooted and relocated outside the gates to allow for the landscaped park. The chimneypieces were of the finest Italian marble, the furniture was elaborately carved and gilded, looking glasses, plasterwork, and rich damasks and velvets adorned every surface. Walpole had covered the walls with the finest paintings he could find. These included works by Poussin (a contemporary favourite; Hervey had one too), Rembrandt, Titian and Raphael.*

The bi-annual Congresses that Walpole held at Houghton were gatherings of his political allies, a sort of eighteenth-century party conference, to which he invited twenty or thirty guests, all men, united by their loyalty to him. His son Horace described these bluff allies of his father's as 'mountains of roast beef'. Sir Robert did not stint on hospitality: when the Duke of Lorraine stayed at Houghton later in 1731, the great hall was lit every night by 130 candles and the saloon by fifty. Walpole spent £15 a night on candles, and a hundred times that on wine each year – which alone was more than one of his tenants could earn in a lifetime.

Hervey and Ste were at the summer Congress together. The Fox brothers (whose father had been a confirmed Tory) had been won over to the Whigs by the combined efforts of Hervey and their mutual friend Thomas Winnington, and now openly supported Walpole. Just before he left, Hervey wrote to Frederick that,

Our company at Houghton swelled at last into so numerous a body that we used to sit down to dinner a snug little party of about thirty odd, up to the chin in beef, venison, geese, turkeys, &c.; and generally over the chin in claret, strong beer and punch. We had Lords spiritual and temporal, besides commoners, parsons and freeholders innumerable. In public we

---

* Early the next century, they were all sold as a job lot to Catherine the Great of Russia to pay off the debts of Walpole's grandson.

drank loyal healths, talked of the times and cultivated popularity; in private we drew plans and cultivated the country.

From a letter of Hervey's to Frederick written from Houghton, it would seem that the Prince was jealous of his friend's lover.

When as you imagine, Sir, that politics can put my old friends (as your Royal Highness is pleased to call them) out of my head, you very much mistake both me and our employments here. Politics have very little share in our conversation, and the friend you mean [has] so great a share in my heart that he is in no danger of being dislodged by that or any other force,

replied Hervey to Frederick's clumsy teasing; it could have been either Fox or Frederick himself to whom the Prince was referring.

The young Prince of Wales took after his father, just as King George had resembled his own. When Frederick arrived in London in December 1728, George happily told Walpole that he did not think him 'a son I need be much afraid of'; this was soon proved to be a mistakenly optimistic view. The archetypal struggle between father and son was played out with particular force by the Hanoverians: George II and his father – Dunce II and Dunce I as they were known – had lived in a state of permanent hostility, just as Frederick and George would. The position of Prince of Wales was almost untenable, with its high status but lack of any real authority or autonomy; sooner or later the heir apparent was bound to chafe against the King, who, simply by living, prevented the fulfilment of his son's ambitions.

Soon after Frederick's début at the English court, Lady Bristol (who, admittedly, had an exaggerated reverence for royalty) described him to her husband as 'the most agreeable young man it is possible to imagine, without being the least handsome; his person little, but very well made, and genteel; a liveliness in his eyes that is indescribable, and the most obliging address [manner] that can be conceived'. Horace Walpole agreed that Frederick was friendly and generous, but added that he was 'really childish'. Hervey's opinion, given years later, was that Frederick was largely unremarkable, neither great nor vicious: 'his behaviour was something that gained one's good wishes, though it gave one no esteem for him'.

Whatever Hervey privately thought of Frederick's strengths and weaknesses, he was able to swallow his criticisms and act as friend and adviser to the rash, immature prince. During Frederick's first years in England, Hervey was as much a mentor to Frederick as one can be to a wilful young heir-apparent. It is evident from their correspondence that Frederick was not only diverted by Hervey's wit, and fond of him but, lacking a close father-figure, also looked up to his sophisticated friend. Like Stephen Fox, Frederick needed an older man to lead him into the adult world; and Hervey was more than happy to play this role once again.

13. 'My dear Chicken'

Despite the positive tone of his letters to Frederick, the excesses of Houghton had done Hervey's health no good and by July 1731 he was very ill for the first time since his return from Italy. At the start of the year he had had an epileptic fit at a Drawing-room in St James's Palace, which he told Ste about 'for fear some officious paragraph in a newspaper should alarm your kindness for me and make you uneasy'. He had been chatting to Frederick 'in as good spirits and health as ever I was in my life', when without warning he had collapsed 'as if I had been shot' at the Prince's feet. Sir Robert Walpole and two friends carried Hervey into Queen Caroline's bedroom, took off his clothes, and ministered to him with hartshorn and gold-powder. Even the King stood by, assisting 'with more goodness than his general good breeding alone would have extracted'. Hervey was taken down to his lodgings, slipping in and out of consciousness, and then blooded in both arms. 'I felt neither pain or sickness the whole time, and feel myself today astonishingly well. The Prince sat with me all yesterday, and has promised to [do] so again today; but all these honours do not compensate for the disagreeable circumstance of this accident having been so public. You know how well I detest being talked over.'

By July, Molly – taunted by her mother-in-law – was panicking, as she wrote to Ste in London days after their return from Norfolk. She did not believe Ste's account of Hervey's health and feared that Lady Bristol's dire hints might be closer to the truth, and was working herself up into a state of mild hysteria. Her mother-in-law, speaking 'in a mysterious frightful sort of manner', had convinced her that Hervey's health might force him to go abroad again. 'Pray don't go out of town (I mean to Somersetshire) 'til he is much better, I wish you could stay some time with him at Hampton Court . . . As long as you stay with him favour me with an account

of him, I'm always impatient yet fearful to receive it.' Molly had
become so used to thinking of Ste as being essential to her husband's
health and happiness that she was willing to implore him to remain
with Hervey.

Lord Bristol was worried too, and blamed Hervey's renewed
ill-health on his excessive consumption of tea.

I can feel little or no abatement of my pain till I hear you are finally
determined to drink no more of that detestable, fatal liquor, which
brought you once before so near to death's door, and which, if persisted
in, will demonstrably hasten your passage through it many years before
you need otherwise experience it; and then what must become of your
country, wife and children, and our forlorn family? Were it in my power
to set you half so much at ease as you might me by so small a sacrifice as
ye self-denial of a cup of tea, I would willingly forgo all ye remaining
satisfactions in life to exchange them for your quiet.

In early August, Hervey was well enough to return to his duties
at Hampton Court. 'I have been out of humour, unpleasing and
unpleased ever since you saw me,' he wrote to Ste; they were to
be apart for three months. While they were together, they had
expanded the codes they used to refer to court figures so that
Hervey could write freely to Stephen even if his letters were
opened. Robert Walpole was called '19' in January, and in his first
letter to Ste after the summer Hervey referred to the Queen as '13',
George as '92', and Frederick as '7'. But two weeks later Hervey
was forced to admit that even with their cypher there was little he
could write about to Ste that he wished to. 'Solomon you know
says, *Speak not in palaces for the walls have ears, nor of princes for the birds
of the air will reveal it.*'

He still felt free to tell Ste how much he adored him, though. At
dinner one day someone called Hervey's neighbour by Ste's name.
Involuntarily Hervey started, and blushed,

and felt just as I imagine your favourite mistress would have done . . .
Don't despise me for these little particulars; but flatter your vanity with
reflecting that to teach such a way of thinking to so good a courtier is not

a less proof of your power, than it would be to establish Christianity in Turkey or chastity in Swallow Street [notorious for its prostitutes].

Despite Hervey's extravagant protestations of affection, his letters had started to betray an underlying tension in their relationship. Hervey persisted in his role of the ardent wooer, forcing Ste, almost by default, into the role of a passive, slightly hesitant party who had continually to be won over by Hervey's demonstrations of abject adoration. 'You are by this time *en train* [on course] (as you call it) at Redlynch,' he wrote later in the year, after Ste had left him in London, 'and as you are generally more desirous to be in *a track* than solicitous about *what* track, I may very fairly for you, and disagreeably for myself, conclude that you are now as well pleased and as well satisfied there as you was a fortnight ago [with Hervey].' This adaptability was convenient for Ste, Hervey concluded, but he could not help begrudging it, since he could not emulate it himself. But the reality was that Stephen really loved Hervey – they simply could not have spent so much time together in such intimacy had he not – and Hervey's constant testing of him, not to mention his often selfish absorption in court life, sometimes became too much for Ste to bear.

At the end of August, when Hervey wrote to him saying that he wished he could love Frederick, his new friend and companion, as much as he loved Ste, he probably wanted to wound Fox for being too content without him. It may also have been a hint of the nature of his relationship with Frederick. Had Hervey seduced Frederick he would hardly have been able to resist boasting to someone about it; and Stephen would have been the only person Hervey could trust with a secret of this magnitude, even knowing the pain his revelation would cause. It is easy to imagine Hervey delighting in debauching the heir to the throne. The Prince, gauche and impressionable, hostile to his parents and uncomfortable around women for all his efforts at conquest, would have been an easy victim for Hervey's charms. Frederick's nicknames for Hervey – 'my dear Chicken' or 'my Lord Chicken' – reveal an intimacy that could be interpreted in several ways; likewise the jealousy Frederick expressed to Hervey in July could be seen either as that of a possessive friend or that of a lover. Certainly, the two men were often publicly in one another's company: when Frederick was ill Hervey was the person he wanted to sit by his bedside; Hervey took pride in using a gold snuffbox that Frederick had given him with the Prince's portrait on it.

There was enough between Hervey and Frederick that Ste might easily have believed they were lovers, even if Hervey had not confessed it to him. Whatever Hervey had meant by his comments about Frederick, Ste took the bait. He wrote back, terrified he would lose his place in Hervey's heart to the Prince. His desperate words struck a chord with his lover, but Hervey refused to apologize, or surrender his role as the older, wiser partner in the relationship. It was always Fox who was wrong, never Hervey.

Hervey claimed he was always readier to grant his pardon than Ste was to ask it; that Ste never showed any repentance to Hervey; that Hervey felt more pain in chastising Ste than Ste could ever feel in deserving his reproaches. 'I wish nothing in this world so much as the constant power of giving you pleasure,' Hervey wrote. If the force of this feeling made him fear that Ste did not return his love or hate their being apart, Ste must forgive him. 'Let my loving you extravagantly, as it is the cause, be also my excuse for loving you disagreeably. The least mark of contrition or affection in you, softens me more than you can imagine, so much, that I fear it is not in your power to commit any crime that it is not in your power to make me forgive.' The tears ran so thickly down his cheeks as he wrote, he said, that he could barely see the page.

He wanted to make a thousand declarations of his fondness but the hackneyed phrases had been debased by being used to describe so many lesser attachments, and too often exceeded the love they represented just as in Hervey's case they would fall short of what he wanted to express.

When I said I wished I loved 7 [Frederick] as I do you, I lied egregiously; I am as incapable of wishing to love any body else so well, as I am of wishing to love you less: God forbid any mortal should ever have the power over me you have, or that you should ever [have] less, who never made me feel that power without thinking slavery the happiest circumstance of my life. Adieu if I was to fill a thousand reams of paper it would be only aiming in different phrases and still imperfectly to tell you the same thing, and assure you that since I first knew you I have been without repenting and still am and ever shall be undividedly and indissolubly yours.

Why should Hervey 'repent' being Stephen's? Perhaps because he was aware of the damage it might do to both of them should the nature of their friendship be revealed; perhaps he would have preferred to pursue Frederick unhampered by old associations. In his next letter, written three days later, Hervey again tried to shift the blame for their argument on to Ste's shoulders, addressing him almost as a spoilt child. It is a testament to Stephen's love for Hervey that this autocratic tone did not rankle, considering the care with which he had nursed Hervey since he had known him and his constant and open affection for him regardless of his own name and reputation.

Hervey promised not to bring up the subject of their last letters again but could not resist one last dig at Ste. 'Here's an end of it: you offended imprudently, I resented it extravagantly; you repented agreeably, I forgave you willingly.' Hervey knew Ste had not meant to displease him, and more importantly, he knew that Ste was devastated once he knew he had displeased him. If Ste was willing to prostrate himself before him, Hervey was willing to reward him with protestations of his enduring love. 'In short I have been prodigiously miserable and prodigiously happy about this silly thing and find every day more and more that whatever impression sinks deep into my mind either of pleasure or of pain must be stamped by you.'

Hervey concluded the letter with a bone thrown to his distraught lover: a plan to meet at Basingstoke, halfway between Hampton Court and Maddington, Ste's hunting-box on Salisbury Plain, later in the autumn. It was only a day's journey for each of them, he thought; and might not Ste use meeting his sister as a ruse? 'In short I long and pine and fret to see you. What does one live for, but to be happy; and what happiness can one have, when one loves one single thing better than all others in the world bundled together, and does not possess it?'

But Hervey, for all these declarations, was so absorbed in his social life – his new intimacy with Prince Frederick and the agreeable pursuit of Anne Vane – that sometimes he could not find time to write to Ste. 'I had the headache so violently all last post-day that I could not lift it from the pillow, and have therefore by this return [of post], contrary to custom, two letters to thank you for.' The post to the south-west was called for two days a week, and arrived at Hampton Court by return; thus one was always writing ahead of one's reader's response. By Ste's last letter, he continued, he saw that Ste thought – hoped Hervey had meant to come to Maddington, but 'you know that is impossible'. And whatever Hervey might wish, he said, he could not stay with Fox at Basingstoke for more than fourteen or fifteen hours.

Hervey was demanding too much of Fox and giving him too little back. His letters were beginning to sound mechanical – not to mention self-absorbed – as Ste's responses to Hervey must have indicated. He questioned Hervey's interest in the ladies at court, demanding reassurances of Hervey's loyalty. 'You guess very ill about the conquest you imagine Lady Tankerville's *agréable folie, naiveté charmante et beauté naturelle* [delightful whimsy, charming naivety and natural beauty] made in a certain heart,' he wrote to Fox in September, after a long letter written two weeks before in which he sang Lady Tankerville's praises.

You must know as little of its sensations to imagine it an easy prize, as you must of its value, if you were to think it a considerable one; for though many have been sojourners there, I promise you there have been but very few governors. And as to *la petite personne* [the little one] you mention [probably Anne Vane], I assure you she has had orders long ago, though not to make room for a successor.

The intensity of their relationship was now such that Ste admitted to seeing women as competition for Hervey's affection; whether Hervey was honest with him in turn about his rivals was another matter. And whether Ste's real rival was a woman or a man was also open to question.

PART THREE

14. Sticks and Stones

Huddled by the fire in his room in the middle of a winter night in 1731, after spending Christmas at Redlynch, Hervey wrote to tell Ste that despite his return to court, his thoughts remained with his lover. 'I have left the King above playing at hazard [a dice game] in a hot, sweaty, stinking crowd, to come and tell you with what content and satisfaction I every moment think of the return of you and happiness,' he began (perhaps a little the worse for wear as his handwriting is less immaculate than usual and his style more rambling). He had dined at Sir Robert Walpole's house in Chelsea, he said, where the conversation had turned to 'the degeneracy of the age and the badness of the world'. Hervey said he had no idea what his companions were going on about: as far as he was concerned, while he had Ste he could imagine no better time or place in which to live.

'To be sure there is muck, mire, and mud in the world; but why people who have eyes need walk into such dirty ways and travel such nasty roads I can not imagine. Or if they must frequent them, let them be but well-clothed and thick-covered, and none of the filth can penetrate or do them any harm. For my own part,' he concluded, 'my mind never goes naked but in your territories. When I stir out of them I am fenced like a stage-coach postillion, and should expect if I was not to be much bespattered.'

Hervey wrote again the following evening ruing the excesses of the night before.

My dear Ste, I am so dispirited, and my head aches so violently with sitting up till three this morning, *ex officio*, that I have not eat a morsel, and have been in bed almost all the day. It is now seven o'clock, and in an hour I must attend his Royal Highness [Frederick] to the Duchess of Marlborough's [Henrietta; Hervey's earlier prediction about their affair had proved accurate] where we are to sup, and I fear will sit up again.

But Hervey's hangover did not prevent him sending Ste an interesting pamphlet, almost certainly 'Sedition and Defamation Display'd', with the words, 'The enclosed I believe you will like; I do.' He wanted to say more, he added, but he was afraid of the other readers of his letters: these thoughts would have to be saved up until they met.

Over the previous year Hervey had written several pamphlets attacking the Opposition, in particular his old friend William Pulteney and Pulteney's patron, Viscount Bolingbroke. Although pamphlets were usually anonymous, the world of politics was so small that individual writers were easily identifiable by their literary styles and modes of attack and much thought and gossip was devoted to determining who had written what. In June 1731, for instance, Molly Hervey wrote to Ste speculating about the author of a pamphlet currently circulating, asking whether or not Ste thought the opinions were the same as those expressed by a friend at her apartments recently: 'there is a paragraph in it that is word for word what a gentleman said on reading the *Craftsman* at our lodgings the other night my Lord and you came to town; don't you remember both the thing and the person? If you do send me word truly whether you think he had any hand in writing it, I don't think 'tis like his style in common discourse but this *rencontre* [coincidence] struck me.'

The pamphlet Hervey sent to Ste had been written by Sir William Yonge (Lord Hardwicke maintained that Yonge had admitted authorship to him years later), with an introductory 'Dedication' by Hervey (according to a note in Hervey's hand on a copy of the pamphlet at Ickworth). The body of the work attacked the Opposition in fairly standard terms.

Our modern disputes have arisen, and been managed by those, who, publicly at least, profess the same principles with those they oppose, and consequently can have no dislike to them on that account. What then must they do to justify their opposition? Their private motives are perhaps unfit to be mentioned, or perhaps would not redound to their honour, and thus a fatal necessity has driven them into a method which I am persuaded many of them dislike in their hearts; and they are forced by personal abuse, and private scandal, to justify their differing, not only from their former friends, but from their own former conduct and behaviour. And I can't help pitying the case of a man of sense, who is reduced so low, as to be capable of so much meanness, as to mention on any occasion the loss of a tooth, or an ungenteel cock of a hat, as an objection to a Minister.

This last sentence was aimed at Pulteney, who in a recent tirade against the government had sniped at Hervey for having a tooth pulled and at Horatio Walpole, Robert's brother, for his notorious scruffiness. A few weeks later, another ministerial writer, William Arnall, also derided Pulteney's personal attacks on Walpole's men: 'Are unmannerly ribald jests, upon the loss of a tooth belonging to one gentleman, or a button belonging to another, a national enquiry?'

The 'Dedication', however, was an entirely more vicious attack intended to discredit personally both Bolingbroke and Pulteney. It described Pulteney at the start of his career as a young man

with all the advantages that recommendation to the esteem, favour and approbation of mankind, caressed and espoused★ by the ministers, loaded with the favours of the crown, promoted to some of the most considerable employments of honour, profit, and trust, and particularly supported by one, who heaped upon him all the obligations that a cordial friendship could ask or give.

The 'one' referred to was Walpole, who had early on spotted Pulteney's political potential and encouraged him, only to be rebuffed in favour of Bolingbroke and Opposition when Newcastle was made Secretary of State over Pulteney in 1724.

The author of the 'Dedication' attributed Pulteney's motives for this desertion to a self-regard that approached monomania:

But being in his own nature ambitious and aspiring, a slave to his passions, impatient and irresolute, unable to bear a superiority; conceiving unjust jealousies and discontents, full of himself, and his own extraordinary

★ In the context of the homosocial atmosphere of Walpolian politics, these are interesting verbs for the author to have chosen.

merit, and determined to hold the highest offices in the state, or to censure and confound *all* the measures of the government, under any other administration; he at length renounced at once all former friendships and principles, vowing the destruction of those who had distinguished him by a peculiar regard, betraying private correspondences, and endeavouring to distress that Prince and that family to which he owed the highest obligations.

Pulteney immediately assumed, presumably from the intimate tone of the 'Dedication', that it had been written by Hervey, and lashed out, utilizing to the full all the skill and venom his years of experience in Opposition had given him. In a letter to the *Craftsman* on 20 January 1731, headed 'A Proper Reply to a Late Scurrilous Libel', Pulteney exacted revenge on his one-time friend. First he asked his readers whether the author of 'Sedition and Defamation Display'd' was a schoolboy, because of the 'laboured jingle' of his style. He speculated next that 'he' might actually be a 'she': a 'forward, pert little boarding-school miss, who was ambitious of becoming, one time or other, a Maid of Honour'. Finally he concluded that it was, in fact, 'pretty Mr Fainlove . . . you know that he is a lady himself; or at least such a nice composition of the two sexes, that it is difficult to distinguish which is most predominant'.

This description reflected the eighteenth-century view, derived from the Greeks, that the difference between the sexes was not set, but on a continuum, spanning a spectrum from the he-man at one end to the simpering helpless girl at the other; in the middle were feminine men, like Hervey, and masculine women, like Charlotte Cibber* who, according to her 1755 autobiography, liked to dress as a male. This explains why eighteenth-century homosexuals were often called hermaphrodites – they were, as Pulteney described Hervey, 'such a pretty mixture of the masculine and feminine gender'.

Having attacked Hervey's sexual identity, Pulteney turned his

---

* She was the daughter of the playwright Colley Cibber, a friend of Hervey's who was also thought to have homosexual tendencies. Not the best poet of his generation, but the most loyal to Walpole, he was created Poet Laureate in 1730 much to Alexander Pope's fury.

attentions to Hervey's ambitions at court, mocking the exaggerated *politesse* that characterized his manners.

O, fie, Master, you should never call names in a declamation, nor foul your pretty mouth with such . . . words as traitor and villain. The dialect of Billingsgate [fish market; another slur against Hervey's sexuality, as it was the Billingsgate fish*wives* who were famous for the obscenity of their language] is very unbecoming a court-education, and will destroy all the pretensions to the character of a fine gentleman, which you have taken so much pains to acquire, and which you would, I dare say, be almost as loath to lose as your place [at court], or even another tooth.

He went on to call into question Hervey's political integrity as well as his status and potential. According to Pulteney, Hervey, like Britain, had been corrupted by Walpole; and both man and nation were accomplices to Walpole's guilt. The author of 'Sedition and Defamation Display'd' had accused the Opposition of being unable to find evidence of the corruption they claimed was endemic to Walpole's government. Pulteney replied that corruption was more difficult than it might seem to prove:

You seem, pretty Sir, to take the word corruption in a limited sense and confine it to the corrupter – give me leave to illustrate this by a parallel case – there is a certain, unnatural, reigning vice (indecent and almost shocking to mention) which hath, of late, been severely punished in a neighbouring nation.* It is well-known there must be two parties in this crime; the pathick [passive party] and the agent [active party]; both equally guilty. I need not explain these any farther. The proof of the crime hath generally been made by the pathick; but I believe the evidence will not be obtained quite so easily in the case of corruption, where a man enjoys every minute the fruits of his guilt.

Pulteney here not only broke an unwritten rule by referring so directly to homosexuality, but also accused Hervey (although he

---

* In 1730–31 in Holland over sixty boys and men were hanged, burned, beheaded, garrotted and drowned for sodomy. See Norton, p. 150.

meant Britain as well) of political prostitution. No matter that he was seeking to attack Walpole through Hervey, no matter that his elaborate metaphors were intended more to strike at the corruption of Walpole's government than to wound his old friend: the insult was too grave to be ignored.

15. Master—Miss

Hervey, who later said of Pulteney's writing that he hardly ever struck 'without exposing himself at the same time, and [was] as open to receive a wound, as dextrous in giving it', in this case saw himself as left with no option but to challenge Pulteney to clear his blackened name. Where Hervey had written (if he did write the 'Dedication') only what he might have shouted at Pulteney across the floor in the House of Commons, Pulteney had used words against Hervey that could not have come from a friend. He had said nothing about Hervey that was not already whispered about him in London's drawing-rooms; but in Hervey's eyes, Pulteney's published words were unacceptable. Hervey waited three days, on the advice of Henry Fox, and then acted.

At Hervey's instruction, Henry Fox formally visited Pulteney to ask if he had written the 'Reply' to 'Sedition and Defamation Display'd'. Pulteney said that he would not answer until Hervey had either denied or admitted being the author of the 'Dedication'. Fox returned with Hervey's reply that he had not written the 'Dedication'. Pulteney, repentant, answered that he was satisfied, if Hervey said he had not written it. Fox insisted that he take back what he had said about Hervey in the 'Reply', and Pulteney, pressed, burst out that regardless of whether or not Hervey was the author of the 'Dedication' he, Pulteney, was ready to stand by what he had written about Hervey 'at what time and wherever Lord Hervey pleased'. This last phrase was the conventional wording of an invitation to duel.

In the early eighteenth century, duelling was still an accepted way for quarrelling aristocrats to settle disputes of honour. According to custom, the offended party would send his second to the insulter to ask him to withdraw his insult, or be willing to fight a duel to clear the injured man's name. A duel could be fought with either pistols or swords. Some duels were fought to the death; others to satisfy honour, in which one or both parties might fire away from each other or parry with swords until one party had been bettered rather than killed. It was unusual for cases to come to court if a dueller was killed because his murderer would either go into hiding in England or escape to the Continent until the affair had blown over. In 1712, the Duke of Hamilton and Lord Mohun both died in a famous duel in Hyde Park which was the culmination of twelve years' bitter wrangling over a rich estate in Cheshire to which both men laid claim. Both seconds were reported by witnesses to have joined in the fray and Hamilton's second, his kinsman Colonel John Hamilton, was sued for murder by Mohun's widow.

Molly Hervey, writing after the fact to her friend Griselda Murray in Scotland, assured her that Hervey had not written the pamphlet – but did not specify whether she was referring to both sections or only part of it. Calling Pulteney's 'Proper Reply' 'that monstrous paper . . . a very improper reply', Molly claimed it, and not the 'Dedication', was the cause of the duel. When Pulteney heard that Hervey was not the author of the 'Dedication', she said, he was shocked, and 'I believe repented as most passionate people do that he had with any certainty of my Lord having done wrong by him done so very unjust and wrong a thing by him'. Replying to Pulteney through Henry Fox, Hervey had stated that the authorship of the 'Dedication' was 'nothing to the business in hand', and demanded satisfaction for the insults he received in the 'Proper Reply'.

The most curious element of this affair is that Hervey denied writing the 'Dedication' to Pulteney, Fox and Molly – perhaps believing that the insults in it might justify Pulteney's 'Reply' – but still noted his authorship on the copy of the pamphlet at Ickworth. The 'Dedication' is in his style, and reflects Hervey's political opinion of Pulteney at this time – albeit in exaggerated form. He did not tell Ste that he had written it when he sent it to him; but then he quite often sent Henry Fox pamphlets he had written without acknowledging authorship, partly in the hope that maintaining anonymity might elicit more genuine criticism, partly because he relied on his friends' recognizing his idiosyncratic style. Most likely, Hervey did write the 'Dedication', but the nature

of Pulteney's response to it perhaps justified the lie in Hervey's
eyes.

Interesting, too, is Henry Fox's strident defence of his and his
brother's friend, acting as Hervey's second in Ste's absence. Possibly
he wholeheartedly disagreed with all Pulteney had written against
Hervey; more probably, he felt that to allow these insults (however
accurate) to pass unchallenged would harm Hervey's reputation –
and by extension his brother's – irredeemably. Whether he guessed
(or knew) that Hervey and Ste actually were lovers may not have
mattered to him; Fox was famously tolerant.

At about four o'clock on the afternoon of Monday 25 January,
Hervey and Henry Fox, and Pulteney and his second, Sir Henry
Rushout, walked through the snowy expanse of Upper St James's
Park (now Green Park) to an appointed clearing behind Arlington
Street, where Pulteney lived. Molly Hervey, who was not told of
the affair till the next day, had not noticed Hervey behaving
strangely that morning. She remembered that he seemed cheerful,
drinking his breakfast chocolate with her and giving her 'a ridiculous
paper of verses to copy' before going off to the House of Commons
where he planned to dine with some fellow MPs. 'I who had been
frightened with the apprehension of what I thought might possibly
happen was easier that day and thought he would answer the paper
["The Proper Reply"] and t'would go off in that manner.'

Leaving the Commons that afternoon Hervey 'met Harry Fox
and from thence they walked across the Park (which was a usual
thing for them to do)', Molly told Griselda Murray. They walked
twice around the lake until Pulteney and Rushout, 'who seemed
to be only walking in Pulteney's garden came out to them'. As they
took off their coats and drew their swords in the dim light, Hervey
told Pulteney 'that if Mr Pultency killed him he had a paper in his
pocket which would secure Mr Pulteney from the ill-consequences
which might otherways attend it'. This apparently moved Pulteney
deeply. The seconds withdrew and Hervey and Pulteney advanced
towards one another, swords unsheathed.

No accounts in the hands of the participants or witnesses of the
duel survive, but according to the varying reports the two men
exchanged scratches – Hervey's slightly worse than Pulteney's, but

none needing any more serious remedy than a bandage – and were then separated by their seconds. At one point, Pulteney

would infallibly have run my Lord through the body if his foot had not slipped and then the seconds took occasion to part them. Upon which Mr Pulteney embraced Lord Hervey, and expressed a great deal of concern at the accident of their quarrel, promising at the same time that he would never personally attack him again, either with his mouth or his pen. Lord Hervey made him a bow, without giving him any sort of answer, and (to use the common expression) thus they parted.

This account (written by Secretary of State Thomas Pelham to the British Ambassador in Paris, Lord Waldegrave) is corroborated by Lady Hervey, who wrote that the impulsive Pulteney had cried, 'Let us contend no more' and embraced Hervey, swearing that if he had killed Hervey he would have been the unhappiest man on earth. The knowledge that Hervey had thought to write a letter pleading for clemency for his potential murderer increased Pulteney's sense of responsibility for the affair. Henry Fox took Hervey back to Ste's house in Old Burlington Street, five minutes' walk away, to have his wounds dressed.

There was keen interest in this encounter. Satirical ballads, poems and discourses appeared almost immediately, some defending Hervey, most deriding him, all speculating on what had actually happened. Many used the characters in *Othello* as cyphers for the principal players in this real-life drama: George II was Othello, Robert Walpole Iago, Hervey Roderigo, and Pulteney Cassio. In an apt displacement in this all-male conflict, Desdemona, the passive figure on whom all the action hangs in the play, became an abstract of political loyalty. In 'Iago Display'd', Walpole's behind-the-scenes machinations were seen as the cause of the duel. The anonymous author opined that Walpole had deliberately allowed Pulteney to believe that Hervey had written the 'Dedication', and encouraged Hervey to smart at Pulteney's 'Reply'; he thought Walpole had seen the loss of Hervey's reputation as a small price to pay for destroying Pulteney's political importance.

But 'Cassio's integrity baffled all Iago's measures, and made them at last fall upon his own head,' the author concluded triumphantly. This view was shared by Pulteney himself, who, convinced by Hervey's assertions that he had not written the 'Dedication', wrote another pamphlet attacking Walpole so unequivocally that Walpole had him struck off the Privy Council. 'Iago Display'd' concluded with an account of the duel itself, and a comment on Hervey's mincing gait and excessive grace. 'Some sneerers add . . . that Roderigo leaping forwards and backwards, advancing and retreating with great art and agility, Cassio told him, "Child, I did not come here to see you dance." '

If the papers generally supported Pulteney, many of his peers believed Hervey had acted honourably in defending his name; even Pulteney, according to Lady Hervey, publicly professed his belief that 'no man ever behaved with more courage and generosity'. In the weeks following the duel, Pulteney did all he could to have the 'Proper Reply' suppressed. Lady Irwin wrote to her father to tell him about the duel. 'I fancy upon the whole [this] will turn to Lord Hervey's service, he knowing well how to make a merit of this at court; and besides, most people had the same opinion of Lord Hervey before Mr Pulteney drew his character with so much wit; but nobody before this adventure thought he had the courage to send a challenge.' Her views corroborate the possibility that it was not what Pulteney thought of him that rankled, but the fact that he had published his views that Hervey took as an insult. And, too, there was Stephen Fox's name and future to think of: any defamation of Hervey by implication brought Ste, well-known to be Hervey's most intimate friend, into disrepute as well.

Political opinion was divided on the rectitude of Hervey's response. Lord Chesterfield thought that the use – by either party – of personal insult to further a political argument was dishonourable. 'A Review of the Whole Political Career of a Late Eminent Patriot', a pamphlet attacking Pulteney published in the year of Hervey's death, decreed that,

The reflections thrown out in Mr **'s 'Proper Reply' were entirely personal to the noble Lord (Hervey's observations in the 'Dedication' had at least their foundation in concern for Pulteney's public character)

and all dispassionate readers thought them foreign to the merits of the question between them. On the other hand, the noble Lord, by sending the challenge to Mr **. . . was a deviation from the strict principles of decorum; since it was never understood that a quarrel, begun with the pen, should be decided with the sword.

Lord Bristol, constitutionally blinkered by loyalty, could only see Hervey's side. His diary entry for 25 January 1731 reads, 'My son Lord Hervey upon the justest provocations sent a challenge to his till then supposed friend, Mr William Pulteney, and fought a duel with him in St James's Park.'

The most material effect of this incident, apart from showcasing the unusual nature of Hervey's private life, was to place him firmly in the pantheon of contemporary satiric figures. Hervey was now associated by the Opposition with his master's corruption; and his unconventional private life was held up as a metaphor for Walpole's perceived pillage of the English nation. The insults and jibes aimed at him early in 1731 recurred throughout the remainder of his political career, to be collated and expanded on, most effectively by Alexander Pope in 1735. Hervey was becoming the stereotype as which he has survived to the present day: the spiteful hermaphrodite, Walpole's creature and the court's darling – pretty, little 'Master–Miss'.

16. Rivals

Perhaps the person most pleased by the public attention given to Hervey's private life as a result of his duel was the Duke of Newcastle, of whom Robert Walpole said, 'his name was Perfidy'. Newcastle and Hervey, despite their nominal alliance under Sir Robert's aegis, were rivals for favour both at court and in Parliament. Newcastle said that Robert Walpole and William Pulteney were not more opposed politically than he and Hervey were personally; for his part, Hervey wrote to Ste that he hated Newcastle 'as much as one can do anybody one so heartily despises [looks down on]'.

The self-important duke was popularly thought to be Princess Emily's lover, and was known at court by the nickname 'Permis' for his habit of prefacing every remark with the ingratiating phrase, '*Est-il permis*? [Is this allowed?]' When Walpole made him Secretary of State in 1724 there was some gossip about why Sir Robert had chosen someone so much less brilliant than William Pulteney, then still allied to Walpole, who had also been in line for the job. 'I can account for it,' commented Lady Mary Wortley Montagu.

If I was a country gentlewoman and came suddenly to a great fortune and set up my coach, I should like to show it in the neighbouring village – but I would not carry you with me, for people might doubt whether it was your coach or mine – but if you would let me carry your cat with you, I would; for nobody would think it was the cat's coach.

On a more prosaic level, Walpole needed the parliamentary seats that Newcastle, one of the country's greatest landowners, commanded. One night at court, reported Hervey, Newcastle was so drunk that he was afraid he had offended the Princess Royal, to whom he had spoken for a long time. The following morning he apologized to her, 'making a thousand excuses for his conduct'. She replied, '*Mon Dieu, vous étiez charmant; vous ne m'avez jamais si bien diverti de votre vie. Je voudrais vous voir toujours ivre* [Oh God, you were charming; never in your life have you amused me more. I wish I could always see you drunk].' The duke was so pleased and proud 'to hear that he was never so agreeable as when he was least himself' that he bowed ten times to the ground. Behaviour like this justified George II's judgement of his Secretary of State: he thought Newcastle an 'impertinent fool'.

When the Duke of Lorraine arrived in London in October 1731, Newcastle held a splendid dinner for forty people in his honour, to which, pointedly, neither Hervey nor Prince Frederick were invited. Frederick commented hotly on the oversight to Hervey, who replied that if someone showed their dislike of Hervey by coupling him with Frederick, he would say, '*Ces affronts sont des faveurs* [These insults are compliments].' The Prince, grateful for Hervey's loyalty, replied, 'You take every occasion to be agreeable, and they to be disagreeable.' Hervey was delighted to observe both that Newcastle noticed how hurt Frederick was, and that Frederick so publicly turned to Hervey for consolation. 'I know it would have been much righter for 7 [Frederick] to have seemed quite indifferent upon this occasion, and for that reason I ought to have been sorry that he did not; but I own I was pleased.'

Missing one dinner was no great sacrifice, though – there were so many. Three days later Hervey went to a great feast held in London for Lorraine by Count Kinski, ambassador to the Holy Roman Empire, whom Hervey described as possessing 'the two imperial characteristics of dullness and pride in the same degree'. There were twenty-six guests, fourteen foreigners and twelve English, who feasted for over three hours. The *pièce de résistance* was a 'dessert of arches, pyramids, giants, beasts, trophies, eagles &c., of barley sugar and sugar plums, painted of different colours [which was] . . . raised to such a monstrous and ticklish height that I believe it had been three weeks building'. For the final two hours of dinner, the doors were opened up to the street, and 'everybody that had curiosity to see, and strength enough to push, came into the room. I never was so hot, so sick, and so tired in my life', complained Hervey, never a fan of contact with the great unwashed.

Despite these ordeals, Hervey liked the Duke of Lorraine. He was, he told Ste, 'as great a romp as you or me'; more importantly, he was the ideal of La Rochefoucauld's *honnête homme*. 'He is well-bred with more nicety, more ease and more constant presence of mind than anybody I ever met with, and has the most beautiful, most sweet, and most sensible countenance I ever beheld.' He repeated his praise to Henry Fox, who was abroad during Lorraine's visit. Lorraine was 'very handsome, cheerful, sensible, well-bred and obliging; and though he seems to do everything with ease and without thought, one never finds he does or says anything that is not proper, or omits anything that is. Never anybody had the good fortune of pleasing so universally.'

As his approbation of Lorraine shows, and despite what his own reputation for superficiality suggests, what Hervey most valued in his friends at court was unaffectedness.

I like the company of my dear, handsome, silly, natural Lady Tankerville, better than that of all those fine ladies put together, who seeing the world has made half-wise, reading novels half-mad, and hearing Lord Chesterfield half-wits. She absolutely and fairly thinks aloud; her mouth is the outlet to everything her eyes and ears take in.

This naturalness was far preferable to the mannered charm of so many court ladies, who 'paint and varnish and polish everything that comes from them, till there is nothing more of nature in their words than there is in Lady Mary's complexion'.*

Lady Tankerville's rival was Lady Deloraine, 'who is grown lean with hearing her commended, and I believe has never slept since Lady Tankerville has taken her place at the King's commerce-table [card table]'. As Mary Howard, Lady Deloraine had been a Maid of Honour in the late 1710s; she married the Earl of Deloraine, who died in 1729. Then she was made governess to the royal children and became one of Hervey's favourite *bêtes noires*. She was very beautiful, and equally ambitious, but had no redeeming streak of either kindness or sense; and she was jealous of anyone with influence at court, such as Lady Tankerville, and even Hervey, as he wrote to Ste. He

---

* Lady Mary Wortley Montagu, once a beauty, was badly scarred from smallpox and wore a great deal of face-powder.

and Miss Fitzwilliams, a rather masculine-looking Maid of Honour, had extolled to Lady Deloraine the beauty of one of her daughters, who was a plump, cherry-cheeked girl, over the other, 'who is in her [Lady Deloraine's] pale, languishing, sickly style and her favourite'. Miss Fitzwilliams and Hervey agreed that the hearty 'cherry-cheeks' would grow up to be the prettier woman, to which Lady Deloraine replied delicacy was an advantage for a girl, for

in her opinion a woman could never look too much like a woman, nor a man too much like a man. Considering the two people she said this to, it was certainly well said; and I can forgive her having bragged of it to every creature she has seen since; as it was the first time she ever chopped upon common-sense, and I dare say will be the last.

Two weeks later, she attracted Hervey's attention again. A beautiful Scottish girl, Miss McKenzie, had been taken into the household as dresser to Princess Louisa, a position under the aegis of Lady Deloraine, governess to the Princesses. Lady Deloraine was so jealous of Miss McKenzie's looks that she went out of her way to make her cry, haranguing her for 'her Scotch Highland awkwardness'. At dinner one day, Lady Deloraine pulled Miss McKenzie's cap off her head to show that she had a high forehead and thin hair, tearing 'off a handful of hair (no doubt) in the operation, and scratched what remained over her temples, crying, "Look here, do you see how bald she is?"' Poor Miss McKenzie sat scarlet through the rest of dinner, while everyone made a point of being nice to her; though, added Hervey,

she sat all the while *coiffée* by my Lady Governess directly like Mrs Cibber in the play of the *Amorous Widow*, when the old aunt had pulled her niece's head [-dress] over one ear to hinder her lover from thinking her pretty.★ *Voilà les scènes dont je m'amuse* [These are the scenes that amuse me]; and whilst her Ladyship is so good to treat the court with such farces, it is impossible to be sorry that the King does not see fit to transport Drury Lane hither.

★ Several years later, jealous of the attentions paid to Miss McKenzie by a Mr Price, Lady Deloraine apparently tried to poison her rival.

Hervey had a holiday from court life in mid-October when, as he had hoped, he and Fox were able to meet for a snatched night at Hertford Bridge, between Bagshot and Basingstoke. Hervey took to his bed for a day on his return to Hampton Court. 'The pain of leaving you would be paying too dear for any pleasure, but that of seeing you; and it was hard that I could not have the one unmixed, nor the other without so disagreeable an added weight.' Everyone at court, he went on, was recovering from the grand ball held to celebrate Lady Diana Spencer's marriage to Lord Russell, heir to the duchy of Bedford. On 9 September Hervey had told Ste of their engagement – Russell was 'at this moment lisping love into her flippant Ladyship's ear at Blenheim' – and the ball was held the day Hervey returned to court. He went to bed, but Lady Hervey had supper in Frederick's apartments where the Prince gave her a delicate lapis lazuli watch set with diamonds. '*La Mouche* [the Fly, Lady Deloraine's court nickname] had no supper, nor no present, and consequently . . . *elle est au desespoir* [she's in despair],' Hervey gloated. He did not say anything else about Molly; his interest in her was limited to his pleasure at her success with his patron.

Lord and Lady Russell came to Hampton Court the week after their wedding. Hervey asked Lady Diana, newly decked in brocade and lace and jewels, if she liked being married; 'she said she thought it was the charmingest thing in the world. Lord John had a very conjugal languor about him; he does not seem [anything] so much as one of those coursers who the first *week* with vigour run.' The old Duchess of Marlborough, Lady Diana's grandmother, was 'as coquette as if she was eighteen, and as rampant as if she were drunk', because of the excitement of the wedding. 'I expect to hear of her soon [en]listing some strapping lusty grenadier in her service or taking some young actor off the stage; if her spirits hold out much longer it is impossible her virtue should.'

The indefatigable Duchess was indeed well pleased with (and invigorated by) her granddaughter's match, as she wrote to Lady Mary Wortley Montagu just before the wedding. 'I propose more satisfaction in it than I thought had been in store for me. I believe you have heard me say that I desired to die when I had disposed well of her; but I desire that you would not put me in mind of it, for I find now I have a mind to last until I have married [off] my Torismond [Lady Diana's brother John Spencer].'

The following spring, the Duchess's grandson Lord Sunderland, the future Duke of Marlborough, became engaged to the only daughter of Lord Trevor. Contrary to everyone's expectations, her Grace erupted with horror at the news of her grandson's betrothal, took immediate steps to disinherit him, and wrote to inform him of her disapproval in no uncertain terms, 'calling the young lady's father a madman, her mother a fool, her grandfather a rogue, and her grandmother a w—[whore]'.

Sunderland responded to her letter by

telling her he found nothing therein to induce him to change his res-olutions, unless she called invectives, persuasions . . . He said it was long since he had either expected or desired to be in her Grace's will; and concluded with telling her that this letter was the last trouble of any kind he should ever give her. 'I am your Grace's grandson, Sunderland,' was his ending,

reported Hervey to his mother, proud of his friend.

Henry Fox wrote long letters to the Duchess pleading his friend's cause but she remained obdurate, as she wrote to her friend Mrs Horner, Henry Fox's mistress, in July. She thought

it a very improper match for a man, what might have had anybody, without being at all in love with the person to marry a woman, whose father is a mighty ridiculous man, a family of beggars and all very odd people. The woman herself (as they say, for I have never seen her) has been bred in a low way and don't know how to behave herself upon any occasion, not at all pretty and has a mean, ordinary look. As to the behaviour, if she has any sense, that may mend. But they say she has very bad teeth: which, I think, is an objection alone in a wife. And they will only get worse with time,

she concluded ominously.

The start of the London season, late in the autumn, brought with it the usual succession of parties; in 1731, the presence of the Duke of Lorraine made them exceptionally lavish. The Prince of Wales planned to attend a masquerade dressed as a shepherd, 'an Adonis, or an Apollo (I have forgot which)'. He would be attended by eighteen huntsmen dressed in green waistcoats, leopard-skins, feathered caps, 'tragedy buskins upon their legs, breeches trussed up like rope dancers', and carrying bows and arrows; one of this number was to be Thomas Winnington. Hervey got out of 'this harlequinade', by pleading 'chicken, headache, fear of sitting up, &c., . . . I blushed with the thought only of being set up in all this prettiness'. But he could not resist going along to witness the Prince and Winnington's display. 'I would fain have them go in at the head of a pack of hounds; nothing else could improve it.'

'I went to the masquerade as I told you I would, and found everything as I thought I should,' he wrote later, with his customary detached amusement.

When I saw that fraternity I had deserted, lugged and twirled about as I imagined they would be when I resolved to desert them, I laughed like Madame Sévigné, *dessous ma coiffe* [behind my fan]: and felt the same sort of pleasure, that I fancy a little *miscarriage* or a child that died in the month [after his birth], would feel in Abraham's bosom, when he looks down and sees the troublesome follies and all the noisy, senseless bustle of a world he was originally designed to be a member of, and which he has had the good luck to slip out of.

Lorraine's visit prompted such an exhausting whirl of parties that Hervey was forced to take to his bed. 'I have been in a fever with the sitting up, and giddy like drunkenness,' he told Ste. 'I have tasted nothing but tea, bread, and hartshorn drops this four-and-twenty hours; and am now freezing by my fire-side, my blood and thoughts quite stagnated, and nothing warm about me but that corner of my heart which you inhabit.'

Despite these precautions, Hervey's health continued to deteriorate, and in the first week of December he had an epileptic attack as he was lighting the King's path on the way to a Drawing-room. Hervey had just enough warning to catch hold of somebody – 'God knows who' – at one side of George's path through the crowd, and stopped to recover his breath till he had passed by. He had enough presence of mind to pretend that he had had a cramp, and that otherwise he was as well as he had ever been. 'I was far from it: for I saw everything in a mist, was so giddy I could hardly walk, which I said was owing to my cramp having not quite gone off, and was so sick I thought I should have vomited in the room.' To avoid suspicion, he forced himself to stay for another ten minutes, talking to people as normally as possible. Only then did he go to his rooms, where he vomited up a great deal of blood.

'I am now far from well,' he concluded,

but better and prodigiously pleased, since I was to feel this nasty disorder, that I contrived to it a *l'insu de tout le monde* [unbeknownst to everybody] . . . The King, Queen, &c. enquired about my cramp this morning, and laughed at it. I joined in the laugh, and said how foolish an accident it was, and so it has passed off. Nobody but Lady Hervey, from whom it was impossible to conceal what happened, knows anything of it.

Although Hervey so blithely ignored his wife most of the time – this is only the third reference to her in his correspondence with Fox – this suggests Molly stayed in her husband's apartments when she came to London.

As the letter to Ste, reassuring him about his health, shows, Hervey was still deeply involved with his lover, despite the distractions of life at court. Hervey was trying to procure a place for Ste in the government, probably because he knew it would require Ste to be more regularly in London, or perhaps to reassure him of his continued commitment to their relationship. But, as Hervey wrote – in code – his attempts had borne no fruit. 'The short of the story is that there [is] going to be a *be by by vba* in the *erg evoobaf*, and my solicitation for *Mbh* has not succeeded. I know you will not care much; and yet, since you care at all, I hate to have miscarried in it.' The whole thing was a puzzle, Hervey said, for there was an available office, and Walpole had seemed sincere about giving it to Ste; what, he wondered, could be the reason for leaving the vacancy unfilled? Sir Robert 'said a thousand obliging things to me, and of you; and, not with the same air that he says those that he does not mean, he assured me he would do anything in his power to please you, and begged me to take care you should not impute what was not his fault to his coolness towards you or his negligence'.

As he said, Hervey believed that Ste must have been refused the place for a reason. 'There is some mystery I cannot fathom. Standish [the Duke of Newcastle], I know, has been monstrous impertinent (if one can properly call what is natural to anybody, monstrous), both to you and to me; but I dare not so much as let him see I know he has been so, for the sake of the canal [channel] of my intelligence.' Had Newcastle, who loathed Hervey, and was jealous of his popularity at court and closeness to Walpole, whispered rumours of Hervey's relationship with Fox, implying that Walpole could not be seen to sanction this scandal by promoting his supporter's lover? It is not unlikely: jealousy, said Horace Walpole of the duke, was 'the great source of all his faults'. Clearly, he had publicly maligned both Ste and Hervey so much that reports had reached them of his defamation.

Whatever Newcastle had said, it was enough to inspire Hervey's undying hatred. 'However, I may have it in my power to return it sometime or other, as strongly and as secretly as I feel it,' he vowed.

Adieu my dear dear creature, I can begin to write on no other subject, I am too much distempered on this to attempt it. I long to see you to talk over a thousand things that are perpetually in my thoughts and never have utterance but to your ear. Once more adieu. For God's sake since you have not this nasty thing [office] never let it be known you asked it: I wish they were all annihilated.

Ste wrote back to assure Hervey that he was unconcerned by his friend's failure.

I received a letter from you yesterday to which I am ashamed to make any answer. All you say in it is sensible and so unanswerable. I showed part of your letter to Sir Robert; he repeated what I told you before, with such an air of sincerity, that if he is so old a courtier to be a hypocrite on this occasion, I own myself so young a one as to have been his dupe.

Ste's calmness and unconcern were a far cry from the petty rivalries and deceptions that filled Hervey's daily life at court, and Hervey, whose head had been turned by recent marks of royal favour, would soon have reason to appreciate Ste once again.

17. Hephaestion Betrayed

At the beginning of November 1731, Hervey was able to take two weeks away from his duties at court to go to Redlynch. 'I have already made my excuse to the Prince for not going to Richmond: with the King you know there, I have nothing to do as Vice-Chamberlain, and hope I shall not be wanted of evenings as Lord Hervey.' In order to waste no time, Hervey planned to leave London at the same time as the King, but he did not think he would manage to get further than Hertford Bridge on that day. (It was at Hertford Bridge they had met for a few snatched hours earlier that autumn; Hervey called it 'a place I shall ever love'.)

In his next letter Hervey expressed his renewed impatience to see Ste now that the date for his leaving court was set. 'Without any exaggeration after the time is once fixed for my returning to you, as I think of little else all day, so I dream of little else every night . . . Next week, thank God, will pass so differently that I shall grudge the hours I sleep, as much as I now covet them and think as little of the past or future as I do now of the present.' He went on to inform Ste of some financial business he had performed for him. 'I wish I was as good a philosopher in everything, as in money matters, and I should know but little disquiet; I should repine much less at being separated from you: but if in that case I was to rejoice less too when I saw you, I retract my wishes for philosophy, and would not balance the account.'

Since their night at Hertford Bridge Hervey had been reminded of how important Ste was as a balance in his life. His love for Ste was a constant, unaffected — at least in his own eyes — by the distractions of Miss Vane and Prince Frederick. Every day, he told Ste, he raged at the necessity of his separation from the only thing that gave him unmitigated pleasure. Without Ste, his life would be a succession of days differing only in name; he would never wish to speed up time to hasten his way to his lover, or slow it down when they were together. But as 'the impression you have made upon me can only wear or decay with the materials on which it is stamped, so till I cease to be anything, I shall never cease to be yours'.

Hervey arrived at Redlynch early in November. He and Ste breakfasted one morning at nearby Wilton with the ancient Earl of Pembroke – by whom (according to Molly) Lady Bristol had been hotly pursued two years before – and his young wife. Pembroke was a keen collector of antiques; Pope described him in 'The Use of Riches' as spending his money on 'statues, dirty Gods, and coins'. He was wearing a stylish pale blue damask dressing-gown, and an old-fashioned black velvet night-cap, which Hervey told Frederick he thought was meant 'to signify the youth of his body and maturity of his head'. Lady Pembroke

knew the history of every *busto* as well as his Lordship, I do not wonder much at his having endeavoured to bring her into a taste for antiques; but I question much, whether her taste is so established that if the antique of her bedchamber was to be exchanged for a modern, she would be much afflicted. I dare say she would have skill enough to find out the difference, but shrewdly suspect that she would hardly be *virtuosa* enough in that case to give antiquity the preference.

The young Prince loved Hervey's *doubles entendres* and witticisms; his own letters, clumsily imitative of Hervey's style (just as Molly's often were), were full of awkward teasing masquerading as wit. 'I have many little drolleries still to tell you,' Frederick concluded one, 'but the time presses, so I end, but being afraid that this letter should be opened if I sent it directly to you so I make a direction to Mr Fox, as if it was written to you by a lady, to make you be teased a little about it.' Did Frederick realize that making his letter look as if it were a *billet-doux* would do more than simply fill Stephen with innocent curiosity? Certainly Hervey did not play down his friendship with Fox to the Prince, sending him a fond verse about Ste.

> *Quant al padrone, Signor Ste,*
> *Le petit drôle, mon cher ami.*
> *Il peste un peu contre la pluie,*

Mais d'un humeur badin, joli,
Amusant, polisson, poli.
Fait les delices de notre vie,
*Rit, cause, et chante, et chasse l'ennui.**

'If it would not be too bold for Hephaestion to pry into the *sanctum sanctorum*, I would ask whether Roxana or Statira is at present in favour?' Hervey continued, referring to himself as Hephaestion, Alexander the Great's closest companion. If Frederick was Alexander — a comparison even Hervey must have seen as incommensurate with Frederick's actual virtues — then Hervey calling himself Hephaestion is close to a confession that Hervey and Frederick were lovers. Alexander called Hephaestion his 'private friend'; when Alexander visited Troy to pay homage at the tomb of his hero Achilles, Hephaestion went through the same rituals before the tomb of Patroclus, Achilles' lover. After Hephaestion died Alexander indulged in wild outpourings of grief; ancient rumour held that he lay on his lover's corpse night and day, before having him honoured as a hero. Roxana was Alexander's first wife, and the mother of his son; Statira, her beautiful Persian rival, Alexander's second wife (whose sister Drypetis Hephaestion married so, Alexander said, that Hephaestion's children should be his nieces and nephews), whom Roxana had murdered after Alexander's death. There is no clue as to which ladies of the court Hervey was referring to as Roxana or Statira, except that they must have been rivals for Frederick's favour, and, implicitly, that they were secondary in importance to Frederick as Roxana and Statira had been second to Hephaestion in Alexander's affections.

Frederick's letters reveal a youthful appreciation of femininity in all its guises, referring practically in one breath to three women: 'dear Lady Dye', the beautiful Duchess of Queensberry and '*ma*

---

* And of my host, Signor Ste,
 The funny little one, my dear friend.
 Good-naturedly he blusters against the weather,
 Prettily, amusingly, politely and charmingly.
 He makes our lives a delight,
 Laughing, chatting, singing and scaring boredom away.

petite brunette'. Since his arrival in England two years earlier he had had affairs with Lady Abergavenny and the young Duchess of Marlborough, and now apparently was interested in Lady Deloraine as well as the three ladies he mentioned to Hervey. Hervey's attitude to Frederick's affairs was indulgent, even encouraging: if he and Frederick were sleeping together, Hervey did not feel threatened by Frederick's interest in women. 'Is La Moscula [Lady Deloraine] still flattered by the Hackney *piper of Dudley's and Trevor's* [presumably Frederick]?' he asked in the same letter. '*Je ne m'étonne point que vous vous ennuyez dans un autre endroit dont vous me parlez*;* but if I was Prince of Wales, healthy and but four-and-twenty years old, I fancy I could find ways to cut out my time in such a manner *que je ne m'ennuyerais pas* [that I would not be bored].'

But from the tone of Hervey's last letter to Frederick from Redlynch, the young Prince's impetuousness had finally begun to grate on Hervey, who had for so long swallowed his pride in an effort to win Frederick's affection. After describing the trial of some poachers on Ste's land, he continued, 'What game you poach, Sir, what you hunt, what you catch, or what runs into your mouth, I don't pretend to guess. If you think fit to tell me, I shall soon be in the way of being informed.' Had Frederick written to Hervey saying, Can you guess what new game I'm chasing? And did the shortness of Hervey's reply show he realized the Prince's quarry was his own mistress, Anne Vane?

Stephen accompanied Hervey back to London from Redlynch and stayed on a few extra days, although not for long enough to satisfy Hervey. 'I did not think you would have gone yesterday, after my showing plainer than I could speak it how great a mind I had to have you stay another day in town; half that hint would once have sufficed to keep you a month,' he complained.

Since you did go, why did you not come to my lodgings for a minute after the opera? I did not stay a quarter of an hour with the Prince. He went immediately to bed; and I came home. As it was uncertain how

---

* It doesn't surprise me at all that you are bored in that place of which you speak.

long he would keep me, I could not ask you to come; but that uncertainty would not have hindered you trying to see me, if you had felt what I did, with thinking it would be two months before we should see one another again.

Maybe Fox did not like being relegated to second place in Hervey's attentions, and his departure was a demonstration of his displeasure; certainly he objected to Hervey's petulance as Hervey's response to his reply a week later showed. Ste's patience was wearing thin, and Hervey knew he had gone too far.

You were in the right to expect thanks rather than reproaches for your late conduct and I in the wrong, and a monster of ingratitude to murmur at your leaving London without saying one word in acknowledgement of your kindness in coming there; all I can plead in my justification or rather in my excuse is, that to love you more reasonably I must love you less warmly; and that whenever I find fault with you, I forget how little I deserve and how much you confer and only reflect how much I desire,

Hervey apologized, uncharacteristically contrite – or maybe, for once, feeling guilty.

Hervey needed Ste's support after his return to London at the end of November as his suspicions that Frederick and Anne Vane were betraying him were confirmed. Hervey's letters to Ste increasingly inveighed against the 'falsehood as well as the folly' of Frederick, and the deception played on him by his friend and his mistress. On 4 December, Hervey was summoned to sit with the Prince after the Opera; 'It is well he is so secret when one is serious, and so entertaining when one is gay, otherwise the frequency of these parties would be too much,' Hervey wrote to Ste, underlining the sentence to show that he meant the opposite. Ten days later, he was forced to write more openly. 'That fool 7 [Frederick] plagues my heart out. He is as false, too, as he is silly, and appears everything he is not at turns but wise.'

Finally, Hervey determined to rise above their betrayal. There was nothing he could do about their falsehood or their wrongdoing.

Let their folly fall on their own head, and their wickedness on their own pate. They shall neither know nor suspect that I have detected them, nor ever shall; for the easiest, the most natural, and the justest revenge one can take upon people who imagine they impose upon one, is to let them fancy they do; and instead of being their dupe, let them make themselves their own,

he resolved philosophically, striving for Montaignian detachment.

I have fretted at their conduct a good deal: but for the future I am resolved to think of it as little as I can, and not speak of it at all. Many reasons will make me silent on this occasion: but I think people with common judgement or common prudence would keep their grievances to themselves as much as their distempers, and never trust the recital to anybody but those who were to cure them.

Despite these stoical words, Hervey was deeply upset by Frederick's behaviour. He wrote to his father about 'the deceit and betrayal by a friend he really loved', without mentioning who it was; Bristol replied that he had read his son's letter ten times over, but 'I am still at a loss whom to condemn and to deliver to Satan for so monstrous a behaviour towards one incapable of deserving it'.

One effect of Anne and Frederick's treachery was to throw into relief Fox's constancy. Over the past year, Hervey had taunted Stephen with his glamorous life at court, and his new friendships and affairs there; he had taken him for granted and expected him to be grateful for any attention Hervey chose to give him. But by the end of 1731 Hervey had realized Ste's value anew, writing on 28 December about his delight at hearing that Ste was bored in the country. 'It is but just that you should feel, by absenting yourself, part of what you inflict. I own I have counted every week I have been from you, and now begin to count the days, and shall come to counting the hours that are to pass until we meet again.' But Ste, hurt and alienated by Hervey's self-absorption, was beginning to draw back from the relationship. Just when Hervey needed his lover most, it seems, his past neglect and selfishness were finally turning Ste against him. It was too little, too late.

In the winter of 1731–2, Hervey's obligations at court were too pressing to allow him to travel to Redlynch at Christmas and New Year for the first time in three years. January saw his former mistress Anne Vane leave court to be installed in a house in Soho Square by her royal lover, with an allowance of £1,600 a year. Some said she had asked the Queen to excuse her from her duties at court, others that she was dismissed 'for her familiarities with the Prince'. She was four months pregnant, and unlike two years earlier when she had written to Mrs Howard denying rumours that she was expecting, this time she was flaunting it; the Dowager Duchess of Northampton said she had never seen anyone 'so proud of a big belly'.

While later evidence suggests Anne Vane had genuinely fallen for Lord Hervey, Frederick's brash awkwardness, crudity and arrogance make it difficult to believe she was with him for any reason other than ambition. She was, in 1731, still unmarried, but with a ruined reputation that made her chances for a good match slim. A liaison with the married Hervey would profit her naught, and Hervey, whose feelings were wrapped up in his old affair with Ste Fox and his new attachment to Frederick, would hardly have offered her any hope of emotional security. But as the recognized mistress of the Prince of Wales, and the mother of his child, Miss Vane would acquire status of which she could only have dreamed as a humble Maid of Honour.

Contemporary pamphlets confirmed that Miss Vane was not ashamed of the proof of her sin and used her story as evidence of the moral dissolution of the court. 'The Fair Concubine: Or, the Secret History of the Beautiful Vanella' described her as 'that fallen angel', one 'whom love and beauty has rendered odious to virtue'. At first the author feigned sympathy for Anne's plight, arguing that the withdrawal method of contraception was unsatisfactory – 'ye will allow, surely, that a moiety of the fruition is wanting, and that it is but a half-pleasure at best' – but went on to condemn her for her beauty, which, it was claimed, was always the foundation of a woman's ruin. Beauty was like the mythical philosopher's stone which might drive a man mad with the longing to possess it; but, once he had grasped it, he would see flaws in what had at first glance seemed so valuable, and inevitably discard what he had so ardently desired to pursue another illusion. A woman's only defences were virtue and chastity, 'the brightest jewels that can adorn a woman; their value is inestimable, their loss irretrievable'.

Another satirical play published in 1732 defended Miss Vane, arguing that she resisted Frederick's advances at first, but that her scruples were overcome by the logic that a Prince's mistress was above scandal: 'can anything be shameful with a Prince?' 'The Humours of the Court; Or, Modern Gallantry' placed the burden of blame squarely on the promiscuous Prince's shoulders, describing his established habits of seducing and abandoning young women at court and depicting Anne Vane as little more than a pawn in Frederick's depraved games. A ballad written by Lady Mary Wortley Montagu (who ought to have known what happened) described Frederick as a puppy (the name his father always used for him) with a cracked bottle – Miss Vane – tied to his tail; Hervey she portrayed as a well-intentioned bystander who tries to remove the bottle, and gets bitten for his trouble.

As with Hervey's duel, no written description of what happened by any of the central figures survives, so satirical pamphlets such as 'The Fair Concubine' offer some clues as to what may have been the course of events. Most agree that Miss Vane, identified variously as Vanella, Vanelia, Viola or Vanessa, had had an affair with one of the Prince's intimates before transferring her affections to him. This man – alternately called Lord Supple, Ingenio or Captain Modish – was obviously Hervey: witty, flirtatious, glamorous and physically beautiful. Interestingly, despite Hervey's effeminacy, he was always portrayed as compellingly attractive to women. That Anne was in love with Hervey was made clear in all of the accounts; she is described as betraying herself by blushes every time her seducer drew near.

Two of the ballad operas on the scandal say that Frederick had asked Hervey to court Anne for him, and that in fulfilling his duties Hervey had fallen for her himself. When the affair between Hervey and Anne Vane became public – whispered abroad by 'Inanis', or George Bubb Dodington, Hervey's successor as Frederick's confidant – Frederick was furious, upbraided Hervey for his disloyalty, and dismissed him from his service. Although from Hervey's letters it would seem that Frederick had stolen Miss Vane from him rather than the other way round, this interpretation of events must not be rejected out of hand: Hervey was quite capable of convincing himself that he was the injured party where in fact he was far from innocent. But Frederick's later behaviour, as well as his proven philandering and his childish desire to impress Hervey, would suggest that he did have a deciding hand in the events that so distressed Hervey at the end of the previous year and which now unfolded before the fascinated general public. The dates, too, corroborate an interpretation which favours Hervey. He apparently started seeing Miss Vane late in 1730, and their affair lasted until the autumn of 1731 – when she began seeing Frederick (still concurrently with Hervey, as well as Lord Harrington) and conceived the child she bore. This was also when Hervey began complaining of her and the Prince's betrayal to Fox and his father.

The mechanics of the erotic triangle that bound together Hervey, Prince Frederick and Anne Vane do not preclude the possibility that the Prince pursued Miss Vane either to hurt Hervey by betraying him or to attract his attention by taking what was his. Perhaps Frederick was frustrated by Hervey's refusal to give Ste Fox up for him. Just as in Shakespeare's sonnets the Fair Youth and the Narrator compete for the Dark Lady – 'the Master–Mistress of my passion' – bound each to each by their shared desire, Frederick must have chosen Miss Vane because of Hervey's interest in her as much as her inherent charms:

> That thou hast her, it is not all my grief,
> And yet it may be said I loved her dearly;
> That she hath thee is of my wailing chief,
> A loss in love that touches me more nearly.

Anne Vane may have been a vehicle through which Frederick could hurt Hervey, the Prince's conscious or unconscious homosexual desire directed heterosexually, through socially legitimate channels.*

---

* See Sedgwick, *Between Men. English Literature and Male Homosocial Desire.* 'Heterosexual love is merely a strategy of homosocial desire': as in the verb to cuckold, which is a sexual act performed on a man by another man, through a passive woman.

The moral to be gleaned from this affair, said Grub Street, was that the court's corruption tainted everyone that came into its sphere.

> Females with double Virtue armed should be,
> Who C[ourt]s frequent, and their Temptations see.

'It shows,' wrote the author of 'Vanelia: Or, the Affairs of the Great', that 'though the great put on an outward form of virtue and probity, yet at the bottom there is little in it but gratifying their passions.' Courtiers were 'black as the devil within', sang a maid, despite their appearance of angels. They were incapable of love – 'it makes people look like fools', said one court lady; her friend Flirtilla replied, 'There is in reality no such thing as love. It is only a phantom which most people conjure up once in their lives to make themselves uneasy: 'tis often talked of, but never found' – and of integrity:

> If you in this Age would quickly rise High,
>   And purchase both Power and Treasure,
> Be sure to each Vice of the great Ones you ply,
>   And carefully pimp for their Pleasure.

Another clue as to what may have happened between Frederick, Hervey and Anne Vane lies in Queen Caroline's passionate interrogation of Hervey in 1737 about Frederick's ability to sire children. 'I know he was so solicitous for the reputation of having a child by Vane that, though you have perjured yourself a thousand times by swearing it was not so, yet I am as sure as if I had heard him do it that he asked you to get one for him,' Caroline said, citing the resemblance between Fitzfrederick, Anne Vane's son born in June 1732, to Hervey's fourth son William, born the month before. They could not have been more like if they had been twins, she said. Hervey agreed that though Miss Vane had told him Frederick was 'in these matters ignorant to a degree inconceivable, but not impotent', he insisted he had not made Anne Vane pregnant in order that Frederick might pass the child off as his own and set the seal on his masculinity. But Frederick may well have harboured fears about his virility. These doubts were perhaps what had led him to cut such a public swathe through the ladies at court in the years after his arrival in London. Hervey, eager to ingratiate himself with Frederick regardless of the cost to his dignity, could conceivably have sunk to these depths, but it must remain an unlikely supposition.

At the end of April, the diarist Lord Percival was told the next episode in this drama by Colonel Schutz, one of Frederick's Gentlemen of the Bedchamber. Until this time Hervey had managed to conceal his resentment of Frederick – together the two men had sponsored and possibly helped write a play, *The Modish Couple*, which was performed for three nights (before derisive crowds) at the Theatre Royal, on Drury Lane, in January.* An arch comedy of manners, the play was no masterpiece, but it is possible that it did especially badly because political opponents of the Prince and Lord Hervey incited the audience to greater than usual displays of disapproval.

During the spring Hervey was forced to admit that the Prince no longer showed him the attentions with which he had once been showered. The months of pandering to Frederick's every whim, of humiliating himself at his hands, had come to nothing. Frederick now spent his days and nights with his pregnant mistress and his new best friend, George Bubb Dodington, a wealthy neighbour of the Foxes' in Somerset. Apparently convinced that it was his former mistress who was responsible for the Prince's change of heart, and determined to be restored to Frederick's circle of intimates despite Frederick's treatment of him, Hervey wrote Miss Vane a letter which he asked his brother-in-law Bussy Mansel (the widower of Hervey's favourite sister Betty who died in 1727) to deliver to her. In order not to arouse Mansel's suspicion, he told his messenger that the purpose of the letter was to recommend a midwife to his former mistress since her *accouchement* was drawing near.

* Curiously, the play was dedicated by the author, Captain Charles Bodens, to Lord Harrington – the other man (apart from Hervey) who claimed to have first seduced Miss Vane.

Mansel delivered the letter and sat with Miss Vane as she read it; to his amazement, she swooned and fainted. When she was revived, he asked her why she had reacted so violently. Anne threw him the letter (no longer extant) and, astonished, Mansel read Hervey's desperate tirade, which accused her of turning Frederick against him, and threatened to 'discover what he knew of her and use her as she deserved' if she did not repair the breach between him and the Prince. Mansel, enraged, swore he would kill his brother-in-law for making him 'the messenger of so great an affront, and for deceiving him'.

Miss Vane told Frederick about Hervey's letter so the Prince would prevent Mansel murdering Hervey for compromising his honour; reluctantly, Frederick made peace between the two men, 'but much resented the ill-treatment of his mistress'. Hervey was forced to apologize formally not only to Frederick and Miss Vane but also to the King, Queen and Prime Minister. They forgave him, but Frederick was to hold his grudge, venting 'his princely resentment even upon women', recorded Horace Walpole ten years later, when the Prince snubbed Lady Hervey at a party. Hervey remained at court as Vice-Chamberlain, but he had been ousted by Bubb Dodington from his unofficial position as royal confidant. The rift between Hervey and Frederick, embittered by the strength of their former intimacy and compounded by each man's sense of having been deeply wronged, was now complete.

On 5 June 1732 Anne Vane's son, the subtly named Fitzfrederick, was born. Both Hervey and Lord Harrington told Robert Walpole that they had sired him; jokes circulated about the boy's father being a triumvirate.

> Of a hundred Amours, she (at least) was accused.
> A hundred! (she cries) Heavens how I'm abused,
> For I'll swear the dear Babe (or else I may starve) is
> The Prince's, or Stanhope's, my footman's, or Hervey's,

ran a verse saved by Lady Mary Wortley Montagu at this time (Stanhope was Harrington's family name). But Frederick was delighted with his son, and convinced enough of his paternity to reward the boy's mother with a grand house in Grosvenor Square the autumn after his birth and to raise her allowance to £3,000 a year.

18. Unconsoled

Hervey still found court life entertaining, but after his humiliation at Frederick and Anne Vane's hands his amusement was increasingly tempered with cynicism about its inhabitants. He had not joined the rest of the court in visiting the annual Bartholomew Fair, he wrote to Henry Fox in 1732, famous for the travelling theatre companies which performed there, because he preferred 'comedies in high life'. Since he was so well entertained at court he did not need to seek amusement in other theatres:

At the other drolls [performances], the dress makes the Harlequin, the Merry Andrew and the Scaramouch. But here it is the reverse. It is not the trappings that make the men ridiculous, but the men the trappings; and as a red and yellow coat there debases the wearer, here a wearer debases a blue or red ribbon [the insignia of royal distinctions like the Order of the Garter]; whilst wealth, titles, and power and honours can no more give sense to the Duke of Newcastle, than paint, patches and brocade can give beauty to the Duchess of Rutland.

Like Lemuel Gulliver at the court of the Lilliputans, Hervey could see the ridiculousness of the world in which he lived; but his ambition and vanity kept him embroiled in it, preventing him from truly distancing himself from the tawdry show in which he played a role as eagerly as his peers.

At this time, Hervey was writing about equally to Stephen and Henry Fox, the latter newly returned from Europe and staying at Redlynch with his brother. In October he forwarded Henry a book (or long pamphlet) that had been sent to him, he said, with the recommendation, ' "There is so much wit and so much wickedness in this paper, that I conclude your Lordship will find it seasoned to your taste"; and as these two ingredients will, I believe, make it full as palatable to you, I send it to you without having read it.' The pamphlet, entitled 'Some Remarks on the Minute Philosopher', was actually Hervey's own response to the recently published 'Minute Philosopher', a work of religious debate marked by its amateurish scepticism. 'If the tenets of Christianity were reconcilable to reason,' Hervey argued in it, 'why were they called Mysteries? If they admitted of demonstration, why would faith be required?' Hervey did not reveal his authorship to Fox, but asked him to show it to the Reverend Sampson, a mutual friend, and added, 'if you should guess who sent it to me I beg you would not say. I guess by the title it will not be a sort of book for . . . Ste to be entertained with.' Henry recognized Hervey's style, and later gave a copy to Voltaire in Paris; Voltaire, ever an admirer and friend of Hervey's, praised it lavishly, saying it was as lucid and witty as Hervey himself.

Although Hervey did not send Ste a copy of his work, he was not neglecting him. Three days earlier he had sent him a political pamphlet written as if during the reign of Charles II – 'I know you love a little dab of history' – but apologized for it as he thought it very poorly written and argued. The author's old-fashioned views, wrote Hervey, turned his stomach: 'there is such an exploded obsolete reverence for majesty, merely for being majesty; such a leaning to divine hereditary right, and such a partiality to a monarchical form of government'. In this, he agreed with Montaigne, who held that subjects owed 'obedience equally to all kings, for that concerns their office; but we do not owe esteem, any more than affection, except to their virtue'. As he wrote in his *Memoirs*, Hervey did not believe kings were necessarily greater than their subjects, and might often be worse: 'I have the conduct of princes in so little veneration, that I believe they act yet oftener without design than other people, and are insensibly drawn into both good and bad situations without knowing how they came there.'

This opinion was shared by Sir Robert Walpole, who told Hervey in 1736 that his ministers ought totally to be able to control King George. 'Whenever our master does wrong, it is the fault of his ministers, who must either want resolution to oppose him, or sense enough to do it with success.' The King imagined that because he was never contradicted he would always be able to do things as he wanted to. He thought of himself as an absolute ruler, with enough courage to back up his claims; 'but if I know anything of him, he is, with all his personal bravery, as great a political coward as ever wore a crown, and as much afraid to lose it'.

According to his *Memoirs*, Hervey sometimes thought that Walpole ought to use his mastery of the King to better ends, thinking as much in terms of posterity as of present advantage. He was not chronicling his age to bring pleasure to future generations, Hervey said, but if he were, he should lament the stability of the times in which he lived. Readers like 'great events, and such were not the growth of this country in the age I am describing'. Walpole's motivation was not lasting fame but temporal power: 'his great maxim in policy was to keep everything else as undisturbed as he could, to bear with some abuses rather risk reformations, and submit to old inconveniences rather than encourage innovations'. He would never assist or encourage any reformation of the law or the church, despite the obvious injustices of both. There were abuses that Walpole had not corrected as fully as he might have, admitted Hervey, citing his master's patch-work repair of the South Sea Bubble at the start of his ministry, and the pitiful state of London's gaols.

But Hervey's progressive views did not mean he wished to see the system under which he lived fundamentally changed. A pamphlet Hervey wrote in 1732 entitled 'The Public Virtue of Former Times, and the Present Age Compared' attacked those in opposition who wanted to reform the government. Hervey agreed with Montaigne, who held that 'the best and most excellent government for each nation is the one under which it has preserved its existence ... Nothing presses a state hard except innovation; change alone lends shape to injustice and tyranny.' Hervey equated dissatisfaction with disloyalty:

Whoever is discontented with the liberty enjoyed in Great Britain at this day, and upon that account desirous of a change, is either a stranger, or an enemy to liberty, and must be for a state of tyranny or confusion ... With peace we enjoy the utmost liberty, all the rights of British subjects, and all the advantages of pursuing by industry and frugality what every man can wish, and the protection of what he enjoys. Whether we owe these blessings to the King and his Ministry, and a Parliament concurring; or to those who have exerted themselves in constant opposition, may as well bear a dispute as the question arising from it: who then are our patriots?

The independent modernism of Hervey's opinion of the pamphlet he sent to Ste was in contrast to the sycophantic tone of his previous letter in which he described the King's arrival at Gravesend from his German capital of Hanover where, according to his habit, George had spent the summer, leaving Caroline behind as Regent. Hervey was a quarter of an hour too late to meet George with the royal barges which went out to the monarch's ship, but galloped up to his coach, shouting for royal permission to cheer with the mob to show his joy at George's arrival. 'He like a very gracious master to a very negligent servant, stopped his coach which was going full gallop and asked me to come in, so that I have already had a conversation of three hours with him, in which he asked me incessant questions, and seemed so glad to see England again, that it was impossible not to be glad to see him.'

Despite the scandal at the beginning of the year and his very public estrangement from Frederick, Hervey's stock at court remained high in the autumn and winter of 1732. The King and Queen – well aware of their eldest son's failings – accepted Hervey's apologies for his rash attack on Anne Vane (and, by extension, on Frederick) and allowed his continued loyalty and discretion to act as a proof of his repentance. But he enjoyed it all much less than he had when his star was in the ascendant, and turned again to Stephen Fox to console him for the soullessness of court life.

If I do not see Redlynch this autumn I shall be miserable; when you go to Goodwood [the Sussex home of their friends the Duke and Duchess of Richmond] I shall go with you; and if you were to go to the ice of Greenland or the hottest furnace in Africa I would, if I could, do so too. From the time I lose sight of you to the time I see you again, I do not reckon I live any more than in the hours I sleep. It is a chasm in which I breathe and dream; but my pleasures are no more real in one case, than my images in the other.

Early in November Hervey wrote to tell Ste that his court obligations would preclude him visiting Redlynch as he had planned. Instead, he tried to persuade Fox to come to London before going to Goodwood, where Hervey hoped to join him in a couple of weeks. 'Can the following a poor woodcock four hours in the four-and-twenty afford you pleasure enough to compensate for the solitary ennui in which you must pass the other sixteen'? he asked. 'Come to London then for a fortnight before you go to Sussex, and instead of seeking pleasure where it is not to be found, bring *one* to me in whom it is never to be missed.' But Ste, who two years before probably would have gone up to town early in order to be with Hervey for a few snatched days, was no longer so amenable to his suggestions: perhaps because so often in the past he had obliged Hervey's caprices and received so little in return, perhaps because now, aged twenty-eight, he was no longer content to place his own interests second to his friend's.

Since he would not be able to visit Redlynch, Hervey planned instead to go to Goodwood at the same time as Ste. He asked Ste to tell his brother Henry that the Duke of Richmond wanted Henry to come to Goodwood too, so that even though they could not all be together in Somerset they could still be united in Suffolk.* A letter written to Ste by Molly Hervey from Goodwood a week later reveals the real reason the Redlynch journey had been put off: Molly's interference. She confessed to Stephen that she had tried to get the Redlynch party transferred to Goodwood so that she could be included in the group, but she was unrepentant. 'You

---

* Twelve years later Henry Fox eloped with Richmond's eldest daughter, Lady Caroline Lennox. The marriage caused a huge scandal, as Horace Walpole gleefully told his friend Horace Mann: 'The town has been in a great bustle about a private match . . . Mr Fox fell in love with Lady Caroline Lennox, asked [for] her, was refused, and stole her. His father was a footman; her great-grandfather a King [Walpole's mistake; actually her grandfather was Charles II; his mistress, Louise de Keroualle, Duchess of Portsmouth, was Richmond's mother]; *hinc illae lacrimae*! All the blood royal have been up in arms.' It was one thing to be friends with the newly rich, but quite another to fall in love with them. Confounding the critics, it was a happy and successful marriage. Their second son was the Whig statesman Charles James Fox. See S. Tillyard's *Aristocrats*.

desire to know how long I shall stay here, it depends entirely on my Lord, for whom I shall stay and with whom I shall return.'

The following year, while Ste and Molly Hervey were staying at Goodwood without Hervey, two masked highwaymen ambushed a carriage holding the duchess, Ladies Hervey and Tankerville, Stephen Fox and Dean Sherwin, a local cleric who was a familiar figure at Goodwood. 'One presented a pistol to the driver while the other rifled the company. Mr Fox and Lady Hervey lost their gold watches, the Countess of Tankerville her gold snuff-box, the Dean eight guineas, the Duchess of Richmond four guineas, and the rest of the company twelve guineas more,' said a newspaper report of the incident. 'Take all!' cried the Reverend Sherwin, after a pistol was discharged close to his head by one of the brigands.

Sherwin related the story again and again over the next few days; each time the horses grew bigger, snorted more loudly and pawed the ground more viciously, there were three robbers rather than two, carrying more guns, threatening more violence; and Sherwin had each time been braver and braver. But in fact, the two highwaymen were none other than Richmond and his trusted servant Ligeois, and the whole incident had been an elaborate practical joke aimed at Sherwin, the only unsuspecting member of the party. The joke was enhanced by Sherwin's increasingly grandiose renditions of the events.

Hervey wrote to Richmond after the prank teasing him about his new role as a criminal — 'all you untaken rogues are so careless notwithstanding to the daily danger you are in of the gallows' — but the joke did not remain secret long. Sherwin himself never believed that he had been played for a fool. He was told that it was a hoax, and informed Richmond about it, saying 'what a ridiculous lying town Chichester is': 'They have actually persuaded my wife and daughters that it was your Grace robbed us, and they never would consider that though you might frighten me, you would never frighten the Duchess or the other ladies.'*

* Several months later, Hervey was much concerned because a joke 'Character', designed as an epitaph, that he had written of Dr Sherwin, and intended for the amusement of the Richmonds, was being circulated privately. 'I am sorry to hear the verses that you say were shown you as written by me on Sherwin are

Hervey, meanwhile, was spending time with old friends in London. 'Excepting the agreeable days I have passed alone with you, I never spent one in a more pleasant male *tête-à-tête* than I did yesterday,' he wrote to Ste on 14 November 1732. He and Lord Chesterfield had breakfasted together, gone to pay their respects at court, and then dined (a meal taken in the mid-afternoon by the aristocracy) at Chesterfield's house in Bloomsbury Square. Hervey's host was in great good humour, 'incessantly entertaining . . . I always listen to him as I read poetry, without hoping for a word of truth. As one values other people in proportion to their adherence to truth, one admires him most when he deviates from it.' This was not to say Chesterfield was a liar, Hervey added: 'his Lordship never thinks of the things he tells being either true or false, and for deceiving you; provided he is sure you like his manner of telling them, he concerns himself no more about the credit you give his narrations, than he does about the authority he has for them. He is a most wonderful composition.'

Lord Chesterfield was two years older than Hervey, and like him had been at court since the 1710s. He adored Molly Hervey, and earlier that year he had been chosen to be godfather to their son William, born in May 1732. Although Chesterfield later became one of the government's most hostile opponents and a close ally of William Pulteney, he supported Walpole at this time, so he and

---

got about; and beg you when you hear them spoken of, to say you have been told they were written for an epitaph on Parson Ford two years ago,' Hervey wrote to Dr Middleton on 15 November 1733, concerned that Sherwin should see his malicious description of him. This ruse apparently worked; as Hervey later informed Henry Fox, 'by the Duke of Richmond's good management' the story was passed on to Sherwin, who 'is now boasting of being abused with me by the *Craftsman* and says it is because he and I are known to be such firm and useful friends to the government'. The printer of the opposition newspaper the *Craftsman* also sent Sherwin a copy of the 'Character', asking him to sign a certificate acknowledging Hervey's authorship of the 'Epistle to a Doctor of Divinity' (see p. 195). Sherwin, believing that Hervey could not have written either the 'Epistle' or the unflattering portrait of Sherwin in the 'Character', sent the publisher's letter to Hervey, saying, 'You see, my Lord, the way that rascal, the *Craftsman*, has taken to pique me into setting my hand to a most notorious untruth. I know nothing at all of the whole matter. Let him print if he dares.'

Hervey were political allies as well as old friends. The letters of advice he wrote to his heir exemplify eighteenth-century aristocratic culture's values and preoccupations, although not everybody thought as much of his wisdom as he himself did. As Dr Johnson famously remarked of him, Chesterfield had 'the morals of a whore and the manners of a dancing master'. His famous charm may have been a way of compensating for his equally famous ugliness: the King called him a 'dwarf-baboon'.

As Hervey said, Chesterfield was 'allowed by everybody to have more conversable entertaining table-wit than any man of the time', but the glittering barbs of his wit 'made him sought and feared, liked and not loved'. Molly agreed, although she admired his conversation, 'that flow of language, Attic elegance, and peculiar manner of stabbing with the genteelest compliments, which he can make more pointed than arguments'. An epigram Chesterfield wrote about Hervey shows the malicious delicacy of his wit, even when it was directed against a friend:

> While Nature H[ervey]'s clay was blending,
> Uncertain what her work would end in,
> Whether a female or a male,
> A pin dropped in, and turned the scale.*

Despite the pleasure he took in Chesterfield's company, Hervey was beginning to look inward, turning his back on the high life of his youth. He was thirty-six, resigned to his continued poor health, and had begun to reassess himself and his life, as he wrote in unusually confessional tone to the Dean of Norwich, a close family friend, several months after losing Miss Vane to Prince Frederick.

I came very early into the world, have lived long in what is called the top of it and had a satiating swing in the showish part of its pleasures; my taste has taken a new turn, the hey-day of my blood (as Shakespeare calls it) is pretty well over; in the midst of a crowded court, I pass many, many

* Probably inspired by an epigram by the Roman poet Ausonius: 'While Nature was in doubt whether to make a boy or girl, thou dids't become almost a girl, my handsome boy' (Horace Walpole's *Letters*, vol. 30, p. 25).

hours alone; I am disgusted of many people I used to love, undeceived in some I used to esteem; and have lowered my opinion of many more I used to admire.

Hervey had reduced his friendships into a narrower compass even than his acquaintances, he said, exchanging the shallow amusement of useless companions for a few useful books. Even though it was his health as much as his inclination that had brought about these changes – he was taking up intellectual pleasures as his physical ones declined – Hervey was determined to gain as much by his new habits as he had lost with his old. '[If] I can enlarge the enjoyments of my mind in the same proportion that time, age and indolence have contracted those of the opposite kind [sensual pleasures], I shall not reckon myself poorer.' Provided the same degree of pleasure was achieved, he said, it was immaterial whether the pleasure was derived from the brain or the senses.

19. A Broken Girdle

Hervey's interest in matters of religion and metaphysics had been stimulated the previous year when his friend Fanny Braddocks committed suicide in September 1731. She had gambled away the last of her money in Bath, and then hanged herself with her girdle over the cupboard door. Another girdle was found broken on the floor, indicating that her first attempt had failed. She had left no suicide note, but a verse written in her hand (though Hervey thought it was not by her) lay on the table.

> Oh! Death: thou certain End of human Woe
> Thou Cure for Life! Thou greatest Good below
> Still mayst thou the Coward and the Slave
> And thy soft Slumbers only bless the Brave.

Her compulsive gambling was well-known, and her death did not come as a surprise to her brother, whose stoical response on hearing of the tragedy was, 'Poor Fanny, I always thought she would play till she would be forced to tuck herself up.'

Hervey thought Miss Braddocks's manner of dying courageous, despite the old-fashioned Christian view which held that she had flown in the face of God by presuming to take her own life. He was, he told Ste, jealous of the strength of character she had shown, and dismayed by the people that detracted from her bravery with foolish remarks. 'I liked her living, and honour her dying. I daresay if it could be known, Adrian, Anacreon, or Petronius did not die with more unconcern.' Hervey's views were coloured by his interest in classical culture and beliefs; writing later in the year about another suicide, he told Ste that he admired the dead man because he had conquered the fear of dying which every living thing involuntarily feels, 'that unaccountable proneness to continue our being'. It made him suspect, he continued, that the will to live was little more than a spell cast upon us to prevent us cutting our lives short before our appointed time was expired.

Hervey refused to enter into disputes about the morality of Fanny's mode of death with those whom he termed the 'orthodox reasoners' – such as Lord Bristol – whose views admitted little independent thought or questioning: 'I should as soon think of reasoning with a kicking horse or a biting dog. All one has to do upon such occasions is to get out of the way.' Where his father unquestioningly accepted every twist of fate, however harsh or unjust, as God's will, Hervey was unable so meekly to submit to such arbitrary dictates. If God's hand was involved in every human event, if not a hair fell to the ground without God's help or permission as well as his knowledge, then how could people like his father have faith in his goodness, mercy and vigilance? he asked himself. What kind of a God could have allowed to occur every link in the chain of misfortunes that brought Fanny to her death? 'What would be said (or what should we not deserve to have said) of you or me? if our voice was health, and our touch happiness, and yet we walked every day through hospitals and prisons with our mouths shut and our hands in our pockets?'

'That there is a God I never doubt,' Hervey continued, but he could not help doubting that God was just, because of the indubitable existence of pain in the world. Pain must be a divine punishment; justice demands that guilt is what is punished. There can be no guilt without evil: but what is evil? From where does it spring? How is it defined? What rules does it obey?

How all this is to be unravelled or reconciled, or when unfolded, are things I am sure I do not know, things I firmly believe I was not designed to know here, and which I often doubt whether I ever shall know hereafter: whenever I think or speak of these things it is as if there was a mist before me which a little help could brush away, and yet 'tis what I never dispel; I endeavour to get forward as one does sometimes in one's sleep, but fret that I can't, and wake out of my reverie as uneasy as I do out of my dream.

Hervey shared these sceptical, deistic beliefs with almost all of his friends, from the Fox brothers to Lady Mary Wortley Montagu to Sir Robert Walpole.

Inspired by this type of free-thinking, many fashionable intellectuals at this time turned away from the church to freemasonry. The association was based on the principles of individual freedom, tolerance for others, brotherhood (it remains an all-male society), and the transcendance of God. It was firmly Whiggish – Sir Robert Walpole was a mason – promoting the ideal of a strong constitutional monarchy supported by a fluid aristocracy. Deist in religious matters, the 1723 Constitution of the Order described God as the Great Architect. An interest in progressive scientific ideas was almost a prerequisite for membership, with over a quarter of the early masons also members of the Royal Society founded by Sir Isaac Newton, himself a mason. Freemasonry's tenets were rational, humanist and intellectual: all principles espoused by Hervey and his friends. Recruits included the Prince of Wales, the Dukes of Richmond, Wharton, Montagu, Newcastle, Norfolk and Cumberland, Lord Chesterfield, the Serjeant-painter to the King Sir James Thornhill, and his son-in-law William Hogarth. Hervey was inducted in 1724; Ste Fox in 1730.

The Augustan belief in the glory of the age in which they lived was tempered by a humanist sense of the fallibility of mankind. Man as an abstract might be perfectable, but all too often the individual fell short. Hervey took the view that one can only look closely at mankind to despise it, and wrote his *Memoirs* almost as an exercise in scientific detachment:

To whom then can a history of such times be agreeable or entertaining, unless it be such as look into courts and courtiers, princes and ministers, with such curious eyes as virtuosos in microscopes examine flies and emmets, and are pleased with the dissected minute parts of animals, which in the gross herd they either do not regard or observe with indifference or contempt?

This dispassionate attitude was typical of the principles that characterized the intellectual climate in early eighteenth-century England.

Hervey concluded his thoughts on Miss Braddocks's death by turning his musings inwards to his feelings for Ste.

One thing I am sure of [is] that whilst I have you, I shall never be tempted to hang myself and that if I was to lose you nothing but want of courage could hinder me; no consideration would tempt me to live though there might be some abject weakness that might make me fear to die . . . You cannot tell how often and how tenderly I think of you, never with indifference, never without emotion; but with the tears starting into my eyes with sorrow at our separation or blushing with pleasure at the thoughts of our meeting.

Hervey began a correspondence with the modernizing Bishop Benjamin Hoadley in the summer of 1733. 'I had a respect for you before I knew you personally and an inclination to be acquainted with you before I was so,' Hervey wrote to him early in their acquaintance. 'The more I knew of you, the more I liked you as an entertaining man, the more I esteemed you an honest one, and the more I loved you as a good one.' Two weeks later he wrote again, teasing the prelate about who was more honest: courtiers or churchmen. 'I do not at all understand the frequent liberties you take of abusing courtiers, and believe you will pique me at last into retaliating upon churchmen; and when our accounts come to be stated, I wonder which class, yours or mine, will find themselves the largest debtors to truth.' He did not want to say that court was the best place to find truth, 'that rare and valuable commodity', but he had heard more truth at a royal reception than he ever had from a pulpit; and was convinced that the only advantage a minister had over a courtier was 'that as he promises nothing but reversions, he is not so easily found out to break his word, and the poor devils that trusted to him are never cheated till it is too late to tell, and too late to complain'.

Hervey's customary flippancy occasionally offended Hoadley. In his next letter, he made a joke to which the bishop responded badly, and Hervey wrote back indignantly to defend himself.

I am very angry with you for what you say about me and puns and Christians; and think, when you was blotting and blurring, as you call it (unless you were infected by one day's conversation with [Canon] Sherwin), that you had much better have blurred your paper a little more, and my reputation a little less, by blotting out the whole paragraph.

Puns were considered the lowest form of humour; according to the *Spectator* in 1711, 'True wit consists in the resemblance of ideas and false wit in the resemblance of words.' The force of Hervey's reply may have been compounded by an awareness that he was letting himself down by indulging in such obvious raillery. The year before, in a letter to Ste, he had nearly scratched out a joke because he thought it might be a pun, 'but because I do not always know a pun any more than I do humour, I will hope I'm mistaken and let it go'.

Despite his disinclination to be teased about them, Hoadley's Low Church, almost deistic, beliefs were similar to Hervey's views, and to those of their friend William Hogarth. Hoadley would be painted in 1741 by Hogarth but had been friends with him for many years before, and it was probably through Hoadley that Hervey met Hogarth for the first time. These classically educated, independently minded men shared many similar opinions. They considered blind subservience to the tenets of a church designed to control rather than enlighten the masses to be archaic and irrelevant to the age in which they lived; sceptical and materialist, they believed in relying on individual contemplation to arrive at a sense of the religious. Politically, they favoured a church subservient to the state, and devoid of papist ritual. A passage describing the papacy in Montesquieu's 1721 fantasy, the *Lettres Persanes*, exemplified this modern view of religion: 'This magician is commonly called the Pope. He will make the King believe that three are only one, or else that the bread one eats is not bread, or that the wine one drinks not wine, and a thousand other things of the same kind . . . He is an ancient idol, worshipped now from habit.'

Hervey echoed this view in his *Memoirs*: 'The fable of Christianity, as Leo X called it, was now so exploded in England that any man of fashion or condition would have been almost as much ashamed in company to own himself a Christian as formerly he would have been afraid to profess himself none.' Even women, he concluded, were careful not to let people think they were bound by Christian prejudices. When the Queen lay near death in 1737 Walpole persuaded the Princess Emily to allow the Archbishop of Canterbury to pray by Caroline's bedside, assuring her that she could tell him to be as quick as she liked. 'It will do the Queen no hurt, no more than any good; and it will satisfy all the wise and good fools, who will call us atheists if we don't pretend to be as great fools as they are.'

20. Complicity

'Politics you hate, and so do I,' Lord Hervey wrote to his friend the Duke of Richmond early in 1733.

Yet I hear nothing else all day long, the worst of politics which are mercantile politics. Excise, wine and tobacco are the three words on which my male companions ring the changes from morning to night; and I am as sick of the two last, as if I had been drinking the one and smoking the other with my Bury [St Edmunds, the closest town to Ickworth and Hervey's constituency] aldermen.

Hervey might protest that he disliked public affairs – at the end of 1731 he had told Ste that he looked 'with more horror on the meeting of Parliament, than my little son does on Monday sennight [every week], when the holidays determine and he is to go to school again' – but really he relished the cut-and-thrust of political life.

Sir Robert Walpole was trying to push through Parliament a new excise scheme in the spring of 1733. It was an unpopular move, and united the previously disparate opponents to Walpole in a grand effort to block the bill and thus destroy his credibility with the King and Queen. But by this time, according to Hervey, Caroline had 'fully possessed his Majesty with an opinion that it was absolutely necessary, from the nature of the English government, that he should have but one minister; and that it was equally necessary, from Sir Robert's superior abilities, that he should be the one'; there was no question that their support for him be withdrawn because of a little dispute over taxes.

Horace Walpole described the curious balance of power that existed between his father and his royal master and mistress:

Though his [George's] affection and confidence in her [Caroline] were implicit, he lived in dread of being supposed to be governed by her; and that silly parade was extended even to the most private moments of business with my father, who, whenever he entered, the Queen rose, curtsied and retired, or offered to retire – sometimes the King condescended to bid her stay – on both occasions [whether she stayed or left] she and Sir Robert had previously settled the business to be discussed.

The power of each depended on the complicity of the other two.

Cesar de Saussure described Queen Caroline in 1727 as having been one of the most beautiful princesses in Europe, but 'grown too stout'. Plump and fair, she had graceful bearing and an impressive bosom which she liked to show to its advantage. Unlike her husband, Caroline was intelligent and learned. She enjoyed witty conversation and intellectual discussions in which George, who prided himself on having eluded all attempts to educate him, neither could nor would participate.

The Queen loved reading and the conversation of men of wit and learning. But she did not dare to indulge herself as much as she wished to do in this pleasure for fear of the King, who often rebuked her for dabbling in all that lettred nonsense (as he termed it), called her a pedant, and said she loved to spend her time more like a schoolmistress than a Queen,

said Hervey. George, he said, used to say he had hated learning as a child not merely because of the boredom, but because 'he felt as if he was doing something mean and below him'.

George was a slow-thinking, stubborn man who, once possessed of an idea, would not willingly relinquish it; he could also be capricious and vindictive, and required careful handling. Only Caroline, who had devoted her life to the study of her husband, could influence him. According to Hervey, her

dominant passion was pride, and the darling pleasure of her soul was power; but she was forced to gratify the one and gain the other, as some people do health, by a strict and painful regime, which few besides herself could have had patience to support, or resolution to adhere to . . . She used to give him [George] her opinion as jugglers do a card, by changing it imperceptibly, and making him believe he held the same with that he first pitched upon.

For this power, Hervey continued, Caroline paid a high cost. She 'governed him (if such influence so gained can bear the name of government) by being as great a slave to him thus ruled, as any other wife could be to a man who ruled her'. Theirs was a complicated relationship, based as much on Caroline's physical hold over her husband as on her intellectual superiority: George desired her but could never possess her because she looked down on him, and Caroline used George's passion to control him.

While Hervey admired Caroline and became increasingly close to her through his role at court, Lady Mary Wortley Montagu believed the Queen was an evil woman who had stimulated and stirred up her husband's resentment of his father, George I. She described Caroline as

so devoted to his [George's] pleasures (which she often told him were the rule of all her thoughts and actions), that whenever he thought proper to find them with other women, she even loved whoever was instrumental to his entertainment, and never resented anything but what appeared to her a want of respect for him; and in this light she really could not help taking notice that the presents made to her on her wedding were not worthy of his bride, and at least she ought to have had all his mother's jewels.

George, then Prince of Wales, distanced himself from his father and the rest of his family because of what he saw as ungenerous treatment of his wife. This alienation only brought him more firmly under Caroline's influence. George I referred to Caroline as 'that she-devil'.

Sir Robert was also skilled in the arts of manipulation. 'Notwithstanding his propensity to laughing, one seldom sees him indulge it in an improper place, or at an improper time,' Hervey wrote to Ste after attending a dinner party at Walpole's house in Chelsea.

'He can suppress a smile when his heart laughs, as well as force one on when it aches. His behaviour in many things that day was, under a seeming openness and negligence, devilish artful.' Like Caroline, Walpole knew how to manage George, to make him think Walpole's ideas were his own, to play to his prejudices and partialities. Sir Robert decided his policies, discussed them with Caroline and sought her approval, entrusting her with securing the King's approval; and then ensured that they appeared to be the act of the King and Council. 'Sir Robert,' said Hervey, 'with a dexterity equal to his power, whilst in fact he did everything alone, was responsible for nothing but in common; whilst those ciphers of the Cabinet signed everything he dictated, and without the least share in honour or power, bound themselves equally with him in case this political merchant should be bankrupt.'

Walpole's steadiness of character and the underlying strength of his ambition served him well in his dealings with his temperamental monarch, and protected him from frustration and cynicism. Hervey expressed surprise that Walpole did not become disillusioned by what he had seen of human nature during his political career. Sir Robert

had more warmth of affection and friendship for some particular people than one could have believed it possible for anyone who had been so long raking in the dirt of mankind to be capable of feeling for so worthless a species of animals. One should naturally have imagined that the contempt and distrust he must have had for the species in gross, would have given him at least an indifference and distrust towards every particular.

Walpole saw things differently after he had been ousted, though, telling his successor-in-waiting, Henry Pelham, 'When you have the same experience of mankind as myself you will go near to hate the human species.'

The Excise Bill was the biggest challenge of Walpole's career since he had consolidated his position as Prime Minister at George II's accession in 1727. The Opposition had apparently already drawn up a list of who would have what job in the ministry they expected to be asked to form after Walpole's imminent defeat.

After a preliminary victory, Walpole was forced to back down and allow the bill to be postponed because the small majority he anticipated if there was a vote would have allowed the Opposition to claim victory. His parliamentary majority during the crisis had fallen from seventy to seventeen.

A howling mob gathered outside the House of Commons during the debate over the bill, 'greeting every member as he passed whom they knew to have been for the excise with ironical thanks, hissings, hallooing, and all other insults which it was possible to put upon them without proceeding to blows', said Hervey; they were also burning effigies of Walpole and a fat woman representing Caroline. According to Lord Percival, local JPs had threatened to read the protesters the Riot Act, 'but these unruly people cried out, "Damn your laws and proclamations."' On hearing that Walpole, as a demonstration of his determination, planned to walk through the mob, Hervey and his friend Charles Churchill walked back through it to accompany their leader. Forty or fifty constables were trying to keep the rioters away from Walpole, walking at the centre of a cluster of his supporters; in the crush, Hervey was wounded in the forehead.*

Walpole declared that the public's attempts to influence Commons policy in this way was illegal, for MPs ought to be independent of outside pressure; ought not, in other words, to be accountable to their electorate or the rest of the population. Hervey spoke in the House of Commons in agreement with Walpole.

If these insolent encroachments of the populace were suffered to grow and were given way to in this matter – if the opinion of the rabble were to be taken on the subject-matter of everything debated here, and in their clamour and not our judgement, to make decisions – in a little time we should expect to see Acts of Parliament passed in London as the Plebiscita were passed in Rome.

Admiration of classical times, then, did not lead to an automatic appreciation of democracy.

---

* Describing the incident in the manuscript copy of his *Memoirs*, Hervey started to elaborate on his bravery, beginning his account of how he was attacked, 'with a broken . . .' but modesty triumphed and he crossed it out.

During the crisis, the King used Hervey as his Commons spy. He made Hervey send him reports by messenger from the Commons throughout the day, and sit up with him when he got back to the palace late at night, to find out who had said what and if the mood in the House was changing. Hervey regaled the indignant George with the Opposition's attacks on Walpole, and Walpole's spirited defence and retaliation. The King, much moved by his minister's courage and perseverance, would 'cry out with colour flushing into his cheeks, and tears sometimes in his eyes, and with a vehement oath, "He is a brave fellow; he has more spirit than any man I ever knew."' This showed, commented Hervey, how much George's ideas of government had changed since he had taken the throne five years previously, when he had had such grand plans of ruling the country himself.

Hervey's loyalty to Walpole during this period and the increased dependence of the King and Queen's moods on his opinion were rapidly making him indispensable to the Prime Minister as well as to George and Caroline. In June, he agreed to accept a peerage in his own right (the title of Lord Hervey that he had held until then was only a courtesy title by virtue of being heir to the earldom of Bristol), take up a place in the House of Lords, and relinquish his seat in the Commons. Walpole needed supporters in the Upper Chamber, and knew that Hervey's seat in Bury St Edmunds was a safe one.

Lord Bristol, who had never been reconciled to Hervey's association with Walpole, wrote to him bewailing his decision to 'exchange ye important House you was a member of for so insignificant a one'; he thought Hervey was sacrificing any chance of real power by accepting being 'kicked upstairs,' but he still paid the £143 for Hervey's patent. Hervey, on the other hand, was delighted, his 'pride and vanity' fed by being singled out for such an honour. He wrote to the King to express his 'double pleasure' at the thought that his elevation would 'in some way be an acquisition Sir to you, as it will strengthen your interests in one house without weakening it in the other'.

Hervey also wrote to Charlotte Digby, Ste's sister, to thank her for her congratulations on his promotion.

You asked so kindly how things went with me, that I cannot help telling you, never better. The clouds that gathered round me last year are dispelled, though I was in so disagreeable a situation, that to justify myself (which I could have done) did not dare to speak; for *that* would have put me in the wrong, though I was not so before, and have led me into the commission of one fault whilst I was clearing myself of another.

Hervey's peerage was, in his eyes, a vindication of the disastrous events of the last year, and the pleasure he took in this mark of favour underlines the growing importance Hervey placed on political success.

Ste Fox accompanied Hervey from London to Ickworth in June 1733 for the election of Thomas Hervey to his brother's old seat in Bury St Edmunds. Despite being with Fox, Hervey chafed at being away from London, complaining of seeing nothing but aldermen, smelling nothing but tobacco, and talking of nothing but taxes. 'This delightful *rondeau*,' he told a friend, 'with all the etcetera comforts of electioning (thank God) is to finish on Sunday, when I shall return to London, in as great haste and much more willingly than I left it.'

Thanks in part to Hervey's efforts, his brother Thomas was duly elected the new Member for Bury St Edmunds. Bristol told his wife that their son had been selected by the Corporation of the town; not one man had voted against him. Several thousand towns-men attended Fox, Hervey and his father (but not the candidate, Thomas) to the Guildhall, crying, 'Long live the honest Earl of Bristol and every branch of his noble family forever.' There were Morris dancers, and the air was filled with the sound of drums, bells ringing and cheering. 'I never remember to have observed more true and cordial affection than on the present occasion, even before they had drunk ten hogsheads of strong beer,' Bristol concluded in his account of the day.

Despite Bristol's naive pride in his son's easy election, he was disappointed that Thomas had not bothered to go to Bury himself to campaign in person, and furious with his wife who had been meddling 'with Corporation affairs'. Tom, who had promised the

Queen in front of Walpole that he would attend the election, had allowed himself to be persuaded by Lady Bristol to boycott it because she disliked Colonel Norton (a relation of hers), the other MP for Bury. It was all very embarrassing for Hervey and distressing for his father, whose initial affection for his second wife had deteriorated to such a point that he had not written to her for four years despite her usual prolonged absences from Ickworth. In October, Lady Bristol wrote with typical self-centredness to tell her husband that Walpole had asked her if she was behaving any better than she had done over the election at Bury. She replied lightly – thinking Walpole was only teasing her – that she was obeying Bristol's orders not to meddle any more in elections. When the Princess Royal, overhearing their conversation, asked what they were talking about, Sir Robert replied, 'Madam, why this Lady would have her Lord ungrateful to the man [Colonel Norton] that has supported her family interest, or else there would not have been a Hervey now in [representing] Bury.'

Bristol wrote to Hervey referring to his wife as the 'Aethiop' [an archaic spelling of Ethiopian; their dark skin was thought to reflect their souls' blackness] but worrying that Hervey was not doing enough to advance his brothers at court. 'I am afraid he [Hervey] is too great a courtier to be very pressing,' thought Lady Bristol. When Hervey failed to secure a promotion for his brother Henry, Bristol warned Hervey that Lady Bristol and her 'few flatterers' would seize on this dereliction of duty to claim that Hervey 'employed your known credit at court more to promote other people than your own brethren'; the implicit meaning was, why do you promote the Foxes ahead of your own flesh and blood? To his wife, he exclaimed, 'Is Harry to remain a cornet [in the army] for ten years more? O! the gratitude of some souls.' But Hervey's brothers were a feckless lot, and he had not recommended them as highly as he did the Foxes because he did not feel he could. Hervey wrote to his brother Thomas in November reproaching him for asking such favours when he was so incapable of living up to them. 'Nor will I add anything more to this tedious letter but to remind you that all your future good or ill in public life depends on your conduct here [at court] and in Parliament. My advice I shall always be ready to give you, my assistance too if you want it, and my good wishes will always attend you.'

PART FOUR

21. Queen Caroline

In 1732 Hervey's new friend William Hogarth had painted some members of the royal family, in a large conversation piece called *A Performance of the Indian Emperor, or The Conquest of Mexico by the Spaniards*. The painting was commissioned by John Conduitt, Master of the Mint, to record a performance at his house of Dryden's play *The Indian Emperor* by his children, the young Lady Caroline Lennox (later to marry Henry Fox), and the son and daughter of the Earl of Pomfret. William Duke of Cumberland sat in a makeshift royal box with his sisters, the Princesses Mary and Louisa; the Duke and Duchess of Richmond were part of the small audience; Lady Deloraine, in her role as royal governess, was in front of the stage with her two daughters, one absorbed by the performance, the other picking up a fan for her mother. The prominent freemason Reverend Desaguliers stood beside the stage acting as prompter for the young actors.

This painting did not lead to a royal commission, even though it depicted members of the royal family; but in all likelihood, Hogarth approached Hervey in the autumn of 1734, hoping to be appointed official painter for the forthcoming wedding of the Princess Royal, Anne, to William Prince of Orange. Hervey was Master of Ceremonies for the wedding and ideally placed to promote the painter of his choice. Queen Caroline initially agreed to use Hogarth, but on the orders of the Lord Chamberlain, the Duke of Grafton – Hervey's superior and father-in-law of the Earl of Burlington, patron of Hogarth's rival William Kent – Hogarth was unceremoniously dumped.

The royal wedding was announced in May 1733 and scheduled to take place in the autumn of that year; in fact, it was delayed until March 1734 because William fell dangerously ill on his arrival in England in November 1733. Although the Prince was, as Hervey said, 'a miserable match both in the point of man and fortune',

Anne was determined to marry – and become independent – at any cost. Her choice was not between two men (there were no other eligible princes in Europe at this time), said Hervey, but between this husband and no husband: 'whether she would go to bed with this piece of deformity in Holland, or die an ancient maid immured in her royal convent at St James's'. William was very short, and physically repellent, but Anne said she was resolved, if he were a baboon, that she would still marry him. Her father responded, 'Well, then, there is baboon enough for you.'* Caroline was equally pessimistic about her future son-in-law. She complained to Hervey about his looks and he replied, 'Lord! Madam, in half a year all persons are alike. The figure of the body one's married to, like the prospect of the place one lives at, grows so familiar to one's eye, that one looks at it mechanically, without regarding either the beauties or deformities that strike a stranger.'

As this intimate conversation shows, Hervey was growing closer than ever both to the King and, especially, the Queen. He wrote to Henry Fox in January 1734, 'I cannot help bragging to you of a present the Queen made me about a fortnight ago of the finest gold snuff-box I ever saw, with all the Arts and Sciences, by her own bespeaking, carved upon it.' In June, she gave him another snuff-box, and, reported Hervey to Henry, 'I am with him or her or both all the day long. They furnish themselves so much to the conversation that it never languishes nor tires one; and I never saw them in better health, humour, or spirits in my life.'

In return, Henry chaffed Hervey about the attentions he was receiving from Caroline. 'You told me in your last I took too much snuff,' Hervey wrote. 'When I tell you the Queen has given me a very pretty horse, and that I hunt twice a week by the side of her chaise, you will say perhaps that I ride too much.' And, he added, George had ordered that his wages be doubled for as long as Hervey held the office; Hervey's successor as Vice-Chamberlain would get

---

* According to Hervey, though, the Princess was no prize herself: she had 'a lively clean look and a very fine complexion, though she was marked a good deal with the smallpox; the faults of her person were that of being very ill-made and a great propensity to fat'.

only the standard salary of £1,000 a year.* 'When I went to his Majesty to thank him for this favour, he was so gracious and so kind that he confirmed by another instance what I have often said of him, which is that, as nobody can disoblige more formidably, so nobody can oblige more agreeably.'

Hervey told Ste of these fresh honours, too. He described his new horse as the 'prettiest and agreeablest' thing ever, with 'infinite spirit, and never makes a false step – two qualities that rarely go together'. On the subject of his retainer, he was more restrained: George had 'said so many obliging things to me in his closet [private room] when he did it, that I should be in as much confusion and as much ashamed to repeat them, as I was to hear them. Praises one is conscious one does not deserve, puts one almost as much out of countenance as reproaches that one does.' But, aware of how important these honours were to his friend, Ste demanded to know exactly what the King had said. Hervey wrote again a week later to inform him fully, returning 'a thousand thanks for the kind part you always take in everything that relates to my pleasure, interest, or character'. He began by saying he hoped Ste knew that he was not repeating George's praise out of vanity, but out of obedience to his wishes. The King had told Hervey that he knew how affectionately Hervey served him, and how well; and that he was ready at any time to please him as he had on this occasion. Hervey replied that although he could say thank you he preferred to let his actions be the measure of his gratitude. 'A great many more, handsome, proper and kind things passed between us but I perceive they do not look so well as they sounded and so I shall cut my narrative short,' he concluded.

It must have been hard for Ste to hear so continually how fond his lover was of the Queen (even though their closeness was filial rather than sexual) and how much she valued his company, when her demands for Hervey meant that Ste was deprived of his company. Although Hervey's relationships with Ste and Caroline were utterly different, his closeness to the Queen can only have deepened

* There was a precedent for this type of gift: both Queen Anne and George I had paid their Vice-Chancellors annuities over and above their Treasury salaries.

the rift that was emerging between the two men, throwing into relief their dissimilarities. Caroline shared Hervey's interests in philosophy, art and literature, they were united by their fascination with the worlds of court and Commons; but Ste, living quietly in the country, could not reach Hervey on these levels.

Hervey was so close to Caroline, according to Lord Percival, that he prevented others suing for her patronage. 'Dr Courage dined with me, and told me he was on Thursday last above two hours with the Queen, but the impertinence of Lord Hervey's staying all that time in the room prevented his speaking to her as fully as he intended about his translation of Father Paul's history'; more likely Hervey had been asked to stay by the Queen in order that she would not have to hear about Father Paul's history. He was also able to recommend people to her. Dr Middleton was a Cambridge academic engaged in writing a biography of Cicero; he had recently become acquainted with Hervey and hoped to find worldly advancement through him; Hervey, in turn, enjoyed discussing ancient history with him. In September 1733 he wrote to assure Middleton that he was doing all he could for him at court. 'You may depend on my doing all the good offices I can to the future Lord Chancellor; I have lately spoken of you to the Queen who gave me leave to tell you how much she liked your letter from Italy which I made her read.'

Although Caroline was fashionably interested in modern theological and philosophical matters, like Hervey, she could also be arrogantly irreverent. One day, her chaplain, Dr Maddox, was saying the daily prayers in a room next to her bedchamber. He commented caustically on a painting there of a naked Venus – 'a very proper altarpiece is here, Madam' – so she ordered the door between the two rooms to be closed, that he might no longer be exposed to it. When the prayers stopped, however, she called out, annoyed, to ask why: 'I will not whistle the word of God through a keyhole,' came the reply.

It was perhaps this incident that inspired a scene in Hervey's vignette of court life, 'The Death of Lord Hervey; Or, a Morning at Court', (Appendix 1) written to amuse the Queen in 1736. Two parsons were saying morning prayers in the room next to the

Queen's as she dressed, and Caroline said to her Mistress of the Robes, 'I pray, my good Lady Sundon, shut a little that door: those creatures pray so loud, one cannot hear oneself speak.' Lady Sundon went to close the door. 'So, so, not quite so much,' instructed her mistress, 'leave it enough open for those parsons to think we may hear, and enough shut that we may not hear quite so much.' Dr Maddox knew who buttered his bread, though; writing from Richmond to Henry in June 1734, Hervey said he had left the King at church, 'and am afraid Maddox knows how to make his court too well to let his sermon allow me to write longer'.

The particular favour Caroline showed Hervey was a bone of contention between her and her estranged son Frederick. He interpreted everything she did for Hervey as being less for Hervey's benefit 'than to insult and outrage him [Frederick], and [thought] that it was extremely hard that a man whom the whole world knew had been so impertinent to him and whom he never spoke to should be picked out by the Queen for her constant companion and her most distinguished favourite.' He told his sisters 'that they knew he had as lief see the devil as Lord Hervey; that the Queen knew it too, and consequently he supposed kept Lord Hervey there to keep him away'. The Princesses responded that although Hervey had wronged Frederick, his crime 'was not of the sort that no repentance could wipe away the remembrance of it; and that if Lord Hervey's past conduct had deserved the Queen's anger, it must be owned too that by his behaviour ever since he had merited her forgiveness'. Hervey had behaved 'with great respect and seeming penitence ever since', Princess Caroline insisted, but the Prince, 'who never forgot an injury or remembered an obligation, was not convinced by these arguments'. Frederick continued to use Hervey's intimacy with his mother as a means to attack her.

But Hervey had, by the summer of 1734, a private cause to feel superior to Prince Frederick: he had revived his relationship with Frederick's erstwhile mistress Anne Vane. Lady Irwin had witnessed their first meeting after Hervey's letter haranguing her for turning Frederick against him: in January 1733 they met by chance at a reception. Hervey addressed her 'in the most supplicant manner'; she afforded him neither a word nor a look. But although she met

Hervey after their falling-out in 1732 'with all the haughtiness of an injured princess', gradually they became reconciled.

Seeing one another in public places and there mutually discovering that both had a mind to forget their past enmity, and renew their past endearments, till from ogling they came to messages, from messages to letters, from letters to appointments, and from appointments to all the familiarities in which they had formerly lived, both of them swearing that there had never been any interruption in the affection they bore to each other, though the effects of jealousy and rage had often made them act more like enemies than lovers.

It was not just Hervey's charm that had led Miss Vane back to his bed, but loneliness. Frederick was widely rumoured to have fathered a child by a chambermaid and was concurrently pursuing both the daughter of the Duke of Ancaster and an opera singer.

At first Hervey and Anne Vane met once or twice a week, in an 'out of the way scrub coffee-house' behind Buckingham House (the London residence of the Dowager Duchess of Buckingham, illegitimate daughter of Charles II; later Buckingham Palace). When the risk of being recognized grew greater, Miss Vane would come up to London from the house Frederick paid for in Wimbledon, and meet Hervey at her house in Grosvenor Square (also maintained by the Prince), having dismissed all the staff but one for the night. Hervey, on foot and swathed in a cloak, would approach the house; at his signal, Miss Vane would distract the servant and run downstairs to smuggle him in through a side door. Their relationship was, said Hervey, more of a risk for Anne than for him: if it was discovered she would be ruined, he merely blamed.

As well as pushing his mistress back into the arms of her former lover, Frederick was determined to assert his independence from his father. During the furore over the Excise Bill the previous year, George had offered his recalcitrant son an allowance of £80,000 a year, the control of his own household, and the choice of three princesses to marry if he would support Walpole's scheme. Frederick, advised by Dodington, refused, and maintained his support of the Commons Opposition to Walpole in defiance of his father.

But he was keen to marry, aware that if he produced a legitimate heir his father would be forced to take more notice of him politically. As it was, George barely acknowledged his eldest son. 'Whenever the Prince was in a room with the King, it put one in mind of stories one has heard of ghosts that appear to part of the company and are invisible to the rest,' said Hervey. 'In this manner, wherever the Prince stood, though the King passed him ever so often or ever so near, it always seemed as if the King thought the place the Prince filled a void space.'

The Prince of Wales's new enthusiasm for the marital state was perhaps encouraged by his sister Anne's wedding to the Prince of Orange in March. He attended the wedding beautifully and extravagantly dressed ('as you may suppose', commented Mrs Delany) and danced 'better than anybody'. Frederick's particular favourites were not the formal French dances such as the minuet, but the country dances – which resembled Scottish reeling – 'for he has a great deal of spirit'. The wedding was a success, and the new Prince and Princess of Orange were so pleased with Hervey's role in organizing it that he was sent to amuse them in Gravesend as they waited for the winds to allow them to set off for Holland in April. There, the Prince of Orange was uncouth enough to try to discuss with Hervey his disagreement with Frederick, acquainting Hervey with 'how often the Prince [Frederick] had entertained him with the recital of his Lordship's ingratitude, and bidding him [Hervey] not to be too proud of that boy [Fitzfrederick], since he [Orange] had heard from very good authority it was the child of a triumvirate, and that the Prince and Lord Harrington had full as good a title to it as himself'.

Earlier that year, Hervey had become a father for the seventh (or eighth, if young Fitzfrederick was his) time, when Lady Hervey gave birth to Emily Carolina Nassau on 24 January. It had been a difficult birth; a month before the little girl was born Molly had taken to her bed, preventing Hervey from going to Goodwood to stay with the Richmonds and Ste as he wished. 'Lady Hervey, without being in direct labour, having been these four or five days enough in pain to apprehend it any moment and keep her room, has desired me not to leave her; which I, like a good husband, as in duty bound, have complied with,' Hervey wrote to Richmond on 27 December 1733. Lady Hervey might have been disappointed to think that it was duty and not love that had kept her husband by her side while she lay in agony. For all her suffering, Hervey was disappointed by the child. 'Lady Hervey is brought to bed of a nasty, shabby girl,' he told Henry Fox in February. She was baptized by Hervey's friend Bishop Hoadley, and her godparents were the Princesses Emily and Caroline, and the Prince of Orange. As Hervey's star rose, he chose progressively grander godparents for his children; but, as with his wife, he seems to have seen them as little more than social accessories. They are mentioned in his correspondence as rarely as his wife, and always with the same wry cynicism he used to refer to Molly. Hervey was not a good husband or a fond father; he had inherited neither uxorious nor paternal instincts from Lord Bristol.

Apart from the Queen, Princess Caroline was Hervey's closest ally within the royal family. The Princess Royal had used to confide in Hervey her dislike of her father's disrespectful attitude to her mother and his ridiculous affectations of heroism, but she had left the court for Holland that spring with her ape-like husband the Prince of Orange. Hervey was estranged from Frederick. Princess Emily, rumoured to have had affairs with both the Duke of Grafton and the Duke of Newcastle, wavered between her brother and her mother and so neither considered her loyal. The only one of the grown-up royal progeny left to Hervey was Princess Caroline. She was a plain, sensible, pious girl, marked, said Hervey, by 'affability without meanness, dignity without pride, cheerfulness without levity, and prudence without falsehood'. Although she may have been a little dull, she and Hervey were united by their love for the Queen, and she adored Hervey's flamboyance; it was said that she never married because of her fruitless love for her mother's favourite. Horace Walpole reported that she was so overwhelmed by Hervey's death that afterwards she refused to appear in public, preferring to live in retirement in St James's Palace. For the rest of her life she devoted herself to looking after the interests of Hervey's children.

By the summer of 1734, Hervey said, he was 'in greater favour with the Queen, and consequently with the King, than ever'.

Queen Caroline petted and fussed over him, calling him her 'child, her pupil and her charge'; she loved his cheekiness and candour. He was her sounding-board and adviser, as well as her dearest friend. 'If your Majesty was never to be told what would be urged in objection to any measure you had a mind to take, how could you be provided with answers to such objections?' he asked her when they disagreed on policy, all the while emphasizing that 'in my situation it is impossible for me to have any interest separate from that of your Majesty and your family'. It was clear to her that he genuinely loved and admired her, and that the 'prodigious court' he paid her sprang from affection as well as self-interest. She in turn said that he only dared to contradict her because he knew she could not live without him.

'It is well I am so old, or I should be talked of for this creature,' she would say, but it was clear to everyone that their relationship was platonic. Hervey replaced the son who had turned against her, and Caroline filled the role Lady Bristol no longer played in Hervey's life. Caroline confessed to Hervey in tears that Frederick's old tutor believed Fretz (as she called him) had 'the most vicious nature and the most false that ever man had, nor are his vices the vices of a gentleman, but the mean base tricks of a knavish footman'. Still, Hervey advocated reconciliation between the Prince and his parents. Although in his *Memoirs* he acknowledged that this policy might make him appear two-faced, he said that he did it simply because if peace was ever made between them and he had not encouraged it thereafter he would be distrusted by everyone involved.

22. Favour

As a staunch Whig whose personal success was a result of his support for the Hanoverian succession, Lord Bristol believed that his son's role as an aristocrat lay in service to the monarchy, and never resented the amount of time Hervey spent at court with his royal master and mistress. But Bristol suspected Walpole's commitment to Hervey's political career. As Hervey said in his *Memoirs*, Walpole always feared that if he turned his back, someone would be working to try to bring him down. 'And how, indeed, could it ever be otherwise? For, as he was unwilling to employ anybody under him, or let anybody approach the King and Queen who had any understanding, lest they should employ it against him, so, from fear of having dangerous friends, he never had any useful ones.' What did this make Hervey, then: useless, or dangerous? It was a question that must have consumed Hervey as it began to grow apparent that Walpole had no intention of promoting him.

His father thought little of the trappings of Hervey's success.

Are there not opiates to be administered for quieting ambition, as well as bark for putting off fits of fevers? And if baubles and bagatelles are found to have a sufficient lulling effect, do you imagine solid benefits are really intended for you? And if any lately have been so, hath not ye mortifying disappointment in Norfolk [the General Election] in some measure spoiled your friend's humour as well as power to serve you?

The Earl thought Walpole, weakened by his struggle over the Excise Scheme and his resources spent by the election, no longer had the power to promote Hervey's interests; and he worried too that his son was growing content with sops to his vanity instead of real power.

The bitter battle Walpole had been fighting for the past year over excise culminated in May 1734 with the General Election.

This election was a crucial one: if Walpole lost too much ground in the Commons he would be forced to resign, and his power-base was as weak as it had yet been because of his determination to pass the unpopular Excise Bill. Hervey and his friends had been working on Walpole's behalf since the previous year. The Duke of Richmond wrote to tell Ste Fox he had been campaigning hard. He had given a ball trying to get the attending women – 'some of them excessive pretty. I believe I kissed fifty women fifty times each' – to influence their husband's votes. He was also travelling round his area of influence in Suffolk, counting the safe seats and encouraging the electorate to vote for the men he supported.

This letter shows Ste through the eyes of someone other than Hervey. Richmond apologized for not answering Ste's letter earlier, but 'in what county, or how to direct to Maddington [Ste's shooting box on Salisbury Plain], may I be damned if I know'; he had had to get Lady Hervey to ask her husband for the address. He was glad, he said, that Ste's campaigning in Shaftesbury was going so well. 'I heartily join in their [the electors'] cry, "A Fox for ever", I don't mean it as a pun, though I *excessively love Foxes*; but without a pun I *entirely* love dear Ste Fox and wish him happiness and success in everything he undertakes.' Ste was known universally as a man of charm and sweetness; every surviving reference to him, like this one, creates a picture of easy good nature and popularity.

Hervey was doing his bit to bring in MPs who favoured the existing government, too. He wrote to Dean Butts of Norwich in October 1733 on behalf of a local candidate, Mr Townshend, 'who desires me to solicit you to procure him as many votes at Cambridge as you can for the next election'. On the same day, Hervey wrote to Dr Middleton, concluding, 'for my sake do Mr Townshend all the service you can, in Cambridge against his next election'.

As the election grew closer, Sir Robert's political credibility was revived by his recent successes in foreign policy: peace had been established in Europe early in 1734, saving Britain 'from all the calamities of war'. Among the government supporters, Hervey, Ste and Richmond had been campaigning busily for nearly a year on Walpole's behalf. Between 11 March and 8 June, 2,050 copies of the *London Journal* were issued by the government, which also subsidized the *Free Briton* and the *Daily Courant*, printed by Sir Robert's brother Horatio Walpole, in a massive propaganda campaign designed to counteract the negative effects of popular Opposition pamphlets and newspapers such as the *Craftsman*. The combined efforts and money of Walpole and Newcastle carried the day in the end, but with a much smaller majority than he had in the last Parliament.

Henry Fox's view of politics was corrupt even for his age but his career serves to demonstrate the eighteenth-century attitude to office and patronage. Like Hervey he was tutored by Walpole in his political apprenticeship. Sarah Duchess of Marlborough wrote to Fox in 1730, as he embarked on his career, returning five guineas he had given to her servants as a tip with a note saying, 'If I were a first minister [as Prime Ministers were referred to before the position was made official], perhaps I might have other sort of notions': the implication was that ministers welcomed bribes. He rose to become Secretary of State and Leader of the Commons in the 1750s and 1760s. Henry Fox's government colleague, the Earl of Lansdowne, described Fox's attitude to politics as, 'I give you so much, and you shall give me in return, and so we'll defy the world and sing Tol de Rol.' Fox 'refused to conceal the fact that he regarded office as the sole object of politics and corruption as the only means to obtain it'. As the historian J. H. Plumb wrote, political patronage 'scarcely bothered to wear a fig-leaf' in the eighteenth century.

The electorate was small and strongly influenced by private interest: Ste Fox, for instance, stood in Shaftesbury (near Redlynch) with the support of the Earl of Shaftesbury. When in 1737 Hervey was trying to procure a barony for Ste Fox, Horatio Walpole told him that George gave honours as reluctantly as he gave cash. Hervey replied that he would ensure, 'if the King is afraid of losing a vote in the House of Commons that Mr Fox shall for nothing [i.e., no payment] bring in anybody you will name in his room [seat] at Shaftesbury'. Paying for votes was not uncommon: Bristol was delighted when his son Thomas was elected member for Bury in 1733 because 'all this unanimity [was] brought about by personal family credit and confidence without one penny given or promised, nay not expected'. Declaration of candidacy was informal, as were

1. William Hogarth: *Lord Hervey and his Friends* (National Trust Photographic Library/John Hammond)

2. Edmé Boucharchon: *Bust of John, Lord Hervey*
(National Trust Photographic Library/James Austin)

3. Enoch Seeman: *Portrait of Stephen Fox* (Private Collection)

4.(*Above*) George Knapton: *Molly Lepell, Lady Hervey* (National Trust Photographic Library/Christopher Hurst)

5.(*Left*) Antonio David: *Portrait of Henry Fox* (Private Collection)

6.(*Above*) Jean–Baptiste
Vanmour: *Lady Mary Wortley
Montagu with her son and
attendants* (National Portrait
Gallery, London)

7.(*Right*) Jonathan
Richardson: *Portrait of
Alexander Pope* (National
Portrait Gallery, London)

9. Thomas Hudson: *Portrait of George II*
(National Portrait Gallery, London)

8. Charles Jervas studio: *Portrait of
Caroline of Brandenburg-Ansbach*
(National Portrait Gallery, London)

11. John Wooton: *Portrait of Sir Robert Walpole as Master of the King's Staghounds in Windsor Forest* (Bridgeman Art Library/Private Collection)

10. Godfrey Kneller: *Portrait of William Pulteney* (National Portrait Gallery, London)

12. Jacopo Amigoni: *Portrait of Frederick, Prince of Wales* (The Royal Collection © 2000, Her Majesty Queen Elizabeth II)

13. Jean-Étienne Liotard: *Portrait of Francesco Algarotti* (Rijksmuseum, Amsterdam)

procedures for registering voters. At the start of his career in 1728, Henry Fox lost a parliamentary by-election at Old Sarum. Thomas Winnington related the story to him: 'It was your fortune to lose the election by one vote only, for [Thomas] Pitt, not suspecting any opposition, had but two voters there except the person who voted for you.' In this environment, the force of character of a man like Walpole counted for a lot; and despite his losses, he was able to retain his place in 1734.

But Walpole's victory was by no means a foregone conclusion. The King and Queen waited for the results of the 1734 General Election at court while Walpole had retreated to Norfolk; Hervey, knowing they needed the reassurance of Sir Robert's presence, anonymously sent to Houghton a quotation from Dryden's *All for Love*:

> Whilst in her arms at Capua he lay,
> The world fell mouldering from his hand each hour.

Walpole recognized his friend's handwriting, understood the allusion, and rushed back to London to assuage his patrons' fears.

Walpole's success enabled him to consolidate the changes he had made to his ministry immediately after the furore over the excise scheme the year before. One of the casualties was Lord Chesterfield, who had been dismissed from government in April 1733 because he refused to support Walpole's stance on the excise. After the election, he was humiliatingly removed from his court post as Lord Steward of the Household when, all unawares, he was stopped by an attendant from entering the Presence Chamber at St James's Palace and handed a summons demanding the white staff of his office.

Barred by his disloyalty to Walpole from a political career as long as Walpole was pre-eminent, Chesterfield turned his attentions to the Prince of Wales. Over the autumn of 1734 he replaced George Bubb Dodington as Frederick's adviser and confidant, just as Dodington had replaced Hervey two years earlier; Dodington, said Hervey, retired to the country 'as much unpitied in his disgrace as unenvied in his prosperity'. Dodington was a neighbour of the

Foxes' in Somerset, and Lord Lieutenant of the county. He was very rich – a valuable asset in the eyes of Frederick whose allowance depended on his father's discretion and was a constant source of conflict between them – but, said Lord Percival, Dodington was also the 'vilest man, vain, ambitious, loose and never satisfied . . . He wants to be a lord, and, when he is that, he will want to be a duke.' His attachment to Frederick had been based on ambition rather than affection; he hoped that when Frederick was King he would be rewarded for his years of loyal service. The two men deserved each other. Hervey records Frederick gloating to his treasurer that he had paid for his London residence, Carlton House, in Pall Mall, with £6,000 of Dodington's money. 'With all his parts I have wheedled him out of a sum of money for the payment of which he has no security if I die, and which, God knows, he may wait long enough for if I live.'

'This is a subject I cannot explain or expiate upon; nor is it enough of a secret for you not to know what I mean, though it is too delicate to admit of a farther disquisition,' Hervey told Henry Fox on 15 August.

Lord Chesterfield is said to have laid the corner stone of the building, whilst Mr Dodington contents himself with the care of the offices and the attic, when the other has had the sole direction of the principal storey. Adieu, my dear Count [Fox's nickname]. If I could write to you with the same safety that I flatter myself I can speak to you, my pen would be as flippant in your absence as you always find my tongue in your presence.

Recent events meant that Hervey could not write as openly on this subject to Henry as he would have liked. 'I am grown more cautious than ever about letters, and never send anything even in an anonymous manuscript that I would not print [publish] with my name.' In December, though, he reported that Frederick had changed the locks of the doors of Carlton House to which Dodington had keys.

Dodington was not the only royal favourite to fall from favour at this time. Molly Hervey's old friend, Mrs Howard (or Lady Suffolk; her husband had succeeded to the title in 1731), George's mistress for nearly twenty years, had finally grown tired of life at court and asked the Queen to allow her to leave her service. Her brutal drunkard of a husband – from whom her connection to the King had protected her – had died the previous September, and for the first time in her life she was financially and legally independent. By the autumn of 1734, the King had stopped visiting her chambers every evening as he used to do, because her friendships with men like Lord Chesterfield and the poets Swift, Gay and Pope, of whose politics he disapproved, made her company distasteful to him. All he addressed to her in the months before she left court, according to Hervey, were 'only some slight common Drawing-room questions'.

George had never really appreciated his mistress. According to Hervey, Lady Suffolk was a woman with 'a good head and a good heart, but had to do with a man who was incapable of tasting the one or valuing the other'. She was a cool, calm woman, whose slight deafness can only have been an advantage in her relationship with the garrulous monarch. George, who loved his wife but believed a King ought to keep a mistress as a mark of his masculinity, had taken Mrs Howard up soon after his arrival in England having been refused by his wife's Maid of Honour, Mary Bellenden. Mary was very beautiful, but poor – 'Oh Gad,' she wrote to Mrs Howard in 1720, 'I am sick of bills . . . I paid one this morning as long as my arm and as broad as my —[ass]' – and George, as he courted her, used to sit beside her counting out the money in his purse. One day, she cried out, 'Sir, I cannot bear it; if you count your money any more I will go out of the room.' George persisted, perhaps thinking that his plan was working if he was able to produce so spirited a response, until finally Mary lost her temper, knocked the purse out of his hands, and ran from the room as the coins skittered across the floor.

Court gossip, as related by Hervey, doubted whether the King had any commerce with Mrs Howard 'that he might not have had with his daughter', but he visited her apartments each evening to keep up appearances. Horace Walpole agreed with Hervey.

The King, though very amorous, was certainly more attracted by a silly idea he had entertained of gallantry being becoming, than by a love of variety; and he added the more egregious folly of fancying that his inconstancy proved he was not governed; but so awkwardly did he manage that artifice, that it but demonstrated more clearly the influence of the Queen.

It was clear to everybody except George that the 'invisible reins' Robert Walpole told Hervey the King could only be led by were held firmly in his wife's hands:

> You may strut, dapper George, but 'twill all be in vain;
> We know 'tis Queen Caroline, not you, that reign –

The Queen, knowing the vanity of her husband's temper, and that he must have some woman for the world to believe he lay with, wisely suffered one to remain in that situation whom she despised and had got the better of, for fear of making room for a successor whom he might really love, and that might get the better of her,

wrote Hervey. But she need not have worried; despite his infidelity, George worshipped his wife. Lady Suffolk remembered in old age, '[Once] the King coming into the room while the Queen was dressing, has snatched off her handkerchief, and turning rudely to Mrs Howard [Lady Suffolk], has cried, "Because you have an ugly neck yourself, you hide the Queen's!"'

Although Hervey said it seemed impossible that Lady Suffolk could have said to the Queen, 'Your husband ill-used me, therefore I am leaving court,' it appears that is what happened. Caroline tried to persuade Lady Suffolk to stay, she told Hervey afterwards.

My good Lady Suffolk, you are the best servant in the world, and, as I should be very sorry to lose you, pray take a week to consider of this business, and give me your word not to read any romances in that time, and then I dare say you will lay aside all thought of doing what, believe me, you will repent, and what I am very sure I shall be sorry for,

she said when Lady Suffolk spoke to her of resigning her position. It was perhaps the attitude of her royal mistress that made Lady

Suffolk determined to leave her service as soon as her future independence was assured.

Caroline had never been able to conceal her hatred for Lady Suffolk, although she had suffered her presence at court in the knowledge that another mistress might have more influence over her impressionable husband – influence that might detract from her own power. For years the Queen had insulted Lady Suffolk behind a mask of genial condescension, calling her 'Sister Howard'. When she was an old woman, Lady Suffolk told Horace Walpole that Caroline had 'delighted in subjecting her to such servile offices [as kneeling before her to hold up a basin of water, and doing her hair; most ladies of gentle blood in the Queen's household performed other, less menial, tasks], though always apologizing to *her good Howard*'.

But George, on hearing of his wife's interference in this matter, angrily asked her why she would not allow him to abandon his mistress. 'I do not know why you will not let me part with a deaf old woman, of whom I am weary.' And so Lady Suffolk left court without stopping to take her leave of the man who had been her lover for nearly two decades. By the following January, as Hervey told Henry Fox, it was as if she had never been there. 'I expected when I came to town to hear a great deal about Lady Suffolk; but they talk of her no more than if she did not exist, or than if she had never existed. One might as well ask questions about Henry II and Fair Rosamund; it would hardly seem a story more out of date.' In 1735 she quietly married George Berkely. No one understood the match, according to Hervey, as they were neither of them young, handsome, healthy or rich, but it was nevertheless a success and presumably a welcome relief after the long years with George – never an easy man as even his daughters acknowledged. 'I wish, with all my heart, he would take somebody else, that Mamma might be a little relieved from the ennui of seeing him forever in her room,' said the Princess Royal after Lady Suffolk's departure from court.

23. Lord Fanny

In January 1733, the poet Alexander Pope published the 'Use of Riches'. Hervey wrote to Henry Fox that Pope's personal attacks in it were so abusive and so pointed 'that it is very probable some of those to whom he pretends to teach the proper use of riches may teach him the proper use of cudgels'. Hervey was bound to think thus of Pope (although he had not been mentioned) because a year before, Pope's first translation of Horace had been published in the *London Evening Post*, with a vicious inscription naming Hervey and describing him in the most sinister terms: 'The man who backbites an absent friend; who fails to defend him when another finds fault; the man who courts the loud laughter of others, and the reputation of a wit; who can invent what he never saw; who cannot keep a secret – that man is black of heart.' But Hervey's views on Pope's latest effort were not pure pique; his reaction to Pope's 'Epistle to Burlington', published in December 1731 (before Pope had attacked him personally) had been similar: everybody agreed, he told Ste, that it was 'dull and impertinent'.

Pope and Hervey had been friends of a sort when they were part of the same group of glamorous young courtiers in the late 1710s and early 1720s. The first sign that they may not have liked one another, or may have fallen out, came after Hervey's marriage to Molly, of whom Pope was fond. The poet accused her of a new insincerity, which he credited to her husband, but which may have been more a manifestation of his own insecurity. But there was another reason Pope hated Hervey.

Pope had harboured a grand passion for Lady Mary Wortley Montagu during the halcyon days at court in the 1710s. In 1716, when she lived with her husband, then ambassador to Turkey, Pope admitted that his feelings for her 'are indeed so warm, that I fear they can proceed from nothing but what I can't very decently own to you, much less to any other'. In 1719 he commissioned her portrait by Sir Godfrey Kneller and wrote a poem in praise of it and her:

> So would I draw (but oh, 'tis vain to try
> My narrow Genius does the power deny)
> The Equal Lustre of the Heavenly Mind
> Where every Grace with every Virtue's joined
> Learning not vain, and Wisdom not severe
> With Greatness easy, and with Wit sincere.
> With Just Description show the Soul Divine
> And the whole Princess in my Work should shine.

Lady Mary and Pope revived their friendship on her return from the Middle East in 1718 but some years later, for a reason neither would explain, they fell out. In almost every poem he wrote after this time it is clear that he felt both betrayed and humiliated by the woman he had once adored. Pope attacked Lady Mary for her excess of cleverness, her reputed lasciviousness, her once-beautiful, now pock-marked, face (it was said at the end of her life that she would not look at herself in a glass because the scars were so disfiguring), her slatternliness and her closeness with money. Lady Mary hinted years afterwards that Pope had tried to make love to her and she had affronted his pride by laughing at him, despite her gravest attempts to keep a straight face; Pope never commented on the incident. He may have felt threatened by Lady Mary's poetic talents, and resented her – a mere woman – for competing with him on his own terms: the insecure poet might have forgiven her for rejecting him romantically, but never for trying to write as well as him.

Hervey, whom Pope knew to be Lady Mary's confidant and suspected of knowing – and ridiculing – Pope's failed attempt to win her, was associated with her by Pope in his humiliation, and punished by him for this perceived complicity; this incident, surely, is the basis for his 1731 attack on Hervey in the *London Evening Post*. But Pope hated Hervey for a variety of other reasons as well: his physical beauty; his apparent political, social and romantic success; above all, for the apparent surety of his self-belief. Pope, by contrast, was hampered by disabilities. As a Catholic and the son of a linen-draper made good, Pope's background precluded his becoming part of the aristocratic Whig establishment he looked towards; and he resented the higher taxes and prohibitions on travel and land ownership imposed on his co-religionists. 'I cannot consider that country mine where I am not allowed to call a foot of ground my own,' he once said. He was also frustrated by his invalid body, and incapable of doing anything – from dressing to bathing to travelling – without constant attendance. He was so weak he had to wear a stiff canvas corset to hold himself upright, and so sensitive to cold that he always wore a flannel waistcoat and fur doublet; he wore three pairs of stockings to give his legs the illusion of bulk. But his weakness also allowed him to live an indulged, pampered life, and he was not above playing on his disabilities to achieve his ends; as Johnson said of him, 'he hardly drank tea without a stratagem'.

Pope liked to portray himself as being above politics, but he supported Lord Bolingbroke and Frederick's Opposition increasingly openly over the 1730s. He professed to despise courts – later using Hervey to exemplify the vices he believed were bred in them –

> . . . quickly bear me hence
> To wholesome Solitude, the nurse of Sense:
> Where Contemplation prunes her ruffled Wings,
> And the free Soul looks down to pity Kings.

but he remained in awe of their noble inhabitants. He was always saying, according to Johnson, ' "I do not value you for being a Lord," which was a sure sign that he did'. He made much of his refusal to accept a pension from a patron; but he did not need to, having made £9,000 from his translation of the *Iliad* alone:

> But (thanks to Homer) since I live and thrive,
> Indebted to no Peer or Prince alive.

In February 1733, Hervey sent Henry Fox Pope's latest work, 'An Imitation of the First Satire of the Second Book of Horace'.

He did not give his opinion of the piece, 'because I am determined to indulge my vanity so far as to believe it would hinder my having your opinion without prejudice; and that either from your particular partiality to me, or your general propensity to contradiction, you would certainly be warped one way or the other'. What he thought, however, would have been clear to his old friend. The opening lines read,

> There are (I scarce think it, but am told)
> Those to whom my Satire seems too bold,
> Scarce to wise Peter complaisant enough,
> And something said of Chartes [the Duke of Charteris]
>   much too rough.
> The Lines are weak, another's pleased to say,
> Lord Fanny spins a thousand such a Day.

This was Pope's first use of 'Lord Fanny', the name with which he was to immortalize Hervey. It was innocently derived, he claimed, from Horace's rival, the Roman poet Fannius; changing it from Fannius to the feminine form Fanny just made it suit the feminine Hervey better.*

Lady Mary was also mentioned, as Sappho:†

> From furious Sappho scarce a milder Fate,
> P-xed by her Love, or libelled by her Hate:

Her resultant fury was unsurprising. She wrote to Pope's friend Lord Peterborough demanding that he get the offending couplet removed from subsequent editions of the poem. Peterborough's

---

* According to the OED it was not until the nineteenth century that the word 'fanny' began being used to mean vagina.

† Sappho was a common cypher for a woman of letters, and an apt name for Lady Mary, whose versifying was well known. The lesbian connotations now associated with the name did not then exist, and Lady Mary did not have a reputation for lesbianism – although Pope may have been happy to suspect her of it as she had turned him down. For more on Lady Mary, see Isobel Grundy's definitive *Lady Mary Wortley Montagu, Comet of the Enlightenment*, Oxford, 1999.

reply only compounded her sense of injury; he said that he could do nothing to help as Pope was intransigent in his assertion that she ought to take no offence.

He said to me what I have taken the liberty to say to you, that he wondered how the town [London Society] could apply those lines to any but some noted common woman [prostitute], that he should be yet more surprised if you should take them to yourself, he named to me four remarkable poetesses and scribblers, Mrs Centilivre, Mrs Haywood, Mrs Manly and Mrs Behn, ladies famous indeed in their generation, and some of them esteemed to have given very unfortunate favours to their friends, assuring me that such only were the objects of his satire.

So Lady Mary took matters into her own hands. With Hervey's assistance, she wrote a poem attacking Pope entitled 'Verses to an Imitator of the First Satire of the Second Book of Horace'. Because she knew Pope so well, Lady Mary was able to strike at him where he was most vulnerable. Well aware of his insecurities about what he called his 'little, tender, and crazy carcass', almost in his own words she attributed 'the universal rancour of thy soul' to 'that wretched little carcass you retain':

> It was the Equity of righteous Heav'n,
> That such a Soul to such a Form was giv'n;
> And shows the uniformity of Fate,
> That one so odious, should be born to hate.

Pope vented his rage indiscriminately, she said – 'to thee 'tis Provocation to exist' – and could not be softened by love or beauty.

> But how should'st thou by Beauty's Force be mov'd,
> No more for loving made, than to be lov'd?

The poem came out anonymously, with the superscription 'by a Lady'. Hervey, who had dealt with publishers before because of his pamphlet-writing, probably arranged for its publication, although there is a theory that Pope saw it in manuscript and had

it published to shame Lady Mary. Although arguments have been
made for Hervey's authorship, the style is Lady Mary's – she was a
much better poet than Hervey for all his pride in his own skills,
which perhaps is why Pope's comments on his spinning a thousand
lines a day so rankled – and there is no reason to suppose that, if he
had been responsible for it, Hervey would have pretended that he
was not. Besides, the insult Lady Mary had suffered was much
graver than that aimed at Hervey. He would have to wait another
two years to bear the full brunt of Pope's venom; although when
he did, it was in part his own fault.

On 20 October 1733 Hervey sent a poem mocking Pope, which
he had written 'to entertain the Richmond-Caravan' that August
to Henry Fox. It was a long verse letter written from Hervey
ostensibly to Sherwin, entitled 'An Epistle to a Doctor of Divinity
from a Nobleman at Hampton Court'. It was common for verses
like this to be circulated in manuscript form, as Hervey himself did
by sending this to Fox (and as had happened with the character of
Sherwin; see p. 150); but Hervey had not anticipated that the
'Epistle' would be published without his knowledge or permission,
as it was the following month. 'I send you enclosed some verses,
which you have already seen in manuscript, and which were printed
without my knowledge,' he wrote to Ste in December.

Despite Hervey's defence of the verses to Pope's friend (and
Hervey's doctor before he went to Dr Cheyne), Dr Arbuthnot –
that Pope 'was a rascal, had begun with me, and deserved it; and
that my only reason for being sorry the verses were printed, which
I did not design they should be, was because I thought it below me
to enter into a paper war with one that has made himself by his late
works as contemptible as he was odious,' – it was as unwise to
attack Pope on paper as it was to make fun of Lord Chesterfield to
his face. Charles Hanbury Williams, a friend of Hervey's at this
time, questioned Hervey's public response to Pope's satire. 'Would
a prudent man choose to engage Mr Pope? His English may not be
grammar, but 'tis intelligible, and his abuse may not be true, but
'tis very lasting.' The King was more blunt: 'My Lord Hervey, you
ought not to write verses; it is beneath your rank: leave such work
to little Mr Pope.' But Hervey could not resist retaliating; he may

not have intended that the 'Epistle' be published but one cannot help feeling he was secretly pleased it had been.

The poem began with Hervey lightly describing how he had given up his academic aspirations when his brother died and he became heir to the earldom, because learning and land-owning were incompatible.

> The very moment therefore I grew great,
> The lazy titled Heir to an Estate,
> For fear my Education might bely,
> By some mean Badge of Sense, my Quality;
> That to good Blood, by old prescriptive Rules,
> Gives Right hereditary to be Fools.

Hervey's implication was that he could have been a scholar, like Pope, but his breeding and the attendant duties it imposed on him had prevented him following this path except as an amateur. Courtiers and nobles, he said, were not so dissimilar to Pope:

> Like you, we lounge, & feast, & play, & chatter,
> In private satirize, in Public flatter.

To Pope, who minded not being of noble blood, this would have been a bitter pill – aggravated by the belittling declaration that Pope's poetry was no more than spite, imitation and envy.

> Such Wits are naught but glittering Ignorance:
> What Monkeys are to Men, they are to Sense;
> Imperfect Mimics, ludicrous and mean,
> Who often bite that Fool they entertain.
> Their Tricks may please, their Quickness may surprise;
> At first we wonder, but at last despise.

Pope, Hervey said, 'with hackney Maxims, in dogmatic strain', trotted out the same old accusations against the same old enemies, celebrating only himself, and repeating:

That Life itself is like a wrangling Game,
Where some for Interest play, and some for Fame;
Whilst ev'ry Gamester at this Board we meet,
Must either be the Bubble [dupe] or the Cheat.
And when the Catalogue he has run o'er,
And emptied of whipt Cream his frothy Store,
Thinks he's so wise no Solomon knows more.

There was a flurry of journalistic activity after the publication of
the 'Epistle' which Hervey was half-appalled and half-delighted by.
'The advertisement you saw was, I fear, for the publication of
genuine things; and all the trouble and bustle I have had to prevent
them coming out, I shall adjourn the recital of till I see you. Pope
is in a most violent fury; and *j'en suis ravi* [I am thrilled],' he wrote
to Ste. In his more detailed account of the events surrounding the
publication of the 'Epistle', written to Henry Fox in February 1734,
Hervey said he had been the load 'of every press, and the song of
every hawker for these last six weeks'. With endearing disin-
genuousness he sent all the pamphlets, those favouring Pope as well
as himself, to Henry in Europe. 'The best things that have been
written against me (though God knows, without prejudice, bad is
the best) I will send you by the next post.' One of the verses he
sent was the following, the only one written by Pope himself, 'To
Lord Hervey and Lady Mary Wortley':

When I call but a flagrant Whore unsound,
  Or have a Pimp or Flatterer in the Wind,
Sappho enraged cries out your Back is round,
  Adonis screams – Ah! Foe to all Mankind!

Thanks, dirty Pair! You teach me what to say,
  When you attack my Morals, Sense, or Truth.
I answer thus, – poor Sappho you grow grey,
  And sweet Adonis, you have lost a Tooth.

Hervey was sanguine about being so attacked. 'A rotten egg more
or less, after so many being thrown, was of no consequence to me,'

he told Henry Fox. Pamphlets, as he said in his *Memoirs*, only 'smart without wounding, and hurt without being dangerous'.

Someone writing for Pope (or Pope himself) quickly published a verse response to the 'Epistle to a Doctor of Divinity' called 'Epistle to a Nobleman', in which the author threw Hervey's insults back at him – 'change but a few words and you'll find it is your own' – and taunted him for being a lesser poet than Lady Mary, despite the advantages his sex ought to have bestowed.

> Sure Nature slept, or else had tippling been,
> And so mistook the mould she cast you in;
> Your Shape, your Countenance, your Hands, your Mind,
> Show for the Toilet you had been designed:
> This from your female Gestures does appear;
> You'll answer, that your Heart is void of Fear,
> From thence conclude that I am in the wrong,
> For Cowardice to women does belong.
> There's a moot point, for Sappho can indite,
> And on occasion Sappho too can fight;
> You fought a Duel, but you cannot write.

Pope's own first reaction to the 'Epistle to a Doctor of Divinity' was a long letter addressed to Hervey called 'A Letter to a Noble Lord' (Appendix 2), which painted the picture of Hervey, the vicious, spiteful courtier, lashing out, without provocation, against the injured innocent, Pope, who lived his quiet, respectable life far from the corruptions of court.

I never heard of the least displeasure you had conceived against me, till I was told that an imitation I had made of Horace had offended some persons, and among them your Lordship. I could not have apprehended that a few general strokes about a Lord scribbling carelessly, a pimp, or a spy at court, a sharper in a gilded chariot, &c. that these, I say, should ever be applied as they have been, by any malice but that which is the greatest in the world, the malice of ill people to themselves.

The 'Letter' was littered with veiled references to the duel Hervey had fought two years before, barbed remarks about his sexuality, as well as unfounded imputations on the friendship between Hervey and Lady Mary, and a detailed and venomous critique of the 'Epistle' to a Doctor of Divinity.

This bitter work of self-defence was not published until 1751, long after Hervey's and Pope's deaths, because the Prime Minister stepped in to protect his friend. Walpole, aided by his brother Horatio, ambassador at The Hague, obtained from Cardinal Fleury, the principal minister in France, the promise of an abbey for Pope's friend Thomas Southcote; in return for this favour, the 'Letter' was suppressed. Judging from his explanation of the situation to Henry Fox, Hervey did not know that Sir Robert Walpole had intervened on his behalf. 'Pope has not written one word but a manuscript in prose never printed, which he had shown to several of his friends, but which I have never seen, and which, I have heard from those who did see it is very low and poor, ridiculing only my person, and my being vain of over-rated parts and the undeserved favour of a court.'

24. Cork Street

Late in November 1733 Ste wrote to Hervey voicing concern that he was ill-suited to London life, and – more importantly – to being Hervey's companion there. 'I must ask you what you mean by talking to me of your living alone till you apprehended your being unfit for my company in London,' Hervey replied, assuring him that 'I should like you rusty, better than any other body polished'. But Ste was right to be insecure, because Hervey's new preoccupations – his paper war with Pope, his service to Walpole, his growing affection for the Queen – meant that he could take less and less time away from court to be with Ste at Redlynch. Even when Ste was in London, Hervey neglected him.

It is possible too that Ste was beginning to chafe at his attachment to Hervey, and was complaining that he was not fit for Hervey's company because he did not wish to be so closely associated with him. The pair had met when Fox was twenty-three, a young man fresh from the Grand Tour in Europe, sheltered by his wholesome life in Somerset. Perhaps because of the early loss of his parents, Ste had responded easily to the devotion Hervey showed him. Hervey, the worldly, educated man, had taken the *naif* under his wing.

Now, aged nearly thirty, Ste was a man, and he wanted his independence. He would no longer drop everything to rush up to town at Hervey's behest. 'I am sorry to hear my dear Ste, that your journey hither is put off a fortnight longer than you once designed,' Hervey wrote late in 1733. 'How can you prefer making your constituents drunk, to making your friends happy; and stay loitering at Hindon or Shaftesbury, whilst I am wishing for you in town?' Even when he did come to London Ste remained aloof, as Hervey indignantly reported to their friend the Duke of Richmond a few days later.

Ste is come to town, but so fine a gentleman, that when I asked him to accompany me to Goodwood, I found it was as impossible to get a direct answer from him, as it would have been to get a direct answer from his Grace of Newcastle [Hervey's enemy, the self-important Secretary of State for Foreign Affairs], if I had asked him anything relating to the present state of Europe.

From January 1734, the two men were together in London for several months, both working for Sir Robert Walpole's re-election. At the opening of Parliament, Ste moved the address in the House of Commons, and Hervey in the House of Lords. 'Your brother and I (as fame reports, and friends and foes allow) behaved well,' Hervey told Henry Fox. 'I hope you will like the Lords' Address [which he enclosed], because every word of it is my own. The King told me in the most obliging manner that it was the best he had ever seen, but that my having said too much of him in it, was the reason he could not say so much upon it as he would to me.'

Henry, who was fond of Molly Hervey, wrote back urging Hervey to be more uxorious – but to little avail. 'One thing that has contributed to my obedience to you is my being a good husband, and coming from Kensington [where the court was] to this place [St James's Palace, where Hervey's permanent apartments were, and where Molly stayed when she was in London] to nurse Lady Hervey, who miscarried last night,' he wrote. '[But] rather than let her inflict herself on me, I chose to force myself on you [by letter].' Hervey still discussed Ste more fondly than he ever did his wife: 'I leave Signor Stephano to give an account of myself,' he wrote to Henry in conclusion of a particularly newsy letter in February.

But despite this continued affection, the passionate intensity of their early years together had faded to be replaced by a more restrained friendship. Hervey could still write to Ste assuring him that 'no business can ever make me neglect what you desire, or prevent my finding time to do anything that you say would give you a moment's pleasure. For absent or present I love you most unfeignedly, and uninterruptedly'; but the sense of total, trusting intimacy had gone. Hervey's letters were fewer, and devoted more space to news than to descriptions of how much he longed for Ste.

For all this, the two men still preferred each other's company to anyone else's, and spent more time together than with anyone else. In August 1734 Hervey wrote to Ste lamenting the fact that Ste had sprained his thigh and would therefore not be able to accompany him to Ickworth. 'I wish you were here and well, to go with me. I am so used to you for these parties, that it is a perpetual want when I go to any of them without you: to be out of London and not with you, is taking poison without my usual antidote; I wish I may survive it.' But after the deluge of almost daily letters that marked the first years of their relationship, by now their correspondence was increasingly sporadic and, one senses, forced.

In 1735 Hervey wrote to another friend, 'I fancy it is with authors as with lovers, each must be warmed by his subject to act with any spirit, and a resolution to write will no more supply the want of choice in one case, than constancy from gratitude and principle will supply the ardour of inclination in the other.' These words came straight from the heart, for Ste had been responding less than ardently to Hervey's still passionate letters, suggesting that he now wrote more from 'gratitude and principle' than inclination. Hervey resisted this trend at first: 'I must now tell you that all your letters in general (but that of yesterday more than any) put me in mind of a Bill in Chancery,' he wrote despairingly.

There are never above three words in a line, nor above three lines in a page; but if you copy the Court of Chancery in the manner of filling your paper, I desire you would copy it too in quantity, and then instead of a sheet in a month you will send me a quire every week. Do not excuse yourself by pleading nothing to say; whenever one thinks, one thinks in words, and whatever these words are, one may write them. Whenever you are awake therefore, you may write.

But Ste did not respond, and Hervey's letters began to sound more like newspaper reports than the love-letters they had once been. 'Can you like to hear how many times a week I go to a Drawing-room, a play, or an opera, how many bows I make at the one, or how many times I yawn at them all? Can it be any diversion to you to hear things repeated from the lips of those who only open them because articulation is a compliment?' he asked Ste wearily, well knowing (if he chose to examine his conscience) that it was partly his own fascination with these court affairs that had alienated Ste from him in the first place.

Hervey accepted Ste's indifference with a lassitude that showed how futile he saw it was to try and cajole him out of it as he had so often in the past. Where, at the start of their association, Hervey had teased Ste with his reluctance, now he saw that it was unfeigned. All he could do was stand steadfast in his loyalty to his old friend, although he could not prevent a note of disappointed disillusion creeping into his thoughts. 'You see my dear friend by the date of this letter, how punctual I am in my obedience to your commands,' he wrote, regretting that he could not fulfil his own inclination as easily as he could obey Ste's request for a letter, to entertain him in the solitary ennui of a gloomy winter evening in Somerset. Hervey could not reply with the 'sentiments, theory and speculation' Ste had asked to hear. He was fed up, sick of it all. Plans and hopes were nothing more than the 'frail, useless, disagreeable cobwebs as a thousand such spiders as myself have, in busied idleness, spun out of the bowels of their own unprofitable brains to catch flies, ever since the world began'.

By the end of 1735 there was a more serious reason behind Ste's change of heart, which Hervey was privy to, and for love of Ste had to support, but which finally signalled the end of their friendship as he had known and treasured it. Over the past two years, Ste had steadily been asserting his independence, while remaining close to his former lover, but in the autumn of 1735 he made a decision that was to alter affairs between the two men irrevocably. He had resolved to go to the gallows, to use an old analogy of Hervey's, and get married.

The girl he had chosen – and girl she was – was the thirteen-year-old daughter of Henry Fox's mistress, Susan Horner: Elizabeth Strangways-Horner, heiress to (among other things) Melbury, a large estate in Dorset. Henry and Susan Horner* had been involved

* She was called Susan, or Susanna, Strangways before her marriage; because she was an heiress, and as rich as her husband, her daughter took both their names. Melbury came to Elizabeth through the Strangways.

for several years, during which time Henry had lived with them off and on in their house at Nice. Mrs Horner, whom Horace Walpole described as 'very salacious', was fourteen years older than Henry, and still married; their relationship was the prototype of the older, sophisticated woman initiating her young lover into the ways of the world. The relationship between Hervey and Ste was an interesting variation of this model; perhaps the two brothers, lacking parents, both unconsciously looked for older lovers to introduce them to adulthood. As Mrs Horner wrote to Ste in January 1735 from Nice, Henry 'studies very hard, and I don't know that I might not make a great man of him'. In his turn, Henry amused himself while staying with her in overseeing her daughter Elizabeth's education, correcting her work and encouraging her studies.

Maybe Henry Fox, knowing Elizabeth, proposed the match to his lover before they all returned to England that summer; maybe Susan Horner, wanting to protect her daughter from the advances of fortune-hunters by marrying her off young, thought Ste would suit her; or maybe Ste and Elizabeth simply fell in love. However it happened, by the autumn of 1735 the match had been settled, and all that remained was to persuade Elizabeth's reluctant father.

So marriage was much on Hervey's mind when he wrote to Ste's sister Charlotte Digby in November (on the same day he had written so despondently to Ste about the futility of spinning cobwebs), continuing what was obviously an ongoing debate about the qualities one should look for in a wife. Unwittingly revealing his misogyny by complimenting her previous letter, he said,

if it had been sent from any hand but yours, [it] would have surprised me as much as it entertained me. I am very ready to acknowledge that no politician argues closer than you do, but no political writer quotes more unfairly, and no Divine reasons from more *postulata* (to few women I would have made use of that word, at least without explaining it).

Charlotte argued that merit was more important than fortune – accusing Hervey of implying that money could be looked at as some kind of consolation for a lack of virtue. Hervey, who agreed with Montaigne that marriage was simply 'a bargain to which only the entrance is free', replied that at least with money one could be sure of what one was getting, while one always took a chance in opting for goodness. 'We both think alike of the value of money, and the value of merit,' he concluded, 'but you imagine one may know the one as well before one marries as the other; whereas I think that in the fortune you may know to a farthing what your wife will be worth.' As there is no way of testing merit except living with someone, he argued, you may marry someone thinking they are good and find out they are not. It was like buying what you thought was gold, wearing it for some time, and then finding out, when your skin became green, that it was an inferior metal. And in marriage, you were 'obliged to wear it on'. The world may think you possess a treasure in your wife, he continued, and envy your happiness; but you, closer to her, know that she is nothing but a counterfeit. Had you never touched her, you might never have been deceived, but the longer you are with her, the clearer the deception grows.

Was Hervey thinking of his own brittle wife, held up as an example of womanly virtue, who had been a beauty but no fortune? He and Molly had married for love, both young and beautiful – each seeing in the other the reflection of themselves – and over the course of their marriage, as Hervey retreated away from his wife, losing himself in other relationships, Molly took on his characteristics as a way of reaching out to him. Her view of herself became what she thought he wanted to see in her. 'I affect an air of grandeur which does not suit my stature, and makes me appear haughty and disdainful,' she wrote of herself the year following Hervey's death.

Raillery is a very great pleasure to me, but I don't love those who slander everybody and everything that is done. I like better that they ridicule in general than particular persons, though the latter diverts me much at the same time that I feel some remorse for being so much pleased with it, and yet would not silence them if I could, nor be silent myself. This is another sign of weakness. Also when I see anyone much more ridiculous than the generality of mankind I cannot help laughing in their face . . . I detest lying as well because it is mean and vile as because it is a crime . . . I am proud to the last degree; nothing equals it but my ambition, which is boundless; there is nothing so ridiculous or impossible in the world but that I have thought to satisfy the one and the other . . . Sometimes I think myself almost worthy to be what I desire, because I cannot be satisfied with less . . . I divert myself very well when alone, and am never tired of myself. I am very passionate, but don't let it appear; I find it beneath me not to be able to disguise it . . . There is no difficulty I cannot surmount to please those I love . . . I had rather be hated than despised. It is the effect of my pride . . . When I take an aversion to anyone I have an incredible desire to affront them.

This description could apply with equal accuracy to her husband as well: Molly had created herself in Hervey's image. Tellingly, he found this wanting. Perhaps some secret self-loathing made Hervey despise his wife the more for wanting to be like him.

Hervey concluded his letter to Charlotte Digby cryptically, 'Pray tell Mrs Horner [who was staying at Redlynch] I wish her not only health but every other happiness; and, as I wish her some things she has not, so I wish too she had not some things she has.'

The type of mercenary match-making favoured by Hervey was deplored by his contemporary Mrs Delany, who had suffered as a young woman by being forced through poverty to marry a much older man whom she did not love. 'Riches and great alliance' were the first considerations for marriage, she said ruefully. 'Beauty, sense, and honour are not required; if thrown into the bargain, why well and good; but the want of them will not spoil a match nowadays.' But the mystery was eternal, according to Lady Mary Wortley Montagu, also unhappily married. 'Where are people matched! I suppose we shall all come right in Heaven, as in a country dance, though hands are strangely given and taken while they are in motion, at last all will meet their partners when the jig is done.'

Hervey's discussion with Charlotte Digby on the value of money over merit in a wife would suggest both that he had been disappointed in his own marriage and that he approved of Ste's match, for Elizabeth Strangways-Horner was a great heiress – such a great heiress that Ste, who was rich enough in his own right, willingly changed his name to Fox-Strangways after their marriage. Perhaps Hervey thought too that her youth and pliability would allow Ste the freedom to maintain the old intensity of his friendship with

Hervey; if Ste had to marry, then an immature, mouldable thirteen-year-old heiress was the best woman for him. Certainly he knew of the match from its inception in the autumn of 1735 and despite his private sadness did all he could to further Ste's suit. Hervey knew it was inevitable, and he accepted it.

But neither Ste's intended wife nor mother-in-law were prepared to ignore his long-standing relationship with Hervey. In November, Hervey wrote a distressed letter to Ste to appraise him of an interview he had just had in Cork Street; he does not say with whom, but it is clear from the text of the letter that he meant Susan and Elizabeth Strangways-Horner. Mother and daughter had been deeply upset by some piece of information they had been given about Hervey and Ste – 'they cried, they scolded, abused me a little, you a little more, and said we were both of us so *sly* and so false, that innocence and honesty could not live with either of us'. Hervey tried to find out who had told them this news, or 'nonsense' as he called it – presumably that he and Ste had been, and perhaps still were, lovers – but they would not reveal their source, although he thought he knew who it was. It could have been his political rival, Newcastle, or Prince Frederick, determined to injure Hervey any way he could, or even a jealous Anne Vane. Hervey's wording and emphasis suggest both that he suspected someone, and that Ste knew whom he suspected.

I laughed at them for listening to every *designing* fool (I thought that word would startle them) that came to tell them lies, assured them I knew nothing at all of what they spoke of, and could not believe there could be any such thing [gossip about him and Fox] in agitation and I not trusted with it – the answer was – *Ah sly devil! but if you were you would not tell* – what struck hardest was your not writing as promised.

Hervey's response does not reveal whether he thought the stories were nonsense because they were untrue, or because his relationship with Ste was irrelevant to his getting married to Elizabeth; he seemed neither shocked nor surprised at the accusation (whatever it was) and his only concern was that they not believe it, in order that Ste's happiness might not be destroyed.

Ste was clearly worried, for in the following week Hervey received three letters from him including one double packet which enclosed a letter from him for Hervey to deliver to Elizabeth. His efforts to calm her fears, reported Hervey, were working: '*She* received the letter she should have had on Friday, the Monday following, after which I saw her, and that letter joined to what I had before said, made her quite easy.'

Once Elizabeth was sure she wanted to marry Ste, and her mother's approval was assured, the only party left to convince was Elizabeth's father, Thomas Horner. He was worried that his daughter was too young to be married in the first place, concerned that Ste was not the right husband for her (less for emotional than political reasons: he was a staunch Tory and thought Ste's adoption of the Whig cause a betrayal), and furious with his wife for allowing the situation to have escalated to the point where it was too late for him to interfere. He forbade the marriage to take place.

But without his knowledge, on 15 March 1736 Stephen married Elizabeth Strangways-Horner in the library of his house at Great Burlington Street, attended by Lord Hervey, Mrs Horner and Mrs Digby. The service was performed by the Reverend Villemain, a parson who owed his living to Ste's patronage, and whom Hervey also knew. A week later, 'in the red damask room up one pair of stairs', the couple were married for a second time, again by Villemain, again with Hervey in attendance, but this time instead of the two female witnesses Ste's friends Thomas Winnington, Charles Hamilton and Lord Falkland were present. The following week, the couple were presented at court, to put the official seal on their match.

Presented with a *fait accompli*, there was little the bride's disapproving father could do except rage at his wife and daughter in private and insist that she remain at home until she was old enough to live with Ste as his wife. Word of the match soon got out. Just three days after the second wedding, Lord Gower reported that 'The Town is at present very much entertained with little Ste Fox's wedding, who on Monday night last ran away with the great fortune Miss Horner, who is but just thirteen years old and very low and childish of her age.' Dr Middleton wrote to congratulate Hervey – as the one who, next to Ste, would take the most pleasure in the pairing – on his friend's happiness, saying, 'This happy event will convince him [Ste], I hope, that whatever else may be transacted there, matches at least are made in Heaven.'

Subsequent events proved that the match was, indeed, an ideal one. For the next three years, Ste and his young wife saw each other (with the connivance of Mrs Strangways-Horner) as much as possible, and corresponded closely using a messenger to deliver their letters without attracting Mr Horner's attention. Six months after their marriage, an emissary wrote to let Ste know he had delivered his letter to Elizabeth safely, '*propria manu* [by hand] as enjoined', adding, 'I scarce believe there is that man in the world, possesses a female heart so entirely as you do hers.'

The following letter, written by Elizabeth the October after their wedding, shows both her artless devotion to Ste and her father's continued disapproval of the match.

Yours, my dearest dear Mr Fox, I received Friday night at Hinsford, where we came the day before, and which we left yesterday for Melbury, a place, I doubt, we must not yet hope to see you at, since Papa designs to be here Tuesday, and though he'll leave us Wednesday, yet he'll return to us again on his way from Taunton to Abbotsbury and stay a day in that visit; which I fear will destroy my poor Mama, for he teases her without end, and insists on Mr and Mrs Ansley's being turned off for selling me to you . . .* Thus you may see, dearest Ste, what a sad way we are in, and

---

* The Ansleys worked for the Horners, and a letter of Susan's written to Lady Sundon, Queen Caroline's Mistress of the Robes, at the same time corroborates her husband's blaming them, as well as her and her daughter, for the match: Mr Horner, she said, was 'more angry than ever with the girl [Elizabeth], without any reason that I know of, and is for discharging all my servants, who he says were at the bottom of the match, though he gives me no reason for believing they were'. Thomas Horner was so angry about his wife's involvement in his daughter's marriage that, even though they had lived separately for many years, he now demanded a formal separation. In Mrs Horner's words, they had realized 'the only way for both of us to spend the rest of our lives in peace was to live separate'. Ste Fox had to stand surety for any debts his mother-in-law might run up. By March 1737, the couple, though permanently separated, were on much better terms. Mrs Horner told Lady Sundon that her ex-husband spoke of her 'in a prodigious handsome manner, and . . . wished me exceedingly well'.

to add to it, to be kept separate from you afflicts me more than you can possibly imagine, and from our uncertainty, to have been the cause of your losing your sport, by leaving Farley sooner than you wished to do, vexes me extremely . . . My dearest dear Ste adieu, I am in a melancholy way and can add no more than that I am happy only in being yours.

Although Ste's wedding meant that he and Hervey spent less time alone than they had once done, partly so as to avoid gossip and partly because Ste's time was taken up with plotting to see his estranged bride, the two men remained close – almost certainly because Hervey had supported Fox in his clandestine courtship and marriage. Except for the bride and groom, and parson, Hervey had been the only witness to both ceremonies. But things had changed: although Lord Bristol could still refer to Ickworth's 'rival, Redlynch', now when Hervey went to stay with Fox he was either accompanied by his wife, or found there the young Mrs Fox and her mother, as well as his beloved Ste.

Something she 'should have despaired of bringing about by any or all methods has come almost of itself', she exulted.

25. The King's Fat Venus

Perhaps in order to distract himself from the failure of his relationship with Ste, or hoping to achieve the success which would be his best defence against Pope's rancour, the thirty-eight-year-old Hervey now submerged himself in life at court. He had his revived relationship with Anne Vane to distract him from private disappointment and public criticism – presumably what Lady Bristol was referring to when she mentioned to her husband the many irons in Hervey's fire, 'some of which I wish were burnt out'. Lady Hervey had gone to France with the Duke and Duchess of Richmond in May,* and so, said Hervey, 'this coast was quite clear'. Prince Frederick, obsessed with Lady Archibald Hamilton, a plain, thirty-five-year-old woman who had borne her husband ten children, was neglecting his erstwhile mistress. So from the summer of 1735 Hervey's relationship with Anne Vane took on a new importance for both of them.

Anne, like Hervey, suffered from delicate health and late one night in bed in Hervey's rooms she fell into violent convulsions; despite Hervey's desperate efforts to revive her with hot towels to her stomach, cordials and gold powder, she became unconscious and her terrified lover thought her 'absolutely dead'. 'What confusion and distress this put his Lordship into is easier to be imagined than to be described,' Hervey recorded in the *Memoirs*. 'He did not dare to send for any assistance, nor even to call a servant into the room, for not one was trusted with the secret. What to do he could not tell, nor what would or would not be said when it should come out, and to conceal it was impossible, that Miss Vane should be found dead in his lodgings'. Just as Hervey was about to summon help and damn the consequences, she came to, and he hurriedly

* They stayed at Aubigny, a château near Orleans, to which Richmond's daughter, the Duchess of Leinster, later moved her family between 1776 and 1779. One of her sons was the Irish revolutionary Lord Edward Fitzgerald.

dressed her and took her down to Pall Mall where he put her into a sedan chair – 'not daring to have one brought to take her up at his lodgings' – to be taken back to her own house in Grosvenor Square and call for a doctor there.

Hervey's panic and rather ungentlemanly haste to get her out of his rooms were as much for her sake as for his own; had they been discovered together she would have suffered more than him, for the Prince would have had no mercy upon a woman who betrayed him with his most bitter enemy. In addition, Lady Archibald, afraid of the continuing influence of the mother of her lover's son, was scheming to force her rival to leave the country or lose the allowance she received from the Prince. She claimed that this was because Frederick was about to be married, and ought not to retain a mistress with a child who might interfere with his new wife. At her instigation, Lord Baltimore was sent as emissary from the Prince to set his offer before Miss Vane. Furiously relating the meeting to Hervey, Anne said that she was quite happy to break with Frederick, indeed that it would give her 'much more pleasure than she had ever found in his acquaintance' – except for the demand that she leave England, her son and Hervey behind her. She begged Hervey to help her reply to the Prince's insulting demands.

Hervey, 'who had a mind to keep Miss Vane in England, and was not a little pleased to have an opportunity of fretting the Prince, undertook this commission very willingly'. Just as, three years earlier, Frederick had used Anne Vane to get to Hervey, now Hervey used her to wound Frederick. He wrote a letter to Frederick in Anne's name, in which he assured him that she would never imagine 'that what was right for your affairs was not to outweigh every consideration of mine'. But he reproached the Prince for his cruelty in trying to break with her using a go-between, and for the further distress her banishment would cause her at a time when, bereft of her lover, she would need the comfort of her family and friends more than ever. The letter rose to a crescendo with a masterful passage of emotional blackmail:

Your Royal Highness need not be put in mind who I am, nor from whence you took me. That I acted not like what I was born, others may reproach me; but if you took me from happiness and brought me to misery, that I might reproach you. That I have long lost your heart I have long seen and long mourned. To gain it, or rather to reward the gift you made me of it, I sacrificed my time, my youth, my character, the world, my family, and everything that a woman can sacrifice to a man she loves. How little I considered my interest, you must know by my never naming my interest to you when I made this sacrifice, and by my trusting to your honour when I showed so little regard, when put in balance with my love, to my own. I have resigned everything for your sake but my life; and, had you loved me still, I would have risked even that too to please you; but as it is, I cannot think in my state of health of going out of England, so far from all friends and physicians I can trust, and of whom I stand in so much need. My child is the only consolation I have left. I cannot leave him, nor shall anything but death ever make me quit the country he is in. Your Royal Highness may do with me what you please; but a Prince who is one day to rule this country will sure, for his own sake, never show he will make use of power to distress undeservedly; and that one who has put herself without conditions into his hands has the hardest terms imposed upon her, though she never in her life did one action that deserved anything but your favour, your compassion, and your friendship; and it is for these reasons I doubt not but your Royal Highness will on this occasion, do everything that will hinder you from being blamed and me from being more miserable than the reflection of what is past must necessarily make one who has known what it is to be happy, and can never expect to taste that font again.

To Hervey's private satisfaction, Anne's brother Harry Vane thought the letter had been written for her by William Pulteney, 'and readily gave in to her sending what he thought had been advised by one whose great understanding and friendship for his sister he had so great an opinion of'. Also to Hervey's satisfaction, Prince Frederick was incandescent with rage when he read the letter to discover that his former mistress would not give in to his demands as easily as he had hoped; but his hands were tied by the submissive tone with which she cloaked her resistance. He could not refuse her request without appearing both cruel and selfish, so he pretended that he had not authorized Lord Baltimore to approach her with the offer. With victory in their sights, Hervey and Anne wrote back, 'It is hard your Royal Highness will not allow me an opportunity to clear myself; but, deal with me as you please, I shall ever pray for your happiness and prosperity, even whilst I reflect it is at least to your love, if not to your hate, that I owe the loss of my own.'

Frederick was forced to assure her he would not try to make her leave England, nor take their son from her; he promised to carry on paying her allowance and gave her the house in Grosvenor Square for life. Hervey had thus accomplished both his objectives: keeping his mistress near him, and thwarting Frederick's plans. He relished having masterminded Anne's triumph. 'Everybody who pretended the least regard for Miss Vane, or for Mr Pulteney, who was generally thought the author, justified that which they would have been the first people to condemn, had they known out of what quiver this arrow had been shot.'

Frederick's move from one mistress to another was mirrored by his father, who had gone to Hanover for the summer, as he regularly did, and there found himself a replacement for Lady Suffolk. In long and detailed letters, George reported his wooing of Madame Walmoden to Caroline in England, adding in 'the account of his buying her . . . [that] the first price . . . was only one thousand ducats – a much greater proof of his economy than his passion,' said Hervey. Rumours of the royal passion for Madame Walmoden held the court transfixed, and its inhabitants waited anxiously to see whether Lady Suffolk's apartments at St James's would be taken over by a new mistress when George came back to England in the autumn. For the first time it appeared that Caroline might have a serious rival.

Hervey publicly pooh-poohed these speculations, telling Horatio Walpole that the Queen had never been in better 'humour, health and spirits' in September as they awaited George's return. But in private he was aware of how much Caroline's confidence was eroded by her husband's new neglect, as well as her fears of the influence a mistress George actually loved might wield.

The King came back to England alone and grumpy, and spent his days writing long letters to his mistress. He would come in the mornings into the long gallery where his family were breakfasting, to snub

the Queen, who was drinking chocolate, for always stuffing [eating], the Princess Emily for not hearing him, the Princess Caroline for being grown fat, the Duke [of Cumberland] for standing awkwardly, Lord Hervey for not knowing what relation the Prince of Sultzbach was to the Elector Palatine, and then carried the Queen to walk, and be resnubbed, in the garden.

He was rude to everybody at court, frequently saying that he preferred Hanover to England, where the men talked 'of nothing but their dull politics, and the [women] . . . of nothing but their ugly clothes'. This opinion was not improved by a poor turnout, both in numbers and extravagance of dress, at his Birthday, as many courtiers were saving their best new clothes for Frederick's wedding the following spring. The English, said George huffily, were a race of 'King-killers and republicans'; in Hanover, 'he rewarded people for doing their duty and serving him well, but . . . [in England] he was obliged to enrich people for being rascals, and buy them not to cut his throat'. Instead of covering up or being ashamed of the insults they received from the King, his courtiers 'bragged of them in mirth'.

He treated the Queen with even more heartlessness than usual to punish her for Madame Walmoden's absence. Not only did he insist on telling and retelling the stories of his seduction of Madame Walmoden to his wife, but he had pictures of these scenes put up on the walls of Caroline's dressing-room 'and was often so gracious to Lord Hervey when he was with their Majesties in this dressing-room for an hour or two in the evening, to take a candle in his own royal hand, and tell him the story of these pictures, running through the names and characters of all the persons represented in them, and what they had said and done'. Hervey would make faces at Caroline over George's shoulder as she sat 'equally afraid of betraying those signs either of her lassitude or her mirth'.

Soon after his arrival in England, George ordered Hervey (as part of his official duties as Vice-Chamberlain) to remove from the royal apartments some paintings by Van Dyck he and Caroline had had brought in to decorate the drawing-room at Kensington, and replace them with the paintings George had previously chosen.

'Would your Majesty have the gigantic fat Venus restored too?' asked Hervey.

'Yes, my Lord,' replied the King. 'I am not so nice [choosy] as your Lordship. I like my fat Venus better than anything you have given me instead of her.' Hervey said he thought, 'though he did not dare to say, that, if his Majesty had liked his fat Venus as well as he used to do, there would have been none of these disputations'.

Robert Walpole was also concerned at the King's distraction, and urged Caroline to use what remained of her influence to throw into her husband's path a mistress who might be more tractable than Madame Walmoden, an unknown quantity. 'If the King would have somebody else, it would be better to have that somebody chosen by her than by him.' Of the two obvious choices he suggested pretty Lady Tankerville – 'a very safe fool' – over Lady Deloraine, who, though beautiful, was rendered dangerous by her ambition. Hervey thought that Caroline, although she had managed to convince Walpole that she took his tactless advice in good part, was hurt by the implication that she had lost her hold over George and might as well surrender it completely in order to retain some vestige of influence; as Hervey said, no woman likes to be told that her physical charms – and with them her power – have faded.

Hervey was closer to the Queen than anybody at this time, and was witness to her every humiliation at George's hands; she could not, he said, speak one word uncontradicted, nor do one act unreproved. One evening, the King began upbraiding her for tipping the servants in the houses she visited. Hervey, in her defence, said generosity was expected from the wife of the monarch.

'Then she may stay at home as I do,' returned George. 'You do not see me running into every puppy's house to see his new chairs and stools. Nor is it for you to be running your nose everywhere, and trotting about the town to every fellow that will give you bread and butter, like an old girl that loves to go abroad, no matter where, or whether it is proper or not.' Caroline blushed, and she began knotting her threads more quickly as tears came into her eyes, but she said nothing. Hervey, who did not care if he 'provoked the King's wrath himself or not, provided he could have the merit to the Queen of diverting his Majesty's ill-humour from her', said that the only way the Queen could see paintings, which she loved, was by going to people's houses to view their collections.

'And what does it matter whether she sees a collection or not?' returned George.

'The matter is, Sir, that she satisfies her own curiosity, and obliges the people whose house she honours with her presence.'

'Supposing,' said the King, 'she had a curiosity to see a bawdy house or a tavern, would it be fit for her to satisfy it? And yet the bawd or innkeeper would be very glad to see her.'

'If the bawd and the innkeeper were used to be received by her Majesty in her palace, I should think the Queen's seeing them at their own houses would give no additional scandal.' Hervey's reply so enraged George that he turned to Caroline, ignoring Hervey who was the only other person present, and poured out a torrent of unintelligible German at her.

The following morning, Hervey went to the Queen's room where she congratulated him on his 'admirable' teasing of the King, 'but I thought you looked at me once as if you thought I was ready to cry'. Hervey had to assure her that he thought she was about to laugh, and could not look at her 'for fear, if he had met her eyes, that they might both have misbehaved'. Hervey, whose treatment of women was barely better than his opinion of them in general, behaved differently with Caroline. He genuinely adored her, and pitied her misfortunes for all he was able to see that it was her pride and lust for power that made her determined to control the King and regret the loss of his affection.

It is strange that Hervey could sympathize with Caroline to the extent he did, and yet extend none of this feeling to his own wife, whom he used arguably worse than George did Caroline. George may have snubbed the Queen in private and insulted her in public, but he respected her opinion – she was always the only person who could change his mind – and remained, until her death, physically in thrall to her (except for the current interlude with Madame Walmoden). But Hervey scorned his wife's efforts to appeal to him either on an intellectual or emotional level, allowing her outwardly to live as his wife, but rejecting her in private. He never referred positively to her, or to their children, in his letters – indeed he hardly referred to her at all –˙ and she was little more than a child-bearing irrelevance to him for most of their married life. Despite her inexplicable adoration of him – amounting almost to hero-worship – he was barely able to bring himself to tolerate her presence. In a letter written to Ste in September 1735 he referred to the 'Duke of Richmond and his caravan' having left Paris on their way home; Molly Hervey was of the party, and had been away for nearly four months, but he did not bother to mention her by name.

The only women Hervey treated as emotional and intellectual equals were those whom he knew intimately, but with whom he was not involved sexually: Queen Caroline, Lady Mary Wortley Montagu and Charlotte Digby, Ste's sister. After Hervey's death, Lady Mary wrote to thank his son for returning their correspondence to her (which she then burned), saying that the letters chronicled 'a long and steady friendship subsisting between two persons of different sexes without the least admixture of love'. Hervey described Mrs Digby as the epitome of La Bruyère's 'receipt for an agreeable woman . . . *le plus charmant commerce qu'il y'est au monde est celui d'une femme qui a touts les agréments d'un honnête homme*':* for a woman to be agreeable to him, Hervey implies, she had to be like a man. These three women were all exceptional in Hervey's eyes – Caroline as anointed Queen, Lady Mary as perhaps the most intelligent woman of her generation, Charlotte Digby as Ste's sister – which perhaps helps explain Hervey's respect for them; normal women, with whom one slept and who bore one's children, were just facts of life up with which one had to put.

Hervey was not unusual in his views on females; as Lady Mary wrote, 'There is no part of the world where our sex is treated with so much contempt as in England.' Chesterfield said that a man of sense only trifled with women, since they were but 'children of a

---

* The most charming relationship that can be had in this world is one with a woman who has all the attractive qualities of an honourable man.

larger growth'. Dr Pringle, a friend of Samuel Boswell's father, was recorded by the young Boswell as saying, 'If I thought Deism the true religion, I would not say so to my wife.' The Duke of Argyll refused to allow his daughters to learn French because 'One language was enough for a woman to talk in.' The woman who could break through these prejudices was rare, and the man who could accept her equally so. Hervey was no less inclined to believe women were intelligent or capable than most of his contemporaries.

But his mother was a difficult, selfish, silly woman whom it is not hard to suppose made Hervey quickly believe that all women were cast in her mould; and as such he treated them. She had cosseted Hervey from childhood (provoking an uncharacteristically harsh warning from Lord Bristol of the consequences of her behaviour), then turned on him with venom when he married, refusing to be civil to her daughter-in-law. In his *Memoirs*, Hervey, with uncharacteristic mildness, described his boastful mother as 'being a little addicted to weave fable in her narratives', adding that he only believed her stories if she were corroborated elsewhere. Lady Bristol wrote to her husband with typical self-delusion on the fortieth anniversary of their wedding, 'to wish all those [years] we are to pass together may prove as happy in our latter days as they were in the beginning'. It had perhaps escaped her notice – or maybe she was blithely ignoring the fact – that her husband had not addressed her as 'dear wife' since 1722 (when gossip, as reported by Lady Mary Wortley Montagu, held that she was having affairs simultaneously with two men) and was not to do so again in his diary until he matter-of-factly recorded her death in 1741.

In many ways, though, Hervey and his mother were more similar than he would have liked to admit. Both were unrepentantly unfaithful to their spouses and neglectful of their children; both sought social advancement, often at the cost of their dignity; both loved gambling, gossip and intrigue; both squandered their health in the pursuit of pleasure. But Hervey was redeemed by his intelligence, and by a highly personal, if sometimes obscure, sense of integrity.

In September 1735 Lady Bristol's behaviour provoked an angry letter from Hervey. It seems that Lady Suffolk had had a snuff-box stolen from her rooms, probably by a woman whom Hervey said had 'been everything but legally convicted of having stolen many other things'. But Lady Bristol was convinced that Felton, her youngest son, had been accused, and mounted a campaign against Lady Suffolk in order to clear his name.

I must own I see no reason any of our family have on this occasion to be angry with Lady Suffolk, and I am apt to think from some things that have been dropped on [the subject], that the turn people will give to your picking a quarrel this year with Lady Suffolk [considering the circumstances; she had just left court] will be rather to your having a desire to make court, than to gratify your resentment,

Hervey informed her sternly. 'Believe me you will have nobody on your side in this affair; you will only do Felly [Felton] no good, he is clear of a very disagreeable suspicion, and your taking it in this way with regard to Lady Suffolk will anger many people (for she has and deserves many friends) and it will oblige nobody: *nobody whatever.*'

He relented enough by the end of the letter to inform his mother that Lady Hervey was on her way back from France, bringing with her the dress Lady Bristol had requested; pandering to his mother's snobbery, he said Molly hoped she would like it, because 'the Duchess of Mazarin helped her to choose it'. Paris was the most chic place to buy one's clothes. Molly's travelling companion, the Duchess of Richmond, came back from Paris in all the latest finery: she appeared at court 'quite in the French mode, very fine and handsome – silver tissue ground and velvet flowers; her head [cap] was yellow gauze, and her lappets [the ties hanging down from her cap] tied with puffs of scarlet ribbon'.

26. Sporus

On 2 January 1735, Alexander Pope published the 'Epistle to Dr Arbuthnot', his public revenge on Hervey for the 'Epistle to a Doctor of Divinity'. The poem was a justification, written in the form of a conversation with his friend Arbuthnot (who died less than a month after the poem was released), of his right as a satirist to attack those figures whom he believed were unfit to wield power – 'Well might they rage, I gave them but their due' – and a defence of his reasons for doing so:

> I ne'er with Wits or Witlings pass'd my days,
> To spread about the Itch of Verse and Praise;
> Nor like a Puppy, daggled through the Town,
> To fetch and carry Sing-song up or down;

At least he was independent, Pope claimed, and his opinions were his own. He was doing no more than observing the corruptions of those who inhabited public life:

> Pretty! In Amber to observe the Forms
> Of Hairs, or Straws, or Dirt, or Grubs, or Worms!

As he wrote to Arbuthnot during the period he was writing the 'Epistle', 'It is truth and a clear conscience that I think will set me above all my enemies.'

And yet despite his disgust with the world he described with such interested malice – which suggested that he felt slighted by not being included in it – all he wanted, he insisted, was to be allowed to live outside the tainted courts his victims decorated, in the manner of the classical poets he so admired.

> Oh let me live my own, and die so too!
> (To live and die is all I have to do:)
> Maintain a Poet's Dignity and Ease,
> And see what Friends, and read what Books I please:
> Above a Patron, tho' I condescend
> Sometimes to call a Minister my Friend.

But while Horace, Pope's model, included his own literary persona in his ironic view of the world, Pope held himself aloft from association with his quarry. He created for himself in this poem a satiric identity which was a composite of three classical ideals, combining the high-mindedness of the *vir bonus*, the modesty of the *ingenu* and the civic spirit of the hero. He portrayed himself as an arbiter of morality observing the corruption of society from the sidelines, untouched by the putrescence of his peers, courageously speaking out against their turpitude.

> The good Man walk'd innoxious through his Age.
> No Courts he saw, no Suits would ever try,
> Nor dared an Oath, nor hazard'd a Lie.
> Unlearn'd, he knew no Schoolman's subtle Art,
> No Language but the Language of the Heart.

He believed it was his duty as the self-appointed commentator on his times to expose vice, either personal or political, where he saw it – 'A lash like mine no honest man shall dread' – and he argued in his defence that his words had little real effect on those he so unflatteringly depicted in verse.*

> Whom have I hurt? Has Poet yet, or Peer,
> Lost the arch'd Eye-brow, or Parnassan Sneer?

---

* Somewhat hypocritically, since he also maintained that the character-sketches he drew were not modelled on real people, and that his victims' assumption that they were, like Lady Mary's indignation over the lines about Sappho in his 1733 'Imitation', merely proved how well they deserved the rapier thrusts of his ridicule.

As he had written to Jonathan Swift after the publication of 'Verses to an Imitator',

I have not the courage to be such a satirist as you, but I would be as much, or more, a philosopher. You call your satires, libels; I would call my satires, epistles: they will consist more of morality than wit, and grow graver, which you will call duller. I shall leave it to my antagonists to be witty (if they can) and content myself to be useful, and in the right.

Although many of Pope's old enemies were mentioned in the 'Epistle' – the bookseller Edmund Curll, the dramatist Colley Cibber, Lady Mary Wortley Montagu – he reserved the full force of his bitterness for Hervey in an extended diatribe against the insidious shallowness of the court of which he saw Hervey as exemplar. It was an inversion of societal norms: Hervey, the aristocrat who counted princes and queens as his friends, was portrayed as a snivelling, servile sycophant; Pope, the low-born hack, had taken on the noble attributes of dignity and measured ease.

> Yet let me flap this Bug with gilded Wings,
> This painted Child of Dirt, that stinks and stings;
> Whose Buzz the Witty and the Fair annoys,
> Yet Wit ne'er tastes, and Beauty ne'er enjoys:
> So well-bred Spaniels civilly delight
> In mumbling of the Game they dare not bite.

Hervey's superficiality was dangerous not only because it disguised weakness and self-interest, seducing onlookers with its illusion of glamour, said Pope, but also because behind the glittering façade lay an overriding willingness to sacrifice one's integrity for access to power.

> Eternal smiles his Emptiness betray,
> As shallow Streams run dimpling all the Way.
> Whether in florid Impotence he speaks,
> And, as the Prompter breathes, the Puppet squeaks;

> Or at the ear of Eve, familiar Toad!
> Half Froth, half Venom, spits himself abroad,
> In Puns or Politics, or Tales, or Lies,
> Or Spite, or Smut, or Rhymes, or Blasphemies.

Eve, at whose ear Sporus, or Hervey, whispered his infamy, was the Queen; the 'prompter' who controlled the puppet's strings was Walpole.

The original Sporus, whose name Pope chose as cypher for Hervey, had been a favourite of the Emperor Nero. Suetonius said that Nero had the young man castrated,

and actually tried to make a woman of him; and he married him with all the usual ceremonies, including a dowry and bridal veil, took him to his house attended by a great throng, and treated him as his wife . . . This Sporus, decked out with the finery of the empresses and riding in a litter, he took with him to the assizes and marts of Greece, and later at Rome through the Street of the Images, fondly kissing him from time to time.

Sporus was with Nero when he fled from Rome and his political enemies, and witnessed his suicide.

It is ironic – or maybe an unconscious admission of guilt – that Hervey devoted two large sections of his *Memoirs* (in 1734 and 1737) to a comparison of Prince Frederick with Nero, detailing their common cruelty and dissolution. It is interesting, too, to reflect that one of Nero's defining sins was his sexual relationship with his mother, Agrippina, whom he later had murdered. Hervey ignored Nero's passion for Sporus and his incestuous relationship with his mother and concentrated instead on the irrational hatred Nero bore for his mother and his disloyalty to his friends. Both Frederick and Nero were, he said, 'as false to their mistresses as to their friends, and no more capable of attachment by constitution to the one than they were of fidelity by principle to the other'. Did Pope know that Hervey and Frederick may have been lovers; or that Hervey himself compared Frederick to Nero thus placing himself – before Pope did – in the role of Sporus?

In the early versions of the 'Epistle', Pope used the name Paris for Hervey, a comment on his physical beauty as well as his destructive vanity, but it was an ambiguous criticism, like the epithet Sappho for Lady Mary, which Pope felt lacked force. In the notes he made while translating the *Iliad*, Pope described Paris as the type of man who might be the protagonist of a romantic novel, softly spoken, 'vainly gay in war as well as love . . . [with] the usual disposition of easy and courteous minds which are most subject to the rule of fancy and passion'. This character-sketch might have annoyed Hervey – he liked to think of himself as being a heavy-weight intellectual as well as a charming courtier – but it would not have caused him much concern or self-doubt since despite his vanity Paris remained in some ways a hero.

In settling on the identity of Sporus, Pope chose to underline Hervey's homosexuality, not simply the effeminacy which the comparison with Paris would have achieved. The castrated Sporus was a hermaphrodite, just as, in Pope's eyes, the overtly homo-sexually inclined Hervey was; and he used Hervey's 'unnatural' deficiency of masculinity, a threat to the normal order of society, as an analogy to the threat Walpole's 'unnatural' corruption posed to England's security.

> Amphibious Thing! that, acting either Part,
> The trifling Head, or the corrupted Heart,
> Fop at the Toilet, Flatt'rer at the Board,
> Now trips a Lady, and now struts a Lord.

These insults were culled in large part from previous political literature attacking Hervey. The phrase, 'now Master up, now Miss', was derived from a line in the ballad 'The Duel' written as a response to Hervey and Pulteney's duel in 1731. A pamphlet of 1734 had satirized Hervey's début in the House of Lords, calling him the 'Lady of the Lords'. Sporus's introduction in the 'Epistle', where the fictional Arbuthnot questions Pope's choice of Hervey as a worthy recipient of his satire,

> What? that thing of silk,
> Sporus, that mere white curd of Ass's milk?

was also taken from this 1734 poem, which includes the lines,

> Tho' when I stand upright,
>> You take me for a Skein of Silk;
> And think me with a Face so white,
>> A perfect Curd of Ass's Milk.

References to the well-known eccentricity of Hervey's dietary habits, these echo the observation of Lord Hailes, who recorded with some exaggeration that Hervey's 'daily food was a small quantity of ass's milk and a flour biscuit; once a week he indulged himself with an apple'. (See the note to p. 10.) The derision with which Hervey had attacked Pope for his imitative style in the 'Epistle from a Nobleman to a Doctor of Divinity' was here justified:

> But had he not, to his eternal Shame,
> By trying to deserve a Satirist's Name,
> Prov'd he can ne'er invent but to defame.

In 1742, Hervey again taunted Pope in 'A Letter to Mr C-b-r [the dramatist Colley Cibber], on his Letter to Mr P –':

I can no more admit that Mr Pope has any merit in this sort of writing [satire], or deserves the title of a satirist, than if I heard a drunken scold of an apple-woman quarrelling with a hackney-coachman . . . [I could say] I had seen . . . two of the keenest satirists I had ever met with in my life . . . He has no more pretence to be called a fine poet, than a good copyist has to be called a fine painter.

Pope's genius lay not necessarily in his originality, but in his skill at drawing together all the various strands of criticism that had been levelled at Hervey over the previous four years and using them to create a more wholly malevolent image of his victim. When Pope first mentions Sporus in the 'Epistle', the fictional Arbuthnot thinks Hervey is no more harmful than a scrap of silk, and derides Pope for selecting him as the object of his censure. But by the time Pope has finished with him, Hervey/Sporus has metamorphosed from a butterfly into a deadly snake: we see him as a being of evil incarnate, with 'a Cherub's face, a reptile all the rest'.

It could be argued that Hervey was no more than a courtier singled out for literary immortality as the personification of sycophancy merely by the ill-luck of having responded to Pope's first insults instead of ignoring them. But Pope's previous relationship with Hervey, the icy malevolence of this attack and, most importantly, the aspects of Hervey's character he chose to attack, show that Pope's hatred for Hervey was personally motivated, as well as politically and poetically expedient. Pope attacked those traits in Hervey which he recognized in himself, as well as what he was envious of, subconsciously selecting a victim through whom he could purge himself of his own demons.

The physical and material differences between Pope and Hervey are the most obvious sources of the poet's enmity. Pope saw Hervey as everything Pope himself was not, everything he affected to scorn, and everything he secretly longed to be: beautiful, charming, polished, secure. Pope, the crippled, gauche outsider, loathed Hervey, whose successes seemed so effortless, for the privileges of person and position that fortune had bestowed upon him, and of which Pope was correspondingly deprived. Hervey's own physical delicacy, mocked in the 'Epistle', was the principal outward sign of their similarity; and Pope may well have believed Hervey's weaknesses were exaggerated for effect (not knowing the extent to which Hervey tried to hide his epileptic attacks from the prying eyes of the court) and resented him the more for this. Although Pope was not above playing on his own ailments to attain his ends, he was – and felt himself to be – far more handicapped by them than Hervey was by his.

As Pope saw it, the only advantage he possessed in life was his ability to write; it was his birthright, his sole inheritance.

> Why did I write? what Sin to me unknown
> Dipt me in Ink, my Parents' or my own?
> And yet as a Child, nor yet a Fool to Fame,
> I lisp'd in Numbers, for the Numbers came . . .

> The Muse but serv'd to ease some Friend, not Wife,
> To help me through this long Disease, my Life.

And yet in the intellectual climate of the day – which extolled moderation and modesty almost above all other virtues – Pope was damned by his unashamed ambition. One could not be seen to try; and publishing one's work in order to make a living was undeniable evidence of trying.

The clearest example of the effect of this mode of thought upon Pope was the way in which he manoeuvred the publication of the first volume of his letters in the same year as the 'Epistle to Dr Arbuthnot' came out. This was a time when, in England at least, correspondence was published only posthumously, if at all. Pope knew that there was a demand for the release of his correspondence, but he did not want to be seen to have arranged for publication because he knew this would be interpreted as intellectual arrogance. His solution was a mark of manipulative – and marketing – genius. He had the manuscript delivered to the office of Edmund Curll, a publisher he had torn to shreds in 1728 in the 'Dunciad', by an anonymous messenger who later revealed that Pope had given him the manuscript and directed him to take it to Curll's office in Rose Street, Covent Garden. Curll, who specialized in shocking and seditious works as well as pirated manuscripts, was gratified to benefit from Pope without having to pay him and had no scruples about publishing the letters. That summer, to underline his triumph over his old enemy, he hung out above his shop a new sign – a picture of Pope's head. Although Curll came out the winner in the short term, ultimately Pope had achieved his objectives: not only was he able to publish his own edition of his correspondence some years later without seeming vain, since some of the letters were already in circulation as a *fait accompli*, but he profited from them even more because of the intrigue surrounding their initial publication.

What stands out most in Pope's vitriolic assaults on Hervey is his obsession with Hervey's sexuality. Pope was famously unsuccessful with women; his hapless passion for Lady Mary Wortley Montagu, exacerbated by Hervey's awareness of the circumstances surrounding his humiliation, was only one of several vain attempts to find love thwarted by his inability to make women see him as a lover rather than a friend. That Hervey, married to one of the most beautiful women of his generation, scorned her in favour of not just a mistress but a male lover as well, must have tormented the lonely poet. His jealousy was heightened by homosexual impulses which Pope struggled to control. There is no evidence of his ever having had a physical relationship with another man – just as there is none for a physical relationship with a woman – but the 'idolatrous homage' with which Pope regarded his patron Lord Bolingbroke was decidedly homoerotic. Even Pope's close friend, and the chief object of his romantic hopes, Martha Blount, a contemporary of Molly Hervey's at court, thought Pope talked about Bolingbroke at a 'strange rate'.

As with Hervey, Pope's interest in classical culture can only have encouraged this tendency. His description of Achilles' mourning for Patroclus in his translation of the *Iliad* reveals his sympathy both for his hero and for the philosophical ideal of homosexual love. Their love heightened their masculinity, and their masculinity glorified their love.

> Restless he roll'd around his weary Bed,
> And all his Soul on Patroclus fed:
> The Form so pleasing, and the Heart so kind,
> That youthful Vigour, and that manly Mind,
> What Toils they shar'd, what martial Works they wrought,
> What Seas they measur'd, and what Fields they fought;
> All past before him in Remembrance dear,
> Thought follows Thought, and Tear succeeds to Tear.

Contemporary criticism of Pope, both as a man and as a poet, often focused on his effeminacy and assumed sexual inadequacy. Because he was crippled, and so small of stature, it was commonly thought that his penis would be correspondingly small and deformed; by an illogical extension, his poetry was thought to lack masculine force. The critic Thomas Bentley's conclusion on Pope's *Iliad* was, 'by a woman too, how the devil should it be Homer?'

'The Poet Finished in Prose', a pamphlet published by Edmund Curll in June 1735, derided Pope for his delicacy. It described him living in fear of being raped by Sappho (Lady Mary Wortley Montagu) – a neat inversion of the situation implying that *her* advances towards *him* had occasioned their schism.

Nothing can be imagined more terrible than a rape, to a gentleman who has not the least passion for the sex . . .'Tis possible his fondness for retirement may have given him this disrelish for the sex; but no doubt he has found out some other amusement, equally entertaining to him in his solitude, and which makes him less solicitous about losing the favour of the ladies.

Pope was aware of this type of criticism, and stung by it. The emphasis in the 'Epistle to Dr Arbuthnot' is on the poet's masculine virtues, integrity and courage. It would, he said,

> . . . be one Poet's praise,
> That, if he pleas'd, he pleas'd by manly Ways.

Opinion was predictably divided on the 'Epistle'. Pope's enemies, such as Curll and Lady Mary Wortley Montagu, expressed their disapproval volubly. The day after the poem's publication, Lady Mary wrote Dr Arbuthnot a letter she asked him to show to Pope. 'I wish you would advise poor Pope to turn to some more honest method than libelling,' she said. 'I know he will allege in his excuse that he must write to eat, and he is now grown sensible that nobody will buy his verses except their curiosity is piqued to see it, to see what is said of their acquaintance, but I think this method of gain so exceeding vile that it admits of no excuse at all.' Her implication was that Pope was writing about a class by which he was ignored, more from spite about his exclusion than genuine concern about corruption. Though she denied that she had written the 1734 'Verses to an Imitator', she did so so perfunctorily that her very denial looks as much like an admission of authorship as a disclaimer: 'I own the design was so well meant, and so excellently executed, that I cannot be sorry they were written.' Voltaire said,

'*Les lecteurs pourront demander si c'est Pope ou un de ses porteurs de chaise qui a fait ce vers.*'* Sir Charles Wyndham thought Hervey's portrayal as Sporus 'moved pity for him rather than mirth'. But Pope's friends and political allies defended him equally forcibly. The Earl of Oxford, a prominent member of the Opposition to Walpole, thought Hervey deserved to be depicted as Sporus, and that the character was 'very proper and very justly drawn'.

Hervey himself made no comment at first, either publicly or in his personal correspondence. Perhaps he had realized, too late, the rashness of challenging Pope on his own territory. The following year, though, in the course of a letter to a friend in which he discussed the varying merits of the English poets, he added, 'I forgot in speaking of the English poets to mention Pope; but you know my opinion of him is that when other people think for him nobody writes better, and few people worse when he thinks for himself.' For all of Pope's insults, Hervey tried to remain objective about him.

Earlier during the dispute with Pope, Hervey's friend Dr Middleton expressed his hope of publishing his correspondence with Hervey on the Roman Senate, but Hervey, chastened by his recent experiences, demurred. He wrote to Middleton from Redlynch, where he was spending a few weeks' holiday from court in June 1734, to explain why he was hesitant. He did not believe the letters were unworthy of publication – he could not, he said, pretend to such uncommon modesty 'considering what wretched company they would keep there' – but 'to own fairly to you the weakness of my mind, I feel my pride would be more hurt in drawing that train of impertinence unnecessarily upon myself, than I could be pleased with any circumstance attending the publication. Therefore,' he concluded, 'as other people print to feed their vanity, I abstain from it, for fear of hurting mine.'

Hervey did, however, show the letters to his father; and Middleton found an ally in Lord Bristol, who saw in this scheme a way of countering the criticism Hervey had lately faced.

---

* The readers may wonder whether it was Pope or one of his sedan chair-carriers who has written this verse.

Let me beg the acquiescence at least in the publication of these [letters], were it only to mortify that little poisonous adder Pope, by showing him yours [Hervey's brain] is far from being of that flimsy texture he endeavoured to represent it, and that the world may judge from this instance how very justly he has dealt by you in every other deprecating lineament he had drawn of you.

In the end, the letters were published after Hervey's death in 1751.

Although he was increasingly reluctant to publish his work, Hervey became more absorbed in his studies as he grew older. He regularly snatched hours 'between the business of Parliament, and the attendance of a Court' to write to Middleton. His scholarship had become a consolation to Hervey for the disappointments he suffered politically and personally, as he told Henry Fox. 'Sometimes you advise me against studying, but you are in the wrong – reading and writing do me more good, when I can force myself to enjoy them, than any other employment; and *no* employment hurts me beyond what you can imagine.' If he allowed his thoughts to take their own course for an hour, he said, he was more drained than if he had spent a night reading Newton's *Principles* by a college lamp; studying was a way to keep himself distracted from the prickling of doubts and fears by which he was increasingly tortured.

Bristol's reasons for encouraging Hervey's studies were more prosaic than the reasons Hervey gave Henry Fox: God, Britain and the Hervey dynasty, in that order. In 1736 he gave Hervey a 144-volume set of the classics,

to assist you in that study you are grown so fond of . . . but as your mind is already completely stored with all the embellishments the *belles lettres* can give it, I hope your next pursuits in knowledge will be chiefly to make yourself more and more acceptable to the Deity, truly useful to your declining country, and at the same time enable yourself to make all just and necessary provisions for our numerous family.

Towards the end of 1736 Hervey wrote to Middleton encouraging him to persevere in the biography of Cicero on which he was working and about which he had often sought Hervey's advice. 'I am extremely sorry to hear you begin work at the life of Cicero as a task, and though it is extremely obliging in you to say you will continue the undertaking for my sake, yet I had much rather for the sake of the work, and for yours, that you should persevere in it from choice, than by complaisance,' Hervey said.

Five years later, Middleton's *Life of Cicero* was published, prefaced by a fulsome dedication to his patron, Lord Hervey, congratulating him for, among other attributes, his scholarship, his classically inspired political detachment, his wit and the inspirational role he had played for Middleton during his work on the book. Soon afterwards, Henry Fielding published *Shamela*, his parody of Samuel Richardson's *Pamela*, which contained a dedication to 'Miss Fanny' by 'Conny Keyber' which mimicked almost exactly the form of Middleton's dedication.

You see, Madam, I have some value for your good nature, when in a Dedication, which is properly a panegyric, I speak against, not for you; but I remember it is a life which I am presenting you, and why should I expose my veracity to any hazard in the front of the work, considering what I have done in the body. Indeed, I wish it were possible to write a Dedication, and get anything by it, without one word of flattery; but since it is not, come on, and I hope to show my delicacy at least in the compliments I intend to pay you.

In the same year, another Fielding novel, *Joseph Andrews*, came out. It contained a portrait of Hervey, as 'Beau Didapper', which was as unflattering as it was strikingly recognizable. The name Didapper derived from a seventeenth-century translation of a classical list of strange 'equivocally generated' creatures. Fielding's Didapper was about 5'4" in height, pale and slender, with soft skin 'like a lady', and an odd hopping gait. His skills included a talent for mimickry, talking a little French, and singing a few Italian songs. 'He had lived too much in the world to be bashful, and too much at court to be proud . . . No hater of women, for he always dangled after them, yet so little subject to lust, that he had among those who knew him best, the character of great moderation in his pleasures.' Hervey's sexual ambivalence was encapsulated by

Fielding's description of Didapper jumping into bed with what he thought was the young girl he had been pursuing, only to find that her place had been taken by a man.

Hervey's political career was also outlined with accuracy, although since Fielding opposed Walpole it was admittedly a biased view.

Though he [Didapper/Hervey] was born to an immense fortune, he chose for the pitiful and dirty consideration of a place of little consequence, to depend entirely on the will of a fellow, whom they call a great-man [Walpole]; who treated him with the utmost disrespect, and exacted of him a plenary obedience of his commands; which he implicitly submitted to, at the expense of his conscience, his honour, and of his country.

To some extent, all these things were true of Hervey; and it was true too that despite his faults he was 'entirely well satisfied with his own person and parts, so he was very apt to ridicule and laugh at any imperfection in another'.

As Didapper, Hervey comes across as a character with whom it is difficult to sympathize, brittle, selfish and tainted by his association with the corruption of Walpole's government. In his youth, Hervey had been content to allow this image to act as a façade, his protection from the eyes of the world; but in the last years of his life, it was becoming his private reality too.

27. A Storm

In the spring of 1736 Anne Vane's son, the three-year old Fitzfrederick, died as a result of his recurring convulsive fits. Miss Vane, already ailing, was unable to recover from this blow, and followed her son to the grave a month later. Hervey's own reactions to this tragedy do not survive, but Prince Frederick – somewhat unexpectedly – was more afflicted by his son's death than the Queen or Princess Caroline had ever seen him, or 'thought him capable of being'.

Frederick's grief was short-lived, though, for he had finally persuaded his father to find him a bride, and on 25 April – less than a month after Anne Vane's death – the young Princess Augusta of Saxe-Gotha arrived at Greenwich to marry him. Seventeen years old, she was tall and pleasant looking, but, said Hervey, despite 'all the finery of jewels and brocade [had] an ordinary air'.

The wedding took place at St James's only three days after Augusta's arrival in London. George, desperate to return to Hanover, his mistress and their new-born son, insisted that the marriage take place with insulting haste so that he could leave the country. In retaliation for this affront, Prince Frederick demanded that he and his bride be seated at their wedding feast on armchairs, rather than stools, and be served on bended knee, as befitted monarchs rather than a mere prince and princess; but his sisters, forewarned, had been ordered by the King to prevent him assuming such majesty. 'I mention these occurrences,' commented Hervey, 'to show from what wise motives the irreconcilable differences in princely families often proceed.'

Determined to assert his virility, Frederick ostentatiously drank a great deal of jelly, a gelatine drink believed to increase sexual potency, at the wedding feast. Princess Augusta was then taken by her new sisters-in-law into the royal bedchamber, where they dressed her in an ornate silver night-dress and lace bed-cap. Then Frederick, also in a night-dress of cloth-of-silver, followed his father into the chamber. The entire court filed through to pay their respects to the couple before leaving them alone together to consummate their union. Lady Bristol reported that the Prince had that night 'tasted all her charms, and was in such raptures in the morning that he squeezed all his servants by the hand, and told them he was the happiest man alive, that his Princess was far beyond any other woman he had ever enjoyed in his life'; but the Queen and Hervey thought the new Princess of Wales looked far too well rested the next morning to have spent the night grappling with her incompetent (if Anne Vane's opinion of his sexual prowess was accurate) husband.*

Despite boasting of his bride's delectability, Frederick continued his affair with Lady Archibald Hamilton. He persuaded the naive Princess Augusta to hire his mistress for offices in her household worth £900 a year. The Princess, who spoke very little English and had brought few servants of her own with her, was soon completely in Frederick's control. 'Poor creature,' said her mother-in-law, 'if she were to spit in my face, I should only pity her for being under such a fool's direction, and wipe it off.'

Queen Caroline, who hoped her husband would be succeeded by her favourite son, the Duke of Cumberland, instead of Prince Frederick, asked Hervey after the wedding if he thought it was possible for the Prince to father children – which would immediately secure his succession – and if not, if it would be possible to substitute someone in Frederick's place in the Princess's bed, without her knowledge, to get her apparently legitimately with child. Hervey replied that he thought it would be, and Caroline replied, 'I love you mightily, my dear Lord Hervey, but if I thought you would get a little Hervey by the Princess of Saxe-Gotha to disinherit my dear William [Cumberland], I could not bear it.'

Legitimate and illegitimate children of the royal family were much in the public eye in 1736, what with the speculation (fuelled by Frederick's very public requests to his coachman to drive softly

---

* In Hervey's description of the wedding in the manuscript of the *Memoirs*, there is a section missing after he recorded this conversation with the Queen, which judging by where the break takes place may well have been an indiscreet disclosure about Frederick's sexuality.

with Augusta in the carriage) about the Princess of Wales being pregnant and the death of Fitzfrederick. The King's mistress, Madame Walmoden, to whose side he had rushed after Frederick's wedding, had given birth to their son in the spring. George was keen to bring them back to England, writing persuasively to Caroline to convince her it would not damage her influence. 'But you see my passions, my dear Caroline!' he wrote.

Vous connaissez mes faiblesses, il n'y a rien de caché dans mon coeur pour vous, et plût à Dieu que vous pourriez me corriger avec la même facilité que vous m'approfondissez! Plût à Dieu que je pourrais vous imiter autant que je sais vous admirer, et que je pourrais apprendre de vous toutes les vertus que vous me faites voir, sentir, et aimer! *

In this matter, Caroline's choice, said Sir Robert, was whether she preferred to 'fear her [Walmoden] at a distance, or despise her near'. Both Walpole and Hervey agreed that Madame Walmoden's power in England would be negligible; within three months, predicted Hervey, she would be 'everything that Lady Suffolk was, but deaf'. In view of how much George talked, she might well have become deaf too.

George's reluctance to return from Hanover – and Caroline's corresponding refusal to move the court to St James's Palace, and open the London season, until his arrival home – was noted by his people who disapproved of his neglect of his wife as much as his fondness for Germany over England. It was thought he was spending English taxes on a Hanoverian whore. A notice pinned to the gate of St James's Palace summed up popular opinion:

Lost or strayed out of this house, a man who has left a wife and six children on the parish [indigent widows and orphans were maintained by their parish]; whoever will give any tidings of him to the churchwardens of St James's Parish, so as he may be got again, shall receive four shillings

---

* You know my weaknesses, there is nothing hidden from you in my heart, and please God that you will be able to correct my faults as easily as you can see into my soul. Please God that I could imitate you as well as I admire you and that I could learn from you all the virtues that you teach me to see, feel & love.

and sixpence reward. N.B. This reward will not be increased, nobody judging him to deserve a crown [five shillings].

But Hervey said reports of these views only made George congratulate himself on his romantic prowess, believing people saw his affairs as evidence of his masculinity.

By mid-October, it had become clear that George would not be in London in time for the official opening of the season, the celebration of his Birthday at St James's Palace on 30 October. Caroline was forced to move to London and his Birthday was marked in his absence. At her request, Hervey stayed with her in London for three weeks in November, instead of going to Redlynch as he usually did, while the rest of the court went to Houghton with Sir Robert Walpole or to their own country seats.

Their main topic of conversation was the Prince of Wales, whom Caroline and her daughters said acted the knave to avoid being thought a dupe. The Queen's example of this (and proof of how fond she had become of Hervey) was what she called his 'betrayal' of Hervey in 1732. Frederick's resentment of his parents, and desire for the throne, was at its peak. Hervey described him as being 'drunk with vanity', with Caroline alone to bear it. When in December news reached London of George being caught in a great storm on the Channel on his way back to London, and there were fears he might be shipwrecked, Frederick's supporters in the Commons 'talked of the King's being cast away with the same *sang-froid* as you would talk of a coach being overturned', said Hervey, adding that the Prince 'strutted about as if he had been already King'. When a fire broke out at the Temple before George's return, Frederick worked all night to help bring the flames under control; 'he exerted himself so much there, that, as he and his people said, several of the mob cried out: "Crown him! Crown him!"'

Caroline was terrified that George might die, less because she loved him than because she feared Frederick becoming King, said Hervey. Knowing his own closeness to her was a constant source of friction between the Queen and the Prince, Hervey offered to leave her service. 'No, my Lord; I should never have suffered that;

you are one of the greatest pleasures of my life,' replied Caroline. 'But did I love you less than I do, I should look upon the suffering you to be taken from me . . . after the manner in which you have lived with me and behaved to me, to be such a reflection upon me, and to betray such a meanness and baseness in me, that I assure you, you should not have stirred an inch from me.'

Except for the pain caused her by Frederick's truculence, Caroline had no problem dealing with affairs of state in the King's stead (much to Frederick's anger, George left her as regent). After all, she was accustomed even when he was in England to deciding affairs with Walpole and then persuading her husband to adopt their views. But her nominal, as well as actual, control was a source of much popular amusement. Hervey included in the *Memoirs* some verses written by William Pulteney on the appointment of county sheriffs in George's absence (although Hervey added that Chesterfield, 'with the same sort of avowing denial that he generally put on when verses were ascribed to him which he had not written, or mistresses he had not lain with', allowed people to think he was the author):

What shall we do! (quoth Walpole to the Queen)
    Unless the Wind turn quick?
The Sheriffs in all times have been
    Chosen by a Prick.

Queen: The Instrument that does the Job
    The King he has about him;
But can't you help me good Sir Bob,
    To do the Job without him?

It turned out the King was not dead, though. The storm had forced his ship back to port, where he waited for the weather to improve enough for him to attempt the crossing again. In October 1735, the journey from Hanover to England had taken him only four days; this time, including delays, it took six weeks. George wrote his wife a thirty-page letter like that 'written by some young sailor of twenty to his first mistress, after escaping from a storm in his first voyage', speaking of his passion for Caroline, his impatience to see her, and the suffering he was enduring as a result. '*Quel galimatias! Quel potpourri!*'* commented Hervey upon reading it; but he and Walpole were forced to admit that they knew of no man who wrote better love letters than their King. If George limited himself to writing to women, said Walpole, rather than talking at and strutting in front of them, 'he would get the better of all the men in the world'.

When he arrived back in London on 15 January 1737, 'everyone was astonished' at the King's open delight to see his wife. The next day, on his way to the Queen, Hervey met Walpole at the foot of the backstairs of St James's Palace, up which courtiers and politicians went privately to see the King. '*Optime, optime, omnia rident* [Very good, very good, everybody is smiling],' said Sir Robert. Hervey quoted from Horace,

> '*Quid si prisca redit Venus*
> > *Diductosque iugo cogit aeneo?*
> *Si flava excutitur Chloe*
> > *Reiectaeque patet ianua Lydiae?*'

and Walpole replied, capping his quotation, '*Dixit ad uxorem,*

> "*Quamquam sidere pulchrior ille est . . .*
> > *Tecum vivere amem, tecum obeam libens.*" '†

Not all of their commentary was so highbrow: Walpole then called out, 'that notwithstanding all this rant, he did not believe Mr Bis [meaning twice in Latin] had been above [upstairs]'. Hervey replied

---

* What rubbish! What a hodge-podge!
† The reference is to Horace, Odes III, 9. I have corrected Hervey's Latin (he missed out a word or two). The following translations are by C. E. Bennett (London, 1924). '*Quid . . . Lydiae*': 'What if the old love come back again and join those now estranged beneath her compelling yoke; if fair-haired Chloe be put aside and the door thrown open to rejected Lydia?' '*Quamquam . . . libens*': 'Though he is fairer than the stars . . . with thee I fain would live, with thee I'd gladly die.' (Walpole added the phrase '*Dixit ad uxorem*', or, 'He said to his wife'.)

that if Mr Semel (once) had been there, it was better than last year at the same occasion.

This was a happy ending to the months of speculation and intrigue at court which Hervey had endured with the Queen. But the stresses of the year had taken their toll on Hervey's health. In September 1736, he was ill enough for Henry Fox to write advising him to take care of himself, but still strong enough to reply telling Henry to mind his own business. 'For the sake of the physician, I have smelt several times at your physic, though I have not swallowed a drop of it; and have found, like smelling at hartshorn, that it raised my spirits while the bottle was at my nose, though none of it went down my throat. In short, my dear Count,' Hervey concluded in a passage of self-analysis that recalls Pope's description of his own 'little, tender, and crazy carcass', 'I have studied my own nasty constitution, my worse temper, my odd body and odder mind so long, that whether I understand it better than anybody else or not, at least the oddness of thinking I do, being yet uncured, I shall act on as if I did.'

28. Old Love, New Love

In March 1736, at the same time as Ste was married, there arrived in London a twenty-four-year-old Italian scholar named Francesco Algarotti, who bore a fond letter of introduction from Hervey's old friend Voltaire. Algarotti, apart from being intelligent and charming (in the words of Thomas Carlyle, he 'had powers of pleasing and used them'), was dazzlingly good-looking, with wavy raven hair swept back from his brow and coal-black eyes: a swarthy stereotype. He had an irresistible effect on almost everyone he met (especially men with homosexual tendencies). People threw themselves at him, strove to beguile him. Voltaire called Algarotti his '*cher cygne de Padue*', Frederick the Great begged him to come and live at the Prussian court; it was almost inevitable that Hervey, too, should fall under his spell.

With youthful enthusiasm, Hervey introduced his new friend into London society, taking Algarotti with him to court and to balls and the opera as he had once done with the young Ste Fox. Many years later, Lord Chesterfield reminded Charles Hanbury Williams, a close friend of the Fox brothers, of Algarotti, 'a led wit of the late Lord Hervey's'; at the same time, Henry Fox said of him,

I knew Algarotti too when he was in England and liked him, though I never thought his parts comparable to the others. But indeed I can form no good judgement of him, for I never saw him but in Lord Hervey's company, which was as a false light to a picture, his Lordship's affection mixed so with and gave such a colour to all conversation that he joined in.

When Algarotti left London in September 1736, he left Hervey and Lady Mary Wortley Montagu distraught and competitive, for Lady Mary, too, had succumbed to Algarotti's charms. Here Hervey (for once) had the advantage of reticence: Lady Mary had chosen

Hervey as her confidant, but she knew nothing of his passion for Algarotti. The night before Algarotti left, he had refused to dine with Hervey, saying he was seeing an old friend – who turned out to be Lady Mary. Her boasting of Algarotti's preference for her provoked Hervey to write to Algarotti belittling Lady Mary: 'How fortunate you are to be gone! The absence that brings sadness to every other lover will fulfil your happiness, for . . . she will not destroy with her countenance the impression she will make by her mind [in her letters].' It was cruel of Hervey to mock Lady Mary for her fading looks, about which he was fully aware she was sensitive. Furthermore, at forty, he was no longer the 'Hervey the handsome' of his youth: Sarah Duchess of Marlborough described him at this time as a ridiculous figure, powdered and rouged, with 'not a tooth in his head', although the previous December he had got himself 'the finest set of Egyptian pebbles [false teeth] you ever saw'.

Lady Mary was completely besotted with Algarotti. After twenty years of an unsatisfactory marriage (like Hervey she had married for what she thought was love, against her parents' wishes, only to find that she and her husband were incompatible), she determined to forsake everything for her autumnal passion, promising Algarotti that she would join him in Italy if he could not return to England to be with her. 'How timid one is when one loves!' she exclaimed – somewhat incongruously, in view of her decision, unprompted by Algarotti himself, to leave England and her husband, for him. 'My thoughts of you are such as exceed the strongest panegyric that the vainest man upon earth ever wished to hear made of himself; and all conversations since I lost yours are so insipid to me that I prefer my own closet [bedroom] meditations to all the amusements of a populous town or crowded court.'

Hervey contented himself with wishing that Algarotti might stay in London. 'I will not say more than you know, but much less than I feel, when I assure you that at present time the thing in the world that I wish most for is to be able to keep you in England for the rest of your life,' he told Algarotti.

A letter he wrote to Henry Fox two weeks after Algarotti's departure revealed Hervey lonely and depressed.

If I was to say I love you better than myself, it might sound like a nauseous, *outré* compliment; but it would be in reality no compliment at all. For at this moment I know nobody I am so angry with, or despise and hate so much. I do not believe there ever was so contemptible or absurd a composition: and have so much benevolence, as well as deference for the rest of mankind, that I hope there is none so disagreeably made, as well as firmly believe there is none so weakly put together . . . I write like a fool, think like a fool, talk like a fool, act like a fool; and have everything of a fool but the content of one. This is no news to you; and if there is anything stirring that would be so I know it not, or can not recollect it. I would not send this letter if I had time to write another, but I had rather you should think anything of me than that I neglect or forget you. Pray burn it as soon as you have read it, and pray allow it the only merit it pretends to, which is being a piece of my silly heart that I would trust to few eyes and few hands but your own.

The colds, sore throats and fevers with which Hervey was beset throughout 1736 were exacerbated by his knowledge that he was without Ste, who seven years before had nursed him so tenderly back to life. Although they remained in close contact, and Hervey's letters appeared on the surface to retain the intimacy that had always characterized them, beneath the wit and patter was a new tone of resigned despair. Hervey bemoaned the fact that he could not write to Ste with any freedom because his letters were always opened.

However I have one comfort even in being [deprived of] the pleasure of entertaining you with any little pieces of secret history by letter, and that is the better being able, by the number of things I have by these means in store, to make our *tête-à-têtes* when we meet, less tiresome to you, when I prolong the pleasure of them to myself; and when you seem in a hurry to be gone, it is with no small satisfaction that I recollect some new story, which I throw out to your curiosity (as Hippomenes did the golden apples) to stop you in your flight.

Where once Hervey could fill reams of paper with assurances of his love and titbits of court gossip, sending letters off every second or third day, from the time of Ste's engagement he struggled to keep the old sense of ease and affection present in his words.

Their friendship had run its course. For their first three years together, they had played out the model of classical pederasty: Hervey, in ardent pursuit of Ste, the ideal youth, whom he initiated intellectually and socially, as well as physically. Gradually, Ste gained in independence, and they met as two men, no longer a man and a boy. As equals, their relationship became less sexual, but no less intimate. Inevitably, Ste married; less inevitably, his wife became the focal point of his life, replacing Hervey as the person in whom he confided and on whom he relied for emotional support. Hervey was left jaded and heartbroken. Montaigne, describing the sense of loss he felt at his lover La Boétie's death, said, 'Since the day I lost him . . . I only drag on a weary life'; Hervey must have felt the same. He once told Ste that without him he would see no point in carrying on living, echoing Horace, whom Montaigne quoted in his essay about La Boétie.

> Since an untimely blow has snatched away
> Part of my soul, why then do I delay,
> I the remaining part, less dear than he,
> And not entire surviving?

For Hervey, Ste had been an antidote to the superficial life he led at court, a much needed balance to the conflicts and humiliations he endured there in the pursuit of social and political success. Ste represented disinterestedness, support, sincere affection: where other lovers – Frederick, for example, or Molly – imitated Hervey in an effort to appeal to him, even going so far as to compete with him, Ste had always remained himself, and apart. But Hervey, in placing his career before his friendship with Ste, had unwittingly relinquished his preeminence in his lover's affections, and once Fox had achieved adulthood, Hervey's only place in his life was as an old, dear friend. Hervey needed Ste as consolation for the emptiness of his life without him; Ste's life had become full whether Hervey was there or not.

Hervey continued to try to obtain for Ste the peerage he so wanted, but despite the regard in which Ste was held 'and backed by the almost quotidian application of Lord Hervey's interest,' he remained unsuccessful. 'I mention this solicitation so particularly,' he said, 'to show with what difficulty even at this time any favour was exhorted from the Court.' In 1737, when Horatio Walpole told Hervey, to console (or taunt) him over his failure, that George gave out honours as reluctantly as he gave away money, Hervey replied, 'I will remove that difficulty on this occasion, with regard to Mr Fox, by pawning my honour Mr Fox shall never ask anything of you besides (if this is done) as long as you are a minister.' He only had his brother Thomas and the Foxes under his protection, he told Sir Robert, and asked nothing for himself; he would always serve Walpole, but could not answer for his dependants' continued fidelity if they received no recompense. What made the situation more difficult for Hervey was that Frederick, seeking parliamentary support, had offered Ste a peerage if he would defect from the government. Ste had refused, and Hervey felt all the more obliged to ensure Ste was rewarded for his loyalty.

Fortune – or Voltaire – had cast the captivating Francesco Algarotti into Hervey's lap just at the moment he most needed a distraction. In the spring and summer of 1736, Hervey channelled all the disappointment he felt at losing Ste into this new friendship. When Algarotti went away, he poured out his heart to him, telling Algarotti of his admiration for him and how much he wished he were in London, trying to create the type of union between them that he and Ste had shared; but these letters say more about his state of mind than any real love for the self-centred Algarotti who was incapable of returning his feelings although he may have submitted to Hervey's advances.

In January Hervey sat down to express his delight to his new friend, then in Venice, at having received a letter when he had almost given up hope of hearing from him. 'Though I know I can send no answer till Friday [when the post to Italy was collected], I cannot deny myself the pleasure of seeming at least to thank you for it immediately. You had been silent just long enough to make me wish to forget you, and at the same time to prove to me it was impossible.' Hervey sounded unsure of Algarotti's affection (these fears enhanced by Algarotti's epistolary negligence; 'I cannot help continuing to desire what I have so little reason to expect,' he told Algarotti in July) and content with Algarotti's friendship if there were to be no more intimate relationship between them. He had not stopped trying to blacken his rival's image in Algarotti's mind, though, snidely commenting of some of the verses that Lady Mary had sent to Algarotti, 'You who do not know that they were most of them taken out of Prior's "Solomon" should have been more lavish in your praises.'

Where his insecurities are most apparent – apart from his inability to restrain himself from making Lady Mary sound like a fool – is in his refuge behind complex language and structure. Hervey's fondness for 'rhetorical flourishes, affected metaphors, and puerile witticisms' had been derided by Pulteney in 1731 and again by Pope in the 1735 'Epistle to Dr Arbuthnot':

> His Wit all see-saw, between *that* and *this*,
> Now high, now low, now Master up, now Miss,
> And he himself one vile Antithesis.

Hervey complained that criticism of his laboured style, in writing but more particularly in speech-making, was unjustified; he often spoke extempore in Parliament, but was always attacked for having over-prepared his speeches. But he did have a tendency to compensate for his uneasiness about expressing himself openly with literary virtuosity, as he did to Algarotti: 'If you could make every place as agreeable to yourself as you must make it to every other body, I should despair of seeing you again; since the consequence of that would be your desiring to change your company as little as your companions desire you should.' All he was saying was that he thought other people would like Algarotti as much as Hervey himself did; what he meant, perhaps, was that he was lonely, and that Algarotti was his only outlet for these feelings since he could not admit to Ste how bereft he felt without him.

Aged forty, Hervey found his age and weakening health made him less inclined to seek gratification in casual friendships or affairs. He was so old, now, that he found conversation the most agreeable of pleasures, he told Lady Mary. How unfair it was of Providence, at the same time as it reduces the number of pleasures one is capable of tasting, to make the pleasures that remain harder to find! And yet when one enjoyed people's minds, rather than their bodies, what could one expect? For there are a thousand people that can satisfy one physically for every person that is mentally compatible.

The difference between Algarotti and Ste was that Algarotti gave nothing back to Hervey. Algarotti liked him, but he was too mercenary to see Hervey as anything more than an entertaining companion and an entrée to English society. He was as ambitious as he was attractive, and if Hervey was prepared to dote on him and introduce him to all his influential friends, then so much the better. He corresponded carelessly with Hervey until he went to Russia, when he wrote regularly; the *Letters to Lord Hervey* were later published. He accepted the devotion Hervey, and Lady Mary to a greater extent, lavished upon him, as if it were his due: it slightly mystified him, but he saw no reason to discourage them. His description of meeting Lady Mary in Turin in 1741, when she had been waiting for him in Europe for a year and a half, is remarkable for its detachment. He told his brother bemusedly that it was 'one of the most curious episodes in his strange life'.★

What Hervey was seduced by in Algarotti was the idealized image of himself as a young man. The similarities between Algarotti, and Hervey at the same age – before disillusion and discontent had set in – were obvious: fêted for their beauty, both men were as charming and brilliant as they were good-looking. As an Italian, Algarotti was heir to the cultural traditions of antiquity that Hervey was so fascinated by; on a more personal level, Algarotti's nationality was a reminder to Hervey of the happy months he spent in Italy with Ste nine years before. In 1737, Algarotti published his *Newtonisme per le Dame*, or 'Newtonism for the Ladies', an explanation of Newton's theories for the lay reader, which was the inspiration for Voltaire's *Eléments de la Philosophie de Newton*. Hervey, who shared these

---

★ When Frederick II came to the Prussian throne in May 1740 he summoned Algarotti to his court. Algarotti left London in haste, borrowing money from Lady Hervey for the journey, and did not return to London until many years later. He and Lady Mary revived their friendship when he retired to Venice in 1753.

academic aspirations, admired Algarotti's combination of intellect and social ease. But where Algarotti was attractive as an abstract, desirable because everybody desired him, Ste's appeal had been to Hervey alone; Hervey loved Algarotti because everybody did, but he had loved Ste because he was his.

PART FIVE

29. Fathers

At the start of 1737, the Prince of Wales, angry at the King's continued refusal to raise his allowance to the £100,000 per year he expected after his marriage (what George had received as Prince of Wales), launched a full-scale campaign against his father. He persuaded William Pulteney to bring forward a parliamentary motion on the issue, with the backing of his regular supporters including Lord Chesterfield, the Dukes of Bedford and Marlborough, Mr Grenville, Thomas Pitt and George Lyttelton, Frederick's secretary, who was a close friend and ally of Lord Bolingbroke and Alexander Pope. On 22 February Pulteney and Walpole, the two best speakers in the House, debated the merits of the Prince's argument. Hervey said that he wished Pulteney well before the motion; Lady Hervey did so too, but with more sincerity.

George's 'rascally puppy of a son', as he called him, lost his motion by thirty votes only because forty-five Tory MPs were absent. The better to control him in future, Walpole advised that Frederick live as part of George and Caroline's establishment, rather than maintaining his own. He was forced to attend all the Drawing-rooms and to dine in state with his parents every Sunday, 'but the King never seemed to see or know he was in the room, and the Queen, though she gave him her hand on all these public occasions, never gave him one single word in private'. Once, said Hervey, Caroline spied her son out of the window of St James's Palace, and cried out, 'Look, there he goes – that wretch! – that villain! – I wish the ground would open this moment and sink the monster to the lowest hole in Hell.' George, for his part, declared he thought his son was a changeling.

Walpole survived Frederick's parliamentary challenge, but his position in 1737 was much weaker than it had been in his heyday ten years earlier, and it was a close-run contest. The members of his government were not as tractable as they had once been:

Lord Hardwicke, who was made Lord Chancellor in February, 'not only felt, but often too plainly showed he felt, how considerable he was become'; Newcastle, mindful of his own career, was gradually shifting his allegiance from Walpole to the up-and-coming Lord Carteret. The Queen, for so long Sir Robert's strongest support, no longer seemed to trust him as she had once done. Quite probably, this was because he insisted on insulting her by bluntly informing her she was too old to retain her husband's love. 'Madam, do not flatter yourself,' he would tell her. 'For pleasure of the body, there must be youth on one side; and believe me, marriage is never so properly called one flesh as after twenty years of marriage, for no husband then knows his wife's flesh from his own.'

Walpole was speaking from experience. The following spring his wife of nearly forty years died, leaving him free to marry his long-standing mistress, Maria Skerritt. Although Pope delighted in calling her Phyrne, after a famous Athenian courtesan, Miss Skerritt was an atypical mistress. She was tall and thin – not pretty but handsome – and devoted to Walpole. Her best friend was Lady Mary Wortley Montagu. Lord Percival described her as a woman of 'extreme good understanding and very agreeable'. Miss Skerritt bore Walpole a daughter at the start of their union in 1725, and was maintained by him for many years in a 'bower of bliss' in Richmond Park, in a house he held by virtue of his Rangership, where he visited her each weekend. Although he took his work there with him he used to say that there 'he put off his cares with his clothes'. Tragically, in June 1738, the second Lady Walpole died of a miscarriage less than three months after their marriage. Walpole was devastated; she had been, he said, 'indispensable to his happiness'.

Queen Caroline was always very curious about Molly Skerritt, and her relationship with Sir Robert. In a comment which, as Hervey said, shed just as much light on her own situation as on Miss Skerritt's,

She said she was very glad he had any amusement for his leisure hours, but could neither comprehend how a man could be very fond of a woman he only got [had] for his money, nor how a man of Sir Robert's age and make, with his dirty mouth and great belly, could ever manage any woman would suffer him as a lover from any consideration or inducement but his money.

But Walpole was right about one thing: although George had lost interest in Madame Walmoden – she was so far away, after all, and he was not the kind of man to remain faithful to a memory – he lost no time in taking another mistress. His choice was Lady Deloraine, governess to the Princesses Caroline and Emily, who had been fluttering her eyelashes at him (and his son Frederick) for years. In Hervey's words, the King 'had conveniently made the governess of his two eldest daughters his whore . . . and the guardian director of his [younger] son's youth and morals his cuckold'.★ Lady Deloraine retained at thirty-five, said Hervey, a bloom that not one in ten thousand women has at fifteen; but her beauty was matched only by her vanity. Several years before she had complained to Hervey that everyone at court was neglecting and avoiding her, and asked him the reason for it. 'I told her I thought it was easy to be accounted for; that envy kept the women at a distance, and despair the men; to which she only answered, "Pshaw," turned to the glass, reflected on her conduct, and believed me.'

By the summer of 1737, everyone at court assumed Lady Deloraine was the King's mistress – not least, because she talked about her conquest so incessantly. She told Hervey that George had been in love with her for two years; 'Who is not in love with you?' Hervey replied. She told Sir Robert that she had not yet yielded to George's advances, but that when she did, she would make sure she was well paid. Once she had succumbed, she asked Princess Caroline – her charge, as well as her lover's daughter – to tell her own husband, Mr Wyndham, about her affair. She boasted that England ought to thank her, because she kept the King from Hanover; presumably she meant it was better that he spend English

★ His younger son the Duke of Cumberland's tutor, Mr Wyndham, whom Lady Deloraine married in 1734. Her first husband had died in 1729.

taxes on an English whore than a German one. When Walpole asked Hervey his opinion of the affair, he replied that while what Miss Skerritt thought was of importance to every man in England, Lady Deloraine might say anything and it would only matter to her and the King.

The Queen affected not to mind, and was glad that her husband's choice meant that he stayed in England, but 'she could not help repining at his being only gone another way abroad, and not come home'. Hervey, whom Caroline saw more of because George now spent his free time with Lady Deloraine rather than his wife, was her constant companion. In a way, Caroline, rather than Francesco Algarotti, had replaced Ste Fox as the person closest to Hervey's heart, although his feelings for her were very different from his feelings for Ste or Algarotti. When Caroline complained that she did not see Hervey enough, he replied, 'he wished with all his heart the King had more love, or Lady Deloraine more wit, that he might have more time with her Majesty, but that he thought it very hard that he should be snubbed and reproved [by Caroline, for not attending her] because the King was old and Lady Deloraine a fool'.

On 5 June, Hervey was called from her side to his father's, who lay ill at Ickworth.

My invaluable son Lord Hervey, hearing I was ill, came to make me a visit at Ickworth, nothwithstanding the Parliament was still sitting, and stayed with me till Thursday ye 30th; for which I hope and pray that God will please to reward him for his fresh instance of his piety towards an aged father, as well as his constant, dutiful behaviour towards me ever since he was born.

One of the most endearing things about Lord Bristol's faith was his simple readiness to give thanks for his blessings.

The old earl was sentimental and demonstrative to a fault, as he admitted to Hervey in 1737; 'my nature inclines me perhaps, as you may have observed, to be sometimes too open in common conversation'. Molly agreed with her father-in-law's self-analysis: according to Bristol's way of thinking, she wrote, 'one should begin to weep for one's children as soon as they are born; for they must die at last, and every day brings them nearer to it'. In 1734, Bristol had written to his eldest son the day after Hervey's birthday – the 'nativity of more importance to me and my family than almost all others' – to tell him that he had worn the grand clothes Hervey had given him to commemorate the day.

I in the first place justly celebrated it with due thanks to God for so signal a blessing as he was pleased to bestow on both by its being your birthday, begging His grace to make you truly sensible of the uncommon gifts He hath endowed you with, and that you may live to use them to His glory and the good of our country and your own happiness; and that I might signalise it in the most extraordinary manner, ventured to appear in all that finery you sent me, which no less occasion could have excused.

Bristol's love for Hervey was a reflection and extension of his passionate sense of duty to God and his country; he saw his son as his family's offering on these combined altars. His pride in Hervey could not be diminished by his private disapproval of the man for whom Hervey worked.

Despite their political disagreements, Hervey adored his gentle, straightforward father. 'I am so unlike most eldest sons,' he assured their family friend Dean Butts of Norwich in 1732, that

one of the greatest afflictions I could have in this world would be the loss of him; the very particular affection he has always expressed for me above any of his other children, and indeed above any other body, has added all the ties of gratitude, to those of nature; and all the attachment of friendship to those of duty . . . As I believe nobody in the world loves me so well as he does there is nobody in the world whose pleasure, welfare and happiness I have more at heart.

Hervey was pleased to be with his father, but the time away from London did lie heavy on his hands, as he wrote to Lady Mary. 'For God's sake how can you talk so like a canting Seneca of the purity of air and the quiet of retirement raising my imagination? You might as well talk of water-gruel raising one's spirits . . . [My imagination] must be cultivated; and I find too that the dunghills I meet with in Town are most excellent manure.'

Hervey wrote to Ste soon after his arrival in Suffolk complaining about being so far from London, wondering how Henry Fox had spoken in Parliament, and what the numbers on the latest vote in the House had been. Two weeks later, he said he had got used to the pace of country life. He began to think he was fitter to live in the country than he had thought. But he still found 'the common pleasures of a country' inferior to those of a town, and, undaunted by the previous consequences of his versifying, could not resist breaking into rhyme ('I find it as difficult to write a letter in plain prose as a dancing-master does to walk into a room'):

> I own, my Friend: my only Pleasures lie
> > In human Creatures, & in Black & White;
> Whilst in my Conduct still I only try,
> > To reconcile what's pleasant with what's right.

The thing that marred his retreat to Ickworth was the presence of his mother there. 'If one mouth in the house I could name was gagged I should like this relaxation very well, but that orifice is so like that of Mount Vesuvius, that everything that comes out of it, that is not fire, is rubbish; everything within the reach of its disagreeable influence is the worst for it.' Lady Bristol was becoming more irritable in her old age. She forbade Hervey from sending his children to Ickworth that spring. Bristol – who adored his grandchildren – 'fell into a violent passion and said he wondered how I come to dare to forbid any of my Lord Hervey's children the house', Lady Bristol reported to her old friend the Duchess of Marlborough, in a letter soliciting her help in turning Bristol against Hervey, 'this treacherous villain'. The year before, mother and son had been on such good terms, curling up for a nap together after the Prince of Wales's wedding, breakfasting regularly with each other, that Lady Bristol had boasted of their closeness; but now she was convinced that Hervey was trying to 'plunder' his father's estates. The next spring she wrote to the Duchess again, begging her 'to find something to lash my wicked pair with; for I don't doubt that they are as infamous in public life as I have felt them in private'.

The reason she may have turned against her 'villainous son', his 'false, bold wife', and their 'young vermin' (her words echoing the Queen's complaints about Prince Frederick), apart from her old patterns of irrational, selfish behaviour, was that Bristol was still trying to bribe his son – although Hervey was by now quite rich in his own right, earning £2,000 a year from his court offices – to desert Walpole. Hervey thought the Scottish Bill, legislation to deal with the Porteous riots in Edinburgh the previous September, which Sir Robert and the King supported, was too harshly punitive; his father suspected that he might have come to Ickworth just as much to avoid the issue as to sit by his sick-bed. Trying to take advantage of Hervey's rare wavering of support for Walpole, Bristol concluded, 'Whenever you find yourself made the least uneasy by any unworthy treatment from those who I know are incapable of setting a due value on your merit . . . you shall at all times be sure to find, not only my house and arms open to receive you and yours with the utmost joy, but my purse so too.'

Hervey returned to London at the end of June having persuaded his father to send Ste one of his best mares with the explanation, 'as you are his particular friend and one I ought ever love and value for the uncommon marks you gave us of that seasonable care and kindness you showed him when he stood in so much need of both'. Bristol wished Henry Fox well, too, 'as a friend of Lord Hervey's', and offered his congratulations on Henry's preferment. Hervey had obtained for Henry the office of Surveyor-General of the King's Works, a position worth £1,100 a year, and Ste had finally been promised his peerage at the next batch of elevations.

Despite Hervey's efforts to please him, Ste Fox was retreating further and further away from his one-time lover. In October 1737, Hervey wrote to Ste, evidently having complained in a previous (missing) letter that his old friend no longer had time for him. Hervey seemed more to be trying to persuade himself, than Ste, that he did not believe Ste could forget him; in parts the language is almost raw, and in parts contrived and artificial, his old refuge and protection. This was Hervey's first acknowledgement, to himself as well as to Ste, of the change in their relationship that had existed since Ste's wedding eighteen months earlier. He had tried to ignore it, tried to pretend that nothing had changed; but to no avail.

How very ill, my dearest of all friends! must I have expressed myself, for you to imagine, by my last letter, that I ever suspected you of forgetting or neglecting me: I deserve too well of you (that is as far as loving you is deserving well) and have too good an opinion of your penetration to doubt of your knowing it well enough to secure me from either of those misfortunes; and whenever I see in you what I should in any other body construe marks of forgetfulness or neglect, I should certainly impute them to chance, inadvertency, or laziness. I have loved you ever since I knew you, which is now many years, so much better than most people are capable of loving any thing.

Ste would not, he could not, be insensible of being so well-beloved; he must want to continue to be so. And yet, Hervey did not want Ste to feel he had imposed an obligation on him, by loving him so much. It was for Hervey's own sake that he had chosen 'to live and converse with you preferably to the rest of my acquaintance', just as when he chose a book in his library it was to please himself, not the book: he returned again and again to favourite books, as to Ste, because they were more agreeable to him than any others. But once again, Hervey's words only emphasized Ste's ultimate passivity in his eyes.

I only wish it was in my power to show you how well I love you, that all your pleasures and wishes depended on me only, and if they did you would find yourself never deprived of the one, or disappointed of the other. There is an air of melancholy rather to be collected from the whole of your letter, than fixed on any particular passage, which gives me great uneasiness; why do you only hint it? Tell me what it is; take my advice and take my assistance, and believe the first will always be as faithful though not perhaps so able as you could wish it; and the last as willing though not as effectual. Adieu; I had the letter you feared was last and I shall expect an answer to this with great impatience.

30. Towels and Tablecloths

On his return to London from Ickworth Hervey found the Queen worried about the impending birth of the Princess of Wales's first baby. Caroline wanted to be present at the lying-in – 'I will be sure it is her child,' she insisted – but Frederick, insulted by her implication, refused to let her. On 31 July, the Prince and Princess of Wales dined in state with the King and Queen at Hampton Court; after dinner, when they had left the rest of the royal family, Princess Augusta went into labour, and her waters broke. Her husband, determined not to allow his mother to witness the birth, put her into a carriage and drove her fifteen miles to St James's Palace. He later told his mother that Augusta's pains were 'so strong he thought he should have been obliged to carry her into some house upon the road to be brought to bed, and that, with holding her and her pillows in the coach, he had got such pains in his own back he could hardly stir'. St James's Palace was closed for the summer, so the Princess was laid to bed on two tablecloths instead of sheets, and there gave birth to a 'little rat of a girl, about the bigness of a good large toothpick case'.

Meanwhile George, Caroline and the Princesses sat at Hampton Court unaware of Frederick's hasty departure, playing cards in cosy domesticity with Hervey as they did most evenings. At ten o'clock they retired to bed, and three hours later someone came to tell Caroline that the Prince had gone to London. The Queen, with Princesses Emily and Caroline, Hervey and the Duke of Grafton set out for St James's, arriving at the palace at four in the morning. Hervey took the precaution of sending for Henry Fox, 'thinking there would be some juggle (as the Queen apprehended) about a false child [there was not], and that he should want some sensible, clever body he could trust to employ in making discoveries'.

When Caroline arrived and greeted her son, it was the first time she had addressed an informal word to him since he had tried to move Parliament against his father six months before. Nine days later, she visited Princess Augusta and her tiny daughter, but Frederick – who would not admit it had been wrong to move his wife such a distance while she was in labour – did not utter one word to his mother, either of thanks for her concern or of apology. George, who still refused to see his son because of the 'deliberate indignity' Frederick had shown him, said Caroline 'was well enough served for thrusting her nose where it had been shit upon already'.

Frederick's insulting rudeness set the seal on his break from his parents. Deliberately, he no longer addressed his mother in letters as 'Your Majesty', claiming that in rank the Prince of Wales was directly beneath the King, but above the Queen. Shamelessly courting popular support, he announced he was going to call his daughter Lady Augusta, in the English fashion, not Princess, as was the custom in Hanover. He hired people off the streets to applaud him when he went to the theatre. George banned foreign embassies from visiting the Prince at his court in Kew (Frederick was now living independently of his parents), and no one who frequented George's court was permitted to attend Frederick's.

Frederick blamed his mother for not trying to make peace between him and his father after his daughter's birth, and his hostility towards her escalated. Caroline, in her turn, became increasingly paranoid about the motives of the people surrounding her. Walpole told Hervey that because she had ruled George for so long by deceiving him, 'it makes her suspect a little of the same play from everybody else, as well as exercise a little of it to everybody else herself'. Their mutual distrust was beginning to corrode the relationship between Caroline and her first minister and,

as the Queen's confidence in Lord Hervey every day increased, Sir Robert Walpole's jealousy of him increased too, not from his being in the rank of a rival to his power, but from a weakness in this great man's composition, which made him grudge this show of favour even where, I believe, he had not the least suspicion, or where, I am very sure, at least, he had no reason given him to justify [the] suspicion that this favour would ever be employed to his disservice.

Caroline turned to Hervey more and more during this period, both to console herself for what she saw as the loss of her son, and to keep her spirits up. She had a bad attack of the gout in August, and flouted convention to take Hervey into her bedchamber to keep her company, saying 'she was too old to have the honour of being talked of for it'. They discussed and analysed Frederick continually. Hervey insisted in his *Memoirs* that he was as objective about the Prince as he could be, and the conversations he recorded do bear this out. He may have held a grudge privately (he was always delighted secretly to work against Frederick's interests), but he did not let it show to Caroline. The Queen, for her part, so favoured Hervey that she no longer believed he had been at fault in his dispute with Frederick five years earlier.

'You once thought, you fool, to be so imposed upon, that he loved me,' she told Hervey.

'I did indeed,' he replied, 'but I never thought people may not alter.'

'You thought too, that he loved you, my poor Lord Hervey. He laughed at you all the while for believing him and for fancying you had any interest in [with] him . . . he cannot love anybody . . . Monster . . . I feel no more of a mother towards him than if he was no relation.'

Caroline, obsessed by her relationship with her son, often questioned Hervey about his parents. Hervey told her of the affection and respect he bore his kind, pious father, concluding, 'He is judicious, dispassionate, just, humane, and a thorough good and amiable man, and has lived long enough in this world to have this character [description] of him (though given by his son) uncontroverted by anyone else.' Caroline, weeping, replied, 'He is a happy as well as a good man to deserve such a son; and your mother is a brute that deserves such a beast as my son [Frederick and Lady Bristol did in fact get on very well]. I hope *I* do not; and wish with all my soul we could change, that they who are so alike might go together, and that you and I might belong to one another.'

At the end of October, the court moved back from Hampton Court to St James's Palace for the King's Birthday celebrations. George and Caroline saw the high attendance as a show of support from the peers for their stance against Frederick, and were gratified. Days later, the Queen came down with a bad case of what she called colic. The King, ever dismissive of illness, berated her for neglecting to greet the Duchess of Norfolk at the Drawing-room that afternoon; Caroline formally apologized to her and then rushed to bed.

Caroline had been very ill over the past few years. In 1733 she had had such a bad case of gout that she had to be 'rolled in and out of the Drawing-room every day in that chair given her by the King of Poland, in which Lady Deloraine played Sea-Goddess [in a masque] last year,' Hervey told Ste. The following autumn saw Caroline struck down again, but George insisted that she fulfil all her official obligations. She was forced to leave Kensington Palace to go to St James's Palace for the celebration of the King's Birthday on 29 October; the King dragged her through 'all the tiresome ceremonies of Drawing-rooms and balls, the fatigues of heats and crowds, and every other disagreeable appurtenance to the celebration of a Birthday'.

There was, said Hervey, a strange affectation of an incapacity of being sick insisted upon by the royal family; it was as if they feared that an admission of physical weakness would be seen as a diminution of their symbolic power. This was not how Walpole saw it. For years he had pleaded with the Queen to defy the King, to insist on resting and looking after her health, but to no avail. 'Your Majesty knows that this country is entirely in your hands,' he warned her. 'I can do nothing without you.'

It was soon apparent that this time the Queen was seriously ill. She did not respond to snakeroot, a strong medicine derived from poison that Hervey sometimes took, or being made to vomit, or having blood – up to twelve ounces at a time – taken from her. Hervey was constantly by her side, never leaving her apartment for more than four or five hours at a time, and more usually only for two hours in the twenty-four; he slept on a mattress on the floor outside her bedroom door. At first George insisted on sleeping on his wife's bed, 'inconveniently both to himself and the Queen . . . where he could not sleep, nor she turn about'.

Frederick came to London from Kew to see Caroline, but George refused him access to her, saying, 'He wants to come and insult his poor dying mother; but she shall not see him; you have heard her . . . very often . . . desire me, if she should be out of her senses, that I would never let him come near her.' The prescience of Caroline's request shows that she was aware of the illness latent within her, and knew that it would surface soon. George was right about Frederick; although he sent every day to St James's (he was staying at his London residence, Carlton House) to find out his mother's progress, the Duke of Marlborough told Hervey that he would say, after seeing the messenger and hearing she was still alive, 'Well, sure, we must have some good news soon. 'Tis impossible she can hold out long. I think I am a very good son, I wish her out of her pain.' According to Walpole, though, Caroline did wish for a reconciliation, telling him that she would have liked to have made her peace with Frederick but that she could not ask to see him because it would embarrass and irritate George.

Caroline kept saying, 'I have an ill which nobody knows of,' but would not explain or allow the doctors to examine her thoroughly. Much against her protests, George finally told them that at the birth of her last child, Princess Louisa, in 1724, she had suffered an umbilical rupture which had not properly healed. Relating this to Hervey, George said that as he told the doctors of her secret, she turned her head away from him and wept the only tears she shed during her whole illness. She had managed to keep her old injury from George until he returned from Hanover in January 1736; and when he found her out, she made him promise that he would tell no one, using his concern to reproach him for being tired of her, blaming the weakness of her body for his weariness of it. She knew her hold over George was sexual as much as emotional or intellectual, and her fear was that an illness of this type would make her seem less of a woman to him.

The doctors proposed an operation, but there was nothing really they could do except try to ease the inevitable. Five days after she fell ill, the wound began to mortify. She bled ceaselessly, a torrent of blood and pus.

> Here lies, wrapt up in 40,000 Towels,
> The only Proof that Caroline had Bowels,

commented Pope. Four days later her gut burst, but she suffered on for another three days. George, desperate to help her but impotent in the face of death, insisted on feeding her 'with a mixture of brutality and tenderness'; she ate to please him, but it caused her obvious pain. Sir Robert Walpole visited her, and he said it was like hearing a corpse speak when she whispered, 'My good Sir Robert, I have nothing to say to you, but to recommend the King, my children, and the kingdom to your care.' She told her husband to promise her he would marry again after her death. George, weeping, stammered, '*Non – j'aurais – des – maîtresses*'; the Queen replied, '*Ah! Mon Dieu! Cela n'empêche pas.*'* Eventually she died at ten on the evening of 20 November 1737. For once, Hervey was away from her bedside, and although he was sent for she died before he arrived.

'I myself, who knew her well, who knew her temper, her strength, her greatness of mind, her patience, her resignation, her mildness, and her indifference to life, could yet have had no conception of her firmness in bodily pain and such acute sufferings,' Hervey wrote to Charlotte Digby the following March.

Knowing the whole time she must die, preserving her senses to the last moment, and behaving to the last as if she had nothing to regret in the place she was leaving, and nothing to apprehend in that she was going to . . . If anything could give me an exalted idea of that dignity of our species which I so often hear of, it would be having known this excellent Queen. But as I know none of the species equal to her, and so few anything like her, it only gives me greater contempt for the odious herd.

In the midst of his own private loss, Hervey, ever the courtier, put his duties before his emotions. He was the first person George sent for after Caroline's death, to talk about how she had died, and how much he had loved her. Then Hervey went straight to the Princess Caroline's apartments, to console her for the loss of her mother, and spent the night there talking to her, 'trying to lighten

---

* No – I would have – mistresses . . . Oh! My God! That should not be an obstacle.

her grief by indulging it, and not by that silly way of trying to divert what cannot be removed, or to bring comfort to such affliction as time only can alleviate'.

Caroline's death meant more to Hervey than the loss of a political asset. 'Upon my word, if I knew her, she was a thorough great, wise, good and agreeable woman,' he told Algarotti in January 1738, 'and the distinctions with which she always honoured me, joined to the satisfaction I had in her company, make me look upon her death to be as great a loss to my interest as to my pleasure, and make my heart regret the loss of her as much as my vanity or my ambition.'

'Lord Hervey is as calm as ever I saw him,' wrote Henry Fox to Ste five days after Caroline's death, 'but afflicted to the greatest degree, and will not soon forget it, nor, I fear, cease to look upon it as the greatest misfortune that could ever befall him, and the loss of so much of the pleasure of his life as makes the rest not worth thinking of . . . He is in health so-so, not so ill as you might expect; but I greatly fear less likely to mend than grow worse.'

Lord Bristol thought Lady Hervey might be able to help her husband to get over the grief at Caroline's death which had made him write to his father during her illness saying that he did not want to go on living himself.

The tedious void your Lord now seems to think this sad accident will occasion in his future life, may in my opinion without doing any natural injury to the memory of the late Queen be amply filled up by you, whose natural talents and your improvements of them can furnish as entertaining a conversation when present, and as agreeable a correspondence when absent, as any of your sex can pretend to,

he wrote, ever hopefully, to Molly from Ickworth. But Ste, the one person who might have been able to console Hervey, remained in Somerset.

Walpole earned himself the lasting animosity of the Princesses Caroline and Emily by advising them to send Lady Deloraine to console George, until they could have Madame Walmoden brought to England, saying, 'People must wear old gloves till they could get new ones'; he knew he could control the King only through a woman and, aware that the Princesses hated him, thought that he might be able to influence George through his mistress. Although he complained she stank of Spanish wine, George continued to see Lady Deloraine, sending 'for this old acquaintance to his apartment from just the same motives that people send casually for a new one to a tavern', said Hervey. But George, faithful in his own way, never did remarry; he later said there was not a woman alive worthy to buckle Caroline's shoe. He desired to be buried next to her, with the sides of their coffins removed so that their corpses might lie undivided by any barrier.

Henry Fox wrote to Ste that he was still worried about Hervey nine days after Caroline's death. Although Hervey was managing to behave as usual, '''tis a total subversion of his thoughts, hopes, pleasures. He loved her, had reason to love her, and lived much and with much delight in her conversation.' Hervey was thin and pale, but insisted that his own health was in no danger, although he slept badly, and found it difficult to distract himself from his thoughts. 'His life is spent in talking of her, which I hope will [ease] his mind to the subject, and help time in weakening the sense, and preventing the effects of this unexpected and sad event.'

Henry Fox had been with Walpole when he first heard that the Queen was dying, according to his grandson, the third Lord Holland. On hearing the news, Walpole walked distractedly round the room,

and said to himself, 'My God, my God, why hast thou forsaken me?' This might be his first reflection, but he soon grew pleased at finding he governed the King alone. He did not love her particularly, for having promoted the quarrel between himself and Lord Townshend [in 1731, see p. 78], in order to make them both dependent on herself.

But George, who resented the tenor of Caroline's last words to Walpole, was in no mood to be managed; and Walpole, whose parliamentary power was in the descendant, could no longer hope to remain in power without George's complete confidence.

31. Carrying Candles

Hervey said that after Caroline's death, some people at court (whom he did not name) endeavoured to persuade him to try to use his own closeness to the King to exclude Walpole from power, 'blowing up Lord Hervey's vanity and ambition, by telling him how capable he was of stepping into Sir Robert's place, and how glad the at present broken Whig party would be to unite under his banner, if he would but set up his standard'. But Hervey had no intention of trying to topple the man he had served so faithfully – and against so much private opposition – for so long; all he wanted was to ensure that he was still close to power. Hervey, 'whilst all the world was speaking of him at this time as the King's first favourite', was fully aware both of the changeability of George's interest, and of Walpole's declining fortunes. He wrote to Walpole two weeks after Caroline's death to, as he said in his *Memoirs*, let him 'see he [Hervey] was sensible he had not been well used . . . to prevent his being worse used'. He did not want to let Sir Robert discard him because his usefulness at court, by virtue of his intimacy with the Queen, was over.

He began by saying that he believed, as he had often told Walpole in conversation, that Caroline's death, although a grievous personal loss, need not necessarily mean Sir Robert would lose his control over the King. 'It may occasion many difficulties in the exercise of your power, but no danger to the possession of it.' This was partly because the dying Queen had recommended Walpole to her husband; and partly because the King, who wanted to refute those who said Walpole was Caroline's minister, not his, would retain Walpole simply to prove them wrong. Walpole's talents and abilities – 'so much superior to anybody I ever knew' – would ensure that 'you may meet with rubs, but you will never find a stop'.

His own situation, continued Hervey, was as well known to Sir Robert as his own: he had, he said,

made it my sole business to please the Queen and you . . . [but] some
honorary titles you have refused me, and other more essential favours
which you have denied, leave me too little room to doubt that either
those who have always been giving you ill impressions of me have made
you afraid or unwilling to distinguish me, or that your own judgement
and knowledge of me have convinced you that I am fit for nothing but
to carry candles and set chairs all my life.

Hervey had often been suspicious about men like his rival Newcastle working to undermine him to Walpole, for example in his
endeavours to obtain positions for the Fox brothers. But all the
same he had never bothered to conceal his closeness to Ste. Then,
too, there was Hervey's public image: could Walpole seriously back
a man who was the butt of every cheap ballad-writer in London?
But Hervey seems to have discounted these factors; he believed
Walpole simply did not regard him highly enough to promote him.
From Walpole's point of view, though, rumours about Hervey's
private life – the ammunition of his enemies at court – can only
have underlined his temperamental unsuitability for high office.
Despite his loyalty to Walpole, his outward refusal to conform
branded him a maverick; and his influence over the Queen had
only aggravated his enemies' resentment.

It was his enduring loyalty to Walpole, Hervey continued, which
had never been rewarded, that made him threaten to quit his post
at court. 'I promised you I never would ask anything for myself of
the Queen but through you, and kept my word; but I own to you
I feel my pride so shocked by many things that have happened to
me of late, that nothing but my not being able to afford to quit has
prevented me.' This last was not strictly true, since Lord Bristol had
always promised to recompense him handsomely if he would leave
Walpole's service; but he would never have left Caroline while she
lived. 'I once had it in my power to serve you (or my vanity gave
me the pleasure of thinking so). That time is over. I know I am
now as insignificant as any other of the dignified cyphers about you
– as insignificant as their envy can make me.

'All I mean to say,' he concluded disingenuously,

is that I will be refused and disappointed no more, for I will ask and expect no more; that my enemies shall not conquer, for I will not struggle; that I could have made my peace with my greatest enemy if I would have done it at your expense; that I scorned it, and do not repent the part I have acted; that I submit to be a nothing, and wish whoever you honour with your confidence, or benefit with your favour, may always serve you with as honest a mind, as warm a heart, and as unshakeable an attachment, as you have been served by your neglected, &c.

The bluff had its desired effect. Walpole sent for Hervey when he received this letter, and told him that after his children he loved no one in England so well as he did Hervey, and felt more obligated to nobody. 'Commit your future interest to my care,' Sir Robert told him, 'and give me leave to think, what I wish to believe, that all the dissatisfaction expressed in your letter is rather the effect of a melancholy present turn of your mind on this unhappy event, than a distrust of my friendship and sincerity.' But Hervey no longer had faith in Walpole's regard for him – he knew him now 'too well to depend much on the most lavish professions of kindness and esteem', and remembered how Sir Robert's envy had made him lie to Hervey when he was afraid that Hervey might have more influence with Caroline than Walpole did himself – and sensed that Walpole's declining fortunes would mean that in his own struggle to retain power, he would not bother to try to promote the man who had served him so faithfully for the last ten years.

There is no denying that Hervey's objectives in seeking power were selfish. He was no idealist, he did not want to change the system in which he lived; but those qualities were rare in politicians of this period. Certainly Walpole lacked them. What Walpole had that Hervey did not was force of character. Hervey was simply too delicate to gain the respect power needs to be accorded: he was bright and able, he was charming, he understood how people worked, but he was slight and precious, his chief weapons malice and manipulation, too effeminate in a world in thrall to masculinity. However loyal he had been to Walpole – and he had been – Hervey's personal weakness combined with Walpole's political weakness meant that Walpole could not reward him as he perhaps would have liked to and as Hervey certainly felt he deserved.

After Caroline died it was as if, knowing that her demise had robbed him of his key to power, Hervey determined to adopt a more aggressive attitude, signalled by his letter to Walpole just after her death. But this newly offensive ambition was tempered by a resignation to the futility of patronage and a disillusion with politics. Early in 1738, he replied to an unknown lady soliciting his help that, despite his closeness to the King, he had no employment in his gift: 'my misfortune like most other people's who have the ear of Princes, is to have credit and interest so much overrated, that I am envied by my enemies for favour I am only thought to possess and often reproached by my friends for not exerting a power in their service which I really have not'. Perhaps he was thinking of how often his mother had berated him for not doing more to assist his brothers' advancement; perhaps he was thinking of the promised peerage for which Ste still waited.

In April 1740 Hervey was made Keeper of the Privy Seal, an official government position which entitled him to sit on the Cabinet. He had waited so long for a distinction like this that he was determined to enjoy his triumph to the full, shamelessly boasting to Lady Mary Wortley Montagu of the jealousy he inspired in his rivals' breasts. 'The King has been so gracious as to reward my little services with the great dignity of Keeper of the Privy Seal; a place of this rank and profit you will easily imagine has not been conferred upon me without my receiving many public congratulations and making me the object of at least as much private envy,' he told her delightedly.

Lord Bristol wrote to Hervey congratulating him equivocally (and convolutedly) on his new post.

The office is certainly an honourable one, but then it must be owned too that you had earned it hardly [with difficulty], not only by a close and slavish attendance for above ten years in a station long since thought much below the merit of your known abilities, but also by having made too successful an use of them on many important national occasions, where very few could, and I know one [Walpole] who would not (had he been master of your talents), have exerted them for the support of many measures tending to the establishment of such a formidable system of power as must in its nature sooner or later endanger liberty.

This had been his perennial concern about Walpole's style of government: that in its quest for unchallenged hegemony it deprived the British nation of the political freedom for which Bristol had fought to bring in the Hanoverian dynasty and a constitutional monarchy. Hervey's political allegiance had, Bristol told him, given him 'many uneasy years' and towards the end of Hervey's life this unease was the cause of hostility between Bristol and his beloved son.

Bristol's comments were the occasion of a row between father and son that dominated their correspondence over the following autumn, during which Bristol attacked Walpole for weakening, if not throwing down, 'the necessary guards and fences of our [British] liberties', for the 'melancholy work' he had made of the government's administration, and for his 'ill-gotten estate'. 'I find myself obliged for your sake to acquaint you with such truths that perhaps nobody but myself dare tell you, because they are such unwelcome ones,' Bristol said. Later that year, he quoted Sir Walter Raleigh to his depressed son (who had tried unsuccessfully to conceal from his father a 'strong and constant' gloom while he was at Ickworth in July 1740): 'Have a care of contracting or continuing a friendship with an overgrown greatness which falling will crush thee, or if likely to stand long, will grow insolently weary of support and proudly spurn those very props that held it up before.'

Hervey was right about the reaction of the political world to his promotion to the office of Privy Seal. Lord Percival thought that Sir Robert had not wanted to give the post to Hervey, but that Hervey had obtained it, 'having much the King's ear and favour'; in fact, Sir Robert, in the face of vigorous opposition, had fought to get Hervey elevated. Hervey's old enemy, the Duke of Newcastle, had spoken vehemently against Hervey's promotion since Walpole announced in autumn 1739 that he intended to bring Hervey into the Cabinet. Relations between Newcastle and his Prime Minister had been strained since 1737 when Newcastle offered to stand surety for the good behaviour of Lord Carteret, a prominent member of the Opposition, if Walpole would take him into government; Walpole told Newcastle unequivocally that he must make his choice between him and Carteret.

Later that year, Hervey could not resist reporting to Ste a '*mauvais mot*' of Newcastle's that revealed the tension under-lying their political relationship. Sir Robert, the Archbishop of Canterbury, 'some more of the *grosses têtes*', and several ladies were dining at the Duchess of Richmond's. As the party sat down,

his Grace said to Sir Robert in his shrill cock-pit voice cross the table, 'Well, Sir Robert, I desire you would not talk in your usual strain to these ladies but remember the Archbishop is here.' Sir Robert answered very gravely, 'I am not conscious of ever having presumed to say anything to these ladies [that] any bishop might not hear'; and with much ado his Grace, after being teased for about an hour for this pretty speech, began to find out he had ingeniously in these few words told Sir Robert he did not know how to behave himself, intimated to the Archbishop that the Duchess of Richmond and the ladies of the Court were accustomed to hear such bawdy as must shock episcopal ears, and that his Grace's presence put a constraint upon the whole company. – Was there ever such an animal?

At first it looked as if Sir Robert might sacrifice his old obligations to Hervey for the sake of retaining Newcastle's support, but by 1740 relations between Walpole and Newcastle were so bad that Sir Robert informed his Secretary of State that he did not care if Newcastle did not want Hervey on the Cabinet. Newcastle saw Hervey's promotion as Walpole's first step towards ousting him from power – 'in this light I do, and ever shall, look upon this step as it relates to myself' – as he wrote to Lord Hardwicke in October 1739. 'What can the world think then to see him [Hervey] Lord Privy Seal, so improper in every respect, as to his rank, his manner of life, and even that scheme which he seems himself to have laid down for his own future preferment?' In Newcastle's eyes, Hervey's 'manner of life' automatically disqualified him from high office;

therefore Walpole *must* be using Hervey to threaten or punish Newcastle.

The world must think that for some reason I am not at present to be laid aside, but to be useless, and that this man [Hervey] was brought in to have the confidence and real trust of the Ministry; for his behaviour towards me has been such that this extraordinary mark of favour towards him cannot be consistent with the least remains of regard towards me.

Newcastle believed, as Hervey had always suspected, that his private life made him unfit for office. He argued, too, that Hervey's low rank in the peerage rendered him unsuitable for high office. What Alexander Pope had so publicly resented about Hervey's apparent successes – his brittle charm, his privileged life, his relationship with Ste – were what actually barred him from any real achievement of them.

Despite Newcastle's continued opposition to his holding office, Hervey managed to hang on to his plum for two years. Walpole, who had lost vital parliamentary ground in the general election in 1741, was forced to resign as First Lord of the Treasury and Chancellor of the Exchequer on 2 February 1742. The disparate forces of Opposition had united to bring him down; only his most loyal supporters, such as Hervey and the Duke of Marlborough, dared to defend him in the House. His unpopularity was such that when he entered the House of Lords for the first time as Earl of Orford two weeks later not one person stood up to shake his hand or congratulate him.

Now in the ascendant were Newcastle, his brother Henry Pelham (Walpole's chosen successor who in three years was to gain control of Parliament as Walpole had desired), Lord Carteret, and Hervey's old antagonist, William Pulteney. The years following Walpole's fall, until Pelham took control, were ones of political upheaval and insecurity: unsurprising, considering they followed a twenty-year period of stability and the entrenchment of Walpole's Whig ideals. As Hervey told the King in July 1742,

Your Court is divided into classes, knots, parties and cabals of men, all with different views, different principles (if they have any), and different interests, contending with one another for power, each thinking to deceive and overreach the other, and all pursuing their own private personal interests, and their own short and narrow views, without considering your Majesty's, the national and general interest, one moment in any action.

For all his fine words (and intentions, no doubt) Hervey was not least among this number.

It was inevitable that Hervey should be dragged down with Walpole, with whom he had always been so closely associated. Prince Frederick, who had refused his father's offer to increase his allowance if he would back down, now had some influence in government, and had waited ten years to avenge himself on his old enemy. Hervey also had his own enemies among Walpole's former supporters – Newcastle chief among them – who hated him for himself, and would not lose the opportunity to get rid of him when Walpole fell even as they scrambled to assert themselves in the new administration. Hervey's prickliness exacerbated his unpopularity, and his pride prevented him making fresh alliances. Although he had been a valuable speaker and writer on behalf of the government, his personality made others unwilling to ally with him, and he did not project the force of character necessary to inspire faith or service in others. Hervey possessed finesse but not force; like a swordsman who fences beautifully with his own reflection in the mirror but cannot beat a real opponent, he was too mannered and too defensive ever to succeed in politics without the support of a powerful patron. But it was easier for him to blame his failure on the shortcomings of those around him – who he felt did not appreciate his talents – than to recognize his own failings.

Since Walpole's retirement, he told Lady Mary in May 1742, 'I am too proud to offer my service and friendship where I am not sure they will be accepted of, and too inconsiderable to have those advances made to me (though I never forgot or failed to return any obligation I ever received) so I remain as illustrious a Nothing in this office, as ever filled it since it was first erected.' But, he told her, he was now so well off (due to the death of his mother the previous May) that it made no difference to him financially whether or not he held office; and from age and infirmity, he said, he had grown almost indifferent to power and rank.

Despite his posturing, Hervey was incensed at being ordered back to London from Suffolk in mid-June, to hand over the seal of his office – which, contrary to custom, he had taken with him to Ickworth – to his successor, Lord Gower. Hervey's description of his interview with George, on learning of his dismissal from office, showed the extent to which his intimacy with the royal family had made him forget that he was, at bottom, only their servant, subject like any other to the whims of majesty. Proudly, he refused the offer of a pension of £3,000 a year to compensate for the loss of his office, insisting that only he could protect the King from the power-hungry politicians circling like sharks around him, and protesting at being sacked to satisfy their envy of him.

'For supposing, Sir (I continued), one of your Majesty's footmen had been beaten for trying to keep an insolent mob off your coach, which mob had shown that they were endeavouring to approach your coach only to insult you – to force you to let them drive it, or else to overturn it – could your Majesty possibly, at the instigation of that very mob, turn away such a footman with the same marks of displeasure that you would do any servant who deserved such treatment by the worst behaviour, and keep only those in your service who had, underhand, encouraged that mob which he has resisted?'

The strange weak answer he made to this can never be guessed, and will scarcely be credited, when I say it was: 'My Lord, there would not be so much striving for a footman's place.'

Charles Hanbury Williams, who hated Hervey, wrote to Henry Fox that after his dismissal Hervey

was complaining in the Rooms [the royal apartments] that everybody was asking him about the King going abroad, that for his part he knew nothing of courts and politics, and was excessively affected about it: and at last turned to me and said, 'What can one do to such impertinent people?' Upon which I answered with great indifference, 'Send 'em to my Lord Gower [Hervey's successor as Lord Privy Seal].'

For all Hervey objected to his removal from office, and insisted to the King that he needed to retain Hervey in his service as the only objective man at court and in the Cabinet, he cannot have been surprised to hear that he had been replaced after the publication of a satirical ballad attacking almost every member of the new government, as well as the King to whose face Hervey professed such loyalty. Horace Walpole sent his friend Horace Mann a copy of the broadsheet, entitled 'The Patriots are Come: Or, a New Doctor for a Crazy Constitution', on 16 May 1742; it was anonymous, but universally acknowledged to be by Hervey with whose style and opinions it corresponds. The song opened with a comment on Frederick's new position of influence,

> And since only of those who have Power I sing,
> I am sure none can think that I hint of the King,

and went on to call Hervey's old superior, the lecherous Duke of Grafton, an old 'booby'; Lady Deloraine, '*virtuous* and *sober* and *wise*'; Newcastle, 'as false as he's silly'; and compared William Pulteney to Phaeton,

> raised for a Day, he shall fall,
> Put the World in a Flame, and show he did strive
> To get Reins in his Hand, though 'tis plain he can't drive

The worst insults were reserved for the King, mocking the bluff manner beneath which he struggled to conceal his impotence, and implying that his only political objective was to have soldiers to play with. 'Cock your great hat, strut, bounce and look bluff,' said the fictional Carteret to his monarch, promising him great armies, 'whate'er debts we make, or whate'er wars we wage'.

> With Cordials like these the Monarch's new Guest
> Revived his sunk Spirits and gladdened his Breast;
> Till in raptures he cried, 'My dear Lord, you shall do
> Whatever you will, give me Troops to review.'

> But oh! my dear England, since this is thy State,
> Who is there that loves thee that weeps at thy Fate?
> Since in changing thy Masters, thou art just like old Rome,
> Whilst Faction, Oppression, and Slav'ry's thy Doom!

Hervey's response to the changing of masters had reconciled him to some old friends including Lord Chesterfield and William Pulteney. Hervey and Pulteney, recently created Earl of Bath to remove his dangerous rhetorical skills from the House of Commons,* were reported to be spending a great deal of time together in Bath in October 1742. There, reported Horace Walpole, they saw a lot of Lord Gower. 'How they must love one another, the late [Hervey], the present [Gower], and the would-be [Pulteney] Privy Seal!' Walpole also related with malicious glee 'a most ridiculous accident' that befell Hervey at Bath.

He used to play [cards] in a little inner room; but one night some ladies had got it, and he was reduced to the public room; but being extremely absent and deep in politics, he walked through the little room to a convenience behind the curtain, from whence (still absent) he produced himself in a situation extremely diverting to the women: imagine his delicacy and the passion he was in at their laughing!

Although Hervey apparently spoke better when he was in Opposition after 1742 than ever before, opposing the new Gin Act in several celebrated speeches, he had become by this time a political joke. From the lofty ambitions he had cherished in the early 1730s he was reduced to a mere caricature of himself. Years after his death, Horace Walpole called Hervey's life a '*chronique scandaleuse*', and refused to commit his memories of it to paper because the details

---

* One of Walpole's last acts in office was to persuade the King to raise Pulteney to the House of Lords, saying that he had 'turned the key of the closet' on his old antagonist. Flattered to be so singled out, Pulteney jumped at the offer – then saw his mistake. He was 'so enraged at his own oversight, that . . . he dashed his patent on the floor and vowed he would never take it up – but he had kissed the King's hand for it, and it was too late to recede' (Horace Walpole's *Reminiscences*, p. 95).

were so sordid. But in reality it was neither Hervey's promiscuity –
he was not particularly promiscuous by the standards of the
day – nor his homosexual tendencies that men like Newcastle and
Horace Walpole found hard to stomach. The difficult thing for his
contemporaries to reconcile themselves to about Hervey was not
that he might have had sex with another man, but that he had been
in love with one. That was what was unforgivable.

32. Elegy

In 1738, Hervey commissioned William Hogarth, whom he had known since the early 1730s, to paint a group portrait of him and his most intimate friends to commemorate their friendship. The group included Stephen and Henry Fox, Thomas Winnington, Charles Spencer Duke of Marlborough and the Reverend John Theophilus Desaguliers. There is no contemporary documentation for the painting, but we know it was painted after March 1738 because Marlborough is wearing the uniform of a colonel of the 38th Foot, a position to which he was appointed at that date. In a later copy of the painting made for Ste Fox which hung at Melbury, the house he moved to from Redlynch with his young wife after Hervey's death, Marlborough's uniform is different, which dates the copy to about 1742. The fact that the original is at Ickworth suggests that the work was originally made for Hervey, and a copy later made for Ste.

The landscape in which the six men stand or sit is lush and romantic, with a sensual profusion of fruits and flowers, while the statue of Athena in the background adds an air of philosophical serenity. It is a scene of exquisite cultivation and repose; these men, one is made to feel, represent the highest ideal of eighteenth-century civilization. They epitomize the graceful negligence of England's Augustan Age. Lord Hervey stands at the centre of the scene: elegant, moderate, refined.

The figures surrounding him are familiar. On the far right sits the witty, detached Thomas Winnington, the man Hervey called Henry Fox's 'politician-quidnunc-correspondent'.* Hervey was

---

* Winnington was closer to Henry Fox than to Ste. In 1740, he made a private will witnessed by Henry Fox providing £500 for a Mrs Mary Smith, and £1,250 each for her two daughters, Charlotte and Mary; to avoid detection Winnington planned to leave the total sum of £3,000 to Henry Fox, who could then dispense it to his mistress and her (maybe their) daughters.

fond of Winnington because he was so close to the Foxes: 'I like to see him for we always talk of you,' he told Ste in 1731. Charles Spencer (second from right) succeeded to the duchy of Marlborough in 1733, at the age of twenty-seven. Hated by George II because his father, the Earl of Sunderland, had been so close to George's own father, George I, Marlborough had gravitated naturally in the 1730s to the court of the young Prince Frederick of Wales, opposed to the hegemony of Walpole and the authority of the King. In 1738, disgusted by Frederick's unfilial behaviour during the illness and death of his mother, Queen Caroline, the previous year, Marlborough defected to the court party; later that year he was made a Lord of the Bedchamber. Welcoming him into his new alliance were his old friends, the Fox brothers, Winnington and Lord Hervey.

Next to Marlborough stands Hervey, with his doll-like face, aesthete's hands and dancer's stance. Hogarth's portrait of Hervey contains within it elements of Hervey's satiric persona – as Sporus, and Lord Fanny, and (later) Beau Didapper – but this time it is a friendly tease, rather than a hostile dig. Here, suggests Hogarth, stands a man of culture and poise, despite his femininity. Tied to Hervey's waist with a pretty bow is the golden key of his office as Vice-Chamberlain to King George II; but (with a hidden twist of irony) the key also represents chastity, and was an accessory Hogarth often gave his female characters, like the central young woman in *Beer Street*, to emphasize their maidenly virtue. Although Hervey is looking out of the canvas at the viewer, he gestures towards architectural plans held by Henry Fox – or perhaps beyond them to his beloved Ste, sitting on the other side of Henry.

These five men – Whig aristocrats, landed and wealthy, all supporters of Sir Robert Walpole and familiar at court – fit naturally together. The men surrounding Hervey were not just his friends, but his political allies. Just as the mood of the painting defines Hervey as an aesthete, so his choice of companions identifies him as a Whig, and a supporter of Sir Robert Walpole. But this painting is far more than a simple commemoration of friendship; and the clue to its meaning – which, as it is undocumented, must remain a mystery – lies in the clerical figure on the far right.

This man not only appears incongruous in this scene, as a church-man rather than a courtier or politician, but his identity has caused some confusion among historians and art historians. One interpreta-tion of the reverend's inclusion in the painting is that the portrait is of Peter Villemain, who performed the clandestine wedding services that married Ste Fox to his child-bride Elizabeth Strang-ways-Horner in March 1736. He was rewarded by Ste with the living of Eisey, near Cricklade, the following year. Hervey also knew Villemain, telling Ste in September 1735 that he had received a letter and two folios from him 'as closely written as any Blue-coat boy [schoolboy] ever wrote the Lord's Prayer and the Belief in the compass of a sixpence. I laughed too twenty times in reading them, which is recommendation enough for any letter.' In the summer of 1736, Villemain was at Ickworth, cataloguing Lord Bristol's library.

The internal evidence that supports this hypothesis is the arch expression on Ste Fox's face as he overturns the chair on which the parson stands. The closeness of Hervey and Fox's friendship was well known, and so Ste's wedding was seen by many as a challenge to the moral authority of the church: he was, metaphorically speaking, upturning the foundations on which the clergyman stood. This interpretation is corroborated by the parson's telescope, turned in the direction of the church on the distant hillside; if the figure is Villemain, the church would be Eisey. The implication is that Villemain would be happy to allow the foundations of his faith to be overthrown as long as he received the living he sought.

But Horace Walpole, generally a reliable source, saw Ste Fox's copy of the painting at Melbury later in the century and stated that the clergyman was not Villemain but the Reverend Desaguliers, a prominent freemason and scientist. Since Walpole visited Melbury during Fox's lifetime it is hard to imagine he was misinformed on this point. On a purely physical basis, the face of the parson in *Lord Hervey and His Friends* exactly matches other portraits of Desaguliers by Hogarth: as the preacher in *The Sleeping Congregation*, and the prompter in *A Performance of the Indian Emperor, or The Conquest of Mexico by the Spaniards* (see p. 173). Finally, because Villemain received the living of Eisey in 1737, and the picture was painted in

1738, the symbolism of his looking hopefully towards a church is a year too late.

John Theophilus Desaguliers (1683–1743) was a Huguenot minister who achieved celebrity during his lifetime as a lecturer on natural philosophy. He was famous enough by 1717 to be invited to speak in front of George I, and ten years later was made chaplain to Prince Frederick. Like his friend, and the godfather of one of his sons, Sir Isaac Newton, Desaguliers was a member of the Royal Society, celebrated for his studies on optics – hence the telescope he holds in the painting. But what Desaguliers was most famous for in his lifetime, and what he has since been remembered for, was his contribution to freemasonry in England. The first Grand Lodge, uniting all English lodges, was founded on 24 June 1717 in the Goose and Gridiron Tavern in St Paul's Churchyard. Desaguliers was Grand Master in 1719, Deputy Grand Master in 1722, 1723 and 1726, and was credited with introducing a combination of aristocrats and academics to the order. Despite all his success in propagating and popularizing the credo of masonry, and his connections with the leaders of society and politics, Desaguliers never had a profitable living, and died a pauper, neglected and ignored.

In this case, then, Hogarth's Reverend, looking hopefully towards an idealized living but unable to focus on it because the integrity of his principles is challenged by unorthodoxy, makes as much sense as Desaguliers as he does as Villemain. It also fits in with the theme of unconventionality and unwillingness to sacrifice oneself for position that marked Hervey's own career, as well as, to a lesser extent, those of the friends with whom he surrounded himself.

Desaguliers introduced Hervey into the Queen's Head Lodge in Bath in 1724; although there is no mention of him in any of Hervey's later correspondence, they would have seen each other regularly at court and in London over the following years. Stephen Fox and Marlborough (then Earl of Sunderland) joined a London lodge in 1730. 'Your brother, Lord Sunderland, and Lord Portmore had last night the honour and pleasure to be admitted into the Freemasons,' Hervey reported to Henry Fox on 25 January. There is no record of Henry Fox or Thomas Winnington being masons, but this does not mean that they were not, merely that if they were the documentation has not survived.

With the introduction of Desaguliers into the equation, the emphasis of the scene and its symbolism is altered – especially bearing in mind that both Hervey, who probably commissioned the group portrait, and Hogarth, who painted it, were masons. Freemasonry becomes an invisible or coded theme. The plans Henry Fox held up for Hervey's approval may refer to Fox's role as Surveyor General of the King's Works, which he had held since 1737, or to some aspect of masonry, since Palladian architecture – epitomized by Houghton, Robert Walpole's grand new house in Norfolk – was associated with masonry. The lawn roller on which Winnington leans is a visual metaphor for God, the Great Leveller. Masonry's secular, rational nature is emphasized by the statue of Minerva, the goddess of wisdom, behind the group, closer to them than the walled-off church is. Desaguliers appears to be directing his telescope towards the statue, representing classicism, rather than the church, on which he ought to be focused by virtue of his calling. The bright colours of the coats of the central figures underline this worldly mood. There is no female presence in *Lord Hervey and His Friends*: no woman mattered enough to be included except the goddess Minerva (whose generous bosom somehow recalls Hervey's much-missed patroness, Queen Caroline), with her masculine attributes of intellect and nobility. What is being celebrated here is the all-male, clubbish, intellectual and political environment in which Hervey and his friends thrived.

The homoerotic, or homosexual, nature of the relationship between the men, particularly between Hervey and Ste Fox, is delineated by Hogarth's use of straight lines, a motif explored in other all-male scenes, such as Tom Rakewell 'Surrounded by Artists and Professors' and the 'Scene in a Gambling House' of the *Rake's Progress*. The telescope, the gateposts, the walking stick with which Ste upturns Desaguliers's chair – all these are symbols of masculinity. The upturned chair, which recurs in scene two of the *Harlot's Progress*, was a metaphor for disorder, or nonconformity. In the marriage scene of *Mariage à la Mode*, the two dogs chained together in the foreground parody the central figures, as they do in the foreground of the *Rake's Progress* 'Married to an Old Maid'; the monkey mimics the cuckolded Jew in scene two of the *Harlot's Progress*. In the Hervey painting, the effeminate dog has taken on the sexually ambiguous characteristics of its masters. Yet for all Hogarth's evident awareness of Hervey's relationship with Ste, he seems not to disapprove or even to judge: the painter is just an observer.

Hogarth's pictorial analysis of the web of relationships that bound this group together is a tenable one, quite apart from the love Hervey and Ste Fox bore for each other. There was a decidedly homoerotic tinge to much of the correspondence of Hervey's circle. Voltaire was rumoured to have had male lovers. Horace Walpole had intensely close (but probably unconsummated) relationships with George Selwyn, the poet Thomas Gray, and his correspondent Horace Mann. Mrs Thrale described Mann as a 'finger-twirler', meaning sodomite. Marlborough's father, the Earl of Sunderland, was exposed as a homosexual in 1723, the year following his death, by the publication of his letters to Beau Wilson, a man he kept as he would have a mistress.

Horace Walpole also had a crush on Lord Lincoln, whom George II thought the handsomest man in England, and who was reputed to have an enormous penis. Fascinated by Lincoln's virility and sexual prowess, Walpole wrote poems to him congratulating him on his conquests, and wishing him a life as long as his manhood. Endless jokes circulated between Walpole, Henry Fox and Charles Hanbury Williams* about Lincoln's sexuality. Williams wrote cryptically to Fox after Hervey's death, saying that Hervey had 'left [Thomas] Winnington a *very handsome legacy* and I suppose he'll *enter* into possession immediately – I suppose Lord Lincoln won't *push* at him any more. If he does, Hervey will certainly appear *backward* to him. Poor Fitzwilliam!' Was the meek Fitzwilliam, who had to postpone his wedding a year later because he was so nervous, Hervey's joking bequest to his old friend Winnington? Regardless

---

* Charles Hanbury Williams had been fond of Hervey until he quarrelled with the Foxes in the 1740s. There is in the archives at Ickworth an undated sheaf of translations of an Ovidian ode on love, signed by Winnington, Williams, Henry Fox and Sir William Yonge, another of Walpole's devotees.

of what this letter actually meant, it does indicate an atmosphere of amused tolerance for homosexuality in Hervey's immediate circle.

The ambiguity of Hogarth's group portrait only emphasizes Hervey's private ambiguity. At first glance, *Lord Hervey and His Friends* looks like a traditional family group, with Hervey and Stephen Fox, a couple *manqué*, surrounded by their friends and political allies instead of their children, in an idealized rural setting by a river. Far off in the background, a sunlit church stands on a hill; baskets of ripe fruit, symbols of fecundity, adorn the foreground; even the family pet is represented – by a dog that resembles nothing so much as a cat, recalling Pope's 'well-bred spaniels' delighting 'in mumbling of the game they dare not bite'. An air of intimacy seduces the observer. It is only when you see the mischievous look on Ste Fox's face as he surreptitiously uses his walking stick to upend the chair on which the pompous clergyman is balancing to look through his telescope that you realize all is not as it seems.

That two figures look out at the viewer, inviting them in as well as challenging them, is rare for Hogarth.* Only in portraits do his subjects usually engage the onlooker directly; and in groups, it is notable if even one figure does so. It is as if, for such an unusual composition, Hogarth used this unexpected complicity to emphasize the scene's unconventionality. Hervey's gaze is direct, but enigmatic. He is holding the key, literally and metaphorically, to a secret only he – and Ste, who looks out with a similarly mocking, ambiguous expression – can unlock. It may be about masonry, or a political alliance, or homosexuality – who knows? They have carried their secret with them.

---

* I have not seen another Hogarth group which has two of the figures looking out of the canvas as Hervey and Stephen Fox do in this painting.

33. A Coffin-face

John Selwyn wrote to Horace Walpole in 1739 to tell him he had delivered Walpole's compliments to Lady Hervey, and told Lord Hervey that Walpole had inquired after his health. Hervey 'bid me say that he is "quite recovered, but I mill [whip to a froth, usually with reference to hot chocolate] myself three or four times a day"'.

'How, my Lord, do you mill yourself?' asked Selwyn.

'Why I am like a cup of chocolate: I grow cold and dead, then I mill myself again and in a little while I am cold again and am good for nothing but to catch dead flies.'

Horace Walpole's views on Hervey, whom he called the 'Fairy Hervey', were representative of most of his peers. Walpole was always morbidly fascinated by Hervey, because of his own unspoken homosexual desires as well as his physical resemblance to Hervey. Both men were slight and witty, and feminine, and walked with characteristic mincing steps. It was said that Hervey's half-brother, Carr, who died in 1722 aged thirty-one, was Horace Walpole's real father, although Horace always firmly asserted that Sir Robert was his father. Sir Robert, though, often referred to Horace, 'with all the *sang-froid* imaginable, [and] called him that boy, got by nobody knows who'. When, as a young man, he first knew Hervey, Horace idolized him, reading his unpublished correspondence with Middleton about the Roman Senate with devoted interest. His friend John Whaley wrote to him in September 1736 with an epigram he had written, 'To Lord Hervey, on his discourse on the Roman Senate':

> How Roman Senates once were fill'd
> From thy judicious Pen we Know;
> That Virtue calls up Britain's Peers
> Yourself to future Times will show.

Much impressed, Whaley described how he had shown this to Hervey, who composed a reply extempore and wrote it on the other side of the sheet of paper:

> I read your Compliment, but there I see
> Not what I am, but what I ought to be;
> *Thus* Trajan's character when Pliny rais'd,
> 'Twas better so to praise, than to be prais'd.

But soon, bored by Hervey's brittle posturing and his inconsistency, Horace Walpole preferred to observe him from a distance. One exception was in the year before Hervey died, when he was too ill to go to the opera. Walpole went to some effort to arrange a private concert for him. Hervey sat watching the performance with 'a coffin-face . . . as full of dirty politics as ever'. This concert had come about some days earlier when Horace called on Lady Hervey, and found her husband there. Hervey, who had always professed great affection for Horace, turned his back on him when he arrived and rushed into a corner to whisper with some other young man. 'Not being at all amazed at one whose heart I knew so well, I stayed on to see more of this behaviour; indeed, to use myself to it,' Walpole told Mann. 'At last he came up to me and begged this music [that Horace had had played for him] which I gave him, and would often again, to see how many times I shall be ill and well with him within this month.' Walpole called Hervey's son George the 'delicate Lord': he 'puts me in mind of his father, who always took pains to ridicule to you the things he had intended to flatter, and was never easy till he had told everybody he was acting a part'.*

By the late 1730s, when Hervey was in his early forties, he had reached a plateau of dissatisfaction from which he would not descend until death released him. It was as if he had given up on life. The once-feted Hervey was seen as repulsive because of his overt homosexual tendencies and bitter because of his thwarted

---

* For all this disapproval, though, Horace Walpole's *Memoirs of the Reign of King George II* self-consciously and deliberately carry on the tradition of Hervey's own *Memoirs*.

political ambition. His looks had faded and his wit was malicious. In his youth he had relied on his appearance and charm to win him friends; then he had had the security of Queen Caroline's public devotion; but now neither looks nor influence remained to him. Everything that had mattered to him was slipping out of his grasp. He was described variously at this time as wretched, vain and ridiculous.

Even his dearest friends began to see Hervey through new eyes. Henry Fox was the first to go. He had supported Hervey immediately after Caroline died, dining with his old friend daily, and reporting his state of mind and health back to Ste in Somerset, but earlier that year he and Hervey had quarrelled. A furious note from Hervey to 'Henry Fox Esq. Neglecter of his Majesty's Works'* shows the bad feeling that was running between the two men at this time:

Which of the devils in hell prompted you to tell the Queen that everything in her library was ready for the putting up of her books? – Thou abominable new broom, that so far from sweeping clean, has not removed one grain of dirt and rubbish. Come to me tomorrow morning to take the rest of your scolding; and go with me to scold all your odious, dilatory subalterns. Bad night.

Hervey's anger was exacerbated by his concern for the Queen, and as Vice-Chamberlain it was his duty to ensure Fox did his job properly; but his tone seems incommensurate with the crime.

It was not until about 1741 that their break became final. Horace Walpole believed that the reason Hervey and Fox fell out was because Hervey had 'betrayed to Mrs Horner Mr Fox's passion for that Duchess [of Manchester]'.† According to Walpole, Hervey had

---

* The note is undated but must fall between Henry's appointment as Surveyor of the King's Works in June 1737 and Caroline's death that November; probably written in August, when Hervey was at St James's, Caroline was still well, and Fox newly in office.

† Hervey had never liked the Duchess of Manchester. In 1734, he told Henry that she 'frets, shrugs and barks there [at her house in Grosvenor Street] as usual; but whether her Grace has swallowed or spit out again, the tips of all the noses she has bit off since you left England I am unable to inform you: the only reason why she has never deprived her dear Duke of his, I suppose is, that she hopes one time or another to lead him by it'.

encouraged Fox to make love to the widowed Duchess, whose fiancé, Lord Scarborough, committed suicide in 1740, in order to reveal Fox's infidelity to Mrs Horner, his mistress of seven years. The Duchess refused Fox's proposal; Mrs Horner, appraised of the offer, broke with Fox but remained friends with Hervey; and Fox blamed his double loss on Hervey. Horace Walpole, who reported the incident, was biased against Hervey, but Henry Fox was not an unreasonable man and would not have dropped his old friend for nothing. Exactly what Hervey did, and why he did it, in view of his deep affection for Fox, his fondness for Mrs Horner and his dislike of the Duchess, is unclear; but that he had done something serious is evident. 'His rule is the same with yours,' Ste told Hervey after the quarrel. 'He as seldom mentions you as you do him.'

The break with Ste was more gradual and far more debilitating for Hervey. Their quarrels had grown more frequent since Ste's marriage in 1736 and Caroline's death, and buried with her Hervey's political hopes, the following year. In a letter of 1738, Hervey had used an expression which offended Ste, and Ste wrote to inform him of his anger. Hervey responded, as ever, by making attack his defence.

I own one of the last things I should have suspected would have been your being angry with me for not *wording* a letter to you as I ought . . . I grieve upon my honour and truth, more for the strain of discontent that runs through your letter, than for any unkindness towards me, because I am sure, the last proceeds from the first, and that you would have been less displeased and less in the wrong to me, if you had been more happy, and more in the right to yourself.

Hervey was at this time far more unhappy than Ste – who was enjoying the first sunlit years of his marriage to Elizabeth – so this accusation reveals more about Hervey, and the bitterness of his state of mind, than it does about Ste. As Hervey wrote to Lady Mary Wortley Montagu, his most faithful correspondent in his last years, 'from an instinctive unaccountable impulse [I] try to live, even though my coolest judgement tells me that living upon the terms I do, is buying mellow apples and mealy potatoes at a guinea a piece instead of a penny a dozen'.

By the following summer, Hervey and Fox were reconciled and Lord and Lady Hervey stayed at Redlynch with Mrs Horner and Elizabeth Fox in June 1739. Three months later Elizabeth Fox moved permanently to Redlynch to begin married life proper. Her letters to Ste before they were united display a touching adoration.

It is out of my power to be grateful enough to you my dearest dear Ste for the many kind obligations I have to you the only way I can aim at returning them is by assuring you that you have and ever will have my most affectionate tender love and you may depend on my giving you all the proofs that lie in my power of my fondness and regard to you the whole study of your Lizzy's life shall be how to please and amuse her only love,

she wrote, her simple devotion contrasting with Hervey's mannered, intellectual correspondence. That Ste returned her affection is certain; one of her last letters to him before she came to live at Redlynch expressed the hope that soon 'we shall be everything we wish to be to one another'.

The match between Stephen and Elizabeth Fox-Strangways (or Ilchester, after his elevation in 1741) exemplified a new form of companionate marriage, in which mutual affection took precedence over practical considerations in choosing a mate. Matches which united great families and great fortunes were still the norm among the aristocracy, but for the first time, in literature as well as in real life, love was considered an important factor in how successfully a marriage would turn out. The romantic weddings of Ste and Henry Fox – both of whom eloped – show a new desire to choose a mate for love, not money (even though both married well, in the eyes of the world). Hervey's marriage, although it began not unidealistically as secret wedding to a young beauty with no dowry, ultimately epitomized the old-fashioned view of a *mariage de convenance*: Lord and Lady Hervey were more like a French couple than an English one, remembered Lady Mary Wortley Montagu's granddaughter Lady Louisa Stuart, 'as well-bred as if not married at all'.

To judge by his previous relationships with the Fox brothers, it would seem more likely that personal matters would provoke the rift with Ste, and politics with Henry; but ironically, it was politics that caused the final argument between Hervey and Stephen in the autumn of 1742. Hervey, forced out of office in June 1742, had to decide whether he would join the Opposition Whigs, or continue to vote with the government that had expelled him. His pride made him scorn to condone what he saw as a grievous personal insult by supporting the new ministry, and he was desperate to persuade Fox to stand with him against it. Hervey's demands put his old friend into a difficult situation, and Ste sought advice from his brother Henry. 'Love your friend without letting him show you to the world in a character most unsuitable to your heart and understanding,' Henry recommended, distancing himself from Hervey with the phrase 'your friend'. While Ste admired Hervey, Henry advised him to remember that he lacked judgement. Ste thought far more highly of Hervey's qualities than he deserved, Henry continued, and should rely on his own, superior, good sense.

Hervey wrote urgently to his old friend in November, hoping that he would be at the opening of Parliament, and offering to release him from the obligations of their friendship, if these would prevent Ste acting one way or the other. He did not want to know how his political opponents had tried to turn Ste against him, or how far they had succeeded in bringing Ste to a political neutrality; but for Ste's own sake he begged him at least to vote, whether he supported Hervey or not. 'The middle way is for ever the worst,' he argued, 'as it not only obliges nobody but disobliges everybody.' Hervey's years in politics had not taught him the art of restraint, but he was desperately aware of the weakness of his position and believed Ste's presence alone would support him both personally and politically.

Ste did not reply to this letter at once, and Hervey was forced to write again on 15 November, expressing his disappointment at having received no word, but hoping that this meant that Ste was on his way to London to vote. 'You must know not only how agreeable it would be to me (though otherwise quite useless I believe) to have your world see one man at least can act rightly to me, but if you will give me leave to say so, because I think . . . it would be as right to yourself.' Just as Hervey's unwillingness to compromise had ruined his political career, so here it deprived him of the solace of Ste's continued loyalty; but he was desperate enough to stake fifteen years of love and friendship for Ste's support on this one point.

Ste's reply to Hervey's first letter crossed the path of his second one. He wrote from Redlynch on 13 November to explain why he was not going to London for the first day of Parliament. Ste's language is both formal and deferential, almost distant, betraying the new coldness of his feelings for the man whom he had once loved. Despite all the obligations he felt to Hervey – 'I have never once forgot that if it had not been for you I should not now have been in the House of Lords' – because he did not seek a political career, he saw no reason to expend his energy by going into active opposition. His only ambition was to live quietly, in tranquillity and obscurity. He was not acquainted with the present ministry, and wanted nothing from them, he said; and so 'their detraction or removal will never give me any degree of uneasiness'. Furthermore, he felt it would be the basest ingratitude to vote against the King who had promoted him to the House of Lords, especially 'at a time when his affairs are difficult and perplexed, when faction runs high, and the favour I have received very recent'.

No one, Ste continued, had ever tried to turn him against Hervey, and whatever he had heard 'about you or against you (and undoubtedly last year there was great clamour against you) I acquainted you with'. What worried him was Hervey's apparent determination to join the Opposition.

I agree it is not uncommon for those who have been ill-used at court, to endeavour to distress the measures of that court, but how anyone, [who] does not quit the court from a dislike of [those] measures, can reconcile such behaviour to themselves or to a desire of preserving a character, I could never understand, unless all character is turned into resentment.

Hervey would only be doing what his enemies hoped he would, Ste reminded him, urging him to call to mind what he had said at their last meeting of soon thinking no more 'of courts or politics or Parliament'. This way of thinking, 'void of resentment and totally dispassionate', seemed to him to be desirable for Hervey. 'I pretend to give no advice, I am not *au fait*, and if I was I know myself unequal to the task, but this I know that I love and regard your Lordship as much as any one person in the world, and I verily believe no one person was more thoroughly concerned at your being displaced [sacked] last year. My Lord,' Ste concluded, 'I write all this with anxiety and uneasiness but let the event be what it will be I beg of you not to construe anything I have written amiss or unkindly or to think I have written with too much freedom, for it is a most certain truth that I am with all possible regard and affection yours.' This is only the first of two letters that survive written from Ste to Hervey, and it displays throughout the reasonableness and affection that Hervey had always valued in his friend; but Hervey was embittered by his political failure, for which on some level he may have blamed Ste, as it was his relationship with him that had been his Achilles heel.

The final letter in their fifteen-year correspondence was written on 20 November 1742 by Ste on receipt of a letter in which a desperate Hervey accused him of failing to honour the obligations of their friendship by refusing to support him in political Opposition, and, no doubt, reminding Fox of all Hervey had done on his behalf. Perhaps Hervey assumed that Ste owed him his political allegiance because he had introduced him to the Whig party, fifteen years earlier.

If a person embarrassed by the difficulties of an uncommon situation, in writing to a friend (upon receipt of a letter taking notice of his embarrassments), opens his mind and lays his whole heart before [him], only for hesitating to take a step scarce ever to be recalled, is to be ranked with one of the strongest instances, in ancient history, of ingratitude, I give up all pretence to the knowledge of the force and signification of the word,

Fox began.

Your Lordship cannot possibly be more conscious of having deserved well towards me than I am, nor more convinced of that truth, than I am desirous of acknowledging it, with regard to the peerage, I am not only convinced I have that obligation to your Lordship, but I have industriously taken every opportunity of publishing it, and with pleasure, for to no one living would I so willingly owe an obligation as to your Lordship.

But my Lord notwithstanding I am desirous of acknowledging every degree of every obligation, and notwithstanding my thankfulness to you, for soliciting, for pressing, and obtaining this favour, does it follow that no return is to be made, no degree of obligation owned to the person from whom it was obtained, and do you really think that I should deserve no reproach, for, the first sessions after my entrance into the House of Lords, endeavouring to distress that King that placed me there, to this part of my 'extraordinary' letter, your Lordship has been pleased to make no answer. Hard indeed is my fate, that when the only motive of my conduct, is to avoid the reproach of ingratitude, that it seems decreed that whether I take this or that part, I must be accused of the crime I most detest and of which I never yet was guilty. My Lord, I will endeavour to act right, but whether I shall do so or no is not certain, because a person in difficulties, especially if not used to difficult situations, with the greatest desire imaginable to act a right part may make great mistakes.

I can't help taking this opportunity of declaring most solemnly that upon the strictest review of my conduct during the fifteen years I have had the pleasure of your acquaintance and friendship, I cannot possibly charge myself with having ever acted wrongly towards your Lordship, I am not conscious, of not having deserved well of you, I am very sure I have never had an unkind, a cool, or an unfriendly thought towards you, much less am I capable of being guilty of such black ingratitude, as your Lordship so freely brands me with, and I have this comfort that I am exceedingly persuaded that I have done nothing, and that I am not arrived at so great a pitch of villainy as to deserve such a letter as I received this afternoon.

This was the end of their friendship. Soon after this interchange Hervey retired to Ickworth to wait to die. He had never tried to disguise his love for Ste, but it had prevented him achieving the political success he yearned for almost as much as he needed Ste; he had never_wanted to neglect Ste, but he had not expected his ambition to destroy their friendship. Hervey's unwillingness to conform to the standards set by his peers meant they excluded him from their number, but his desire for worldly recognition destroyed the love that had set him apart in the first place.

34. Ennui Relieved

Hervey's last extant letter was written to Lady Mary Wortley Montagu from Ickworth on 18 June 1743, just two months before his death, in a weak, barely legible script quite unlike the youthful confidence of his usual copperplate hand. 'The last stages of an infirm life are like filthy roads, and like all other roads, I find the farther one goes from the capital, the more tedious the miles grow, and the more rough and disagreeable the ways.'

It may have been the physical suffering Hervey endured (as well as the potent medicines he took) at the end of his life that made him so irritable and unpleasant. Hervey's health had grown steadily weaker since the mid-1730s. At the start of 1738 he wrote to Dr Cheyne, questioning whether 'at my time of life, when all passions begin to subside, and consequently the sources of all pleasure begin to slacken their supplies, be worth preserving is another question . . .

> By an instinctive folly still we choose
> Unpleased possessing, what we fear to lose.'

The physical pain Hervey suffered made him less tolerant of others, and exaggerated the sharpness of his wit. Just after hearing of Ste's match, he had written unusually openly to his mother about his fears of growing old and unwell.

Whatever it is, I find a great change, without any in the things or persons that come my way, in my manner of thinking of them; I grow peevish with people I used to laugh at, yawn with some that used to entertain me; am uneasy at things I used to be indifferent to; think oftener of what I hate and seldom of what I like; and hate more, and like fewer things than I used to; I am apter to suspect people I love, to think things will happen that I dislike and nothing that I do like; in short I have the same unentertaining and unentertained gloom hanging about me, that one sees so often.

This sense of ennui dominated his emotions over the last years of his life as, alone and morose, he brooded over his failures and flaws while he waited for death.

> Mankind, I know their Nature and their Art,
> Their Vice I own, their Virtue by a *Part*
> Ill-played so oft, that all the cheat can tell,
> And dangerous only when 'tis acted well . . .
> To such Reflections when I turn my mind,
> I loathe my Being and abhor Mankind.

Hervey had always prided himself on his detachment, but as he grew older this contrived disinterest became the predominant element of his makeup. When the mask slipped, as it did in his last contact with Ste, a bitter face was revealed. Ever defensive, Hervey now preferred to accuse others than admit he was wrong, preferred to push people away than draw near to them. He could not bring himself to accept the love of his family that should be the solace of old age.

Despite the hope his father had expressed after Queen Caroline's death, Hervey found no relief in his wife's company. Nor did Lady Bristol's campaign against them bring the couple together. Hervey's marriage only deteriorated as he approached death. He and Molly still lived together if they happened to be in the same place at the same time, but perfunctorily. Gossip held that Lady Hervey had been in Bath in search of 'fresh pleasures' in the autumn of 1738. However, the summer Hervey died, she was at Ickworth with him, writing to the Reverend Edmund Morris, her sons' tutor, asking for 'any news you can pick up; for though I am not very solicitous about it myself, yet those whom I wish to please here are always glad to be told anything, whether foreign or domestic, material or trifling; in short, news and information is what they like, and I like to please them'. She was, she said, reading Hervey Humphrey Oldcastle's *Some Remarks on the History of England*.

But Hervey apparently refused to have her near him just before he died, and in his will, dictated on 23 June 1743, he specified that all his money was to go to her younger children (his eldest would inherit from Lord Bristol on his death) 'born in wedlock' – a strange phrase implying that Molly had at some point been unfaithful to him. Even more strangely, he desired that his youngest daughter, Carolina, be brought up by Mrs Horner, and not her mother. There is a letter from Molly Hervey dated 10 September 1743 from Ickworth, not addressed, which is in the Holland House letters. This was probably Molly's reply to Mrs Horner's refusal to adopt Carolina. 'I am not surprised at any proof of esteem given you by my dear late Lord, knowing the great friendship he had for you, Madam,' she wrote, 'and I am as little so at the very right manner in which you have acted on this occasion.' The terms of the will, markedly unlike the contents of other wills of the same period, suggest that far from merely being dismissive of his wife, Hervey was in fact actively hostile to her. For her part, Molly greeted his death with a sanguinity which hinted of relief: 'I see and feel the greatness of this last in every light, but I will struggle to the utmost, and though I know, at least I think, that I can never be happy again, yet I will be as little miserable as possible, and will make use of the reason I have to soften, not to aggravate, my affliction.'

When Hervey died on 5 August, 1743, Horace Walpole's comment was that it was lucky for him, 'for he had outlived his last inch of character'. Disillusion had embittered the man who had once seemed to have everything at his fingertips. But instead Hervey had lost his only love, watched the woman he loved like a mother die, and failed to fulfil his political potential. He had had it all: looks, charm, breeding, landed wealth, favour at court, the ear of the Prime Minister, an adoring wife and children. A glittering butterfly (or 'tinsel insect', in Pope's words), he floated apparently effortlessly through life. But he died alone, a failure in his own eyes, estranged from the one person he had truly loved, decrying his disillusion with the world and his place in it. Beneath the gilded exterior Hervey had become by the end of his life a broken man who had sacrificed both love and ambition and gained nothing in return.

Alexander Pope died quietly in 1744, after receiving absolution from a priest. He was buried by Twickenham Church.

Sir Robert Walpole died in 1745, having seen his chosen successor, Henry Pelham (brother of the Duke of Newcastle), rise to power.

Prince Frederick died in 1751, after being hit by a tennis ball, leaving Augusta with five sons and two daughters. His son, the future George III, succeeded to the throne in 1760 on George II's death.

Lord Bristol died in 1751. He left orders that he wished to be buried with a packet of his first wife, Isabella Carr's, letters, and a 'blue turkey-stone' (turquoise) ring she had given him.

Lady Mary Wortley Montagu lived in Italy for nearly another two decades. She returned to England in 1761 after her husband's death, and died the following year.

Francesco Algarotti lived at the court of Frederick the Great of Prussia until 1753, when ill-health took him back to Italy. He died in 1764.

Molly Hervey died in 1768, after an apparently happy widowhood. She lived in a small, impeccably decorated house off St James's Park where she held a French-style salon that attracted celebrated visitors such as Lord Chesterfield, Thomas Carlyle and Horace Walpole. Her friendship with the Fox brothers continued for the rest of her life.

Henry Fox had a long and distinguished political career culminating in his creation as Lord Holland in 1763; he died nine years later. His son, Charles James Fox, later became Foreign Secretary.

Stephen Fox and his wife Elizabeth had nine children and a long and happy marriage. Ste received his long-promised title in 1741 when he was made Lord Ilchester; in 1756 the barony was elevated to an earldom. The motto he chose – a reminder to himself of the person to whom he owed his honour – was *Faire sans dire*: to do without saying. He died in 1776.

Appendix 1

THE DEATH OF LORD HERVEY;
OR, A MORNING AT COURT
A DRAMA

ACT I

SCENE. – *The Queen's Gallery. The time, nine in the morning.*

Enter the QUEEN, Princess EMILY, Princess CAROLINE, *followed by* Lord LIFFORD *and* Mrs PURCEL.

Queen. Mon Dieu, quelle chaleur! en vérité on étouffe. Pray open a little those windows.

Lord Lifford. Hasa your Majesty heara de news?

Queen. What news, my dear Lord?

Lord Liff. Dat my Lord Hervey, as he was coming last night to *tone,* was rob and murdered by highwaymen, and tron in a ditch.

Princess Caroline. Eh! grand Dieu!

Queen [*striking her hand upon her knee*]. *Comment, est il véritablement mort?* Purcel, my angel, shall I not have a little breakfast?

Mrs Purcel. What would your Majesty please to have?

Queen. A little chocolate, my soul, if you give me leave; and a little sour cream and some fruit.   [*Exit* Mrs PURCEL.]

Queen [*to Lord L.*]. *Eh! bien, my Lord Lifford, dites nous un peu comment cela est arrivé.* I cannot imagine what he had to do to be putting his nose there. *Seulement pour un, sot voyage avec ce petit mousse – eh bien?*

Lord Liff. Madame, on sçait quelque chose de cela de Mon. Maran, qui d'abord qu'il a vu les voleurs s'est enfui et venu à grand galoppe à Londres, and after dat a waggoner take up the bady and put it in his cart.

Queen [*to Princess Emily*]. Are you not ashamed, *Amalie,* to laugh?

Princess Emily. I only laughed at the cart, mama.

Queen. Ah! that is a very *fade plaisanterie.*

Princess Em. But if I may say it, mama, I am not very sorry.

Queen. Ah! fie donc! Eh bien! my Lord *Lifford!* My God, where is this chocolate, Purcel?

Re-enter Mrs PURCEL, *with the chocolate and fruit.*

Queen [*to Mrs Purcel*]. Well, I am sure Purcel now is very sorry for my Lord Hervey: have you heard it?

Mrs Purcel. Yes, madam; and I am always sorry when your Majesty loses anything that entertains you.

Queen. Look you there now, *Amalie*; I swear now Purcel is thousand times better as you.

Princess Em. I did not say I was not sorry for mama; but I am not sorry for him.

Queen. And why not?

Princess Em. What, for that creature!

Princess Car. I cannot imagine why one should not be sorry for him; I think it very *dure* not to be sorry for him. I own he used to laugh *malapropos* sometimes, but he was mightily mended; and for people that were civil to him he was always ready to do anything to oblige them; and for my part I am sorry, I assure.

Princess Em. Mama, Caroline is *duchtich*; for my part I cannot *paroître.*

Queen. Ah! ah! You can *paroître* and be *duchtich* very well sometimes; but this is no *paroître*; and I think you are very great brute. I swear now he was very good, poor my Lord Hervey; and with people's lives that is no jest. My dear Purcel, this is the nastiest fruit I have ever tasted; is there none of the Duke of Newcastle's or that old fool Johnstone's? *Il étoit bien joli quelquefois*, my Lord Hervey; was he not, Lifford?

Lord Liff. [*taking snuff*]. Ees, ended he was ver pretty company sometimes.

Princess E. shrugs her shoulders and laughs again.

Queen [*to Princess Emily*]. If you did not think him company, I am sorry for your taste. [*To Princess Caroline.*] My God, Caroline, you will twist off the thumbs of your glove. *Mais*, my Lord *Lifford, qui vous a conté tout ça des voleurs, du ditch, et des wagoners?*

Lord Liff. I have hear it at St James, *et tout le monde en parle.*

Queen [to Mrs Purcel]. Have you sent, Purcel, to Vickers about my clothes?

Mrs Purcel. He is here, if your Majesty pleases to see the stuffs.

Queen. No, my angel, I must write now. Adieu, adieu, adieu, my Lord Lifford.

QUEEN *and the two* PRINCESSES *alone.*

Queen. Mais, diable, Amalie, pourquoi est ce que vous voulez faire croire à tout le monde que vous êtes dure comme cette table? [*Strikes the table with her hand.*]

Princess Em. En vérité, mama, je n'ai jamais fait semblant de l'aimer pendant qu'il étoit en vie, et je ne sçais pas pourquoi donc je devrois faire semblant de le pleurer à cette heure qu'il est mort.

Queen. Ah! psha; n'y a-t-il point de différence entre pleurer les gens et rire de leur malheur. Outre cela vous aviez grandissime tort même quand il étoit en vie; car il s'est comporté envers vous avec beaucoup de respect; et jamais je crois a-t-il dit le moindre impertinence sur votre sujet.

Princess Em. Pour moi, je crois qu'il en a dit cent milles.

Queen. Vous faites fort bien de dire que vous le croyez pour vous excuser.

Princess Car. Pour moi, je ne le crois pas; je ne dis pas que la Emilie n'a pas raison de le croire; parce qu'il y a mille gens qui pensent faire leur cour en disant qu'ils l'ont entendu parler impertinemment; mais je n'ai jamais entendu de ces choses dans son stile, et je connais son stile; et outre cela il m'a paru s'être fait une règle de ne le point faire.

Queen. Eh bien! adieu, mes chères enfans, il est tard. Dites un peu en passant que la Mailbone soit prête. [*Exeunt.*]

ACT II

SCENE. – *The Queen's Dressing-room. The* QUEEN *is discovered at her toilet cleaning her teeth;* Mrs PURCEL *dressing her Majesty's head; the* PRINCESSES, Lady PEMBROKE *and* Lady BURLINGTON, *Ladies of the Bedchamber, and* Lady SUNDON, *Woman of the Bedchamber, standing round. Morning prayers saying in the next room.*

1 *Parson* [*behind the scenes*]. '*From pride, vainglory, and hypocrisy, from envy, hatred, and malice, and all uncharitableness,*'

2 *Parson*. '*Good Lord deliver us!*'

Queen. I pray, my good Lady Sundon, shut a little that door; those creatures pray so loud, one cannot hear oneself speak. [*Lady Sundon goes to shut the door.*] So, so, not quite so much; leave it enough open for those parsons to think we may hear, and enough shut that we may not hear quite so much. [*To Lady Burlington.*] What do you say, Lady Burlington, to poor Lord Hervey's death? I am sure you are very sorry.

Lady Pem. [*sighing and lifting up her eyes*]. I swear it is a terrible thing.

Lady Burl. I am just as sorry as I believe he would have been for me.

Queen. How sorry is that, my good Lady Burlington?

Lady Burl. Not so sorry as not to admit of consolation.

Queen. I am sure you have not forgiven him his jokes upon Chiswick. I used to scold him for that too, for Chiswick is the prettiest thing I ever saw in my life. But I must say, poor my Lord Hervey, he was very pretty too.

Lady Burl. [*colouring and taking snuff*]. I can't think your Majesty does Chiswick any great honour by the comparison. He was very well for once, like a party to Vauxhall, where the glare and the bustle entertain one for a little while, but one was always tired of one as well as t'other in half an hour.

Queen. Oh! oh! I beg your pardon. I wish all the Vauxhalls were like him, I assure you — I would divert myself exceedingly with Vauxhall; and for your half-hour, I am your humble servant; he has entertained me, poor my Lord Hervey, many and many half-hours, I can promise you; but I am sure you thought he laughed at you a little sometimes, as well as Chiswick. Come, own the truth.

Lady Burl. I never thought enough about him to think whether he did or did not; but I suppose we had all our share.

Lady Sund. I must say I never in my life heard my Lord Hervey make or give into any joke upon people that he professed living at all well with. He would say a lively thing sometimes, to be sure, upon people he was indifferent to, and very bitter ones upon people he was not indifferent to; and I believe we are all glad enough to do that when we have a fair opportunity; the only difference amongst us is, who does it best and worst.

Princess Em. [*to Lady Sundon*]. Did you really love him? [*Laughs, and mutters something in German to the Queen.*]

Lady Sund. I had a great deal of reason, for he was always very particularly civil and kind to me.

Lady Burl. If he was very civil to you, it was being very particular to you, that's certain.

Queen. I beg your pardon, he was very well bred.

Lady Burl. Where it was his interest, perhaps; he was very well bred to your Majesty, I dare say.

Lady Sund. I am sure he loved the Queen.

Princess Em. That is, you are sure he said so, my good Lady Sundon, and so will all mama's pages and gentlemen ushers.

Lady Sund. But he has said it in a way that I think I could see whether he felt what he said or not; he has often said that the Queen had a thousand good and agreeable and amiable qualities that one should like in a private person, and that he could not conceive why those qualities were not to be loved because they were in a Queen – and one felt the justness of that way of thinking; and I assure your Royal Highness I think the Queen will have a very great loss of him, for, besides the use he was of in Parliament, which I do not pretend to be a judge of, he was certainly a constant amusement to the Queen in private, and gave up his whole time to amuse her; and I must say I do not think it is everybody (if they would give their whole time to it) is capable of amusing the Queen.

Queen. Oh! upon my word he amused me exceedingly. I pray give me the basin to wash. [*Lady Pembroke kneels and gives the basin.*] I am afraid, my good Lady Pembroke, you *　　* 　　* 　　* 　　*

Princess Em. *　　*

Lady Pem. *　　* 　　* 　　*

Lady Burl. You might *say* what you pleased, but I don't see how you could *think* what you pleased *　　*

Lady Pem. I don't know; one flatters oneself, you know, and then Mr Mordaunt was out of his wits about it.

Lady Burl. But you must be out of your wits too, – *　　* 　　*

Queen. I beg pardon. *　　* 　　* 　　* * Oh! poor my Lord Pembroke; he was the best man in this world, and loved you prodigiously.

Lady Pem. I believe there was nothing in the world he would not have done for me *　　* 　　* 　　* 　　*

Queen. *   * I must say my Lady Pembroke was the best wife in the world, and you will be, I am sure, as good a wife to Mr Mordaunt.

Lady Pem. I am sure I should deserve to be hanged if I was not, for he is the best husband in the world.

★   ★   ★   ★
★   ★   ★   ★

Before I was married he used to nurse me almost as much as he did afterwards; indeed it was that prodigious good nature that made me marry him; for in so young a man, showing so much compassion and good nature to be sure is very engaging.

Enter Lord GRANTHAM.

Queen. Oh! *mon Dieu!* there is my Lord Grantham just come from Scarborough. How do you do, my good Lord Grantham? How does your vapours, and how does Mr Clarke? I am prodigious glad to see you again, my good Lord Grantham.

Lord Grantham. I am sure I am glad to see your Majesty; for when I am not with your Majesty I am always as de goose out of de water.

Lady Burl. Then now your Lordship is like the goose in the water.

Queen. And so he is. I know nobody can swim better in a Court than my Lord Grantham.

Lady Sund. And it is not in Court-waters as in other waters, where the lightest things swim best.

Queen. They must not be too heavy neither. But what news do you bring us, my Lord Grantham?

Lord Grant. Your Majesty has hear de news of poor my Lord Hervey?

Queen. Ah! *mon cher* my Lord, *c'est une viellerie; il y a cent ans qu'on le sçait.*

Lord Grant. I have just been talking of him to Sir Robert. Sir Robert is prodigiously concerned; he has seen Monsieur – how you call – *Maraut.*

Queen. Maran, vous voudrez dire. I must ask Sir Robert a little what that poltroon, Mr *Maraut*, as you call him, says of his Lord. I pray, my good child, take away all these things, and let Sir Robert come in.

Lord GRANTHAM *brings in* Sir ROBERT WALPOLE, *and all but* Sir ROBERT *and the* QUEEN *go out.*

Queen. Come, come, my good Sir Robert, sit down. Well, how go matters?

Sir Rob. Everything very well, madam, pure and well. I have just had intelligence out of the City – all is very quiet there.

Queen. But we must hang some of these villains.

Sir Rob. We will, if we can, madam. I had my Lord Chancellor and my Lord Hardwicke with me this morning, and I told them the circumstances of the fellows we had taken.

Queen. I must do my Lord Chancellor and my Lord Hardwicke justice. They have behaved both exceeding well; exceeding well, upon my word. I am sure they will hang these rogues.

Sir Rob. I told my Lord Chancellor, madam, that these fellows that the soldiers had seized were some of the most clamorous and most audacious, that they were halloaing in a very tumultuous manner at the head of the mob, and crying 'Come on! come on!' and all that kind of stuff.

Queen. And what did he say? I am sure he was very zealous. He is the best man in the world.

Sir Rob. Madam, after hearing my story out, he paused some time, and seemed to decline giving any opinion at all; at last he asked, and very significantly, whether the hour given by the Riot Act for the dispersing of the mob was expired before the men we proposed trying were taken.

Queen. Mon Dieu! that is always those silly lawyers' way, as if the soldiers were to go against people in rebellion with watches in their pockets, or to be asking what is o'clock when they should be serving their Prince. And what said my Lord Hardwicke?

Sir Rob. He said too, madam, that it was impossible to condemn these fellows upon the Riot Act unless the hour was expired.

Queen. Ah! *mon Dieu!* they are all so *ennuyant* with their silly forms and their silly Acts. But what did he say about pulling down and disfacing – how do you call it? – the houses.

Sir Rob. He said on that too, madam, that unless it could be proved that the men we have taken assisted in the defacing the houses, that their being in company with those that did was not capital; for though in murder all present are deemed principals, yet in this law, none were deemed criminal but those who were proved accessory.

Queen. There is your fine English liberty! The *canaille* may come and pull one by the nose, and unless one can prove which finger touched one's nose, one has but to put a plaster to one's nose, and wait to punish them till they pull it again; and then, may be, they shall pull one's eyes out of one's head too.

Sir Rob. I am afraid, madam, there are inconveniences and imperfections attending all systems of government, and these are ours; but we will see what's to be done, and if they are to be come at, they shan't escape. But what news from Hanover, madam?

Queen. There is a letter of five-and-forty pages I have received from the King; I have not time now, but there are some things in it I must talk to you about.

Sir Rob. I have had a long letter, too, from Horace.

Queen. Oh! *mon Dieu!* not about his silly ladder-story again. My good Sir Robert, I am so tired and so sick of all that nonsense, that I cannot bear to talk or hear of it any more. Apropos – poor my Lord Hervey, I swear I could cry!

Sir Rob. Your Majesty knows I had a great partiality for him; and really, madam, whatever faults he might have, there was a great deal of good stuff in him. I shall want him, and your Majesty will miss him.

Queen. Oh! so I shall; and that fiddle-faddle Duke of Newcastle I am sure will be glad; but if he or his sleepy friend the Duke of Grafton come with any of their silly raillery about him, upon my word I will give them their own. Adieu, my good Sir Robert, I believe it is late – I must go a moment into the drawing-room; do you know who is there?

Sir Rob. I saw the Duke of Argyll, madam.

Queen. Oh! *mon Dieu!* I am so weary of that *Felt-marshal*, and his tottering head and his silly stories about the Bishops, that I could cry whenever I am obliged to entertain him. And who is there more?

Sir Rob. There is my Lord President, madam.

Queen. Oh! that's very well; I shall talk to him about his fruit, and some silly council at the Cock-pit and the Plantations: my Lord President loves the Plantations.

Sir Rob. He had plantations of his own for several years together, madam, in Leicester Fields, but your Majesty would not let them grow.

Queen. He was, poor man, just the reverse of those people in the Gospel who reaped where they had not sowed, for my good Lord President sowed where he did not reap. But who is there beside?

Sir Rob. There is my tottering Lord Harrington.

Queen. Oh! *mon Dieu!* I wish he tottered till he fell quite down, that I might not have the fatigue of being obliged to entertain him. The slowness of that drone is a fatigue to me that is inexpressible; he must have six hours in the morning for his chocolate and his toilet, and the newspapers; six hours more for his dinner; six hours more for his nasty *guenipes* and for supper; and six more for sleep; and there is the twenty-four very well disposed: and if ever he gives by chance six hours to his business, it is for what might be done in six minutes, and should have been done six days before.

Sir Rob. Ha! ha! ha! Poor Harrington; I wonder he need take six hours to dress, when your Majesty shows you can *dress* him in six minutes, with six words.

Queen. Adieu, adieu, my good Sir Robert; I must go, though you are today excellent conversation.

ACT III

Scene changes to the great Drawing-Room — all the Courtiers ranged in a circle.

Enter the QUEEN, *led by Lord* GRANTHAM, *followed by the* PRINCESSES *and all her Train.* [QUEEN *curtsies slightly; Drawing-Room bows and curtsies very low.*]

Queen [*to the Duke of Argyll.*] Where have been, my Lord? One has not had the pleasure to see you a great while; and one always misses you.

Duke of Argyll. I have been in Oxfordshire, madam; and so long, that I was asking my father here, Lord Selkirk, how to behave: I know nobody that knows the ways of a Court so well, nor that has known them so long.

Lord Selkirk. By God! my Lord, I know nobody knows them better than the Duke of Argyll.

Duke of Arg. All I know, father, is as your pupil; but I told you I was grown a country gentleman.

Lord Selk. You often tell me things I do not believe.

Queen [*laughing.*] Ha! ha! ha! You are always so good together, and my Lord Selkirk is so lively. [*Turning to Lord President.*] I think, my Lord, you are a little of a country gentleman too – you love Chiswick mightily; you have very good fruit there, and are very curious in it; you have very good plums.

Lord President. I like a plum, madam, mightily – it is a very pretty fruit.

Queen. The green-gage, I think, is very good.

Lord Pres. There are three of that sort, madam – there is the true green-gage, and there is the *Drap-d'or* that has yellow spots and there is the *Reine Claude* that has red spots.

Queen. Ah! ah! One sees you are very curious, and that you understand these things perfectly well: upon my word, I did not know you was so deep in these things – you know the plums, as Solomon did the plants, from the cedar to the hyssop.

Queen [*to the first Court Lady*]. I believe you found it very dusty.

First Court Lady. Very dusty, madam.

Queen [*to the second Court Lady.*] Do you go soon into the country, madam?

Second Court Lady. Very soon, madam.

Queen [*to the third Court Lady.*] The town is very empty, I believe, madam?

Third Court Lady. Very empty, madam.

Queen [*to the fourth Court Lady.*] I hope all your family is very well, madam.

Fourth Court Lady. Very well, madam.

Queen [*to the fifth Court Lady.*] We have had the finest summer for walking in the world.

Fifth Court Lady. Very fine, madam.

Queen [*to the Duchess of Hamilton.*] One cannot help wishing you joy, madam, every time one sees you, of the good matches your daughters have made.

Duchess of Hamilton. Considering how they behaved, I wonder indeed they had any matches at all; but for any other two women of quality, one should think it no great catch for one to be married to a fool and t'other to a beggar.

Queen. Oh, fie, fie! my good Duchess! One cannot help laughing, you are so lively; but your expressions are very strong.

Queen [*to the Duchess of Rutland.*] Come, come, my good Duchess, one is always glad to see you.

Duchess of Rutland. Your Majesty is always very kind to · an old woman and a poor widow, that you are so good to let torment you about her children: and, madam, I must beg your Majesty – [*whispers to the Queen*].

Princess Caroline [*at the other end of the room to the Duke of Grafton.*] I vow I think it is very brutal to laugh at such things.

Duke of Grafton. Dans ce monde, il faut – il faut – il faut – se consoler dans tous les malheurs. [*To the Duke of Newcastle.*] Have you cried for my Lord Hervey? Princess Caroline says one should – one should – shed a little tear for my Lord Hervey.

Princess Car. I say no such thing. I said there was not *de quoi rire* for anybody; and that, for my own part, I am very sorry; and that he used to entertain me very often.

Duke of Graft. Well, I knew people used to say – and that – of his wit; but, upon my word, it may be, perhaps – you know everybody does not – just alike, and so – in those things – or may be, when I saw him – but I swear then – entertaining and all that – why now, *Madame la Princesse*, it did not, I own, strike me; and there was something – I don't know how to say it – but, in short, you know what I mean.

Princess Emily. Well, I swear I think now the Duke of Grafton is in the right: to be sure there was a vivacity, and a great many words, and all that – *mais je vous jure que le tout ensemble ne me plaisoit pas.*

Duke of Newcastle [*picking his nose, his ears, his teeth, &c., one after another.*] Well said, *Madame la Princesse!* I think the Princess Emily has hit that off well: there was, to be sure, things in him, but altogether it did not do well; at least, it did not please me: and there was something, I don't know how to describe it, and perhaps I may be told I am prejudiced, and therefore –

Duke of Graft. Why now there is Chesterfield – I don't love Chesterfield – but then my Lord Chesterfield has – has – my Lord Chesterfield has certainly wit – and that –

Duke of Newc. Well, I think Chesterfield has ten times more wit than my Lord Hervey; and in the House of Lords, though Sir Robert, you know, is partial to one and against the other, in my opinion there is no comparison.

Queen [*comes up to the Dukes of Grafton and Newcastle*]. You are talking of poor my Lord Hervey, I believe; well, I am sure now the Duke of Grafton is very sorry, for *au fond* the Duke of de Grafton is not what one calls *hard — je l'ai toujours dit*.

Duke of Graft. Your Majesty will want him by your chaise a hunting — oh! no — I think he did not hunt of late.

Queen. No, my Lord, he did not hunt; but though he did not love nor understand hunting so well as *votre Grace*, there are many occasions in which I shall want him very much; the King will want him too. Do you not think so, Duke of Newcastle?

Duke of Newc. I think the King can't want a Vice-Chamberlain; I dare say his Majesty will find people enough will be glad of the office.

Queen. I must say, my good Duke of Newcastle, this is *une très platte réponse* — to be sure, the King will find Vice-Chamberlains enough, though my Lord Hervey is dead; as he would find Secretaries of State enough, if we had the misfortune to lose our good friend *Permis*; but I dare say he would never find such another —

Duke of Newc. As which?

Queen. Just as you please; I leave it with you.

Enter Lord GRANTHAM *in a hurry.*

Lord Grantham. Ah! dere is my Lord Hervey in your Majesty gallery; he is in de frock and de bob, or he should have come in.

Queen. Mon Dieu! My Lord Grantham, you are mad!

Lord Grant. He is dere, all so live as he was; and has play de trick to see as we should all say.

Queen. Then *he* is mad — *allons voir qu'est ce que c'est que tout ceci*.

[*Exeunt omnes.*]

Appendix 2

A LETTER TO A NOBLE LORD
ON OCCASION OF SOME LIBELS WRITTEN AND
PROPAGATED AT COURT, IN THE YEAR 1732-3

MY LORD,   Nov. 30, 1733

Your Lordship's Epistle has been publish'd some days, but I had not the
pleasure and pain of seeing it till yesterday: Pain, to think your Lordship
should attack me at all; Pleasure, to find that you can attack me so weakly.
As I want not the humility, to think myself in every way but *one* your
inferiour, it seems but reasonable that I should take the only method
either of self-defence or retaliation, that is left me, against a person of
your quality and power. And as by your choice of this weapon, your pen,
you generously (and modestly too, no doubt) meant to put yourself upon
a level with me; I will as soon believe that your Lordship would give a
wound to a man unarm'd, as that you would deny me the use of it in my
own defence.[1]

I presume you will allow me to take the same liberty, in my answer to
so *candid*, *polite*, and *ingenious* a Nobleman, which your Lordship took in
yours, to so *grave*, *religious*, and *respectable* a Clergyman:[2] As you answered
his *Latin* in *English*, permit me to answer your *Verse* in *Prose*. And tho'
your Lordship's reasons for not writing in *Latin*, might be stronger than
mine for not writing in *Verse*, yet I may plead *Two good* ones, for this
conduct: the one that I want the Talent of spinning *a thousand lines in a*
Day (which, I think, is as much *Time* as this subject deserves) and the
other, that I take your Lordship's *Verse* to be as much *Prose* as this letter.
But no doubt it was your choice, in writing to a friend, to renounce all
the pomp of Poetry, and give us this excellent model of the familiar.

When I consider the *great difference* betwixt the rank your *Lordship*
holds in the *World*, and the rank which your *writings* are like to hold in
the *learned world*, I presume that distinction of style is but necessary, which

you will see observ'd thro' this letter. When I speak of *you*, my Lord, it will be with all the deference due to the inequality which Fortune has made between you and myself: but when I speak of your *writings*, my Lord, I must, I can do nothing but trifle.

I should be obliged indeed to lessen this *Respect*, if all the Nobility (and especially the elder brothers) are but so many hereditary fools, if the privilege of Lords be to want brains, if noblemen can hardly write or read, if all their business is but to dress and vote, and all their employment in court, to tell lies, flatter in public, slander in private, be false to each other, and follow nothing but self-interest.[3] Bless me, my Lord, what an account is this you give of them? and what would have been said of me, had I immolated, in this manner, the whole body of the Nobility, at the stall of a well-fed Prebendary?

Were it the mere *Excess* of your Lordship's *Wit*, that carried you thus triumphantly over all the bounds of decency, I might consider your Lordship on your *Pegasus*, as a sprightly hunter on a mettled horse; and while you were trampling down all our works, patiently suffer the injury, in pure admiration of the *Noble Sport*. But should the case be quite otherwise, should your Lordship be only like a *Boy* that is *run away with*; and run away with by a *Very Foal*; really common charity, as well as respect for a noble family, would oblige me to stop your carreer, and to *help you down* from *this Pegasus*.

Surely the little praise of a *Writer* should be a thing below your ambition: You, who were no sooner born, but in the lap of the Graces; no sooner at school, but in the arms of the Muses; no sooner in the World, but you practis'd all the skill of it; no sooner in the Court, but you possess'd all the art of it! Unrivall'd as you are, in making a figure, and in making a speech, methinks, my Lord, you may well give up the poor talent of turning a Distich. And why this fondness for Poetry? Prose admits of the two excellencies you most admire, Diction and Fiction: It admits of the talents you chiefly possess, a most fertile invention, and most florid expression; it is with prose, nay the plainest prose, that you best could teach our nobility to vote, which, you justly observe, is half at least of their business: And, give me leave to prophesy, it is to your talent in prose, and not in verse, to your speaking, not your writing, to your art at court, not your art of poetry, that your Lordship must owe your future figure in the world.

My Lord, whatever you imagine, this is the advice of a Friend, and one who remembers he formerly had the honour of some profession of Friendship from you: Whatever was his *real share* in it, whether small or great, yet as your Lordship could never have had the least *Loss* by continuing it, or the least *Interest* by withdrawing it; the misfortune of losing it, I fear, must have been owing to his own *deficiency* or *neglect*. But as to any *actual fault* which deserved to forfeit it in such a degree, he protests he is to this day guiltless and ignorant. It could at most be but a fault of *omission*; but indeed by omissions, men of your Lordship's uncommon merit may sometimes think themselves so injur'd, as to be capable of an inclination to injure another; who, tho' very much below their quality, may be above the injury.

I never heard of the least displeasure you had conceived against me, till I was told that an imitation I had made of *Horace* had offended some persons, and among them your Lordship. I could not have apprehended that a few *general strokes* about a *Lord scribling carelessly*, a *Pimp*, or a *Spy* at Court, a *Sharper* in a gilded chariot, &c. that these, I say, should be ever applied as they have been, by *any malice* but that which is the greatest in the world, *the Malice of Ill people to themselves*.

Your Lordship so well knows (and the whole Court and town thro' your means so well know) how far the resentment was carried upon that imagination, not only in the *Nature* of the *Libel* you propagated against me, but in the extraordinary *manner*, *place*, and *presence* in which it was propagated; that I shall only say, it seem'd to me to exceed the bounds of justice, common sense, and decency.[4]

I wonder yet more, how a *Lady*, of great wit, beauty, and fame for her poetry (between whom and your Lordship there is a *natural*, a *just*, and a *well-grounded esteem*) could be prevail'd upon to take a part in that proceeding. Your resentments against me indeed might be equal, as my offence to you both was the same; for neither had I the least misunderstanding with that Lady, till after I was the *Author* of my own misfortune in discontinuing her acquaintance. I may venture to own a truth, which cannot be unpleasing to either of you; I assure you my reason for so doing, was merely that you had both *too much wit* for me; and that I could not do, with *mine*, many things which you could with *yours*. The injury done you in withdrawing myself could be but small, if the value you had for me was no greater than you have been pleas'd since to profess. But surely, my Lord, one may say, neither the Revenge, nor the Language you held, bore any *proportion* to the pretended offence: The appellations of *Foe* to *humankind*, an *Enemy* like the *Devil* to all that have *Being*; *ungrateful*, *unjust*, deserving to be *whipt*, *blanketed*, *kicked*, nay *killed*; a *Monster*, an *Assassin*, whose conversation every man ought to *shun*, and against whom *all doors* should be shut; I beseech you, my Lord, had you the least right to give, or to encourage or justify any other in giving such language as this to me? Could I be treated in terms more strong or more atrocious, if, during my acquaintance with you, I had been a *Betrayer*, a *Backbiter*, a *Whisperer*, an *Evesdropper*, or an *Informer*?[5] Did I in all that time ever throw *a false Dye*, or palm *a foul Card* upon you?[6] Did I ever *borrow*, *steal*, or accept, either *Money*, *Wit*, or *Advice* from you? Had I ever the honour to join with either of you in one *Ballad*, *Satire*, *Pamphlet*, or *Epigram*, on any person *living* or *dead*? Did I ever do you so great an injury as to put off *my own Verses* for *yours*, especially on *those Persons* whom they might *most offend*? I am confident you cannot answer in the affirmative; and I can truly affirm, that, ever since I lost the happiness of your conversation I have not published or written, one syllable of, or to either of you; never hitch'd your *names* in a *Verse*, or trifled with your *good names* in *company*.[7] Can I be honestly charged with any other crime but an *Omission* (for the word *Neglect*, which I us'd before, slip'd my pen unguardedly) to continue my admiration of you all my life, and still to contemplate, face to face, your many excellencies and perfections? I am persuaded you can reproach me truly with no great *Faults*, except my *natural ones*, which I am as ready to own, as to do all justice to the contrary *Beauties* in you. It is true, my Lord, I am short, not well shap'd, generally ill-dress'd, if not sometimes dirty: Your Lordship and Ladyship are still in bloom; your Figures such, as rival the *Apollo* of *Belvedere*, and the *Venus* of *Medicis*; and your faces so finish'd, that neither sickness nor passion can deprive them of *Colour*; I will allow your own in particular to be the finest that ever *Man* was blest with: preserve it, my Lord, and reflect, that to be a Critic, would cost it too many *frowns*, and to be a Statesman, too many *wrinkles*! I further confess, I am now somewhat old; but so your Lordship and this excellent Lady, with all your beauty, will (I hope) one day be.[8] I know your Genius and hers so perfectly *tally*, that you cannot but join in admiring each other, and by consequence in the contempt of all such as myself. You have both, in my regard, been like – (your

Lordship, I know, loves a *Simile*, and it will be one suitable to your *Quality*) you have been like *Two Princes*, and I like a *poor Animal* sacrificed between them to cement a lasting League: I hope I have not bled in vain; but that such an amity may endure for ever! For tho' it be what common *understandings* would hardly conceive, Two *Wits* however may be persuaded, that it is in Friendship as in Enmity, The more *danger*, the more *honour*.

Give me the liberty, my Lord, to tell you, why I never replied to those *Verses* on the *Imitator of Horace*? They regarded nothing for my *Figure*, which I set no value upon; and my *Morals*, which, I knew, needed no defence: Any honest man has the pleasure to be conscious, that it is out of the power of the *Wittiest*, nay the *Greatest Person* in the kingdom, to lessen him *that way*, but at the expence of his own *Truth*, *Honour*, or *Justice*.

But tho' I declined to explain myself just at the time when I was sillily threaten'd, I shall now give your Lordship a frank account of the offence you imagined to be meant to you. *Fanny* (my Lord) is the plain English of *Fannius*, a real person, who was a foolish Critic, and an enemy of *Horace*: perhaps a Noble one, for so (if your Latin be gone in earnest) I must acquaint you, the word *Beatus* may be construed.

> *Beatus Fannius! ultro*
> *Delatis capsis et* imagine.

This *Fannius* was, it seems, extremely fond both of his *Poetry* and his *Person*, which appears by the pictures and *Statues* he caused to be made of himself, and by his great diligence to propagate *bad Verses* at *Court*, and get them admitted into the library of *Augustus*. He was moreover of a delicate or *effeminate complexion*, and constant at the Assemblies and Opera's of those days, where he took it into his head to *slander poor Horace*.

> *Ineptus*
> Fannius, *Hermogenis* laedat *conviva Tigelli*.

till it provoked him at last just to *name* him, give him a *lash*, and send him whimpering to the *Ladies*.

Discipularum inter jubeo plorare cathedras.

So much for *Fanny*, my Lord. The word *spins* (as Dr *Freind* or even Dr *Sherwin* could assure you) was the literal translation of *deduci*; a metaphor taken from a *Silk-worm*, my Lord, to signify any *slight, silken,* or (as your Lordship and the Ladies call it) *flimzy* piece of work. I presume your Lordship has enough of this, to convince you there was nothing *personal* but to *that Fannius,* who (with all his fine accomplishments) had never been heard of, but for *that Horace* he injur'd.

In regard to the right honourable Lady, your Lordship's friend, I was far from designing a person of her condition by a name so derogatory to her, as that of *Sappho*; a name prostituted to every infamous Creature that ever wrote Verses or Novels. I protest I never *apply'd* that name to her in any verse of mine, *public* or *private*; and (I firmly believe) not in any *Letter* or *Conversation*. Whoever could invent a Falsehood to support an accusation, I pity; and whoever can believe such a Character to be theirs, I pity still more. God forbid the Court or Town should have the complaisance to *join* in that opinion! Certainly I meant it only of such modern *Sappho's*, as imitate much more the *Lewdness* than the *Genius* of the ancient one; and upon whom their wretched brethren frequently bestow both the *Name* and the *Qualification* there mentioned.

There was another reason why I was silent as to that paper – I took it for a *Lady*'s (on the printer's word in the title page) and thought it too presuming, as well as indecent, to contend with one of that *Sex* in *altercation*: For I never was so mean a creature as to commit my Anger against a *Lady* to *paper*, tho' but in a *private Letter*. But soon after, her denial of it was brought to me by a Noble person of *real Honour* and *Truth*.[9] Your Lordship indeed said you had it from a Lady, and the Lady said it was your Lordship's; some thought the beautiful by-blow had *Two Fathers*, or (if one of them will hardly be allow'd a man) *Two Mothers*; indeed I think *both Sexes* had a share in it, but which was *uppermost*, I know not: I pretend not to determine the exact method of this *Witty Fornication*: and, if I call it *Yours*, my Lord, 'tis only because, whoever *got* it, you *brought it forth*.

Here, my Lord, allow me to observe the different proceeding of the *Ignoble poet*, and his *Noble Enemies*. What he has written of *Fanny, Adonis, Sappho,* of who you will, he own'd he publish'd, he set his name to: What they have *publish'd* of him, they have deny'd to have *written*; and what they have *written* of him, they have denied to have *publish'd*. One of these was the case in the past Libel, and the other in the present. For tho' the parent has own'd it to a few choice friends, it is such as he has been obliged to deny in the most particular terms, to the great Person whose opinion *concern'd him most*.[10]

Yet, my Lord, this Epistle was a piece not written in *haste*, or in a *passion*, but many months after all pretended provocation; when you was at *full leisure* at Hampton-Court, and I the object *singled*, like a *Deer out of Season*, for so ill-timed, and ill-placed a diversion. It was a *deliberate* work, directed to a *Reverend Person*,[11] of the most *serious* and *sacred* character, with whom you are known to cultivate a *strict correspondence*, and to whom it will not be doubted, but you open your *secret Sentiments*, and deliver your *real judgment* of men and things. This, I say, my Lord, with submission, could not but awaken all my *Reflection* and *Attention*. Your Lordship's opinion of me as a *Poet*, I cannot help; it is yours, my Lord, and that were enough to mortify a poor man; but it is not yours *alone*, you must be content to share it with the *Gentlemen* of the *Dunciad*, and (it may be) with many *more innocent* and *ingenious men*. If your Lordship destroys my *poetical* character, *they* will claim their part in the glory; but, give me leave to say, if my *moral* character be ruin'd, it must be *wholly* the work of *your Lordship*; and will be hard even for you to do, unless I *myself co-operate*.

How can you talk (my most worthy Lord) of all *Pope*'s Works as so many *Libels*, affirm, that *he has no invention* but in *Defamation*, and charge him with *selling another man's labours printed with his own name*? Fye, my Lord, you forget yourself. He printed not his name before a line of the person's you mention; that person himself has told you and all the world in the book itself, what part he had in it, as may be seen at the conclusion of his notes to the Odyssey.[12] I can only suppose your Lordship (not having at that time *forgot your Greek*) despis'd to look upon the *Translation*; and ever since entertain'd too mean an Opinion of the Translator to cast an eye upon it. Besides, my Lord, when you said he *sold* another man's works, you ought in justice to have added that he *bought* them, which very much *alters the Case*. What he gave him was five hundred pounds:[13] his receipt can be produced to your Lordship. I dare not affirm he was as *well paid* as *some Writers* (much his inferiors) have been since; but your

Lordship will reflect that I am no man of Quality, either to *buy* or *sell* scribling so high: and that I have neither *Place*, *Pension*, nor Power to reward for *secret Services*. It cannot be, that one of your rank can have the least *Envy* to such an author as I: but were that *possible*, it were much better gratify'd by employing *not your own*, but some of *those low and ignoble pens* to do you this *mean office*. I dare engage you'll have them for less than I gave Mr Broom, if your friends have not rais'd the market: Let them drive the bargain for you, my Lord; and you may depend on seeing, every day in the week, as many (and now and then as pretty) Verses, as these of your Lordship.

And would it not be full as well, that my poor person should be abus'd by them, as by one of your rank and quality? Cannot *Curl* do the same? nay has he not done it before your Lordship, in the same *kind of Language*, and almost the *same words*? I cannot but think, the worthy and *discreet Clergyman* himself will agree, it is *improper*, nay *unchristian*, to expose the *personal* defects of our brother: that both such perfect forms as yours, and such unfortunate ones as mine, proceed from the hand of the same *Maker*; who *fashioneth his Vessels* as he pleaseth, and that it is not from their *shape* we can tell whether they are made for *honour* or *dishonour*.[14] In a word, he would teach you Charity to your greatest enemies; of which number, my Lord, I cannot be reckon'd, since, tho' a Poet, I was never your flatterer.

Next, my Lord, as to the *Obscurity of my Birth* (a reflection copy'd also from Mr *Curl* and his brethren) I am sorry to be obliged to such a presumption as to name my *Family* in the same leaf with your Lordship's: but my Father had the honour in one instance to resemble you, for he was a *younger Brother*. He did not indeed think it a Happiness to bury his *elder Brother*, tho' he had one, who wanted some of those good qualities which *yours* possest. How sincerely glad could I be, to pay to that young Nobleman's memory the debt I ow'd to his friendship, whose early death depriv'd your family of as much *Wit* and *Honour* as he left behind him in any branch of it.[15] But as to my Father, I could assure you, my Lord, that he was no Mechanic (neither a hatter, nor, which might please your Lordship yet better, a Cobler) but in truth, of a very tolerable family: And my Mother of an ancient one, as well born and educated as that *Lady*, whom your Lordship made choice of to be the *Mother of your own Children*; whose merit, beauty, and vivacity (if transmitted to your posterity) will be a *better present* than even the noble blood they derive *only* from *you*. A Mother, on whom I was never oblig'd so far to reflect, as to say, she *spoiled me*. And a Father, who never found himself oblig'd to say of me, that he *disapprov'd my Conduct*. In a word, my Lord, I think it enough, that my Parents, such as they were, never cost me a *Blush*; and that their Son, such as he is, never cost them a *Tear*.

I have purposely omitted to consider your Lordship's Criticisms on my *Poetry*. As they are exactly the same with those of the *foremention'd Authors*, I apprehend they would justly charge me with partiality, if I gave to *you* what belongs to *them*; or paid more distinction to the *same things* when they are in your mouth, than when they were in theirs. It will be shewing both them and you (my Lord) a *more particular respect*, to observe how much they are honour'd by *your Imitation of them*, which indeed is carried thro' your whole Epistle. I have read somewhere at *School* (tho' I make it no *Vanity* to have forgot where) that *Tully* naturaliz'd a few phrases at the instance of some of his friends. Your Lordship has done more in honour of these Gentlemen; you have authoriz'd not only their *Assertions*, but their *Style*. For example, *A* Flow *that* wants skill *to restrain its* ardour, – *a* Dictionary *that gives us nothing at* its own expence. – *As luxuriant branches* bear *but little fruit, so Wit unprun'd* is *but raw fruit* – *While you* rehearse ignorance, *you still* know enough *to do it in Verse* – *Wits* are *but glittering* ignorance. – The *account of* how *we pass our time* – and, *The weight on Sir R. W – 's* brain. *You can* ever *receive from* no *head more than such a head* (as no head) *has to give*: Your Lordship would have said *never* receive instead of *ever*, and *any head* instead of *no head*: but all this is perfectly new, and has greatly enrich'd our language.[16]

You are merry, my Lord, when you say, *Latin* and *Greek*

> *Have quite deserted your poor* John Trot-head,
> *And left plain native English in their stead.*

for (to do you justice) this is nothing less than *plain English*. And as for your *John Trot-head*, I can't conceive why you should give it that name; for by some papers I have seen sign'd with that name, it is certainly a head *very different* from your Lordship's.[17]

Your Lordship seems determined to fall out with every thing you have learn'd at school: you complain next of a *dull Dictionary*,

> *That gives us nothing at its own expence,*
> *But a few modern words for ancient Sense.*

Your Lordship is the first man that ever carried the love of Wit so far, as to expect a *witty Dictionary*. A Dictionary that gives us *any thing but words*, must not only be an *expensive* but a very *extravagant Dictionary*. But what does your Lordship mean by its giving us but *a few modern words* for *ancient Sense*? If by *Sense* (as I suspect) you mean *words* (*a mistake not unusual*) I must do the Dictionary the justice to say, that it gives us *just as many modern words as ancient ones*. Indeed, my Lord, you have more need to complain of a bad Grammar, than of a dull Dictionary.

Doctor *Freind*, I dare answer for him, never taught you to talk

> *of Sapphic, Lyric, and Iambic Odes.*

Your Lordship might as well bid your present Tutor, your Taylor, make you a *Coat*, *Suit of Cloaths*, and *Breeches*; for you must have forgot your Logic, as well as Grammar, not to know, that Sapphic and Iambic are both included in Lyric; that being the *Genus*, and those the *Species*.

> *For all cannot invent who can translate,*
> *No more than those who cloath us, can create.*

Here your Lordship seems in labour for a meaning. It is that you would have Translations, *Originals*? for 'tis the common opinion, that the *business* of a Translator is to *translate*, and not to *invent*, and of a Taylor to *cloath*, and not to *create*. But why should you, my Lord, of all mankind, abuse a Taylor? not to say *blaspheme* him; if he can (as some think) at least go halves with God Almighty in the formation of a *Beau*. Might not Doctor *Sherwin* rebuke you for this, and bid you *Remember your* Creator *in the days of your Youth*?

From a *Taylor*, your Lordship proceeds (by a beautiful gradation) to a *Silkman*.

> *Thus* P—pe *we find*
> *The Gaudy* Hinchcliff *of a beauteous mind.*

Here too is some ambiguity. Does your Lordship use *Hinchcliff* as a *proper name*? or as the Ladies say a *Hinchcliff* or *Colmar*,[18] for a *Silk* or a *Fan*? I will venture to affirm, no Critic can have a perfect taste of your Lordship's works, who does not understand both your *Male Phrase* and your *Female Phrase*.

Your Lordship, to finish your Climax, advances up to a *Hatter*, a Mechanic, whose Employment, you inform us, is not (as was generally imagined) to *cover people's heads*, but to *dress their brains*. A most useful Mechanic indeed! I can't help wishing to have been one, for some people's sake. – But this too may be only another *Lady-Phrase*: Your Lordship and the Ladies may take a *Head-dress* for a *Head*, and understand, that to *adorn the Head* is the same thing as to *dress the Brains*.

Upon the whole, I may thank your Lordship for this high Panegyric: For if I have but *dress'd* up *Homer*, as your *Taylor*, *Silkman*, and *Hatter* have *equip'd your Lordship*, I must be own'd to have dress'd him *marvellously indeed*, and no wonder if he is *admir'd by the Ladies*.

After all, my Lord, I really wish you would learn your *Grammar*. What if you put yourself awhile under the Tuition of your Friend *W—m*?[19] May not I with all respect say to you, what was said to *another Noble Poet* by Mr Cowley, *Pray*, *Mr* Howard, *if you did read your* Grammar, *what harm would it do you*?[20] You yourself wish all Lords would *learn to write*; tho' I don't see of what use it could be, if their whole business is to *give their Votes*: It could only be serviceable in *signing their Protests*. Yet surely this small portion of learning might be indulged to your Lordship, without any Breach of that *Privilege* you so generously assert to all those of your rank, or too great an Infringement of that *Right* which you claim as *Hereditary*, and for which, no doubt, your noble Father will thank you. Surely, my Lord, no Man was ever so bent upon depreciating himself!

All your Readers have observ'd the following Lines:

> *How oft we hear some Witling pert and dull,*
> *By fashion Coxcomb, and by nature Fool,*
> *With hackney Maxims, in dogmatic strain,*
> *Scoffing Religion and the Marriage chain?*
> *Then from his Common-place-book he repeats,*
> *The Lawyers all are rogues, and Parsons cheats,*
> *That Vice and Virtue's nothing but a jest,*

> *And all Morality Deceit well drest;*
> *That Life itself is like a wrangling game, &c.*

The whole Town and Court (my good Lord) have heard *this Witling*; who is so much every body's acquaintance but his own, that I'll engage *they all name* the *same Person*. But to hear *you* say, that this is only – *of whipt Cream a frothy Store*, is a sufficient proof, that never mortal was endued with so humble an opinion both of himself and his own Wit, as your Lordship: For, I do assure you, these are by much the best Verses in your whole Poem.

How unhappy is it for me, that a Person of your Lordship's *Modesty* and *Virtue*, who manifests so tender a regard to *Religion, Matrimony*, and *Morality*; who, tho' an Ornament to the Court, cultivate an exemplary Correspondence with the *Clergy*; nay, who disdain not charitably to converse with, and even assist, some of the very worst of Writers (so far as to cast a few *Conceits*, or drop a few *Antitheses* even among the *Dear Joys* of the *Courant*) that you, I say, should look upon Me alone as reprobate and unamendable! Reflect what *I was*, and what *I am*. I am even *Annihilated* by your Anger: For in these Verses you have robbed me of *all power to think*, and, in your others, of the very *name* of a *Man*! Nay, to shew that this is wholly your own doing, you have told us that before I wrote my *last Epistles* (that is, before I unluckily mention'd *Fanny* and *Adonis*, whom, I protest, I knew not to be your Lordship's Relations) *I might have lived and died in glory*.

What would I not do to be well with your Lordship? Tho', you observe, I am a mere *Imitator of Homer, Horace, Boileau, Garth*, &c. (which I have the less cause to be asham'd of, since they were *Imitators of one another*) yet what if I should solemnly engage never to imitate *your* Lordship? May it not be one step towards an accommodation, that while you remark my *Ignorance in Greek*, you are so good as to say, you have *forgot your own*? What if I should confess I translated from *D'Acier*? That surely could not but oblige your Lordship, who are known to prefer *French* to all the learned Languages. But allowing that in the space of *twelve years* acquaintance with *Homer*, I might unhappily contract as much *Greek*, as your Lordship did in *Two* at the University, why may I not forget it again, as happily?

Till such a reconciliation take effect, I have but one thing to intreat of your Lordship. It is, that you will not decide of my *Principles* on the same grounds as you have done of my *Learning*: Nor give the same account of my *Want of Grace*, after you have lost all acquaintance with my *Person*, as you do of my *Want of Greek*, after you have confessedly lost all acquaintance with the *Language*. You are too generous, my Lord, to follow the *Gentlemen* of the *Dunciad* quite so far, as to seek my *utter Perdition*; as *Nero* once did *Lucan*'s,[21] merely for presuming to be a *Poet*, while one of so much greater quality was a *Writer*. I therefore make this humble request to your Lordship, that the next time you please *to write of me, speak of me*, or even *whisper of me*, you will recollect it is full *eight Years* since I had the honour of *any conversation* or *correspondence* with your Lordship, except *just half an hour* in a Lady's Lodgings at Court, and then I had the happiness of her being present all the time. It would therefore be difficult even for your Lordship's *penetration* to tell, to what, or from what *Principles*, *Parties*, or *Sentiments*, Moral, Political, or Theological, I may have been converted, or perverted, in all that time. I beseech your Lordship to consider, the Injury a Man of your *high Rank* and *Credit* may do to a *private Person*, under *Penal Laws* and many other disadvantages,[22] not for want of *honesty* or *conscience*, but merely perhaps for having too *weak a head*, or too *tender a heart*. It is by *these alone* I have hitherto liv'd excluded from all *posts* of *Profit* or *Trust*: As I can interfere with the *Views* of *no man*, do not deny me, my Lord, *all that is left*, a little *Praise*, or the common Encouragement due, if not to my *Genius*, at least to my *Industry*.

Above all, your Lordship will be careful not to wrong my *Moral Character*, with T H O S E under whose *Protection* I live, and thro' whose *Lenity* alone I can live with Comfort. Your Lordship, I am confident, upon consideration will think, you inadvertently went a little *too far* when you recommended to T H E I R perusal, and strengthened by the weight of your *Approbation*, a *Libel*, mean in its reflections upon my poor *figure*, and scandalous in those on my *Honour* and *Integrity*: wherein I was represented as '*an Enemy* to Human Race, a *Murderer* of Reputations, and a *Monster* mark'd by God like *Cain*, deserving to wander accurs'd thro' the World.'

A strange Picture of a Man, who had the good fortune to enjoy many friends, who will be always remember'd as the first Ornaments of their Age and Country; and no Enemies that ever contriv'd to be heard of, except Mr *John Dennis*,[23] and your Lordship: A Man, who never wrote a

Line in which the *Religion* or *Government* of his Country, the *Royal Family*, or their *Ministry* were disrespectfully mentioned; the Animosity of any one Party gratify'd at the expence of another; or any Censure past, but upon *known Vice, acknowledg'd Folly*, or *aggressing Impertinence*. It is with infinite pleasure he finds, that *some Men* who seem *asham'd* and *afraid* of *nothing else*, are so very sensible of *his Ridicule*: And 'tis for that very reason he resolves (by the grace of God, and your Lordship's good leave)

> *That, while he breathes, no rich or noble knave*
> *Shall walk the world in credit to his grave.*[24]

This, he thinks, is rendering the best Service he can to the Publick, and even to the good Government of his Country; and for this, at least, he may deserve some Countenance, even from the GREATEST PERSONS in it. Your Lordship knows of WHOM I speak. Their NAMES I should be as sorry, and as much asham'd, to place near *yours*, on such an occasion, as I should be to see *You*, my Lord, placed so near *their* PERSONS, if you could ever make so ill an Use of their Ear as to asperse or misrepresent any one innocent Man.

This is all I shall ever ask of your Lordship, except your pardon for this tedious letter. I have the honour to be, with equal *Respect & Concern*,

My Lord,

Your truly devoted Servant, A. Pope

Notes to Appendix 2

(For more detailed notes, see R. Cowler, ed., *The Prose Works of Alexander Pope. Vol. II: The Major Works, 1725–1744*, Oxford: 1986.)

1. References to Hervey's recent duel with William Pulteney.
2. Canon Sherwin, to whom Hervey's 'Epistle' was addressed, who was little more than a figure of fun to Hervey.
3. All deliberately misrepresented references to the text of Hervey's 'Epistle'.
4. 'Verses Address'd to the Imitator of the First Satire of the Second

Book of Horace. By a Lady' – Lady Mary Wortley Montagu and Hervey's 1733 attack on Pope.

5. References to Hervey's role at court.

6. References to Hervey's love of gambling.

7. This claim would be proved false a year later with the publication of 'Epistle to Dr Arbuthnot'.

8. Pope was seven years older than Hervey and one year older than Lady Mary.

9. Dr Arbuthnot.

10. Hervey may have been forced officially to deny his hand in the 'Verses Address'd to an Imitator' because of his court position as Vice-Chamberlain.

11. Sherwin.

12. Pope collaborated with another poet in his translation of the *Odyssey*, which brought him his first taste of fame and wealth.

13. Pope probably made more like ten times this amount from the *Odyssey*.

14. 2 Timothy 2:20: 'But in a great house there are not only vessels of gold and of silver, but also of wood and earth; and some to honour and some to dishonour.'

15. Pope seems to have been genuinely fond of Lord Carr Hervey, who died in 1723.

16. All references to Hervey's 'Epistle'.

17. Pope's political patron, Lord Bolingbroke, had written letters to the *Craftsman* as 'John Trot, yeoman'.

18. Thomas Hincliff was an eminent London mercer and Thomas Colmar a merchant.

19. Probably William Windham, undertutor to the Duke of Cumberland.

20. Edward Howard, an undistinguished poet and dramatist, was one of Dryden's brothers-in-law.

21. The Emperor Nero forced Lucan to commit suicide after the poet conspired against Nero's tyranny.

22. Laws against Catholics.

23. Another critic of Pope's poetry.

24. From 'The First Satire of the Second Book of Horace, Imitated'.

Bibliography

Works by and about Hervey

R. Halsband, *Lord Hervey, Eighteenth Century Courtier*, Oxford: 1973

Ilchester, Lord, *Lord Hervey and his Friends 1726–1738*, London: 1950

Letters between Lord Hervey and Dr Middleton Concerning the Roman Senate, London: 1778

R. Sedgwick, ed., *Lord Hervey's Memoirs*, London: 1931 (first published edition by J. W. Croker, 1848)

Pamphlets attributed to Hervey (all published in London)

'Observations on the Writing of the Craftsman', 1730

'Farther Observations on the Writings of the Craftsman', 1730

'Sequel to a Pamphlet Intitled Observations on the Writings of the Craftsman', 1730

'Remarks on the Craftsman's Vindication of his Two Honourable Patrons in his Paper of May 22 1732', 1732

'The Publick Virtue of Former Times, and the Present Age Compar'd', 1732

'Ancient and Modern Liberty, Stated and Compar'd', 1734

'Epistle from a Nobleman to a Doctor of Divinity', 1734

'A Letter to Mr C-b-r, on his Letter to Mr P –.', 1742.

'The Difference between Verbal and Practical Virtue, with a prefatory Epistle from Mr C-b-r to Mr P –.', 1742

'Some Remarks on the Minute Philosopher', 1752

Some pamphlets concerning Hervey (all published in London)

'Sedition and Defamation Display'd: In a Letter to the Author of the Craftsman', 1731

'A Proper Reply to a Late Scurrilous Libel, Intitled Sedition and Defamation Display'd', 1731

'An Epistle from Little Captain Brazen to the Worthy Captain Plume',
1731

'Iago Display'd', 1731

'The Countess's Speech to her son Roderigo, upon her first seeing him,
after he was wounded in his late Duel', 1731

'The Duel: a poem inscribed to the Right Honourable W-- P--y, Esq.',
1731

'The Humours of the Court; Or, Modern Gallantry', 1732

'The Fair Concubine: Or, the Secret History of the Beautiful Vanella',
1732

'Vanelia: Or, the Amours of the Great', 1732

'Verses Address'd to the Imitator of the First Satire of the Second Book
of Horace', 1733

'Advice to Sappho Occasion'd by her Verses on the Imitator of the First
Satire of the Second Book of Horace', 1733

'The Knight and the Prelate; A New Ballad', 1734

'Epistle to a Nobleman', 1734

'Tit for Tat', 1734

'Tit for Tat Part 2', 1735

'Vanella's Progress', 1736

'The Court Spy; Or, Memoirs of St J-m-s's', 1744

Works by Hervey's contemporaries

F. Algarotti, *Letters on Russia*, London: 1769

W. Bingley, ed., *Correspondence between Frances Countess of Hertford and
Henrietta Louisa Countess of Pomfret, between the years 1736 and 1741*,
London: 1805

C. Bodens, *The Modish Couple*, London: 1732

J. Bradshaw, ed., *Chesterfield's Correspondence*, London: 1892

Bristol, Lord, *Diary and Expenses*, Wells: 1894

—, *Letter-books*, Wells: 1894

J. J. Cartwright, ed., *Wentworth Papers 1705–1739*, London: 1883

W. Coxe, ed., *Memoirs of the Reign of King George II*, London: 1798

J. W. Croker, ed., *Letters of Lady Hervey*, London: 1821

—, *Letters to and from Henrietta, Countess of Suffolk, and her Second Husband,
the Hon. George Berkely, 1712–1767*, London: 1824

H. Fielding, *Joseph Andrews & Shamela*, Oxford: 1980

J. Gay, *The Beggars' Opera*, London: 1727

R. Halsband and I. Grundy, eds., *Essays and Poems of Lady Mary Wortley Montagu*, Oxford: 1977

C. Hanbury Williams, *Collected Works*, London: 1822

B. Hoadley, *A Plain Account of the Nature and End of the Sacrament of the Lord's Supper*, London: 1735

W. S. Lewis *et al.*, eds, *Horace Walpole's Correspondence*, London: 1937–83

Llanover, Lady, ed., *Mrs Delany's Autobiography and Correspondence*, London: 1861

S. Marlborough, *Opinions*, London: 1788

Memoirs of the Life of Sir Stephen Fox, London: 1717

C. Middleton, *The History of the Life of Marcus Tullius Cicero*, London: 1741

R. A. Roberts, ed., *Diary of Viscount Percival*, London: 1920

G. Sherburne, ed., *Pope's Correspondence*, Oxford: 1956

G. S. Thompson, ed., *Letters of a Grandmother*, London: 1943

K. Thompson, ed., *Memoirs of Viscountess Sundon, Mistress of the Robes to Queen Caroline*, London: 1847

P. Toynbee, *Letters of Horace Walpole*, Oxford: 1903

P. Toynbee, ed., *Horace Walpole's Reminiscences*, Oxford: 1924

—, 'Horace Walpole's Journals of Visits to Country Seats', *Walpole Society XVI*, 1927–8

H. Walpole, *Memoirs of the Reign of King George II*, London: 1847

H. P. Wyndham, ed., *Diary of the Late George Bubb Dodington . . . 1749–1761*, London: 1784

Works about Hervey's contemporaries

W. Andrews, *Voltaire*, New York: 1981

J. Brooke, *King George III*, London: 1972

A. Calder-Marshall, *The Two Duchesses*, London: 1978

K. Campbell, *Sarah Duchess of Marlborough*, London: 1932

J. L. Clifford and L. A. Landa, eds, *Pope and his Contemporaries*, Oxford: 1949

E. Dowden, *Michel de Montaigne*, Port Washington, NY: 1972

B. Fothergill, *The Mitred Earl. An Eighteenth Century Eccentric*, London: 1974

—, *The Strawberry Hill Set*, London: 1983

V. Glendinning, *Swift*, London: 1998

D. Green, *Sarah Duchess of Marlborough*, London: 1967

I. Grundy, *Lady Mary Wortley Montagu, Comet of the Enlightenment*, Oxford: 1999

R. Halsband, *The Life of Lady Mary Wortley Montagu*, London: 1956

B. W. Hill, *Sir Robert Walpole, 'Sole and Prime Minister'*, London: 1989

W. R. Hurst, *An Outline of the Career of John Theophilus Desaguliers*, London: 1928

Ilchester, Lord, *Henry Fox, First Lord Holland*, London: 1920

Ilchester, Lord, and Mrs Langford Brooke, *Life of Charles Hanbury Williams*, London: 1928

W. H. Irving, *John Gay's London*, Cambridge, MA: 1928

S. Johnson, *Life of Pope*, London: 1917

C. H. G. Lennox, *A Duke and his Friends*, London: 1911

M. Mack, *Alexander Pope, A Life*, New Haven, CT: 1985

L. Melville, *Lady Suffolk and her Circle*, London: 1924

T. Mowl, *Horace Walpole. The Great Outsider*, London: 1996

R. Northcott, *A Tribute to Algarotti*, London: 1917

G. Paston, *Lady Mary Wortley Montagu and her Times*, London: 1907

A. Ponsonby, *English Diaries*, London: 1929

D. A. Ponsonby, *Call a Dog Hervey*, London: 1949

F. A. Pottle, ed., *Boswell's London Diary*, Harmondsworth: 1966

J. H. Plumb, *Sir Robert Walpole. The King's Minister*, London: 1956

T. W. Riker, *Henry Fox, First Lord Holland*, Oxford: 1911

P. Rogers, *Alexander Pope*, Oxford: 1993

F. Rosslyn, *Alexander Pope: A Literary Life*, London: 1990

D. M. Stuart, *Molly Lepell, Lady Hervey*, London: 1936

S. Tillyard, *Aristocrats*, London: 1994

C. C. Trench, *George II*, London: 1973

J. Uglow, *Hogarth: A Life and a World*, London: 1997

W. H. Wilkins, *Caroline the Illustrious*, London: 1901

General/miscellaneous eighteenth-century books

J. Ashton, *The History of Gambling in England*, London: 1898

R. Bayne-Powell, *Eighteenth Century London Life*, London: 1937

—, *Housekeeping in the Eighteenth Century*, London: 1956

W. Besant, *London in the Eighteenth Century*, London: 1902

J. Brewer, *The Pleasures of the Imagination. English Culture in the Eighteenth Century*, London: 1997

J. Brewer and R. Porter, eds, *Consumption and the World of Goods in the Seventeenth and Eighteenth Centuries*, London: 1993

A. F. Calvert, *The Grand Lodge of England*, London: 1717

E. B. Chancellor, *The Eighteenth Century in London*, London: 1920

J. L. Clifford, ed., *Man versus Society in Eighteenth Century Britain*, Cambridge, MA: 1968

R. Foster Jones *et al.*, *The Seventeenth Century*, Stanford, CT: 1951

P. Fritz and D. Williams, eds, *The Triumph of Culture: Eighteenth Century Perspectives*, Toronto: 1972

M. D. George, *London Life in the Eighteenth Century*, London: 1925

—, *England in Johnson's Day*, London: 1928

M. Girouard, *Life in the English Country House*, New Haven, CT: 1978

J. Hamill, *The History of English Freemasonry*, Addlestone: 1994

C. Hill, *Reformation to Industrial Revolution*, Harmondsworth: 1969

G. Holmes and D. Szechi, *The Age of Oligarchy: Pre-Industrial Britain 1722–1783*, Harlow, Essex: 1993

J. Ingamells, *A Dictionary of British and Irish Travellers in Italy, 1701–1800*, New Haven, CT: 1997

M. C. Jacob, *The Radical Enlightenment*, London: 1981

J. P. Malcolm, *Anecdotes of London in the Eighteenth Century*, London: 1956

G. E. Mingay, *English Landed Society in the Eighteenth Century*, London: 1963

T. Nugent, *The Grand Tour*, London: 1778

Mrs Oliphant, *Historical Sketches of the Reign of George II*, London: 1869

J. H. Plumb, *England in the Eighteenth Century*, Harmondsworth: 1950

—, *Georgian Delights*, London: 1980

R. Porter, *English Society in the Eighteenth Century*, London: 1982

J. Redwood, *Reason, Ridicule and Religion: the Age of Enlightenment in England 1660–1750*, London: 1976

M. Reed, *The Georgian Triumph*, London: 1983

A. E. Richardson, *Georgian England*, London: 1931

L. Stone, *An Open Elite?*, Oxford: 1986

W. Thackeray, *The Four Georges*, London: 1866

E. R. Wasserman, ed., *Aspects of the Eighteenth Century*, Baltimore, MD: 1965

Select Trials, London: 1734

Costume

A. Buck, *Dress in Eighteenth Century England*, London: 1979

G. Squire, *Dress, Art and Society 1560–1970*, London: 1974

C. Willet-Cunnington, *Handbook of English Costume in the Eighteenth Century*, London: 1957

Art and architecture

E. Einberg and J. Egerton, *The Age of Hogarth*, London: 1988

H. Honour, *Neo-Classicism*, London: 1968

A. Laing, *In Trust for the Nation: Paintings from National Trust Houses*, London: 1995

—, 'In Trust for the Nation', *Apollo*, April 1996

M. Levy, *Rococo to Revolution, Major Trends in Eighteenth Century Painting*, London: 1995

E. Lucie-Smith, *Eroticism in Western Art*, London: 1972

R. Paulson, *Hogarth: High Art and Low 1732–1750*, Cambridge: 1992

—, *Hogarth's Graphic Works*, New Haven, CT: 1965

M. Pointon, *Hanging the Head*, New Haven, CT: 1993

J. Summerson, *Architecture in Britain 1530–1830*, London: 1953

M. Webster, *Hogarth*, London: 1979

R. Wendorf, *The Elements of Life: Biography and Portrait Painting in Stuart and Georgian England*, Oxford: 1990

Letter-writing and literature

H. Anderson *et al.*, eds, *The Familiar Letter in the Eighteenth Century*, Kansas UP, KA: 1966

A. Beljame (trans. E. O. Lorimer), *Men of Letters and the English Public in the Eighteenth Century, 1660–1744: Dryden, Addison, Pope*, London: 1948

D. F. Bond, *Critical Essays from the Spectator*, Oxford: 1970

J. Boone, *Tradition Counter Tradition: Love and the Form of Fiction*, Chicago: 1987

B. Boyce, *The Character Sketches in Pope's Poems*, Durham, NC: 1962

J. L. Clifford, ed., *Biography as an Art: Selected Criticism 1560–1960*, London: 1962

H. Deutsch, *Resemblance and Disgrace. Alexander Pope and the Deformation of Character*, Cambridge, MA: 1996

P. Dixon, *The World of Pope's Satires*, London: 1968

P. Fussell, *The Rhetorical World of Augustan Humanism*, Oxford: 1965

J. V. Guerinot, *Pamphlet Attacks on Alexander Pope 1711–1744*, London: 1969

G. W. Hatfield, *Henry Fielding and the Language of Irony*, Chicago: 1968

W. I. Irving, *The Providence of Wit in the English Letter Writers*, Duke UP, NC: 1955

C. Lowenthal, *Lady Mary Wortley Montagu and the Eighteenth Century Letter*, Athens, GA: 1994

M. Mack, 'The Muse of Satire', *Yale Review 41*, Autumn 1951

J. Mullan, *Sentiment and Sociability, The Language of Feeling in the Eighteenth Century*, Oxford: 1988

E. Olson, 'Rhetoric and the Appreciation of Pope', *Modern Philology 37*, 1939

C. J. Rawson, *Henry Fielding and the Augustan Ideal under Stress*, London: 1972

B. Redford, *The Converse of the Pen: Acts of Intimacy in the Eighteenth Century Familiar Letter*, Chicago: 1986

P. Rogers, *Hacks and Dunces*, London: 1980

—, *Eighteenth Century Encounters*, Brighton: 1985

S. Shesgreen, *Literary Portraits in the Novels of Henry Fielding*, DeKalb, IL: 1972

Foreigners' views of London

Madame du Boccage, *Letters Concerning England, Holland, and Italy*, London: 1770

M. Marais, *Journal et Mémoires*, Paris: 1863

H. Misson, *Memoirs and Observations of his Travels over England*, London: 1719

Muralt, *Letters Describing the Characters and Customs of the English and French Nations*, London: 1726

C. Saussure, *A Foreign View of England*, London: 1902

S. G. Tallentyre, ed. and trans., *Voltaire in his Letters*, London: 1919

Voltaire, *Letters on England*, London: 1889

Writers Hervey would have read

C. J. Betts, trans., *Montesquieu's Persian Letters*, Harmondsworth: 1977

D. S. Carne-Ross and K. Haynes, eds, *Horace in English*, London: 1996

I. Kidd, ed., *Plutarch's Essays*, London: 1992

M. Massey, ed., *Society in Imperial Rome. Selections from Juvenal, Petronius, Martial, Tacitus, Seneca and Pliny*, Cambridge: 1982

J. C. Rolfe, trans., *Suetonius's Lives of the Caesars*, London: 1914

L. Tancock, ed., *La Rochefoucauld's Maxims*, London: 1981

—, *Mme de Sévigné's Letters*, London: 1982

K. Walker, ed., *Rochester's Poetry*, Oxford: 1984

On sexuality

H. Barker and E. Chalus, *Gender in Eighteenth Century England*, London: 1997

C. Bingham, 'Seventeenth Century Attitudes towards Deviant Sex', *Journal of Interdisciplinary History I*, 1971

P. Bouce, ed., *Sexuality in Eighteenth Century Britain*, Manchester: 1982

J. Campbell, 'Politics and Sexuality in Portraits of John, Lord Hervey', *Word & Image VI, 4*, Oct.–Dec. 1990

R. D. Cottrell, *Sexuality/Textuality. A Study of Montaigne's Essais*, Columbus, OH: 1981

J. Davidson, *Courtesans and Fishcakes*, London: 1997

K. J. Dover, 'Classical Greek Attitudes to Sexual Behaviour', *Arethusa 6*, 1973

L. Dowling, *Hellenism and Homosexuality in Victorian England*, Ithaca, NY: 1994

W. R. Dynes and S. Donaldson, *Homosexuality in the Ancient World*, New York: 1992

M. Foucault, trans. R. Hurley, *The History of Sexuality*, New York: 1978

R. Lane-Fox, *Alexander the Great*, Harmondsworth: 1973

M. McIntosh, 'The Homosexual Role', *Social Problems 16*, 1968

R. Norton, *Mother Clap's Molly House, The Gay Subculture in England 1700–1830*, London: 1992

G. S. Rousseau and R. Porter, *Sexual Underworlds of the Enlightenment*, Chapel Hill, NC: 1988

A. L. Rowse, *Homosexuals in History, a Study of Ambivalence in Society, Literature and the Arts*, London: 1977

E. K. Sedgwick, *Between Men, English Literature and Male Homosocial Desire*, New York: 1985

R. Sennett, *Flesh and Stone. The Body and the City in Western Civilisation*, London: 1994

A. Soble, ed., *The Philosophy of Sex*, Lanham, MD: 1997

C. Spencer, *Homosexuality: A History*, London: 1995

L. Stone, *The Family, Sex and Marriage in England 1500–1800*, London: 1977

R. Trumbach, 'London's Sodomites: Homosexual Behaviour and Urban Culture in the Eighteenth Century', *Journal of Social History II*, 1977

—, *Sex and the Gender Revolution. Heterosexuality and the Third Gender in Enlightenment London*, Chicago: 1998

R. Trumbach and G. S. Rousseau, essays in *Eighteenth Century Life 9*, 1985

P. Wagner, *Eros Revived*, London: 1988

C. D. Williams, *Pope, Homer and Manliness*, London: 1993

Politics

J. M. Beattie, *The English Court in the Reign of George II*, Cambridge: 1967

J. Brewer, *Party Ideology and Popular Politics at the Accession of George III*, Cambridge: 1976

M. D. George, *English Political Caricature*, Oxford: 1959

I. Kramnick, *Bolingbroke and his Circle. The Politics of Nostalgia*, Cambridge, MA: 1968

J. Loftis, *The Politics of Drama in Augustan England*, Oxford: 1963

Notes

Hervey's letters to Stephen Fox are stored at the West Sussex Record
Office (Ick) and in the Holland House Papers (HH) at the British
Museum. Those in Sussex are mostly copies made by a secretary in the
eighteenth century; the Holland House ones are the originals sent to Ste,
which he saved. By comparing the total number to the number at
Ickworth it is clear Fox destroyed a large proportion of the letters he
received. Also included in the Holland House Papers are Hervey's letters
to Henry Fox, Henry Fox's letters to his brother and Thomas Winnington, and Molly Hervey's correspondence with both Fox brothers.
The first twenty-six pages of the first letter-book in Bury have been cut
out; there is no way of knowing what they dealt with, but Hervey's

previous biographer Robert Halsband speculates that they were to a previous lover of Hervey's whom Ste succeeded. Also in Sussex are some letters Hervey wrote to his other correspondents: Lady Mary Wortley Montagu, Conyers Middleton, Prince Frederick and so on. Only two of Ste's letters to Hervey survive, both in the Holland House archives. Most probably, after Hervey's death, his son George returned them to Ste (as he returned Lady Mary Wortley Montagu's letters to her) and Ste then destroyed all but the last two which he kept (presumably) as a reminder of his sad, difficult, loving friend.

One person who read this book in draft speculated that Hervey may have imagined or exaggerated the nature of his friendship with Fox. This is impossible to prove, since Ste's letters do not survive, but I refute it for several reasons. First, the fact that Ste saved many of Hervey's letters to him indicates they were important to him. Second, Hervey's responses to Ste often reveal a passion and possessiveness on Ste's part, particularly from 1727 to 1732. Third, Hervey and Ste would not have spent eighteen months abroad together, or shared a London house, or spent so much time publicly together had they not been in a reciprocal relationship. Finally, it is Hervey who convinces me of their love: he was too proud, at the same time as being too realistic about people, to have made up a connection that was not there.

Hervey's *Memoirs of the Court of King George II* are in manuscript form at Bury St Edmunds, and were published in two editions in the mid nineteenth and mid twentieth centuries (see Bibliography). The later version is complete. The section that deals with the turbulent events from May 1730 to late summer 1732 was destroyed after Hervey's death by his grandson, the first Marquess of Bristol.

I have not noted who letters were written by, and to whom they were written, if this is clear from the text; in the Notes, if the recipient is not noted, the letter was written to Stephen Fox. With many quotations, for example all correspondence to and from Lord Bristol and much of his wife's, as well as his diaries, there is only one source (for the Bristols, his *Letter-Books* and *Diary and Expenses*); in these cases I have not noted them. These instances include Mrs Delany's diaries and letters, Horace Walpole's correspondence, Lord Chesterfield's correspondence, Lady Mary Wortley Montagu's correspondence, Viscount Percival's diaries, Cesar de Saussure's observations, Misson, Montaigne and Suetonius. I have done this only if I am sure that it is clear from the text who is writing and that the reference will be easy to find in the Bibliography.

I have modernized spelling, extended abbreviations ('though' instead of 'tho', 'Sir Robert' instead of 'Sr. Robt'), removed capitals for nouns, and altered the grammar a little (for example, in the eighteenth century a colon was often used for a full stop), but only to make the text easier to read. In some places the letters do not make complete sense – if Hervey was angry or in a hurry – but I have not altered them. In quoting poetry, I have tried to remain as true to the eighteenth-century originals as possible with capitalized nouns, spelling and so on.

Introduction

p. 4   'cat scratchant . . .': HWC, XXXV, p. 109. Horace Walpole to John Chute, 6.3.59

p. 5   'Few Men . . .': Ick; written by Hervey in 1742 as his own epitaph, and given to his father

PART ONE

1 – Childhood

p. 7   'a tenant's old house . . . ever saw': ML, p. 80, 1731

2 – *Jeunesse Dorée*

p. 14   'I believe . . .': *Dress in Eighteenth Century England*, p. 20

p. 14   'the most perfect . . .': Rem, p. 60

p. 14   'made up of every . . .': Mem, p. 41

p. 17   'Now let me . . .': Pope, II, p. 41

p. 17   'lazy titled heir . . .': Hervey's 'Epistle from a Nobleman to a Doctor of Divinity'

p. 18   'my Lord Fanny's . . .': LS, p. 62, 1737

p. 19   'hard as flint . . .': M, 13.9.27

3 – Stephen Fox

p. 20   'They all jog on . . .': 'An Account of my own Constitution and Illness, with some Rules for the Preservation of Health; for the Use of my Children', reprinted as Appendix II of Sedgwick's edition of Hervey's *Memoirs*

p. 21   'I have an . . .': Ick, 23.11.26

p. 21   'What amusements . . .': Ick, 27.12.26

p. 21   'I hate your . . .': Ick, 19.1.27

p. 22   'his time here . . .': Holland, p. 24

p. 22   'good-for-nothing . . .': HH, undated

p. 23   'everybody's . . .': Ick, 17.8.31

p. 23   'I dote on . . .': Ick, 25.11.29

p. 24   'is such a . . .': HH, 28.9.53

p. 24   'I have thought . . .': Ick, 29.5.27

4 – Sir Robert Walpole

p. 26   'I shall be . . .': Ick, 15.6.27

p. 26   'My time has . . .': Mem, p. 24

p. 26   'I shall certainly . . .': Rem, II, p. 285

p. 27   'dazzled with . . .': Mem, p. 24

p. 27   'New leeches . . .': Mem, p. 48

p. 28   'There I am sure . . .': Rem, II, pp. 294–5

p. 28   'did not seem . . .': Mem, pp. 39–40

p. 28   'no Cuzzonist . . .': Ick, 13.6.34

p. 28   'who had been all . . .': HH, 10.8.34

p. 28   'An anti-Handelist . . .': Mem, p. 274

p. 31   'flat as a pancake . . .': Mrs Delany actually says Duchess of Queensborough, but she must have got the name wrong as this title did not exist, and the Duchess of Queensberry was a famous beauty

p. 31   'all the pageantry . . .': Mem, p. 66

5 – Remembrances

p. 33   'Though I have . . .': HH, 3.7.27

p. 33   'What charming . . .': *Sentiment and Sociability*, p. 5

p. 34   'it seems to have . . .': *The World of Pope's Satires*, p. 17

p. 36   'whom I loved . . .': 'An Account of my own Constitution and Illness'

p. 36   'who loved me . . .': Ibid.

p. 37   ''tis imposible . . .': M, 27.9.27 to Griselda Murray

p. 37   'yet I think . . .': M, 25.9.27 to Griselda Murray

p. 38   'you will not find . . .': Ick, 1.6.27

p. 39   'Do not, for the . . .': ML, p. 15

p. 39   'There is a great deal . . .': M, 11.3.29 to Griselda Murray

p. 40   'You once told me . . .': Ick, 28.12.27

p. 40   'I have told you . . .': Ick, 30.12.27

p. 41   'I would no more . . .': Ick, 2.1.28

p. 41   'As to your . . .': HH, 9.1.28

p. 41   'nothing but *politiquer* . . .': Ibid.

p. 42   'Pray make my . . .': Ibid.

p. 42   'Mr Fox never . . .': An Account of my own Constitution and
         Illness'

p. 42   'Walk often through . . .': Ick, 18.6.28

p. 43   'I beg my . . .': Ick, 20.6.28

p. 43   'I prefer the . . .': Ick, 25.6.28

p. 44   'They have no good . . .': HH, 27.6.28

p. 44   'With an affection . . .': 'An Account of my own Constitution
         and Illness'

6 – Eros and Agape

p. 45   'We rise . . .': Sun, II, p. 285

p. 45   'Fashions are come . . .': Ick, 30.9.28

p. 46   'no attempt . . .': *Journal et Mémoires*, ii. p. 320

p. 50   'mutual devotion . . .': *Arethusa 6*, p. 67

p. 50   'While I was dear . . . shadow': *The Converse of the Pen*, pp. 104–
         111

p. 51   'to show how . . .': Ick, 30.12.27

p. 51   'Thou dearest youth . . .': Ick; reproduced in Lady Mary Wortley
         Montagu, *Essays and Poems*

p. 51   'There is only . . .': *Lighting in the Domestic Interior*, p. 96

7 – In Sickness and in Health

p. 53   'I beg my Lord . . .': HH, 20.9.28

p. 53   'thoughts as much . . .': M, 14.7.28 to Griselda Murray

p. 53   'How does he . . .': HH, 9.12.28

p. 54   'or revive the . . .': ML, p. 72

p. 54   'I know laudanum . . .': M, 21.12.29 to Griselda Murray

p. 55   'out of all . . .': HH, 25.1.29

p. 55   'I looked so . . .': 'An Account of my own Constitution and
         Illness'

p. 57   'The clergy say . . .': Ick, 2.7.29

p. 57   'Within an hour . . .': Ick, 24.6.29

p. 58   'If you had not . . .': Ick, 16.7.29

p. 59   'But sick or well . . .': Ick, undated

p. 59   'His good sense . . .': 'An Account of my own Constitution and
         Illness'

PART TWO

8 – Allegiance
p. 63   'I don't send . . .': Ick, undated
p. 63   'I am already . . .': HH, 18.11.29
p. 64   'It seems her little . . . hanged': HH, 13.11.29
p. 65   'Prudes wonder . . .': Ick, 2.12.34 (misdated; must be 1729)
p. 65   'It is the way . . .': *The Family, Sex and Marriage in England 1500–
        1800*, p. 506
p. 66   'O would kind . . . ended there': reproduced in Lady Mary
        Wortley Montagu, *Essays and Poems*
p. 67   'It might very . . .': Mem, p. 261
p. 67   'equal to any . . .': ML, p. 78
p. 67   'no more to be . . .': MHL, p. 20
p. 67   'yet there is . . .': MHL, p. 24
p. 68   'Every day produces . . .': HH, 9.1.28
p. 68   'I am so . . .': HH, 5.2.30
p. 69   'the Crown was . . .': Mem, pp. 281–2
p. 69   'the King loved . . .': Mem, pp. 257–8
p. 70   'What was there . . .': *Bolingbroke and his Circle. The Politics of
        Nostalgia*, p. 205
p. 71   'was false, loved . . .': Mem, p. 108
p. 71   'at last forced . . .': Ibid.
p. 71   'I began the day . . .': Ick, 15.11.29
p. 71   'My own affairs . . .': Ick, 25.1.30
p. 72   'I have been very . . .': Ick, 22.11.29
p. 72   'If these four days . . .': HH, 5.11.29

9 – Perceptions
p. 73   'One should never . . .': HH, 13.11.29
p. 73   'I *must* see you . . .': Ick, 15.11.29
p. 73   'Your letter . . .': Ick, 25.11.29
p. 74   'A letter I received . . .': Ick, 2.12.34 (misdated; it is 1729)
p. 74   'A *guignon* . . .': Ick, undated
p. 75   'As to our manner . . .': Ick, 29.12 (year unmarked)
p. 76   'I shall *Fox*-hunt . . .': HH, 18.11.29

p. 76 'time in a hum-drum . . .': Ick, 17.2.30

p. 77 'went afterwards . . .': Ick, 3.3.30

10 – The Back Stairs

p. 78 'My Lord there is . . .': *Caroline the Illustrious*, I, p. 147

p. 78 'As long as the firm . . .': Coxe, *Memoirs of the Reign of King George II*, II, p. 390

p. 78 'six hours to . . .': Mem, p. 346

p. 79 'alchemy of ritual . . .': *Aristocrats*, p. 121

p. 80 'We jog on . . .': Ick, 14.9.30

p. 80 'No mill-horse . . .': Sun, II, p. 231

p. 80 'one Birthday . . .': Ick, 31.10.32

p. 82 'only of a size . . .': *Dress in Eighteenth Century England*, p. 28

p. 83 'Nobody can carry . . .': *The English Court in the Reign of George II*, p. 248

p. 84 'It is pleasant . . .': *Alexander Pope, A Life*, p. 609

p. 84 'be proud . . .': *Chesterfield's Correspondence*, II, p. 656

p. 85 'there is one article . . .': M, 8.8.(1730)

p. 85 'courts are . . .': *Chesterfield's Correspondence*, II, pp. 655–6

p. 86 'to come hither . . .': Rem, p. 91

p. 86 'reversed the manners . . .': Mem, p. 67

11 – Gilded Cages

p. 88 'I cannot help . . . have already': Ick, 13.6.30

p. 88 'Why are you not . . .': Ick, 19.7.30

p. 89 'I have you now . . .': Ick, 22.7.30

p. 89 'What are the royal . . .': Ick, 21.8.30

p. 90 'sits as uneasily . . .': Ick, 22.7.30

p. 90 'I beg you would . . .': Ick, 21.8.30

p. 90 'It is quite . . .': Ick, 21.12.31

p. 91 'Lady Hervey, by . . .': LS, p. 62

p. 91 'Or were I . . .': reprinted in LS, pp. 60–61

p. 92 'suffered a good . . .': M, 1.8.30

p. 92 'How this happened . . .': Ick, 24.9.30

p. 92 'we chickens . . .': Ick, 9.9.30

p. 92 'I have been so tied . . .': Ick, undated

p. 93 'They are so taken . . .': Ick, 4.9.30

p. 93   'I write today . . .': Ick, 14.9.30

p. 93   'Not that I . . .': Ick, 16.9.30

p. 94   'I long to be . . .': Ick, 8.12.30

p. 94   'which I told . . .': Ick, 12.12.30

p. 94   'I thought you seemed . . . forever': Ick, 8.12.30

12 – Miss Vane

p. 95   'a folio-collection . . .': LS, I, p. 67

p. 95   'I confess the . . .': Ibid.

p. 95   'a Maid of Honour . . .': H. Walpole, *Memoirs of the Reign of King George II*, I, p. 75

p. 95   'No one is shocked . . .': *Sexuality in Eighteenth Century Britain*, p. 12

p. 95   'And pray tell . . .': LA, I, pp. 175–6

p. 96   'I shall always . . .': HH, 6.1.31

p. 97   'I have kept . . .': HH, 14.6.31

p. 98   'As to the cheeses . . .': HH, 18.11.29

p. 98   ''Tis impossible to tell . . .': HH, 3.7.31

p. 98   'The base, or . . .': Ick, 14.7.31

p. 99   'very great expense . . .': Earl of Oxford quoted in *Sir Robert Walpole. The King's Minister*, p. 82

p. 99   'mountains of roast . . .': *The Strawberry Hill Set*, p. 18

p. 99   'Our company . . .': Ick, 21.7.31

p. 100   'When as you . . .':xIck, 16.7.31

p. 100   'a son I need . . .': Mem, p. 95

p. 100   'his behaviour . . .': Mem, p. 97

13 – 'My dear Chicken'

p. 102   'for fear some . . .': Ick, 11.1.31

p. 102   'in a mysterious . . .': HH, 26.7.31

p. 103   'I have been . . .': Ick, 12.8.31

p. 103   'Solomon you know . . .': Ick, 26.8.31

p. 103   'and felt just . . .': Ick, 17.8.31

p. 104   'You are by this . . .': Ick, 20.11.31

p. 105   'I wish nothing . . . indissolubly yours': Ick, 31.8.31

p. 106   'Here's an end . . .': Ick, 2.9.31

p. 107   'I had the headache . . .': Ick, 9.9.31

p. 107   'You guess very ill . . .': Ick, 18.9.31

PART THREE

14 – Sticks and Stones

p. 111   'I have left . . .': HH, 6.1.31
p. 111   'My dear Ste . . .': Ick, 7.1.31
p. 112   'there is a paragraph . . .': HH, 14.6.31
p. 113   'Are unmannerly . . .': Arnall, 'Observations on a Pamphlet Entitled an Answer', 1731

15 – Master–Miss

p. 117   'without exposing . . .': Mem, p. 263
p. 118   'that monstrous . . . attend it': M, 2.2.31 to Griselda Murray
p. 121   'no man . . .': M, 11.2.31 to Griselda Murray
p. 121   'I fancy upon . . .': BLMR; to Lord Carlisle

16 – Rivals

p. 123   'his name was . . .': Rem, II, p. 164
p. 123   'as much as one . . .': Ick, 30.9.31
p. 123   'I can account . . .': *Lady Mary Wortley Montagu, Comet of the Enlightenment*, p. 262
p. 123   'making a thousand . . . *ivre*': Ick, 30.9.31
p. 124   '*Ces affronts* . . . was pleased': Ick, 23.10.31
p. 124   'the two imperial . . .': Ick, 26.10.31
p. 124   'as great a romp . . .': Ick, 25.11.31
p. 125   'He is as well-bred . . .': Ick, 23.10.31
p. 125   'very handsome . . .': Ick, 8/19.12.31, to Henry Fox
p. 125   'I like the company . . . commerce-table': Ick, 4.9.31
p. 126   'who is in her . . . the last': Ick, 18.9.31
p. 126   'her Scotch Highland . . . hither': Ick, 30.9.31
p. 127   'The pain of leaving . . .': Ick, 12.10.31
p. 127   'she said she thought . . .': Ick, 19.10.31
p. 127   'I propose more . . .': WLM, p. 20
p. 128   'it a very improper . . .': BLMS, Duchess of Marlborough to Mrs Horner, 14.7.32
p. 129   'an Adonis . . .': Ick, 2.12.31
p. 129   'I went to the . . .': Ick, 4.12.31

p. 129   'I have been in . . .': Ick, 27.11.31
p. 130   'I was far . . . of it': Ick, 7.12.31
p. 130   'The short of . . . all annihilated': Ick, 14.12.31
p. 131   'the great source . . .': Rem, I, p. 65
p. 131   'I received a letter . . .': Ick, 23.12.(31)

17 – Hephaestion Betrayed

p. 133   'I have already . . .': Ick, 23.10.31
p. 133   'Without any . . .': Ick, 26.10.31
p. 134   'the impression . . .': Ick, 21.10.31
p. 134   'to signify the youth . . .': Ick, 6.11.31
p. 134   'I have many little . . .': Ick, undated
p. 134   '*Quant al padrone . . . m'ennuyerais pas*': Ick, 6.11.31
p. 136   'What game you . . .': Ick, 10.11.31
p. 136   'I did not think . . .': Ick, 18.11.31
p. 137   'You were in the . . .': Ick, 25.11.31
p. 137   'falsehood as well . . .': Ick, 25.12.31
p. 137   'It is as well . . .': Ick, 4.12.31
p. 137   'That fool 7 . . .': Ick, 14.12.31
p. 138   'Let their folly . . .': Ick, 25.12.31
p. 138   'It is but just . . .': Ick, 28.12.31
p. 139   'for her . . .': *Diary of Viscount Percival*, i, p. 218
p. 139   'so proud . . .': Halsband, *Hervey*, p. 135
p. 142   'I know he was . . . not impotent': Mem, pp. 615–16
p. 144   'discover what . . . his mistress': *Diary of Viscount Percival*, I, pp. 264–5
p. 144   'his princely . . .': ML, p. 114

18 – Unconsoled

p. 146   'comedies in high . . .': Ick, 7.9.32
p. 146   'There is so much . . .': Ick, 10.10.32
p. 147   'I know you love . . .': Ick, 7.10.32
p. 147   'I have the conduct . . .': Mem, p. 507
p. 147   'Whenever our . . .': Mem, p. 364
p. 149   'He like a very . . .': HH, 26.9.32
p. 149   'If I do not see . . .': HH, 7.10.32
p. 150   'Can the following . . .': HH, 7.11.32

p. 151 'One presented . . .': *A Duke and his Friends*, p. 267

p. 151 'all you untaken . . .': Ick, 18.7.33

p. 152 'Excepting the . . . composition': HH, 14.11.32

p. 153 'allowed by . . .': Mem, p. 71

p. 153 'that flow of . . .': MHL, p. 31

p. 153 'I came very early . . . myself poorer': Ick, 14.11.32

19 – A Broken Girdle

p. 155 'O! Death: thou . . .': Ick, 1.10.31, to Henry Fox

p. 155 'Poor Fanny . . .': *Horace Walpole's Letters*, iii, p. 334

p. 155 'I liked her . . .': Ick, 27.9.31

p. 158 'I had a respect . . .': Ick, 7.7.33

p. 158 'I do not at all . . .': Ick, 28.7.33

p. 158 'I am very angry . . .': Ick, 14.8.33

p. 159 'but because I do . . .': HH, 13.8.32

20 – Complicity

p. 161 'Politics you hate . . .': Ick, 17.2.33, to Richmond

p. 161 'with more horror . . .': Ick, 28.12.31

p. 161 'fully possessed . . .': Mem, p. 152

p. 162 'Though his affection . . .': Rem, p. 71

p. 162 'The Queen loved . . .': Mem, p. 261

p. 162 'dominant passion . . .': Mem, pp. 253–4

p. 163 'so devoted to his . . .': WLM, pp. 122–3

p. 163 'Notwithstanding . . .': Ick, 30.12.31

p. 164 'Sir Robert with . . .': Mem, p. 18.

p. 164 'had more warmth . . .': Ibid.

p. 164 'When you have . . .': Ibid.

p. 165 'greeting every . . .': Mem, p. 164

p. 166 'cry out with . . .': Mem, p. 153

p. 167 'You asked so kindly . . .': Ick, 5.7.33

p. 167 'This delightful . . .': 11.33 to Middleton

p. 168 'Nor will I add . . .': Ick, November 1733

PART FOUR

21 – Queen Caroline

p. 173   'a miserable . . .': Mem, pp. 192–3
p. 174   'I cannot help . . .': Ick, 20.1.34
p. 174   'I am with him . . .': Ick, 9.6.34
p. 174   'You told me . . .': Ick, 15.8.34
p. 175   'prettiest and . . . one does': HH, 10.8.34
p. 175   'a thousand thanks . . . narrative short': HH, 16.8.34
p. 176   'You may depend . . .': Ick, 6.9.33
p. 176   'a very proper . . .': *George II*, p. 155
p. 177   'than to insult . . .': Mem, p. 274
p. 178   'with all the . . .': Mem, pp. 388–9
p. 179   'Whenever the . . .': Mem, p. 371
p. 179   'how often the . . .': Mem, p. 290
p. 179   'Lady Hervey . . .': Ick, 27.12.33
p. 180   'Lady Hervey is . . .': Ick, undated
p. 180   'affability without . . .': Mem, p. 276
p. 180   'in greater favour . . . this creature': Mem, pp. 348–9
p. 181   'the most vicious . . .': Mem, p. 306

22 – Favour

p. 183   'some of them . . .': HH, 2.10.33
p. 183   'who desires me . . .': Ick, 15.10.33
p. 183   'for my sake . . .': Ibid.
p. 184   'If I were a first . . .': HH, 11.8.30
p. 184   'I give you so . . .': Croker's edition of Hervey's *Memoirs*, p. lix
p. 184   'refused to conceal . . .': Ibid.
p. 184   'scarcely bothered . . .': *The Triumph of Culture: Eighteenth Century Perspective*, pp. 370–71
p. 184   'if the King is afraid . . .': Mem, p. 669
p. 185   'It was your fortune . . .': *The Triumph of Culture*, pp. 369–70
p. 185   'Whilst in her arms . . .': Mem, p. 294
p. 185   'as much unpitied . . .': Mem, p. 312
p. 186   'With all his parts . . .': Ibid.
p. 186   'This is a subject . . .': Ick, 15.8.34

p. 187 'only some slight . . .': Mem, p. 381

p. 187 'a good head and . . .': Mem, p. 42

p. 187 'Oh Gad . . .': *Caroline the Illustrious*, I, p. 303

p. 187 'that he might not . . .': Mem, p. 41

p. 187 'The King, though . . .': Rem, p. 62

p. 188 'invisible reins': Mem, p. 152

p. 188 [Once] the King . . .': Rem, p. 68

p. 189 'My good Lady . . .': Mem, p. 474

p. 189 'delighted in . . .': Rem, p. 68

p. 189 'I do not know . . .': Mem, p. 474

p. 189 'I expected when . . .': Ick, 13.1.35

23 – Lord Fanny

p. 190 'that it is very . . .': Ick, 16.1.33

p. 190 'Dull and impertinent . . .': Ick, 21.12.31

p. 192 'I cannot consider . . .': *Men of Letters and the English Public in the Eighteenth Century 1660–1744*, p. 375

p. 193 'because I am . . .': Ick, February 1733

p. 194 'He said to me . . .': Twickenham edition of Pope's collected poems, p. xvii

p. 195 'I send you enclosed . . .': HH, 6.12.33

p. 195 'was a rascal . . .': Ick, undated, to Henry Fox

p. 195 'Would a prudent . . .': *Collected Works*, p. 112

p. 195 'My Lord Hervey . . .': Sun, II, p. 224

p. 197 'The advertisement . . .': HH, 6.12.33

p. 197 'of every press . . .': Ick, undated, to Henry Fox

p. 197 'A rotten egg . . .': Ick, 14.2.34, to Henry Fox

p. 198 'smart without . . .': Mem, p. 68

p. 199 'Pope has not . . .': Ick, undated, to Henry Fox

24 – Cork Street

p. 200 'I must ask . . .': HH, 29.11.33

p. 200 'I am sorry to hear . . .': HH, 6.12.33

p. 200 'Ste is come . . .': Ick, 27.12.33

p. 201 'Your brother and I . . .': Ick, 20.1.34

p. 201 'One thing that . . .': Ick, 7.10.34

p. 201 'I leave Signor . . .': Ick, undated

p. 201 'no business . . .': HH, 10.8.34

p. 202 'I wish you were . . .': HH, 16.8.34

p. 202 'I fancy it is . . .': Ick, 29.11.35 to Middleton

p. 202 'I must now tell . . .': Ick, 11.9.35

p. 202 'Can you like . . .': Ick, 13.11.35

p. 203 'You see my . . .': Ibid.

p. 204 'studies very hard . . .': Holland, I, p. 39

p. 204 'if it had been . . . wear it on': Ick, 13.11.25

p. 205 'I affect an air . . .': Ick, 1744

p. 206 'Pray tell . . .': Ick, 13.11.35

p. 206 'Where are people . . .': *Collected Letters*, I, p.11

p. 207 'they cried, they . . . as promised': Ick, 18.11.35

p. 208 '*She* received the . . .': Ick, 25.11.35

p. 208 'in the red . . .': *Henry Fox, First Lord Holland*, i, p. 45

p. 208 'The Town is . . .': BLMR, 25.3.36

p. 209 'This happy event . . .': BLMR, 30.3.36

p. 209 '*propria manu* . . .': HH, 11.9.36

p. 209 'Yours, my dearest . . .': HH, 3.10.36

25 – The King's Fat Venus

p. 211 'this coast was . . .': Mem, p. 477

p. 211 'absolutely dead . . . been shot': Mem, pp. 478–83

p. 214 'the account of . . .': Mem, p. 458

p. 215 'the Queen, who . . .': Mem, p. 490

p. 215 'of nothing but . . . in mirth': Mem, pp. 485–6

p. 215 'and was often so . . . her mirth': Mem, p. 528

p. 216 'Would your Majesty . . . disputations': Mem, p. 489

p. 216 'If the King . . .': Mem, p. 491

p. 216 'Then she may stay . . . have misbehaved': Mem, p. 502

p. 218 'a long and steady . . .': ML, p. 95

p. 218 'receipt for an . . .': Ick, 6.10.35, to Charlotte Digby

p. 218 'There is no part . . .': *England in Johnson's Day*, p. 63

p. 218 'children of a larger . . .': *English Society in the Eighteenth Century*, p. 24

p. 219 'If I thought Deism . . .': *Boswell's London Journal* (ed. F. A. Pottle, 1966), p. 303

p. 219 'One language . . .': *The Family, Sex and Marriage*, p. 347

p. 219   'being a little addicted . . .': Mem, p. 380

p. 220   'I must own . . .': Ick, 9.9.35

p. 220   'the Duchess of . . .': Ibid.

26 – Sporus

p. 224   'as false . . .': Mem, p. 308

p. 225   'vainly gay in war . . .': *Pope, Homer and Manliness*, pp. 98–9

p. 226   'daily food . . .': *Opinions*, p. 43, note

p. 229   'by a woman too . . .': *Pope, Homer and Manliness*, p. 70

p. 231   '*Les lecteurs . . .*': ML, p. 98

p. 231   'moved pity for . . .': *Lord Hervey and his Friends*, p. 178

p. 231   'very proper . . .': *Sexuality in Eighteenth Century Britain*, p. 10

p. 231   'I forgot in . . .': Ick, 30.10.36, to Algarotti

p. 231   'considering what . . .': Ick, 27.6.34

p. 232   'between the . . .': *Letters between Lord Hervey and Dr Middleton Concerning the Roman Senate*, p. 61

p. 232   'Sometimes you . . .': Ick, 4.9.36

p. 232   'I am extremely . . .': Ick, 29.11.35

27 – A Storm

p. 235   'all the finery . . .': Mem, p. 551

p. 235   'I mention these . . .': Mem, p. 552

p. 236   'Poor creature . . .': Mem, p. 565

p. 236   'I love you mightily . . .': Mem, p. 617

p. 237   'But you see . . . but deaf': Mem, p. 603

p. 237   'Lost or strayed . . .': Mem, p. 610

p. 238   'drunk with vanity . . .': Mem, pp. 643–4

p. 238   'No, my Lord . . .': Mem, p. 640

p. 239   'with the same . . . without him?': Mem, p. 651

p. 239   'written by some . . . the world': Mem, p. 642

p. 240   'everyone was . . . had been above': Mem, pp. 649–50

p. 241   'For the sake of . . .': Ick, 4.9.36

28 – Old Love, New Love

p. 242   'a led wit of the . . .': Charles Hanbury Williams, *Collected Works*, p. 204

p. 242   'I knew Algarotti . . .': Ibid., p. 207

p. 243   'How fortunate you . . .': 9.9.36; *Lord Hervey and his Friends,*
         p. 200

p. 243   'not a tooth . . .': *Opinions,* p. 42

p. 243   'the finest set . . .': *Mrs Delany's Autobiography and Correspondence,*
         I, p. 544

p. 243   'How timid . . .': *Life of Lady Mary Wortley Montagu,* p. 157

p. 243   'My thoughts . . .': *Collected Letters,* II, p. 111

p. 243   'I will not say . . .': 14.8.36; *Lord Hervey and his Friends,* p. 199

p. 244   'If I was to say . . .': Ick, 16.9.36

p. 244   'However I have . . .': HH, 4.12.36

p. 245   'and backed by . . . a minister': Mem, p. 669

p. 246   'Though I know . . . your praises': Ick, 16/27.1.37

p. 247   'If you could . . .': Ick, 16/27.1.37

p. 248   'one of the most . . .': *Collected Letters,* II, p. 232, note

PART FIVE

29 – Fathers

p. 253   'but the king never . . .': Mem, p. 693

p. 253   'Look, there he . . .': Mem, p. 681

p. 254   'not only felt . . .': Mem, p. 659

p. 254   'Madam, do not . . .': Mem, p. 656

p. 254   'he put off his . . .': Mem, p. 534

p. 254   'She said she was . . .': Mem, p. 421

p. 255   'had conveniently . . .': Mem, p. 745

p. 255   'I told her . . . with you': Ick, 21.12.32

p. 256   'she could not help . . . a fool': Mem, p. 745

p. 257   'I am so unlike . . .': Ick, 14.11.32

p. 257   'For God's sake . . .': Ick, 18.6.37

p. 260   'How very ill . . . great impatience': HH, 15.10.37

30 – Towels and Tablecloths

p. 261   'I will be sure . . .': Mem, p. 757

p. 261   'so strong he . . . discoveries': Mem, p. 761–2

p. 262   'was well enough . . .': Mem, p. 795

p. 262   'it makes her suspect . . .': Mem, p. 788

p. 262   'as the Queen's . . .': Mem, p. 809

p. 263   'she was too old . . .': Mem, p. 799

p. 263   'You once thought . . .': Mem, p. 812

p. 263   'He is judicious . . .': Mem, p. 820

p. 264   'rolled in and . . .': HH, 6.12.33

p. 264   'all the tiresome . . .': Mem, p. 372

p. 264   'Your Majesty knows . . .': Mem, p. 373

p. 264   'inconveniently both . . .': Mem, p. 881

p. 264   'He wants to . . . her pain': Mem, p. 886

p. 265   'I have an ill . . . *n'empêche pas*': Mem, p. 883

p. 266   'with a mixture . . .': Mem, p. 911

p. 266   'My good Sir Robert . . .': Mem, p. 898

p. 266   '*Non – j'aurais* . . .': Mem, p. 896

p. 266   'I myself who . . .': Ick, 4.3.38

p. 266   'trying to lighten . . .': Mem, p. 914

p. 267   'Upon my word . . .': Ick, 15/26.1.38

p. 267   'Lord Hervey is . . .': HH, 24.11.37

p. 267   'People must wear . . . tavern': Mem, p. 919

p. 268   ''tis a total . . . sad event': HH, 29.11.37

p. 268   'My God, my God . . .': *Lord Hervey and his Friends*, p. 275

31 – Carrying Candles

p. 269   'blowing up Lord . . . and esteem': Mem, p. 924

p. 272   'my misfortune . . .': Ick, 4.2.38

p. 272   'The King has been . . .': Ick, 21.4.40

p. 274   '*mauvais mot* . . . an animal': HH 10.9.37

p. 274   'in this light . . . towards me': *Hardwicke*, pp. 229–33

p. 275   'Your Court is . . .': Hervey to Lord Bristol, in the *Letter-Books*

p. 276   'I am too proud . . .': Ick, 20.5.42

p. 277   'For supposing . . .': Hervey to Lord Bristol, in the *Letter-Books*

32 – Elegy

p. 282   'I like to see . . .': Ick, 15.10.31

p. 283   'as closely written . . .': Ick, 11.9.35

p. 284   'Your brother, Lord . . .': Ick, 25.1.30

p. 286   'left Winnington a . . .': HWC, XVIII, pp. 167–8

33 – A Coffin-face

p. 288   'bid me say . . .': HWC, XL, pp. 27–8
p. 288   'How Roman Senates . . .': HWC, XL, pp. 21–2
p. 289   'puts me in mind . . .': HWC, XXX, p. 52
p. 290   'Which of the devils . . .': Ick, undated
p. 291   'His rule is . . .': HH, 13.11.42
p. 291   'I own one . . .': HH, 7.12.38
p. 291   'from an instinctive . . .': Ick, 5.11.41
p. 292   'It is out of . . .': HH, 28.12.38
p. 293   'as well-bred . . .': WLM, I, p. 69
p. 293   'Love your friend . . .': HH, 28.10.42
p. 293   'The middle way . . .': HH, 6.11.42
p. 293   'You must know . . .': HH, 15.11.42
p. 294   'I have never . . . affection yours': HH, 13.11.42
p. 295   'If a person . . . afternoon': HH, 20.11.42

34 – Ennui Relieved

p. 298   'The last stages . . .': Ick, 18.6.43
p. 298   'at my time . . .': Ick, 31.1.38
p. 298   'Whatever it is . . .': Ick, 27.12.35
p. 299   'Mankind, I know . . .': Ickworth; reprinted in Croker's edition
             of Hervey's *Memoirs*
p. 299   'any news . . .': MH, p. 12
p. 300   'I am not surprised . . .': HH, 10.9.43
p. 301   'I see and feel . . .': MH, p. 14
p. 301   'for he had outlived . . .': HWC, XVIII, p. 294

Acknowledgements

I would like to thank the following people for all their generous help with this book: the staff of the British Library and the manuscript room there, the West Sussex Record Office, the London Library and Westminster Archives. Susan Sloman from the Victoria Art Gallery, Elizabeth Bevan of the Bath Central Library, Katrina Jowett, Assistant Librarian at Freemasons' Hall in London and Alastair Laing from the National Trust all kindly replied to my queries. Nino Strachey helped me a great deal with her knowledge of the Hervey family and allowed me to look around Ickworth House. Judith Watt, Clare Naylor, Roy Porter and Orlando Fraser read drafts and supplied suggestions. Euan Rellie and my mother, Davina Miller, patiently went through the manuscript with me; Euan also thought of titles and rescued me when my computer broke down. Jenny and Stuart Woodhead took wonderful care of me when I worked in Bury; my aunt Willa Elphinstone kindly had me to stay while I looked at the archives at Mellerstain House belonging to Binning and Jane Haddington; and Philip and Soh Yung Smiley lent their writing room and Korean desk. My stepfather Josh Miller suggested some useful reading, as did Bill Montgomery. The Hon. Mrs Charlotte Townsend for her friendly interest in the book. My agent, Georgina Capel, for her encouraging words and work. My gratitude to everyone at Penguin – Jessica Ward, Keith Taylor, Richard Duguid, Bela Cunha (and her son Paul) for the copy-editing, Helen Smith for the index, Sarah Day, Kate Barker, Joanna Prior, John Bond and Peter Bowron – for all their hard work and enthusiasm, especially Andrew Kidd, whose calm and creative editing has improved this book immeasurably. And finally, thanks to my friends and family, whose varying forms of support during what has not always been an easy process have been invaluable and are vastly appreciated.

Index

Numbers with an asterisk indicate information found in notes at bottom of page.